Ephesians

Recovering the Vision
of a Sustainable Church
In Christ

by

Phillip A. Ross

PILGRIM
platform books

Marietta, Ohio

ISBN: 978-0-9839046-6-3
Edition: 1.1.2020

Published by

Pilgrim Platform
149 E. Spring St., Marietta
Ohio, 45750
www.pilgrim-platform.org

Biblical quotations are from the English Standard Version, Standard Bible
    Society, unless otherwise cited.

Printed in the United States of America

"I have this against you, that you have abandoned the love you had at first ... Yet, I know your works, your love and faith and service and patient endurance, and that your latter works exceed the first" (Revelation 2:4, 19).

for Christ's church scattered and gathered in the 21ˢᵗ Century

Books by Phillip A. Ross

The Work At Zion—A Reckoning, Two-volume set, 772 pages, 1996.

Practically Christian—Applying James Today, 135 pages, 2006.

The Wisdom of Jesus Christ in the Book of Proverbs, 414 pages, 2006.

Marking God's Word—Understanding Jesus, 324 pages, 2006.

Acts of Faith—Kingdom Advancement, 326 pages, 2007.

Informal Christianity—Refining Christ's Church, 136 pages, 2007.

Engagement—Establishing Relationship in Christ, 104 pages, 1996, 2008.

It's About Time! — The Time Is Now, 40 pages. 2008.

The Big Ten—A Study of the Ten Commandments, 105 pages, 2001, 2008.

Arsy Varsy—Reclaiming The Gospel in First Corinthians, 406 pages, 2008.

Varsy Arsy—Proclaiming The Gospel in Second Corinthians, 356 pages, 2009.

Colossians—Christos Singularis, 278 pages, 2010.

Rock Mountain Creed—The Sermon on the Mount, 310 pages, 2011.

The True Mystery of the Mystical Presence, 355 pages, 2011.

Peter's Vision of Christ's Purpose in First Peter, 340 pages, 2011.

Peter's Vision of The End in Second Peter, 184 pages, 2012.

The Religious History of Nineteenth Century Marietta, Thomas Jefferson Summers, 124 pages, 1903, 2012 (editor).

Conflict of Ages—The Great Debate of the Moral Relations of God and Man, Edward Beecher, 489 pages, 1853, 2012 (editor).

Concord Of Ages—The Individual And Organic Harmony Of God And Man, Edward Beecher, D. D., 524 pages, 1860, 2013 (editor).

Ephesians—Recovering the Vision of a Sustainable Church in Christ, 417 pages, 2013.

Galatians: Backstory/Christory, 315 pages, 2015.

Poet Tree—Root, Branch & Sap, 72 pages, 2013.

Inside Out Woman—Collected Poetry, Doris M. Ross, 195 pages, 2014 (editor).

God's Great Plan for the World—The Biblical Story of Creation and Redemption, 305 pages, 2019.

John's Miracles—Seeing Beyond Our Expectations, 210 pages, 2019.

TABLE OF CONTENTS

INTRODUCTION

"The church is the community of God's people rather than an institution, and must not be identified with any particular culture, social or political system, or human ideology" (*The Lausanne Covenant*, John Stott, Lausanne Library, 2009).

The kingdom of God is the environment in which Christ's church exists. It is the environment in which humanity exists, and Christ's church is manifest in God's kingdom, in the environment, as the body of Christ. The Bible is actually a very Green book.

Green became the color of a number of European political parties in the 1980s that were organized around environmental issues. The color green was chosen because of its association with nature, health, and growth. Green Parties are concerned about ecology, health, wholeness, grassroots democracy, nonviolence, and social justice; and are found in over one hundred countries.

However, in the current political landscape the Green Movement and Christianity, broadly conceived, both believe themselves to be in opposition to one another. Thus, contrary to popular opinion, to say that the Bible is Green means that the human environment or habitat is a central biblical concern. The concerns of the Green Movement are, in fact, central to the Bible's concerns about salvation. Making this argument is the intention of this book.

The burden of proof is the responsibility of the greater truth to edify the lesser truths, if only because a lesser truth cannot successfully persuade a greater truth that its perspective is superior. And in every case, the greater truth is always God's truth. As much as I'd like to persuade the Green community about the environmental perspective of the Bible, this is more an effort to persuade the Christian community about God's reality and the reality of Christ's salvation in the twenty-first century. The argument is that Christian salvation is God's effort toward human sustainability on earth, as it is in heaven.

It is not an argument that the twenty-first century has suddenly discovered some lost biblical truth that has been obscured in previous centuries. Rather, it is the argument that human sustainability has always been God's central concern, and the failure to receive God's message of salvation by too many people is coming to a head in the twenty-first century. The argument here is that God's message of salvation is not opposed to science or technology, but that science and technology are part of God's gifts to humanity, and as such they have an important role to play in God's kingdom. The effort of this book is to reignite the Bible's grand vision of the role of humanity through the body of Christ in the world, and in the world's environment—the universe. Indeed, the scope, scale, and vision of the Bible are necessarily grand, and that vision must be freed from its captivity by the narrow-minded and self-centered perspective of modern individualism that infects too many Christians and their churches.

Consequently, this book also presents a challenge to the new atheism movement—people who think that history has outgrown Christianity. For the most part, atheists misunderstand the Bible, and they learned most of what they know from Christians who don't understand the Bible or the faith. The god that most atheists reject is not the God of the Bible, but is a god of their own imaginations. And because so many Christians don't understand the grand view of Christianity, much of this book will appear to be foreign to them, as well.

Christians in the emergent/emerging camps will find some familiar themes in these pages, but they might be shocked by the expression of biblical fidelity to historic doctrine and rejection of the tenets of liberal progressive Christianity as being far too slippery and weak to support the gravitas of the biblical gospel. The perspective of these pages is not so much a call for the church to do something new, as it is for the church to continue doing what she has always done—make the gospel speak to the genuine spiritual needs of the age. Or course, there must be doctrinal continuity with the past, but that continuity must not become grounds for a retreat from the future. Christians are not chained to the rotten corpse of past genius, nor addicted to the passion of some imaginary future. Rather, Christians must be appropriately adapted, in the light of Christ, to the moment in which they actually live.

Regardless of what you think about Rick Warren, the opening words of his mega-successful book, *The Purpose Driven Life*, are spot on: "It's not about you." God is not here to satisfy our personal desires and purposes, we are here to serve His. The success of modernity through the development of science and technology has proven to be an Achilles' heel, in the same way that ancient Israel's success, its wealth and prosperity during Isaiah's time, worked to undermine their faith in God, which in turn corrupted the foundations of Isaiah's society. The lack of familiarity with Isaiah's story stands as an accusation of contemporary biblical illiteracy.

The problem in Isaiah's society was not its success or its wealth, but the lapse of faithfulness to the God of the Bible. And the same thing is true today. Our problem is not American success, or capitalism, or science, or technology, or Western wealth. Our problems stem from our lapses of faithfulness to Jesus Christ, who is the God of the Bible. As such, our problems cannot be blamed on unbelievers, or governments, or Wall Street, or education. Rather, the blame for a lack of faithfulness can only be applied to those who *ought* to be faithful. The blame falls to the church(es), to both leaders and followers because you can't have one without the other. The church as a whole is at fault, and so this book is directed at the church as a whole.

The purpose of this book is neither dogmatic nor academic, but is systemic in that it endeavors to provide a reading of Ephesians and a biblical perspective that issue out of the wholeness of the Bible. It labors to hold various themes, lessons, and aspects together in order to display the Bible's sustainable depth and breadth in the light of Christ in the twenty-first century. Elsewhere I have argued for the progressive revelation of Christ in history,[1] and here I apply that argument to produce a twenty-first century reading of Paul's letter to the Ephesians. We must remember that the Holy Spirit accused the Ephesian church of having "abandoned the love you had at first" (Revelation 2:4), and charged them to "do the works you did at first" (Revelation 2:5).

---

1   For a discussion of the progressive revelation of Christ see: Ross, Phillip A. *Peter's Vision of Christ's Purpose in First Peter*, 2011; and *Peter's Vision of The End in Second Peter*, Pilgrim Platform, Marietta, Ohio, 2012.

This is a very interesting charge in the light of Protestantism's understanding of works-righteousness. Of course the Ephesian church was not charged to *achieve* salvation by *doing* various things, but was charged to manifest the love—agape, or the deeds of love—as a *consequence* of salvation, in the sense discussed in the book of James. So, while Protestantism's argument against works-righteousness is justified, it is not complete. It's not the whole truth of salvation. But neither is this admission an attack on the doctrine of *Sola fide*. No doctrine stands alone in the sense of being all by itself. There are five solas, all of which testify to the multi-centrality of various Christian doctrines: *Sola scriptura* (by Scripture alone), *Sola fide* (by faith alone), Sola gratia (by grace alone), *Solus Christus* or *Solo Christo* (Christ alone or through Christ alone), and *Soli Deo gloria* (glory to God alone)—all are necessary. This concern will come up in the text in several places.

The central idea of this book follows Paul's letter to the Ephesians, and his effort to explicate the nature and character of Christ's church. An early question that inspired this book was whether Abraham Lincoln was a Christian. Would Christ count him a member of His church? It's a more difficult question than might be first supposed. From what the historians know about Lincoln, his parents were Hard-shell Baptists who joined Little Pigeon Baptist Church near Lincoln City, Indiana, in 1823. That means that Abraham would not have been baptized as an infant. Historian Mark Noll reports that "Lincoln never joined a church nor ever made a clear profession of standard Christian belief."[2] Yet, Lincoln's religious concerns and attitude are legendary.

Noll argues that Lincoln was disgusted with organized Christianity as a young man because of the excessive emotion and bitter sectarian quarrels of various camp meetings and traveling preachers. Lincoln enjoyed the work of deists, such as Thomas Paine. And he wrote a lot that would be considered to be religious. But because people thought he was hostile to Christianity, which almost cost him a congressional bid, he mostly kept his religious beliefs to himself. The guiding religious tenet that Lincoln seemed to hold throughout his life was the doctrine of necessity, also known as predestination, which

---

2   Noll, Mark A. *A History of Christianity in the United States and Canada,* Eerdmans Publishing Company, 1992.

informed his understanding of the Civil War, and shaped his mature religious thinking.

Col. John G. Nicolay, a close friend of Lincoln in Washington, said of him,

> "Mr. Lincoln did not, to my knowledge, in any way change his religious ideas, opinions, or beliefs from the time he left Springfield to the day of his death."

Judge David Davis, a lifelong friend and the executor of Lincoln's will, said the same thing: "He had no faith in the Christian sense of the term." Colonel Lamon, a contemporary Lincoln biographer, said:

> "Never in all that time did he let fall from his lips or his pen an expression which remotely implied the slightest faith in Jesus as the son of God and the Savior of men."

Yet, the question remains: Was Lincoln a Christian? Did the Lord count him a friend? Was he saved? Did Lincoln contribute positively to the church of Jesus Christ? No particular church claimed him as a member, nor did he claim membership in any particular church. Yet, nine out of ten people I informally polled answered immediately in the affirmative. *Of course he was!* He was a great American. But what was his relationship to Christ's church?

Keep that question in mind as you read because the deeper question is not about Lincoln, but is about the church. Another way to ask the question is: Was the church at that time in such a state of confusion and apostasy that it chased Lincoln away? Was the fault of Lincoln's failure to become a church member a matter of his faithlessness? Or the faithlessness of the churches he knew? And if that was true then, what is the condition of the churches today? This is the theme of this book. And I commend it to you with fear and trepidation, knowing that many of the questions and issues it raises will be difficult to grasp—not because they are hard to understand, but because they run against the grain of contemporary Evangelical Christianity of nearly every stripe. So, I pray for your patience. I'm not saying that I have all the answers, or any answers. But I do have some important questions for your consideration.

Semper Reformanda!

I am grateful for those who have contributed directly or indirectly to the completion of this book. First on the list, as always, is my wife, Stephanie, without whom I could not do what I do. I'm grateful for her endurance. My sons, Adam, Austin, and Justin—now all theologians in their own right, have also contributed in many ways, most of which are unknown to them—various discussions, prayers, etc. Special thanks to Austin for reading an early version and providing some editing ideas. Other readers of an earlier manuscript include Scott Craig Mooney, whose initial response proved to be very helpful, Gary Combs, Mic Cox, Dr. Mark Hamilton (Ashland University), Timothy Lyzenga, Barry Sheets, Dr. David Torbett (Marietta College), and others who read it without comment. Many changes have been made in light of the help that these men provided. Thank you!

Phillip A. Ross
Marietta, Ohio
February 2014

1. FAITHFUL SAINTS

Paul, an apostle of Christ Jesus by the will of God, to the saints who are in Ephesus, and are faithful in Christ Jesus.
                                                                    –Ephesians 1:1

True to the form for ancient letters of this sort Paul identified himself as the author of the letter to the Ephesians. Whether Paul was claiming formal apostleship is difficult to know because we have transliterated the Greek word ἀπόστολος directly into English as *apostle*. But it could also be translated as *delegate* or *ambassador*, referring to Paul's function rather than his office. Regardless, Paul was simply re-presenting Jesus Christ to the saints.

His authority to represent Jesus Christ was given to him by the will of God. Several of his letters contain this mention. Paul's history as a persecutor of Christians probably made him sensitive to various concerns about his authority in the church. So, he addressed the issue of church authority in order to clarify it. Unlike civil government, the church does not have the power of coercion—force. Rather, the authority of the church is moral declaration and persuasion.

Paul was answering the question that could be raised by those who would not honor his authority. *Who made you the boss of me?* False apostles could simply dismiss Paul's self-claimed authority for a variety of reasons, unless it came directly from God—which it did. Paul made this claim because of his Damascus Road conversion where he was drafted into the service of Jesus Christ. Paul was not engaged in self-service. He was not doing what he had always wanted to do with his life. He had been drafted by the Lord Himself into a life of service, sacrifice, and suffering.

1

There is no question that Paul was writing to the *saints* (ἅγιος). However, in Greek the word is more like an adjective than a noun. It could be read as *saintly*. Though again, the word means sacred, pure, consecrated or set apart. This phrase might also be read as *to the consecrated* or *separated unto God*, though Paul was not suggesting a special category of Christians called *saints*, as if some Christians are specially consecrated and some aren't. We know this because Paul argued everywhere for Christian unity and the elimination of all subgroup identity politics in the church. The distinction was between Christians and non-Christians, not between Christians and special Christians.

BAPTISM

He was writing to Christians, so the consecration would be baptism. The thing that separates Christians from non-Christians is not what they say they believe, though there are significant differences. Nor is it some sort of personal testimony about God or Jesus or the Holy Spirit, though testimonies are important. It's too easy to say all sorts of things that might be true or not, with no way of proving that people mean what they say. Indeed, self-delusion is all too common. Rather, actions speak louder than words. What sets Christians apart from the world, in the eyes of the world, is baptism. The best evidence to unbelievers for Christianity is the sacrament (sacred act) of baptism. The unbaptized are not Christian, and the baptized are—regardless of their stated beliefs or behaviors.

Please don't let your mind wander into wild speculations about what this means before I'm finished with it. I'm not suggesting that all Christians are faithful Christians, only that being baptized puts one's name on a list over which Christ's church has jurisdiction. Paul was writing to the saints in Ephesus, to those who were under the authority of Christ's church. And he was using moral and persuasive authority, not coercion.

Of course, being under the authority of the church does not necessarily mean that one is obedient to that authority, which ought to be obvious. Therefore, Paul further identified the people he was writing to. He narrowed the list by adding the qualification of faithfulness. Paul used two terms to describe those he was addressing: the *saints*, separating the baptized from the unbaptized, and the *faithful*, separating intentional believers from nonbelievers. Such a distinction reflects Paul's understanding of the character of the church he discussed in Romans, where he observed that "not all who are descended from Israel belong to Israel" (Romans 9:6).

The church is a mixed bag because it is a dynamic institution of growth and maturity in Christ. The purity of the church is relative in the same sense that the perfection of any individual Christian is relative. Paul acknowledged this in Romans 7:19 where he admitted that he could not always accomplish what he intended, where his own sin continued to dog his walk. Even Paul could not claim perfection this side of the grave. And if Paul couldn't personally perfect his own Christianity, there is no reason to expect that any church will contain only perfectly faithful members.

Perfection

This insight ought not to be used as an excuse for faithlessness, and where it is so used it is contrary to the teaching of Scripture. The fact that people cannot be perfectly faithful is not an excuse for not making every effort to strive for such perfection. Everything that excuses or interferes with the pursuit of Christian perfection is sinful and should be avoided. Jesus calls us to "be perfect (τέλειος), as your heavenly Father is perfect" (Matthew 5:48). We are called to the perfection of God Almighty, and we must not deny this high calling.

However, some idea about this perfection to which we are called is needed. The Greek word (τέλειος) doesn't mean flawless or sinless, it means complete or whole. We are not called to some sort of Gnostic, abstract idea of mathematical flawlessness, but to completion and wholeness. We are to become complete, mature or fully grown—even ripe. The Greek word literally means *brought to its end*, or *finished*. And we cannot be at the end when we are still in the middle. We cannot be perfect until our purpose is fulfilled. We cannot be finished while we are still running the race. The call for perfection is actually a call for endurance to the end—perseverance. We are not called to be perfectly sinless, but we are called to sin less over time.

The fact that perfection or completeness is not immediately attainable is immaterial to the call itself. The fact of its instant unattainability is central to the gospel of Jesus Christ because it provides for the reality that salvation is by grace alone, but not by grace exclusively. We are called to seek perfection with every fiber of our being, and to know that *we* cannot fully achieve it—and yet we are to trust that God will provide what we cannot achieve. That trust is ours because He sent the Holy Spirit to inhabit the lives of His people, to lead, to guide, to provide, and to comfort. Were we able to attain perfection on our own, there would be no need for Christ or His Holy Spirit.

Because the church is a dynamic institution of growth and maturity in Christ it is filled with people on such a journey. People are always coming into her and going out from her, being born and dying, joining and leaving. And the people who comprise the church are not static, either. They are continually growing and changing. And, indeed, such personal growth is an essential element of Christian character, supplied by the Holy Spirit through regeneration.

Conversely, those who are not growing and maturing in faithfulness ought not to be church members, at least not voting members. Growth and maturity are evidence of faithfulness. Just as stagnation and immaturity are evidence of faithlessness.

Faith

Our contemporary world speaks about faith quite a bit, but it speaks about it generically as if having faith in something—anything —is the main thing. The popular ideas of faith speak in ways that are foreign to Scripture. For instance, people speak about the Baptist faith, the Methodist faith, the Presbyterian faith, etc. Scripture doesn't do this, but it could have. It could have mentioned the Pharisee faith, the Sadducee faith, priestly faith, levitical faith, Matthean faith, Pauline faith, Johananine faith, etc. But it doesn't.

Scripture doesn't speak of faith in this way because doing so creates false ideas about faith. It is not that the faith of Baptists is different from the faith of Methodists, but their emphasis about what's most important, their practice or choreography of what they do in worship and how they are organized that is different. For instance, the Baptists don't baptize infants, but Methodists (some of them, anyway) and Presbyterians do. The Presbyterians may celebrate communion with wine, but Baptists generally don't. Baptists generally don't have elders, but Presbyterians do. Such things, while important in some ways, have little to do with having Christ as the object of faith. All Christians have Christ as the object of their faith, which is the basis of Christian unity.

In addition, things like justification, love, hope, satisfaction, etc., are found in Christ, not only in the sense that these things belong to Christ as His possessions, but in the sense that we have access to them only by being *in Christ* ourselves. Our access to His possessions comes from being in Him.

In Christ

The phrase *in Christ* is used seventy-eight times in the New Testament, making it an important concept. Sometimes it means that Christ is the object of faith, sometimes it suggests that something is available in or through Christ, and sometimes it suggests that Christians inhere or dwell in Christ. Of course, all of these are always true, but it is instructive to understand where the emphasis of a particular verse is placed.

Being *in Christ* can be understood literally. Jesus said, "I am in My Father, and you in Me, and I in you" (John 14:20), like Russian nesting dolls. This is not magic or mysterious, but is quite ordinary. John later clarified this idea:

> "Whoever keeps his commandments abides in God, and God in him. And by this we know that he abides in us, by the Spirit whom he has given us" (1 John 3:24).

We note three things from this: first, that abidance is a function of obedience; second, that knowledge of abiding in Christ comes from the Holy Spirit; and third, being in Christ is an identity matter.

Of course, obedience is not the only element of abiding in Christ. In fact, it's the last element because obedience is the result. Abiding begins in the heart of God because He has provided the means. God provides it because of His love, grace, and mercy, and not because of anything in us or anything that can be done by us apart from Him. It is His idea, not ours. Our faithfulness does not mean that we initiate the idea, but that we simply agree with God and His ideas. It means that we receive what He provides.

First, He provided His Son, Jesus Christ, to atone for our sin. And second, Christ has dispatched the Holy Spirit as the means or way for redeemed and repentant sinners to have union with God. That union involves the *touch* of the Master's hand that heals our brokenness and restores our wholeness. Salvation and the restoration of human wholeness in Christ are different ways to say the same thing.

Restoration of Wholeness

Christ provides the wholeness of humanity in three ways. First, He restores our broken relationship with God the Father so that God can play His proper role in our lives and we can play our proper roles in His life. Second, Jesus Christ restores God's covenant with humanity by providing the covenantal archetype for the human manifestation of a new humanity, a new human identity in Christ. And third, Christ has sent His Holy Spirit to inhabit His people and provide for the unity, guidance, and function of His church.

The restoration of the human/divine relationship involves both our identity (who we *think* we are) and our being (who we *actually* are). First, with regard to identity, there are three possible ways that the human/divine gulf can be bridged. The human side can be absorbed into the divine such that the healing of the relationship implies the divination of humanity. This is the ancient desire for mystical unity where human ego or identity is fused with God.[1] Here man becomes God, or he *thinks* that he does, because it is actually not possible for what is finite to be infinite.

The second way that the human/divine relationship is bridged takes the opposite approach by absorbing the divine into the human, such that the divine is seen as both illusory and imaginary.[2] Here the divine is absorbed into the human such that the bridging of the relationship implies the complete humanization of the divine. What is divine is thought to be an illusion. This is the Modern humanistic desire for the absence, unreality, and/or denial of the divine, and is usually called *atheism*. Here man denies God. But the denial of God has no effect on God, other than breaking His heart and confirming that the person who does the denying is not a believer and, therefore, cannot inherit the blessings of God.

The third way to approach the broken human/divine relationship is provided by Jesus Christ alone as the only mediator between God and man. Here both the divine and the human are gathered together in Christ, which then constitutes the needed healing. The Christian healing of the human/divine relationship is neither the absorption of man into God (mysticism) nor the absorption of God into man (atheism), but is the union of God and man *in Christ*. Union with Christ allows God to be God and man to be man by acknowledging the Trinitarian character of God-in-Christ through the Holy Spirit as the archetype of humanity in Christ. Here both human and divine identities are not only preserved but God's cause is enhanced by the product of the union.[3]

---

1   Meister Ekhart (1260-1327) was one of the most famous Christians of this type.

2   Friedrich Nietzsche (1844-1900) was one of the most famous atheists of this type.

3   Ross, Phillip A. & Nevin, John Williamson, in *The True Mystery of the Mystical*

Paul points to this Christian union by his use of the phrase "in Christ" (v. 1). Thus, we see that Paul was writing to those who were already in Christ, and to those who would at some future point find themselves *in union* in Christ. Consequently, we see that union with Christ is not a simple relationship between the individual believer and Christ, but is the complex relationship between all believers and Christ, such that there is both a human/divine dimension and a human/human dimension to the relationship.

The human/divine dimension of the relationship involves what is traditionally understood as the Christian's personal relationship with Jesus Christ and all of the various aspects of personal Christian spirituality that are therein implied. The human/human dimension of the relationship is not simply the relationship of one person to another person, but involves the moral relationship of one person to another person *in Christ*.

Christians share more than their humanity with one another, they share a primary and common relationship with Jesus Christ, which means that they share the light or wisdom of Jesus Christ.[4] This sharing is necessarily a corporate or community thing, and not simply a personal or individual thing. The wisdom of Christ is available to those who gather in His name, and not simply to isolated individuals. Part and parcel of that wisdom comes from its corporate character. The wisdom of Christ emerges as faithful Christians engage Scripture and one another faithfully.

BEING & MORALITY

Consequently, Christianity has both ontological (physical) and moral (behavioral) elements. It involves the being or identity of humanity, both individually and corporately. And it is because of this simultaneous individual and corporate character or dimension that Christianity involves the manifestation or incarnation of biblical morality, both personally and socially. Christianity has a unique individual element that is usually called a *personal relationship with Jesus Christ*. It is this relationship that provides for individual conscience and sanctification, or maturity in Christ.

Alongside of this personal, individual dimension is a social, corporate dimension that is usually called *fellowship* or *the church*. The

---

Presence, Pilgrim Platform, Marietta, Ohio, 2011.

4   Ross, Phillip A. *The Wisdom of Jesus Christ in the Book of Proverbs*, Pilgrim Platform, Marietta, Ohio, 2006.

definite article (the) belongs with the name because it indicates that the church is one, a whole or indivisible unity. One cannot be Christian apart from being *in Christ*, and being in Christ brings individuals into personal, spiritual intimacy with Jesus Christ and with one another in a way that involves the union of the finite individual with the infinite God-in-Christ. It is *one* because Christ has only one body and *the* church is His body. Furthermore, this union exists only *in Christ* because Christ is the only mediator between man and God. There can only be one mediator because the function of the mediator is the restoration and maintenance of the wholeness of humanity, and such wholeness cannot be divided. Wholeness or oneness means the lack of division into parts. The mediator—Jesus Christ—is one because the wholeness of humanity is one *in Christ*.

In addition, the fact of being in union with God-in-Christ also brings the individual into unity with other individuals who are similarly—but not identically—in union with God-in-Christ. This corporate union in Christ is a manifestation of *the church*. And the church, being a product of the union of trinitarian individuals with the Trinitarian God-in-Christ or the Trinity, also has a trinitarian character. The church or body of Christ is manifest wherever two or three are gathered in the name of Jesus Christ (Matthew 18:20). The many different gatherings do not destroy the unity of the body.

The fact that the Lord provided specific numbers is important because those particular numbers provide description and instruction regarding the constitution of the church. The minimum gathering that can be defined as an instance of the church is *two*. *One* cannot gather with himself, so while a solitary person can most certainly be a Christian in union with God-in-Christ, one person does not constitute an instance of the church. But two people can gather together. Of course, two people do not constitute the whole church. But in fact, the whole church cannot ever be gathered in one place. It's too big for that. But because of its unity, wherever two or three are gathered, the wholeness of the church is represented.

In order to constitute an instance of the church, such a gathering must be in the name of Jesus Christ. It must be an intentional and conscious coming together in the explicit name of Jesus Christ. Jesus' name is not a magic talisman, but it does have power. To do something in the name of Jesus Christ means doing it in the character of Jesus Christ, and doing it for the purpose of Jesus Christ. Acting in the character of Christ means taking on the character qualities of Jesus

Christ, imitating Him (2 Thessalonians 3:9). It means becoming the character that God created you to be, becoming who God wants you to be *in Christ*. Serving the purpose of Jesus Christ means serving the purpose of God, because Christ is God by the power of the Holy Spirit.

Christians are baptized "in the name of Jesus Christ for the forgiveness of ... sins, and ... receive the gift of the Holy Spirit" (Acts 2:38). Those who gather must first be baptized because baptism functions as the initiating ceremony of church membership or inclusion in Christ. It is not that the ceremony of baptism does something magical or mystical, but that the ceremony of baptism provides a public and legal acknowledgment that the person being baptized is to be considered to be a member of the body of Christ from that point forward. It is legal because it is public. The ceremony is the public acknowledgment of the reality of the thing symbolized in the ceremony.

The baptism is not a private concern merely for the individual or even for the church. From the time of John the Baptist baptism has been a public confession of Christ's ownership. Both the individual and corporate elements are important, and should not be separated. Baptism functions as a kind of public marking of the person being baptized. The whole community in which the person resides is put on notice that the baptized person now belongs to Jesus Christ first and foremost. Baptism is a public declaration and recognition of inclusion *in Christ*.

2. Grace & Peace

Grace to you and peace from God our Father and the Lord Jesus Christ. —Ephesians 1:2

Here Paul blesses the church at Ephesus by invoking God's grace and peace upon them. We might think of the mention of grace and peace as the announcement of Paul's themes for this letter, which opens and closes with the invocation of grace and peace (Ephesians 6:23-24).

Paul was not writing to any particular saint at Ephesus, but to all of them—not to any part of the church, but to the whole church. This fact will grow in significance as we work through this letter and see Paul's catholic (whole or universal) emphasis. Paul always and everywhere teaches the unity and wholeness of the church, and this will become increasingly important to understand as he alludes to various doctrinal concerns in this letter. This blessing, as indeed the whole letter, is for the whole church.

We must take care not to think of grace (χάριν) as a noun or a thing. It is neither, but is a quality or attribute, and serves here as an adverb or a modifying word. The bestowal of God's grace is the bestowal of His graciousness and favor toward people. To enjoy God's grace is to enjoy His favor, or the favor of His blessings in our lives. Grace is not a thing that can be given, or handed down. Paul was praying that God would treat the church at Ephesus favorably, with kindness and mercy.

Enjoying God's grace does not mean that people get whatever they want, nor that their lives will be forever rosy. Rather, the specific favor that Paul evoked upon them is the love and protective care that God has for His own Son. Because the church exists in Christ, she

11

(the Person of Christ as the church) enjoys and shares the blessings and loving care that God has for His Son. God will treat Christians the same way that He treats His Son. This is what it means to be *in Christ.*

God treats His Son faithfully. God is faithful to His promises. Though it was necessary for His Son to atone for human sin, and though that atonement required the death of His Son, God was also faithful not to abandon His Son in death, but to suffer with Him and resurrect Him into eternal life with Himself. God treated His Son with both justice and mercy. And those who are in Christ cannot expect to be treated differently, except that Christ's atoning death on the cross happened once for all.

Christians are not called to atone for human sin, that job has been accomplished. But Christians are called to death in the waters of baptism and new life in Christ through regeneration. It is essential that Christians come to terms with their own death and objectify their understanding through the motifs of death and resurrection as reflected in the biblical understandings of baptism and regeneration because the fruit of baptism and regeneration is peace.

God has promised redemption for humanity on the basis of Christ's obedient propitiation on the cross, and God's promise is trustworthy. It is trustworthy, however, because God made it, not because we believe it. Human belief adds nothing to the promise of God. That promise is true whether people believe it or not. The failure of individual belief does not make God's promise false. But if this is true, then why should people pay any attention to it? If nothing will stop God from fulfilling His promise to save humanity through the propitiation of Christ on the cross, what difference does it make whether any particular individuals believe it or not?

It makes the same difference that believing in any truth makes. Sustainable human life must be grounded in the truth of the human condition and situation. This is true ecologically, financially, scientifically, socially, and religiously. False beliefs produce false ways of living, and false ways of living undermine and destroy the sustainability of human culture. Unbelief cuts the unbeliever off from the ultimate benefit—salvation. Unbelievers are excluded from sustainable human culture by their own unbelief. Follow this logic: What is true is believable, and what is untrue is unbelievable. Therefore, unbelievers believe what is not true.

NEW CREATION

Paul's blessing of grace and peace from God provides a communique from God to humanity by one of God's ambassadors. God is building a new humanity-in-Christ, and sent a message of blessing to that new humanity-in-Christ through Paul. It means that God has recognized this new humanity-in-Christ as an actual and viable creature in His realm. This new humanity is a creature that is as significant as the creation of Adam and Eve (old humanity) in the Garden. This new humanity-in-Christ is a new biblical kind, a new species of human being that is as different from homo sapiens as are apes. However, the differences are not biological, but are of a completely different order. The differences are spiritual. But keep in mind that body and spirit are not different entities, but always occur in unity. Humanity-in-Christ involves a new way of being human or way of life.

With the introduction of this new biblical kind, the church of humanity-in-Christ, and the identification of the essential character of the church as spiritual, comes the danger of misunderstanding. This danger issues from the fact that the word *spiritual* has a long and sad history of misunderstanding and abuse that has issued from false belief and false religion dating far back into antiquity. Indeed, this history stretches back into the dark recesses of the dawn of humanity. And because misunderstanding has always attached itself to considerations of spirituality, we must be suspect of all definitions and uses of the term. The word *spiritual* today means so many different things that it actually means nothing in particular.

As a category, we must suspect all pre-Christian uses and understandings of spirituality because we now know that Christ's incarnation provided the fullness of the only actual God in existence by manifesting the Son of God, the Second Person of the Trinity in human flesh. Following that manifestation, Christ Himself authorized and sent the Holy Spirit to indwell all subsequent human flesh by grace through faith. The process of that indwelling has been underway for two millennia, and has produced the most profound changes the world has ever seen. It has been laying the foundations for the birth of humanity-in-Christ.

However, that process still has a long way to go to fulfill God's promise of human salvation in Christ. Though Christianity is the largest religion in the world today, it still occupies a minority of humanity. In addition, the growth of Christianity has not been steady, but has been in fits and starts, two steps forward and one back. It has always been this way, and is a reflection of human stubbornness and sin.

As the church advances in the world through evangelism it increasingly brings Christ-like character qualities to more and more people through regeneration by the power and presence of the Holy Spirit. But in that process the church also absorbs some of the worldly and ungodly character qualities from the sinners and new converts it brings into her ranks. There is a cross-pollination of character qualities as the church advances into the world of sin and corruption. In order to change people it must interact with people who are not regenerate. This cannot be avoided, but must be treated seriously in order to maintain the church on the course that God has set for her.

This program of evangelism and membership maintenance in the church involves the ongoing preaching, teaching, and discipline of sanctification or maturity in Christ. All levels of growth and maturity must always be actively engaged because there are always new people coming on board, and people don't all grow and mature in the same ways or at the same rates. Therefore, there must be a broad variety of perspectives, understandings, theories, and theologies that are mutually harmonious in order to maintain the unity of the church in face of human diversity and maturity. Indeed, this variety provides fuel for growth and sanctification as the various perspectives and understandings require mutual love and patience to maintain the cords of harmonious participation in the great cause of Jesus Christ.

PATIENCE

Common participation and harmonious cooperation in the face of diverse perspectives, opinions, and understandings of Jesus Christ must be maintained in the church in order for sanctification and maturity in Christ to be genuinely effective. When participants divide from or renounce other faithful Christians, they break the bonds of harmony and sanctification, and thereby thwart and stunt their own spiritual maturity in Christ by cutting off dialog. Christians cannot renounce other Christians and expect the Lord to be pleased with them.

The issue here is understanding and accepting the definition and limits of Christian orthodoxy (doctrine) and orthopraxy (polity). We are called to maintain the peace and purity of the church, and yet at any given time in history the church will not be perfectly peaceful nor perfectly pure. The boundaries of acceptable Christian faithfulness are not static, but are dynamic and even somewhat porous, which means that the issue of who is actually in Christ and who is not is a perpetual concern.

The most important aspect of this issue is that individual Christians are not at liberty to decide the answers for themselves. No individual Christian should anathematize another person—period. Rather, the decisions regarding the acceptable limits of orthodoxy and orthopraxy are the responsibility of church elders, not individual members. If Christians will accept this rule, then they are free to enjoy theological and doctrinal discussion and debate with all comers (everyone, regardless of their associations), understanding that the topics of discussion and debate are beliefs and ideas, not persons. And where people suspect serious deviation of doctrine, belief, or principle, they should discuss it with their own church elders and allow the elders to deal with it, or not. Such determinations should always be formal decisions made by the corporate body, not individuals.

We must understand that people are not saved by what they believe, as if believing the "right things" unlocks the door of salvation. It just doesn't work that way. Rather, people are saved in order that they may trust Jesus Christ to bring them into agreement with God and ultimate salvation. It is trusting in Christ and not believing in particular doctrines that provides the ground for salvation—and for sanctification. We must not separate salvation from sanctification. They always work together because salvation is not an end to attain, but a means to engage. Right belief is not static doctrine, but involves dynamic growth in Christ, and different individuals begin from different places and grow in different ways and at different rates in order to come to harmonious conclusions.

Consequently, Paul's blessing and/or call for the peace that issues from God's grace comes from his commitment to Christian unity in the face of the diversity that he experienced in his travels. Paul set the limits of orthodoxy and orthopraxy in his letters and Christendom is bound by them. We are to imitate Paul, who imitated Christ in this regard.

Paul's letter to the church at Ephesus was directed to this end and it will behoove Christians everywhere to trust and embody this letter in its entirety. May God grant us the grace to live in peace and harmony with one another.

3. FOUNDATIONAL BLESSINGS

Blessed be the God and Father of our Lord Jesus Christ, who has blessed us in Christ with every spiritual blessing in the heavenly places, even as he chose us in him before the foundation of the world, that we should be holy and blameless before him. In love... —Ephesians 1:4

In verse 2 Paul brought God's blessing to the church. In verse 3 he returned blessings to God. The blessing goes both ways. It comes from God to the church, and the church then prays blessings upon God. Each blesses the other because each is a blessing to the other. And as Paul models this behavior between God and church, so individual Christians and their churches are to engage in this kind of mutual blessing, as well. Blessings are a lot like friends, in that if you want one you need to be one.

Paul's acknowledgment that God is the Father of Jesus Christ provides a statement of Christ's divinity and of the Lordship of Christ over His church. Paul provided assurance that the church and the Ephesians were not engaged with false gods. Rather, God, being their Father, would protect, preserve, and persevere with them.

To instruct and insure them that they were not engaged in works-righteousness Paul used the past tense to describe what Christ had already done for them. They were not trying to earn God's blessing. They couldn't! It had already been given in abundance. Paul wasn't exaggerating when he said that *every* spiritual blessing in heaven had been given to them. To understand what spiritual blessings are and how they work, we need only indicate their source—Jesus Christ. All spiritual blessings come through Jesus Christ because of Christ's role as Messiah and position as the archetype of the new humanity in Christ. Christ is the only mediator between God and humanity, so He is the only source of spiritual blessings from God to humanity. And because Christ has already come, all spiritual blessings have already come with Him. They are not complete, but they have come.

This provided much assurance for the Ephesian church, which had been infiltrated with false teachers and apostles. Paul was writing to correct the church, and understanding that Christian salvation was accomplished by Christ, and not by our belief in Christ, provided much needed help. People are forever falling back into the ideas and habits of religious works-righteousness that insists that we must earn our salvation.

Chrystostom suggested that Paul had emphasized the word *spiritual* here in order to contrast the Mosaic blessings of the law with Christ's spiritual blessings that fulfilled the law and thereby made the law efficacious. Prior to the advent of Christ, the law could only point to human sin and our inherent inability to live in obedience to the law. In this way, the law served to set up the advent of Christ because apart from Christ the law would be an unattainable, eternal curse.

However, because the law set up the advent of Christ, and the church is the resurrected body of Christ, the law also has a function in the church—seeing the law in or through Christ. *In Christ* the law took on new meaning and effectiveness because *in Christ* it can be engaged and obeyed to the best of our inadequate ability, knowing that our abilities are insufficient, but resting in the fulfilled promise that the Messiah provides for us what we cannot provide ourselves. And that is great news indeed!

ELECTION DECISION

Verse 4 provides the classic proof text for the doctrine of election. Because the gospel of Jesus Christ is not a matter of works-righteousness but works "by grace through faith" (Ephesians 2:8), we must be clear that it is not *our* faith that causes us to be included in Christ. Rather, it is Christ's faith in God's promises that allowed Him to provide propitiation for human sin. And His propitiation opened the gates of the church. Because Christ gave His life while we were yet sinners, when we were unable and unwilling to even be concerned about God or Christ, we can be in Christ, not because of some decision we have made, but because of the decision God made to send

Christ and the decision Christ made to provide propitiation for human sin on the cross.

Of course, believers assent to God's plan,[1] but it is not our choosing to be in Christ that puts us in Christ. Rather, people find themselves in Christ, and then choose to agree with God, His Word, and His plan. It's not that the language of "giving ourselves to Christ" is wrong—it isn't. But the truth is that it was God's firstgiving that lands people in Christ, not their decision. Again, our giving of ourselves comes after the fact of God's presence in our lives, and constitutes the simple affirmation that we have been given to Christ.

If I want to give something to you, I have to have a relationship with you before I give the gift. And the same thing is true regarding God. For us to either receive something from or give something to God, we must have a relationship prior to the giving. We must think carefully here, lest we confuse ourselves and others. I'm not saying that there is no human decision to be made regarding faith in Christ, clearly there is. However, our decision does not *determine* our salvation. It does not put us in Christ. Rather, our decision is simply a confirmation of what God has already done. We cannot be grateful to God until we realize that we are already included in the salvation He has provided. To find ourselves not included in God's salvation, but challenged to accept what we do not know, understand, or experience amounts to a call to blind faith. God does not call people to blind faith. Rather, He cures blindness. God is opposed to blind faith because it is a function of ignorance. God calls people to intelligent faith, not ignorance.

By the time people become aware and/or seriously concerned about God, Christ, and salvation in their own lives, the critical decisions have already been made by God—and usually by them, as well. Some people say that God prevenes or precedes our decisions with His grace. By the time that we feel the urgency of God's concerns, we feel them because God has already shown us our inadequacies and needs. All we do is confirm what God has already done.

If we find ourselves in Christ, we will at some point simply assent to the fact. We agree with what God has already done because we find that it is true in our own lives. And those who don't find themselves in Christ, well … the truth is that they don't *find themselves* at all. They simply remain lost in the mindset and circumstances of

---

1   *God's Great Plan for the World—The Biblical Story of Creation and Redemption*, Phillip A. Ross, Pilgrim Platform, Marietta, Ohio, 2019.

Adam, and are unconcerned about Christ or salvation. We may wish things to be otherwise, but the lost simply ignore and/or deny the truth, reality, and power of God. They deny God's prevening grace and choose to ignore God.

Sure, people pine about the gods of their own imaginations. Lost people do sometimes speak about God and Jesus, but they do so without genuine care or real understanding because of their prior denial. What they mean by the words *God* and *Jesus* is not the God or Jesus of faithful biblical interpretation, but the "god" and "jesus" of unbelief, of denial. The words themselves do not invoke the power or presence of God or Jesus. They may as well be speaking about imaginary characters in a fictional story because the characters *they* imagine to be associated with those names are in fact *imaginary*. And they often acknowledge this by saying that the God of the Bible is imaginary—because He is imaginary *to them*.

A lot of people misunderstand the doctrine of election by thinking about it from a godless perspective. But as evidenced from the above discussion, believers and unbelievers do not understand the same ideas in the same way. Belief or lack thereof colors our understanding. It shapes how we see reality. Those who believe in God see the world through a *God-lens*, and those who don't, see the world through a *not-God-lens*. There is no neutral or objective position between belief in God and belief in not-God (or unbelief) because the God issue determines the definition of what is usually called *objective neutrality*. Thus, the doctrine of election understood by the elect is quite different from the doctrine of election understood by the non-elect. And this fact has given rise to much misunderstanding over the centuries.[2]

The traditional doctrine of election issues out of the doctrine of God's sovereignty, out of the idea that God is all-powerful and noth-

---

2   Traditionally, Calvinists think that Arminians are not believers, and Arminians think that Calvinists are not believers because the theologies of Calvinism and Arminianism have been crafted out of mutually exclusive doctrines. Both are internally consistent and logically valid positions from within their universe of assumptions. And because those assumptions are projected upon the Bible, they both identify themselves as being biblically faithful and consistent. For a theological discussion that transcends these traditional perspectives see: Beecher, Edward. *Conflict of Ages—The Great Debate of the Moral Relations of God and Man* (2012), and *Concord of Ages—The Individual And Organic Harmony Of God And Man* (2013), Phillip A. Ross, editor, Pilgrim Platform, Marietta, Ohio.

ing can stop Him from doing exactly what He wants to do. We find the idea of election clearly stated in Deuteronomy 7:6:

> "The LORD your God has chosen you to be a people for his treasured possession, out of all the peoples who are on the face of the earth."

Paul also embraced it, reminding the Romans of God's words through Moses:

> "I will have mercy on whom I have mercy, and I will have compassion on whom I have compassion" (Romans 9:15).

God decides who receives His mercy and compassion, which is equivalent to salvation for our purposes here.

INITIATOR

Again, it is important to note that this does not mean that individuals have no say with regard to their own salvation. No one is saved who doesn't want to be saved, and no one who wants to be saved is left unsaved. Clearly salvation and the desire and willingness to be saved always go together. All I am saying is that God is the initiator in salvation. God leads and we follow. God commands and we obey. God offers and we accept. There is no salvation apart from the acceptance, the following, and the obedience. All who are saved agree with God's initial decision, and all who are not saved agree with God's decision to pass them by.

Louis Berkof said that God's

> "knowledge is all immediate and simultaneous rather than successive like ours, and His comprehension of it is always complete. And the decree that is founded on it is also a single, all-comprehensive, and simultaneous act. As an eternal and immutable decree it could not be otherwise. There is, therefore, no series of decrees in God, but simply one comprehensive plan, embracing all that comes to pass. Our finite comprehension, however, constrains us to make distinctions, and this accounts for the fact that we often speak of the decrees of God in the plural. This manner of speaking is perfectly legitimate, provided we do not lose sight of the unity of the divine decree, and of the inseparable connection of the various decrees as we conceive of them."[3]

---

3 Berkof, Louis. *Systematic Theology*, 1932, 1938, Erdmans, 1996.

To speak of God's decree, purpose, or plan are simply different ways to talk about God's intention. According to Matthew 1:21, Mary "will bear a son, and you shall call his name Jesus, for he will save his people from their sins." Here we see that Jesus will save "his people" (τον λαόν). This first mention of salvation in the New Testament points to the corporate element of our human identity. To understand this we need to see the difference between *a people* and *some persons*. A people is a group who share significant similarities of genetics, character, and culture, whereas a group of persons is simply a random collection of individuals who may or may not have much in common.

The reason that this distinction is important is because of the role that it plays in Christian unity. The fact that Christ came to save *a people* unto Himself means that He was saving human unity or the wholeness of humanity. To better understand the importance of this distinction we can consider the future of humanity apart from Christ's salvation.

EXTINCTION

If Christ had not come, if there would be no such thing as God's salvation in Christ, Humanity would perish as a species because "all have sinned and fall short of the glory of God" (Romans 3:23), no one would be saved. Humanity as a kind or species would become extinct if no one is saved because there is both a heavenly and an earthly element to salvation. One of the things that salvation means is sustainable human life on earth.

This is the context of God's salvation, and is a consequence of the meaning of the sure death[4] that Adam acquired in the Fall. It is not that Christ came to save a few good people out of a rotten humanity for a pristine life in some nether world called *heaven*. Rather, Christ came to save the human genome, humanity as a species from extinction. Keep this thought in mind, but realize that it paints only half of the picture.

Compare the above idea of corporate salvation with Matthew 10:22: "... the person (οὗτος) who endures to the end will be saved." Here the Lord is speaking about those *individuals* who endure. Here we see Christ's emphasis upon the salvation of the individual rather

---

4   Genesis 2:17, מות תמות. Ross, Phillip A. *Arsy Varsy—Reclaiming The Gospel in First Corinthians*, Pilgrim Platform, Marietta, Ohio, 2008, chapter 47: "Death."

than the soul.[5] We must keep in mind that human identity requires the manifestation of a specific instance of a type, kind, or species—an individual. No human being exists in a vacuum and no individual can exist without other human beings. Every individual is a product of two other human beings. That product (embryo) becomes a specific instance of humanity, and carries the essential genetic structure of humanity. This is the other half of the picture.

When we ask, *who did Christ come to save*, we must acknowledge that He came to save humanity from extinction, but humanity cannot be saved apart from saving particular individuals. Thus, it is these dual elements of human identity that entail both human individuality (uniqueness) and human corporality (groupness) that gives rise to the confusion regarding the doctrine of election. God chose to save a people, the wholeness and unity, not merely particular individuals, but *a people*, a particular type, kind, or species. When we try to decide whether the wholeness or the particularity of humanity is more important, we find ourselves in a quandary because the individuality and the corporality of human identity cannot be separated without damaging the reality of life.

However, it is clear that God chose Israel out of the mass of humanity to be His treasured possession. He infected them with the desire for righteousness. The Old Testament is the story of God's selection of a particular type or kind of person to be saved. God did not choose to save every kind or type of person, but has consistently chosen particular individuals to represent the kind or type of person He intends to save. When God created humanity, He began with one person, Adam. But it was the whole person of Adam, and so God is concerned about the whole person of Christ. And from Adam's type (or genome) he formed Eve to be Adam's complement. All of humanity has come from Adam and Eve—and God. God's involvement is essential.

But Adam and Eve separated themselves from God, so God separated them from Himself. And God was not pleased with what humanity had become apart from Him in their rejection and sin, so He drowned them all in a flood—all except Noah (the archetypal individual) and his family (the corporality). Later God chose Abraham to be His representative (archetype) and promised him many sons (corporality). Then He applied the same promise to Isaac, and then to Jacob.

---

5 See "Wholeness & Soulness" p. 66.

God always chooses a particular type of individual out the midst of many possible types.

In Jacob, then, God planted His flag as He created the nation of Israel (corporality) out of Jacob (the archetypal individual). God had reshaped Jacob from his original type to a new type who was touched by an angel, and changed forever. The important thing about Jacob was that God reshaped him, and that Jacob represented the kind of person that God wanted to save—those who can be reshaped by the Lord.

However, the final lesson of the Old Testament is found in the Book of Acts. The final lesson of the Old Testament was the destruction of Jerusalem and the Temple. It was not sufficient for God to simply reshape people into a better likeness of Himself on the foundation of Adam (or on the typology of Adam). God sent His Son, Jesus Christ, to serve as Messiah in order to birth a new human archetype for human emulation. Humanity needed to be reborn into a completely new image, a better image on a better type, an image that was free from the sorry history of humanity prior to Christ.

Reshaped

The reshaped image of Jacob carried too much old history. It was not simply that Jacob's reshaped moral character was lacking, but that the other nations of the world had too much old history with Jacob's ancestry. They could not let go of that history, and were determined to hold on to their revenge against Jacob and his people. Their identity was caught up in family and clan, and they could not release themselves from their historic commitments of family honor that produced the religions of revenge. In fact, that old human urge for revenge has continued to plague humanity for our entire history. Indeed, the Old Testament is full of ongoing sin—faithlessness, wars, revolutions, betrayal, intrigue, etc.

In order to escape the historic momentum of human sin, betrayal and revenge, God needed a particular archetype to represent a new humanity who did not bring the baggage of sin and revenge with him, someone apart from the baggage of human history. But there was no one on earth or in earth's history who could serve such a role. So God sent His Son, Jesus Christ, who had no previous history on earth as a human being—which is the significance of His virgin birth. In Christ, humanity could begin again with a clean slate. Jesus Christ would serve as the new human archetype for a new humanity-in-Christ.

Christ, then, came to provide a new human archetype that was worthy of God's salvation. The incarnation of Christ brought that archetype into human flesh and human history as a reality. And Christ's obedience unto death on the cross provided the evidence that this archetype could be manifest as a reality in the world.

It was as though God had sent a non-cannibal into a tribe of cannibals to teach them how to stop cannibalizing. The only way to accomplish it was to have the non-cannibal model life apart from cannibalism, but doing so would mean that he would be cannibalized himself. But before he was cannibalized he would teach a few others the joy and beauty of life without cannibalization. The community of his followers and the historical record of his life without cannibalism would preserve the new archetype so that it could be adequately presented to the tribe as a viable lifestyle in future generations.

TWO EDGES

Indeed, such was the mission of Jesus Christ, who came to save humanity by regeneration into the unity of His own likeness, according to the Messianic archetype described in Scripture. God's salvation focus is double-edged. One edge involves particular individuals, and the other edge involves the wholeness or unity of those individuals in the corporate body of Christ. Again, Christ is saving only a particular type of individual out of a humanity that is currently composed of many types. The particular type of individual that the Lord is saving is the kind who belongs to Jesus Christ, who imitates Christ's character, who follows Christ's leadership, and who lives in Christ. Such an individual must die and be born again in Christ in order to put an end to the human history that clings to him and his family history like barnacles on a ship.

Christ is not just saving a random assortment of human individuals, but He is saving a unified people who will serve as His body in this world and the next. He is saving the church in all of her holiness and wholeness, which is the new ark of humanity that is currently being built in the midst of the fullness of the accumulated sin of the world. Those who are not in this arc[6] cannot be saved. Those who are

---

6   The analogy between the ancient Ark of Noah and corresponding arc of God's wake or train in human history is intended.

not in unity with the Ark of Christ (the Arc of Christianity) will perish in the disunity of the progeny of Adam's sin.

Individuals cannot be saved apart from being in the Ark of Christ, which means that the Ark—the church of Jesus Christ—must also be saved as a whole. The Ark is the wholeness and the unity of the individuals who are in Christ. And this is the object of God's salvation.

Paul said that this decree, purpose, and/or plan was conceived by God "before the foundation of the world" (v. 4). This simply means that God plans before He acts, but since God doesn't live in time like we do, He doesn't experience time sequences like *before* or *after*. Thus, using the word *before* here indicates a logical priority rather than a time sequence. Another way to say it is that God acts with intent and purpose, and takes time to accomplish His intentions.

Holy Perfection

Paul said that *we*, the church, should be holy and blameless before God (v. 4). But there is a serious difficulty here in that if the standard is *perfection* (Matthew 5:48), then no individual Christian will qualify this side of glory. So we are given a moral directive that cannot be satisfied if we hold on to some sort of ultimate form of perfection that every individual must achieve. The requirement of an individualistic, ultimate form of absolute perfection undermines the reality of God's mercy and human growth, development, and maturity—and smacks of Gnosticism. Perfection, therefore, cannot mean what most Christians think it means. Rather, it is a process of growth and maturity.

When Jesus calls His people to be perfect in Matthew 5:48, he calls *them* as a group to a particular understanding and practice of perfection. The Greek word translated as *perfection* (τέλειος) literally means complete or whole. The whole people of God are to embrace the wholeness or unity of the people of God-in-Christ. And that wholeness or unity is not a static characteristic, but an unfolding process that is related to the progressive revelation of Christ in history.[7] This wholeness or unity is a present fact because it is a teleological projection, not simply an abstract or intellectual construct, but an actual, historical projection in the sense of being a historically accumulative dynamic reality. Think of it as the course of a ship, airplane, or spacecraft, where the target of *projection* is the destination, and the actual *route* is the dynamic path it takes to that destination based

---

7   See footnote 1 on p. iii.

upon its initial point of departure and the varying conditions encountered along the way. A better word for it might be *end* or *goal*.

The progressive revelation of Jesus Christ in history produces an accumulation of wisdom and knowledge that is passed forward by preceding generations of faithful Christians through literature and tradition. Each new generation of faithful Christians inherits this accumulated wisdom and knowledge—not perfectly, but adequately—as they encounter and engage Christ through His literature and traditions. But their job is not to simply receive and pass forward what they have received. Rather, their job is to glorify what they have received by adding their own understanding of it to the Ark of Christ, the Arc of God's history in the world.

Thus, the perfection that belongs to the church as a whole, exists through the decree of God outside of time, or in the fullness of time. The destination of the trip is not part of the trip because the trip ends when the destination is reached. The end is not part of the means. And yet, the engagement of that perfection must be manifest in time, which means that it grows and matures over time in the consciousness of particular Christians who are dependent on Christ and interdependent with one another. Another way to say it is that the decree of God calls Christians to perfection in Christ through engagement with other Christians in the body of Christ. This consciousness produces contemplation, consideration, and discussion among Christians of every sort and era that calls contemporary Christians (or the current and ongoing generation of Christians) to progressive sanctification in Christ through prayer, worship, study, and service.

OUR LOVE

Verse 4 ends in the *English Standard Version* with a sentence fragment, "In love...." The *Authorized Version* assigned these words to the preceding sentence,

> "According as he hath chosen us in him before the foundation of the world, that we should be holy and without blame before him in love" (v. 4).

The Greek does not have punctuation, so sentence structure is a matter of interpretation. The *Authorized Version* interpretation says that our holiness and blamelessness are a function of our being *in* God's *love*. The *English Standard Version* interpretation says that God's predestination issues out of God's love. Both ideas are biblically true, but which is the correct reading here?

To ask about *the* correct reading assumes that there is only one correct reading. Yet, both readings produce true statements, so both are correct. Therefore, we must inquire into God's purpose in providing this apparent dilemma. However, we must keep in mind that it is only a dilemma if there is only one correct interpretation. And because there are at least two correct interpretations, we must conclude that God has not provided a dilemma, but an opportunity to better understand God's character, which is Trinitarian or multi-perspectival.[8]

Because the Godhead is both one and three, both unitary and manifold at the same time, we can understand the question of the correct reading here in terms of the multiple perspectivity of God Himself. Each Person of the Godhead provides a unique perspective that is in complete unity with the other unique perspectives of the other Persons of the Godhead. Doing so brings us to the conclusion that God intends us to find this issue and understand it in the light of God's Trinitarian character. Thus, both readings are true and each adds clarity and articulation to our progressive understanding of God. To choose one or the other readings exclusively diminishes our understanding of the wholeness of God. The fact that both are true adds to the uniqueness of God's Trinitarian reality.

Understood from the *Authorized Version* perspective we see that our holiness and blamelessness are a function of being in *love* (ἀγάπη, *agape*). Paul's choice of words here draws us away from a romantic or emotional definition of love and into the practical love of *agape* that is also known as *charity*. *Agape* is love with legs, love that serves others with no expectation of reward or return. Love that is holy and blameless is neither romantic nor other worldly, but issues out of selfless service. Indeed, such service, such love is holy and blameless, and it issues our of our humanity in Christ.

GOD'S CHOICE

From the *English Standard Version* perspective, we learn from verse 4 that God's choosing was itself an act by God that put those whom He chose in Christ. Here we see that God's choice was not

---

8   *A Primer on Perspectivalism,* John M. Frame, https://frame-poythress.org/a-primer-on-perspectivalism/.

simply a function of God's desire that Christians be holy and blameless as they come before Him, but that God's decision to put them *in Christ* is the very thing that makes them holy and blameless. This does not mean that those in Christ no longer sin. Rather, it means that those in Christ rely upon the perfection of the archetype of Christ to guide them into personal holiness and corporate wholeness in Christ over time.

Here our holiness and blamelessness are not a function of our own love or charity, but are a function of God's electing love, which teleologically puts particular individuals into Christ's church or body, like putting marbles in a bag. Of course, Christ is holy and blameless, and we are called to be like Christ. But how on earth are people supposed to accomplish such a high calling? People are full of sin, Christ is not. People are finite, Christ is infinite. The call to be like Christ calls people to do or become what they cannot of themselves do or become. Coming to this realization of our own personal inability is the purpose of God's electing love. We can't do it ourselves!

If it is going to happen at all, it must first happen as a function of God's action, God's selection, God's electing love—not ours because we are inadequate. Only God *can* do it, and He *has* done it through Christ! Only Christ has lived in perfect obedience. And because Christ has done it in the flesh, He has opened the way for those who will follow Him. But He didn't merely open the way, He also sent the Holy Spirit to both initiate and complete the process. He sent the Holy Spirit as His Agent to be our helper (John 14:16, 14:26, 15:26, 16:7).

It is critical that we understand who and/or what God has elected (selected). The idea that God "chose us in him" (v. 4) means that God made a choice. The *us* (ἡμᾶς) that God chose is plural. He chose a group or type of people. Of course groups are composed of individuals, and in this case the individuals of the group are self-similar.[9] Thus, those who emulate Christ's character are in the group, *in Him*. It's not that God was choosing random individuals before time, but that God choose to save a particular type of character, which Christ modeled perfectly and we emulate as best we can, trusting that God will complete what He began, and that Christ's model has sufficient power to provide what is needed.

---

9   In mathematics, self-similarity means exactly or approximately similar to a part of itself (i.e. the whole has the same shape as the parts). Here self-similar means that the group has or will have the same character as Christ.

Seed Principle

In the beginning God created Adam as a human seed, and out of this one seed all humanity through all of history has proceeded or issued out of Adam. And prior to the creation of Adam, God had a plan, a decree or purpose regarding Adam—humanity. That plan involved the billions of people who have since lived, and who will continue to live, on earth. That plan also involved Jesus Christ, His Son, and redemption in Christ. God's plan was not merely to preserve human seed from extinction, but to provide for a massive human population on earth (Genesis 22:17). God's plan was not simply to save random individuals from eternal death, but to save a particular kind or type of renewed individual from extinction.

God was aware of the individuals He intended to save, not because of their individual human uniquenesses, but because of their Christian commonalities.[10] God is in the process of saving *Christians*, people whose character qualities are like Christ's character qualities—not identical, but similar. God chose to save a particular kind or type of human being, those like Christ, His Son. Thus, we can understand that God's election involves, not random individuals, but a particular group, kind, or type of individual. It is not that God randomly chooses individuals and then conforms or changes them to fit the criteria of the group. But rather, God planted the seed of the Holy Spirit in Christ, who then incarnated into human flesh in order to spawn His Spirit in humanity in order to bring humanity into increasing conformity with Christ's character.

God's intention is to save humanity, both individually and corporately, because humanity can only be truly saved when both the individuals and the wholeness of humanity are saved. To save only individuals without also saving human wholeness would not be human salvation. And to save only the wholeness of humanity but not particular individuals would amount to a salvation that includes no one. Consequently, both parts and whole must be involved in salvation.

God has therefore chosen to save both particular individuals and humanity as a whole. People invite confusion when they seek to know too much detail because the details of reality are far more complex than they think or want or can comprehend. All of the details are not provided in Scripture. Rather, Scripture provides an outline of

---

10 Human uniqueness is enhanced not destroyed by our relationship to Christ. See "more unique," p. 68.

God's plan, and with regard to election we find only brief allusions to the whole, and not concrete explanations of the details. This means that we can understand God's election to be His decision to save a particular kind of individual. He intends to conform humanity to the character of Christ. Precisely which individuals will be saved and which won't be is not revealed—except that those who will be saved will conform to the character of Christ over time. Nor are we to speculate as individuals beyond our own personal inclusion. The question is not whether this or that person will be saved, but will I (you) be saved?

Since God's intention is to save the whole of humanity from extinction, it behooves us not to doubt the salvation of others, but to assume that God's grace and mercy in this regard are far greater than our own. In addition, the assumption of the salvation of others provides them with a kind of encouragement to fulfill that expectation. It provides a kind of glue that contributes to social cohesion and harmony.

4. GOD'S FORELOVE

In love he predestined us for adoption as sons through Jesus Christ, according to the purpose of his will, to the praise of his glorious grace, with which he has blessed us in the Beloved.

—Ephesians 1:5-6

Understood from the *English Standard Version* perspective we learn that God's predestination issues out of God's love. Because He loves us He makes plans for our future well-being. God's predestination isn't that odd or strange. To predestinate is nothing more than to plan. It should be no surprise that God plans. Nor should it be a surprise that God accomplishes what He plans.

The Greek word (προορζω, *predestined*) literally means to limit in advance. God set limits—boundaries, borders, and distinctions. And this is perhaps one of God's most important activities.

> "In the beginning God created the heavens and the earth. The earth was without form and void, and darkness was over the face of the deep" (Genesis 1:1-2).

Boundaries, borders, and distinctions were the first result of God's creation. God created a separation between heaven and earth. Having created heaven and the earth (Genesis 1:1), God turned His gaze to the earth, but there were no distinctions or separations on the earth. At that point the earth was an amorphous, distinctionless, dark (חשֶׁךְ) blob. Note that the earth was not nothing, but lacked form (תהו). It was an empty wilderness (בהו). We need to rethink the idea of creation *ex nihilo*.

"God said, 'Let there be light,' and there was light" (Genesis 1:3).
It should not go unnoticed that God created heaven and earth before
light was mentioned, because it has far reaching implications regarding the creation, evolution, and origins debates. It is usually thought
by all parties that the first thing created was light, but that is not what
the Bible says. One of the implications of this is that the light (אוֹר)
that God mentioned may not be what the scientists think of as light.
A closer reading of Genesis will also reveal that it does not say that
God *created* light. Rather, after God created heaven and earth, He
brought light to illuminate them. But this is a conversation of a different order.

Then God separated or distinguished light from darkness (Genesis 1:4), again setting boundaries, borders, and distinctions. This is interesting because light in-and-of-itself provides the distinction
between itself and darkness. God recognized the distinction, and by
recognizing it He authorized it. Then God separated the waters in the
sky from the waters below (Genesis 1:6). Note again how God used
division, which requires boundaries, borders, and distinctions. In the
beginning, God created boundaries, borders, and distinctions which,
as it turns out, provide the foundation for life. All creatures are by
definition distinct from their surroundings, their environment. Each
created creature is a kind of whole, distinct from its environment.

God subsequently created Adam, and then made Eve from
Adam's rib. He differentiated them. Later, God gave the Ten Commandments, which set limits—boundaries, borders, and distinctions—
on human behavior. Then God separated the nation of Israel from the
other nations, etc. You get the point. God distinguishes things by
creating limits, distinctions, boundaries, and borders. This activity of
God helps us to distinguish one thing from another, to make distinctions and judgments, all of which are critical to life and living. Life
involves the interaction of various distinct things, and without
boundaries, borders, and distinctions life could not exist. This is what
God does. And it is all a kind of predestination in the sense that God
has a plan for the world to support life, and that plan distinguishes one
thing from another as it unfolds.

Adoption

Paul tied predestination to adoption in verse 5, and adoption is
also about the borders and boundaries of inclusion and exclusion.
Adoption is about family membership. Adoption takes someone who

is not a natural member of a family and makes him a legal member. Adoption is a legal process that institutes what is otherwise limited to family or blood identity. Family members are related by blood—or by adoption.

Adoption changes one's identity and provides for inheritance rights, or intergenerational transfer of property and ownership. Adoption involves no necessary change in the individual person who is being adopted, but is entirely dependent upon the person who is doing the adopting. Similarly, divine adoption is entirely an action that only God can take, human beings can contribute nothing to their adoption, other than their agreement.

Paul's concern in this verse was to indicate that adoption was part of God's plan, that He predestined it for no other reason than it contributes to His purpose. It not only fit into God's plan, but it is a key element of God's plan. There has been much discussion in Christian history about the relationship between Christian adoption and regeneration. Are they the same things? If not, what is the difference? Is one logically and/or temporally prior to the other? Are they equivalent?

John Murray said of this concern:

> "In a word, the representation of Scripture is to the effect that by regeneration we become members of God's kingdom, by adoption we become members of God's family."[1]

Interestingly, Murray's definition is the opposite of what most Evangelicals think. Regeneration garners much more attention and print among Evangelicals than does adoption. It is commonly believed in Evangelical circles that regeneration brings people into the family of God by spiritual birth, which identifies them as Christian. And adoption, being a legal term, just doesn't get the attention—presumably because it is associated with legalism. Adoption is found in the historical and technical literature of Evangelicalism, but it isn't mentioned much in popular church culture. However, Murray's analysis is worthy of our consideration.

KINGDOM

Murray suggests that membership in God's kingdom is different than membership in God's family. And because Jesus redefined His

---

1   Murray, John. *The Collected Writings of John Murray*, 4 volumes, *Adoption*, Edinburgh, Banner of Truth Trust, 1982.

family as being "whoever does the will of my Father in heaven" (Matthew 12:46-50), and because doing God's will means being *in Christ*, God's family is another term for the church, the people of God or body of Christ. According to Murray, regeneration puts people into God's kingdom, and adoption brings them into the church, which is a subset of the greater kingdom. Prior to regeneration, people are neither in the kingdom nor the church, but are in Adam, that is, in sin.

People are born in sin, in Adam, and Christians are baptized into the Trinitarian name of Jesus through the Father, Son, and Holy Spirit. By baptism people receive the name of Christ, and are to be considered Christian by everyone—at least that is the intention of baptism. Because Christian baptism is a public ceremony, it announces to the world, not just to the church or the kingdom, that the baptized individual has been marked by the name of Jesus Christ.

We must take care to be aware that Scripture is not as technically precise as we twenty-first century, scientific people want it to be. The whole idea of the change from being a non-Christian to being a Christian is described in Scripture in a variety of ways with a variety of terms. Sometimes the term *baptism* is so used to describe the change of character, and sometimes it simply refers to the ceremony of baptism. Sometimes the change is referred to as *regeneration, conversion,* or *adoption.* Of course, there are subtle differences between these things, but they all contribute to the change of character that God intends.

The ceremony of baptism celebrates and symbolizes adoption and points the baptized person to the fulfillment of regeneration and conversion, to the process of sanctification. And while there are a variety of ways to organize these terms, they must all be engaged for the process of salvation to be complete. However we choose to organize them intellectually, we must distinguish between the ceremony of baptism, the psychology of regeneration, the new way of thinking and behaving that results from conversion, and the formal legalities of adoption. It's not as neat and tidy in Scripture as we want it to be.

Baptism

The baptismal ceremony simply initiates and symbolizes the change with its imagery of dying to the world and being reborn in Christ. The symbolism of baptism is death and resurrection in Christ, the beginning and end points of the process. The ceremony marks the beginning of the decent into symbolic death by publicly acknowledging that the baptized individual is under God's jurisdiction, suffering from the consequences of Adam's sin. It is the acknowledgment that the individual is responsible to God's covenant. Baptism is not a guarantee of individual faithfulness, whether we are talking about infant or believers' baptism. It is, however, the public announcement that the individual is under God's jurisdiction and the care of Christ's church.

Baptismal resurrection in Christ is symbolically equated with regeneration. It is rising in new life, a new beginning in Christ. Sometimes the process of new birth in Christ is dramatic, and sometimes it is subtle. Different people need and experience it differently. The quality and/or reality of regeneration is not tied to our subjective experience of it, whether dramatic or subtle. But whatever our experience, the result of regeneration is the birth of a new interest and passion for God-in-Christ. And again, that passion may be strong or weak, but whatever else it is, it must be real.

The symbolism of regeneration originates in baptismal resurrection (or fruition) in Christ. Baptism begins with a public ceremony and concludes with the reality of new life in Christ. Sometimes these two elements of baptism (death and resurrection) appear close together in time, and sometimes there are years or even decades between them. Nonetheless, the time involved is immaterial to God. The significant result of regeneration is the conscious acceptance, reception, and confession of Jesus Christ as personal Lord and Savior. This confession should also be a matter of public proclamation or confirmation that begins a process of discipleship—study and training.

New Life

The birth of new life in Christ brings the individual into the kingdom of God, according to Murray. Note that entry into the kingdom of God involves the conscious, intentional and free will confession of Christ as Lord and Savior by the individual. Entry into the kingdom of God is where human free will is exercised in the process of salvation, whether through the Baptistic symbolism of choosing to be baptized, or the Reformed symbolism of choosing to be confirmed or to own the covenant.[2] However, more is required to actually be in Christ than our personal consent or agreement to follow God-in-Christ because of the temptation and reality of self-delu-

2 See Appendix, Baptism Parallels, p. 408.

sion. People are gullible, and self-centered. Self-justification is too simple.

God's Doing

One day Jesus was talking about false prophets and how to recognize the fruit of the gospel.

> "Not everyone who says to me, 'Lord, Lord,' will enter the kingdom of heaven, but the one who does the will of my Father who is in heaven. On that day many will say to me, 'Lord, Lord, did we not prophesy in your name, and cast out demons in your name, and do many mighty works in your name?' And then will I declare to them, 'I never knew you; depart from me, you workers of lawlessness'" (Matthew 7:21-23).

Those whom Jesus rejected here thought that they had experienced personal regeneration, and had even made public profession of Christ, and were probably baptized. We know this because they were leaders in that they were prophesying, healing, and doing miracles—all activities associated with leadership. But they lacked something essential.

What they lacked was adoption. They lacked what only God can supply. Only God can initiate and complete adoption into His family. In a sense, He must sign the papers to make it real. Matthew 7:21-23 shows us that human desire or will is not sufficient for church membership. Jesus said that "whoever does the will of God, he is my brother and sister and mother" (Mark 3:35). Paul acknowledged that "the Spirit intercedes for the saints according to the will of God" (Romans 8:27).

> "Do not be conformed to this world, but be transformed by the renewal of your mind, that by testing you may discern what is the will of God, what is good and acceptable and perfect" (Romans 12:2).

In Matthew 7:21-23 we see the symbolism of God's sovereignty in salvation that stands against what we can do in our own free will decisions to adopt Christ for ourselves. We can accept Christ and do all sorts of great things in His name, but if God Himself does not officially and legally adopt us into His family, we have no inheritance in Him. This is a hard and difficult teaching because it stands against what is false—false teaching, false belief, false testimony, false confession, etc. What is false is what is not perfect truth, not whole or complete truth. Partial truth is always false truth because it is incomplete. It is not the whole truth, or the holistic truth, or the wholeness of truth. Ultimately, this suggests that people cannot become members of Christ's church apart from God's adoption, apart from His approval and signature—His will.

God's signature, His mark is a sign from God that the individual sufficiently conforms to the likeness of Jesus Christ. This sign or mark is manifest by the godliness of the life of the individual. This does not mean that people must be perfectly godly, but it does mean that their level of godliness improves over time. There is a moral element of Christianity that grows and matures over time, that results in increased godliness or Christ-likeness (Romans 6:17, Ephesians 2:2). The idea of God's signature or mark is an analogy, and does not simply mean that a piece of paper must be authorized by some church. Nor does the analogy oppose such a piece of paper. However, the reality is the godly life of the believer, not the paper.

But it also suggests that membership in Christ's church involves a legality, in that Jesus accused the people in Matthew 7:21 of being workers of lawlessness or illegality. They claimed something—membership in Christ's church—that requires some sort of legal sanction that they did not have and could not provide. It should be noted here that the law involved is God's law, and not necessarily civil or church law. Interestingly however, the elements of church membership (baptism and confirmation/confession—acknowledgment of regeneration) involve a public ceremony of announcement. Of course, such ceremonies do not require any action, legal or otherwise, by civil authorities. Like marriage, God's adoption or church membership doesn't require any civil approval, though it is available for civil recognition. Civil approval is only necessary for civil benefits, while recognition is mere acknowledgment.

The creation of the church through adoption is, Paul said, "according to the purpose of his will" (v. 5), God's will. The church is the extension of God's purpose and God's will, which makes sense since the church is the body of God-in-Christ. His body should be subject to His will. Humanity engaged in the actual doing of God's will in Christ is the new humanity created by God-in-Christ. Only God can create new species, so it is appropriate that the action of creation—adoption—is God's action, not ours.

In Christ

Verse 6 begins with the Greek word εἰς, which literally means in this context: *for the purpose of.* All that takes place in verse 5 is for the purpose of "the praise of his glorious grace" (v. 6). God's predestination of our adoption, His plan to bring us into Christ, is not for our good or benefit—though it benefits us greatly. Rather, it is for God's own purpose of causing Christians to praise His grace. It is for the enhancement and ornamentation of God's mercy and grace. The purpose of God's predestination is to bring humanity into a state of worship—thankfulness, humility, and obeisance, wherein God-in-Christ is the object of worship.

Though God acts for His own purposes, His own glory, Christians derive a secondary benefit from God's graciousness simply because we are the recipients of God's grace "which ... has blessed us" (v. 6). Though God plans and executes it for His own benefit, those who are brought into Christ also receive benefit. God's primary concern is for the wholeness of the body of Christ, not for the benefit of the parts that comprise it—though the health and well-being of the parts contribute to the health and well-being of the wholeness.

Compare it to our own individual bodies. We want to be healthy and whole ourselves and if a body part becomes diseased or threatens the well-being of the whole, we will sacrifice the part for the sake of the whole. A diseased organ will be surgically removed, or a gangrenous foot will be amputated to preserve the well-being of the whole.[3] Indeed, we even make plans by securing health insurance to cover the cost of such surgery. And, in fact, the elimination of diseased parts positively contributes to the wholeness of individuals.

Such planning on our part is not all that different from God's predestination plan and the health and wholeness of His body, the church. God's predestination plan is to encourage and incorporate spiritually healthy individuals into His body, to heal the sick, and eliminate those who refuse to be spiritually healthy. It's God's body so He defines spiritual health and wholeness, and He has done so in Scripture. People are free to disagree with God's definitions, but they are not free to become or remain in His body against His will when they oppose His biblical definitions of spiritual health.

God's blessings function "in the Beloved" (v. 6), a reference to Jesus Christ which is confirmed in verse 7. The church, Christ's body is

---

3   Note that the loss of a part does not necessarily destroy the wholeness. Wholeness is of a different order than the parts. Amputees are still whole persons.

composed of all who are *in Christ*, or "in the Beloved." This book is a discussion of the meanings and implications of being *in Christ* as Paul discusses it in his letter to the Ephesians.

5. Summa Christos

In him we have redemption through his blood, the forgive-
ness of our trespasses, according to the riches of his grace,
which he lavished upon us, in all wisdom and insight making
known to us the mystery of his will, according to his pur-
pose, which he set forth in Christ as a plan for the fullness of
time, to unite all things in him, things in heaven and things
on earth.   —Ephesians 1:7-10

Redemption, another of the words that describe the change from faithlessness to faithfulness, is found *in Christ. Redemption* (ἀπολύτρωσις) is essentially an exchange. It could also be translated as *ransom,* and provides both the means of salvation and the essential element of Christian worship. As the means of salvation, sinners exchange their worthlessness for Christ's worthiness. Sinners are completely and entirely unable to save themselves because they cannot satisfy God's demand for perfect righteousness. God cannot be in direct union with imperfect beings because their lack of perfection will mar and therefore destroy His perfection, which is why He needed to send Jesus. Human beings must be in relationship with God through Christ in order to be perfect or whole.

Christ manifested perfect righteousness because He is perfectly divine. Only what is divine can be perfectly perfect. We might understand this in the sense that what is time-bound is subject to time, which makes it subject to change and decay. Everything in time decays over time, according to the Second Law of Thermodynamics. So, what is perfectly perfect must necessarily be outside of time or timeless. People are in time, and therefore perfection is not available to them.

Christ can be in relationship with imperfect sinners because of His dual nature. Christ, the Second Person of the Trinity, who is both human and divine without obscuring either, came from outside of time and kept one foot in time (His humanity) and one foot outside of time (His divinity). As such, He was able to represent humanity to God by perfectly keeping God's law. In this way Christ was able to maintain relationship with God as a human being. But because He represented humanity to God, He also had to take on and suffer the consequence of human sin as a human being—death—because God's law is perfect and cannot change.

God could not simply forget the consequences for disobedience of the first human beings. Those first human beings (Adam and Eve) provided the archetypal pattern for all further human behavior. Humanity is a biblical *kind* (Genesis 1:25) or species, which means that natural reproduction only works among humans and humans only produce humans. Like kind produces like kind, a species does not naturally produce another species. At a very fundamental level, all human beings share a common character or gene pool.

This simply means that children are not fundamentally different from their parents. We all share a common humanity. And such is the case regarding humanity (the children) and Adam and Eve (the first parents). Children were not born to Adam and Eve until after their Fall, which means that the Fall became an inherited aspect of all children born after Adam and Eve.[1] Consequently, in order for humanity to overcome the Fall and the consequent sin entwined therein, a new biblical kind or species would need to be created. One that does not naturally and habitually include sin.

From a time-bound perspective, the God who created Adam and Eve had a small time-investment in humanity because humanity was created during the first week of creation. While God does not change over time, our time-bound human understanding of God does. Nei-

---

1   Can God impute Adam's sin to Adam's progeny and maintain the kind of justice that the Bible teaches? One of the upgrades of the Old Testament is found in Ezekiel 18:20, "The soul who sins shall die. The son shall not suffer for the iniquity of the father, nor the father suffer for the iniquity of the son. The righteousness of the righteous shall be upon himself, and the wickedness of the wicked shall be upon himself." Accordingly, children are not liable for the sins of their parents. How can God hold Adam's progeny guilty for Adam's sin? For a discussion of this see, *Conflict of Ages—The Great Debate of the Moral Relations of God and Man*, Edward Beecher, 1853, Phillip A. Ross, editor, Pilgrim Platform, Marietta, Ohio, 2012.

ther human understanding nor identity are static. We mature into God's likeness, or we mature apart from it. In addition, we grow both individually and corporately. We cannot escape the bonds and bounds of the society in which we live. Our individual growth and maturity are always related to the society in which we live. We are social beings. Consequently, the limitations of our individual maturity are the reasons why it is necessary for God to manifest in three Persons.

No individual can take in the infinitude of God's being in the span of or within the limitations of a single individual life. The being of God is so large, so to speak, that He cannot fit into or be conceived or comprehended by any one individual. The wholeness of individuality is of a different order[2] than the life of the individual. In order to more perfectly manifest as the character of God, three unique divine Persons are necessary. The Trinity provides the only way to understand God for human beings bound in time. Thus, from God's perspective His oneness and threeness are both perfectly unified and perfectly distinguished, and from our perspective God's Oneness could only be perfectly manifest in three Persons.

The fullness of the manifestation of *Yahweh Elohim* necessarily requires the manifestation of Jesus Christ, who then sent the Holy Spirit to dwell with His people. However, for human beings to understand God's divinity, a lesson in divinity was required prior to the advent of Jesus Christ. That lesson is found in the whole of the Old Testament story, and apart from it the revelation and understanding of God is impossible. That lesson set up history so that humanity could rightly perceive, conceive, and receive the character of God. In order to know what God is and how God operates, we must know His character. Apart from such knowledge, God cannot be recognized.

It is not that people must understand God in the fullness of all that He is, but that people must understand God correctly—analogically, to know Him personally like we know a friend. Only then can we value Him sufficiently to live in obedience to Him. Or perhaps it would be better to say that we must value God sufficiently to trust Him, so that we do not exceed the bounds of disobedience that result in death. This is the death that God warned Adam about, "for in the day that you eat of it you shall surely die" (Genesis 2:17). The lesson there is that getting good and evil wrong leads to the death or extinction of humanity.

---

2   See Appendix, Cardinal and Ordinal numbers, p. 405.

Every biblical kind has a particular habitat in which it is able to exist. Every kind or species, however, also has the ability to destroy its own habitat. Such destruction usually occurs from overpopulation. For instance, Buffalo over-grazed their supply of grass for food in North America. Humanity, however, was given the responsibility of dominion of the whole earth (Genesis 1:28), which means that humanity has the ability to tend or destroy every habitat because the human habitat includes almost every habitat on the whole earth. Again, human extinction is the death that God warned Adam about (Genesis 2:17).

THE BLOOD

Paul said that "we have redemption through his *blood*" (αἷμα, v. 7). The Greek word means *bloodshed* by implication, and Paul meant to imply that we have redemption through Christ's death on the cross. Nonetheless, he said *blood* not *death* because of the Old Testament teaching about atonement. The first dozen or so verses of the first chapter of Leviticus pertain to atonement, sacrificing for the forgiveness of sin. And that sacrifice involved blood, the ritual killing of the animal and the liturgical use of its blood in the process (Leviticus 1:5). Blood was sprinkled about the alter as a kind of purification rite. The salient points here are the necessary death of the sacrificial animal and the ritual use of its blood.

When Christ made Himself the ultimate sacrifice for the sin of humanity, His death was necessary. But what about the ritual use of Christ's blood?

Just as Christ's death was a substitutionary death for His people, so the ritual use of communion wine provides the ritual substitute for His blood. The fact that wine is substituted for His blood underscores the fact of His substitutionary death, His shedding of blood for His people. The ritual of communion symbolizes the reality of substitutionary atonement, which is the very heart of Christianity. *Blood* has a rich symbolic life in the Bible, New Testament and Old, and is at the heart of redemption.

The next phrases of verse 7 provide the content of the redemption exchange: "the forgiveness of our trespasses, according to the riches of his grace." Our sin or trespasses (παράπτωμα, literally *deviations*) are exchanged for the inheritance of His resources. We give God our sin or deviations from obedience to Christ, and God gives us the inheritance of His resources. Notice that when we give God our sin, we no longer have it. The exchange is our trespasses or deviations for God's inheritance. Christ's takes our trespasses upon Himself, and we take God's gifts of grace upon ourselves.

It's a kind of forgiveness. The Greek word translated as *forgive* (but not used in Ephesians) is ἀφίημι, and literally means *to send away*. The idea of forgiveness is the surrender of one's right and desire for revenge, to *give* it up without conditions, or to give it up first —*fore*. To receive God's forgiveness is to have God give up His demand for retribution and vengeance against you for some infraction or offense you have caused Him to have. It does not actually involve something that we receive, but involves something that we don't receive—God's wrath and damnation. When people are forgiven they don't receive what they deserve—vengeance and retribution.

God's forgiveness restores our relationship with God, yet God cannot sanction sin and ill-perfection. Those who hold on to their own sin, their deviations from Christ's archetypal norm, cannot receive God's forgiveness. It's not that God doesn't want to give it, but that God's perfection cannot abide sin and remain perfect. So, the sin must go or be neutralized. People who identify themselves on the basis of their sin—some desire, preference, or behavior that falls short of Christ's perfect righteousness—define themselves apart from God. Their deepest understanding of themselves excludes conformity to the archetypal character of Christ.

And in one way or another and to one degree or another, we all do this. So, God insists that our original identification in Adam, our original humanity must die, so that we can release all sense of identity apart from Christ. Our self-identity in Adam must completely cease to exist in order that a new identity in Christ can replace it, an identity that finds unity with Christ, with Christ's perfect righteousness.

This does not mean that Christians immediately reflect and manifest the perfection of Christ's righteousness. Rather, it means that Christians *genuinely want* to live on the basis of Christ's righteousness. Sure, we do a lousy job of it. But because Christ Himself inhabits Christians, there is no doubt that He will complete the process that He began. It is not that people have to work up the desire to want Christ—that turns the whole thing into more works-righteousness. Rather, Christ Himself has already slain or defeated the archetype of human identity in Adam. That identity even has a name—Satan.

Humanity *in Adam* is the body of Satan in the same way that humanity *in Christ* is the body of Christ. Adam is the old archetype and

Christ is the new archetype. Their archetypal roles are similar. The original impetus to resist God's plan—God's rules for life on this planet, God's determination of good and evil—originated not from Eve and Adam but from the Serpent, whom Scripture identifies as Satan. Satan provided the archetype for all who do not follow Christ. Thus, all those who do not follow Christ belong to Satan because they vivify the archetype of humanity *in Adam*, the fallen humanity of Adam and Eve.

The risen Lord, critiquing the church at Smyrna, mentioned "a synagogue of Satan" in association with those "who say that they are Jews and are not" (Revelation 2:9). He repeated the phrase in Revelation 3:9. Here we see that just as there had been false teachers who pretended to be Christians, there were also false teachers who pretended to be Jews. It is likely that the same pretense involved both groups. It is the pretense of faithfulness, and the first victim is the self.

From the Fall of Adam and Eve forward, God has been working to restore to humanity the wholeness that is only found *in God*. Humanity had been cast out of the Garden as a consequence of sin, of failing to ground their lives by trusting God. Rather than trusting God, they trusted the ruse of Satan, who said that they could trust their own judgment. Such were the people who said they were Jews, but were not, and who said they were Christians, but were not. Like Balaam,[3] they said that they were faithful to God—and even believed it themselves! But they were not!

Real Christians trade the fallen archetype of Adam for the archetype of Christ, the new Adam. The old Adam is really the archetype of Satan, of those who are separated from God by their sin, their refusal to trust God. Redemption involves the exchange of these archetypes, which changes the model, mode, and identity of being human from that of Adam to that of Christ. The original, pre-Fall model of humanity has been recovered by Jesus Christ, who serves as its archetype.

But it is not that Christians have to reproduce the archetype of Christ in their own lives, but that Christ Himself reproduces Christians in His image. It is not that Christians have to work up the gumption to incorporate Christ into their lives, but that Christ incorporates Christians into the gumption of His life. This is what it means to be *in Christ*.

---

3   For a discussion of Balaam see, *Peter's Vision of The End in Second Peter*, Phillip A. Ross, Pilgrim Platform, 2011, "Balaam," p. 98-ff.

Moola

Paul's mention of the "riches (πλοῦτος) of his grace" (v. 7) points to a connection between God's grace and wealth, literally money and possessions. The relationship between God's grace and wealth issues from Christ's character qualities involved in the imitation or reproduction of Christ's likeness in the lives of Christians. It is not that God simply arranges circumstances that serendipitously bring money to Christians, but that Christ's character qualities of honesty, integrity, and industry cause Christians to love work enough to excel at it in one way or another. And when a society has a sufficient number of such people, they are able to increase social wealth through their love of honest work.

When people do what they love, they tend to get good at it; and getting good at something often brings financial rewards. Not always, of course, but often. The biblical connection between work, wealth, and Christianity is not aimed at individuals, but at societies. Christian societies tend to have a better standard of living than non-Christian societies. History knows this phenomena as the Christian Work Ethic. Societies that promote honesty, integrity, and industry are better able to improve through advancements in science and technology. And this has been the historical reality.

God's forgiveness triggers the exchange of the life and values of Adam, the Old Man, with the life and values of Christ, the New Man. God's forgiveness brings people into Christ where He showers them with the riches of God's grace, "which he lavished upon us, in all wisdom and insight" (v. 8). It is by God's wisdom and insight that He provides His inheritance for His people. And by receiving that inheritance His people receive *all* wisdom and insight. The *Authorized Version* translates it as "wisdom and *prudence*" (φρόνησις). The Greek word literally means mental activity, intellectual and/or moral.

God's wisdom and insight was provided by "making known to us the mystery of his will, according to his purpose, which he set forth in Christ" (v. 9). Knowing God's will, God's purpose, is the key that unlocks abundant life on earth, and the more individuals who know it, the greater the abundance of God's blessings. God's will is not a secret *mystery* (μυστήριον) that we must strive to find. Rather,

> In the NT it denotes, not the mysterious (as with the Eng. word), but that which, being outside the range of unassisted natural apprehension, can be made known only by divine revelation, and is

made known in a manner and at a time appointed by God, and to
those only who are illumined by His Spirit.[4]

God's will cannot be *found* through Bible study and prayer,
though it cannot be known without these, either. God's will is not
found or discovered at all, it is revealed. God gives His people ears to
hear and eyes to see His truth, and apart from receiving God's gift of
seeing and hearing His Holy Spirit, it remains unknown.

Once the gift is received, we can note that God's will is perfectly
aligned with His purpose in Christ, His purpose for sending Christ to
manifest in human flesh as Messiah. All of God's will, everything that
God has done is about the accomplishment of Christ's purpose in the
world. Christ is the center of everything, not just spiritually but in
*every*thing. Nothing can be known properly and fully apart from
God's purpose for it in Christ.

In the service of that purpose, Paul added that there is "a plan for
the fullness of time, to unite all things in him, things in heaven and
things on earth" (v. 10). The *Authorized Version* translated the phrase
as "the *dispensation* of the fullness of times." And the Greek word
οἰκονομία (*dispensation*) means *administration* or *economy*, the same
word that we use for national budgets and employment statistics—
moola, money. It is composed of two Greek words: οἶκος, which
means *dwelling* and νόμος, which means *law*. It's about household
management, which includes the management of money, but is not
limited to money.

In God's plan or economy all things will be united in Him. The
Authorized Version translated the word *united* (ἀνακεφαλαίομαι) as
"he might gather together in one" (v. 10). At the root of this complex
Greek word is the idea of head or headship (κεφαλή) and κεφάλαιον,
which indicates "a principal thing, that is, main point; specifically an
amount (of money), a sum."[5] The mathematical definition of *sum* is a
set containing all and only the members of two or more given sets.
For our purposes those two sets are represented by the Christian's dual
citizenship. One is earthly and one is heavenly.

Sum

We are to understand this unity of all things in Christ analogously in the same way that we understand the sum of a column of

---

4   Vine, W.E. *Vine's Complete Expository of New Testament Words*, public domain,
     1940, "Mystery."

5   Strong, James. *Strong's Hebrew and Greek Dictionaries*, 1890-2007, G2774.

numbers. The sum is the value of the whole of the parts, and the wholeness is greater than the simple sum of the parts. The sum adds something to the parts (the column of numbers to be added) that the parts don't have in themselves. The sum is different from all of the individual numbers, and represents their wholeness or integration. As a calculation the sum exists in a different order than the parts, while simultaneously representing the totality of the parts.[6] The sum has a greater or different magnitude than any of the parts. It is a construct of a different order. This kind of mathematical language provides important information about Jesus Christ and His role and function on earth. It provides a dimension to Christ's purpose that is otherwise not discerned. Indeed, it greatly helps us to better understand the reality of what it means to be *in Christ*.

Verse 10 tells us that "things in heaven and things on earth" are held in unity in Christ. Christ bridges the infinite and the finite in His own person, being both fully divine and fully human. And He bridges the sum, wholeness, or integrity of humanity with individual human beings through representation. In an analogous way, just as an individual body is composed of interrelated parts that conform to a central will or purpose, humanity as a whole is also composed of interrelated parts that conform to a central will or purpose. Just as an individual body grows and matures over time, so humanity as a whole also grows and matures. There is a collective aspect of being human that becomes increasingly important as humanity grows and matures.

The maturation of humanity, which involves the manifestation of large populations that are increasingly interrelated, produces an increase in complexity regarding their maintenance and sustainability. More people living on earth means greater social complexities, and part of God's covenant and promise is to provide increasing populations with sufficient skills and abilities to supply and satisfy those needs. This growth is a reflection of the progressive revelation of Jesus Christ in history.[7]

The larger the population, the greater the need to rely upon the gifts and graces provided by Jesus Christ for human sustainability. The truth is that there are not too many people on earth, but that there is too much sin. The reduction and elimination of sin in society through the increase of honesty, integrity, and industry in Christ will allow for much greater population growth than is otherwise possible.

---

6   See Appendix I: Membership & Set Theory, p. 405.

7   See footnote 1, p. iii.

Those who define human freedom as the freedom to sin will be supplanted by those who define human freedom as the freedom to be what God has created us to be in Christ.

6. FOREHOPE

In him we have obtained an inheritance, having been pre-destined according to the purpose of him who works all things according to the counsel of his will, so that we who were the first to hope in Christ might be to the praise of his glory. —Ephesians 1:11-12

There is so much in these two verses! The central subject is the inheritance that we have in Christ. This inheritance pertains to the Parable of the Tenants (Matthew 21:33-41, Mark 12:1-9, Luke 20:9-16). In that parable a vineyard or garden was planted and developed by the owner of the land, who had leased it to tenants while he was away on a trip. The owner then sent a representative to get some of the harvested fruit. The tenants not only refused to give the representative any of the harvest, but they beat him. Another representative was sent, only to receive the same treatment. And another. Finally, the owner sent his son to sort things out, and they killed him with the intention of seizing the son's inheritance—ultimate ownership of the vineyard.

The story is obviously an allusion to Israel and their treatment of God's prophets. Nonetheless, the inheritance Paul mentioned is the inheritance of the saints in Christ—the blessings and riches of God.

Note also that this is not an inheritance that is yet to be received, but Paul's language is in the past tense. It has already been received. This reception happened *in Christ*. People get in Christ by receiving the gift of the Holy Spirit, by acquiescence to the character of Christ. This gift renews, regenerates, reconfigures, or redefines them in such a way that their being, their persons, their individualities, their most fundamental identities—including their morality and behaviors—are

53

changed by God to increasingly reflect the character of Jesus Christ. To be in Christ is to understand yourself to be a lesser person who is being directed by a Greater Person. Our wants, desires, preferences, and purposes are to give way to God's wants, desires, preferences, and purposes for *us*, for humanity—not merely for *me* as an individual.

Jesus Christ demonstrated that such living is possible for human beings because He did it perfectly. And by doing it perfectly—completely, by living in perfect obedience unto death, not simply to God's law but living in perfect obedience to God's every desire, Jesus modeled ideal Godliness in human form. That model is archetypal. Thus, to live *in, by,* or *according to* the model is to live in Christ.

Fortunately, we don't have to imitate Christ's model perfectly in order to begin. Perfection is not instantaneous, it takes time. Nor is perfection individually attainable, it takes the wholeness in Christ of a community. As people surrender their own personal wants, desires, preferences, and purposes in the hope of better modeling Christ over time, Christ's model itself will complete the process because Christ's model is self-correcting, it will correct itself into perfection over time. The mechanism of self-correction is called sanctification. The Spirit of Christ continues to mold people into His likeness, both individually and corporately.

Predestined

To predestine is to plan. God has a plan that He uses to accomplish His purposes. God has a plan for the world. This is not a difficult idea to understand, yet people get themselves all twisted up around the idea of God's predestination. Scripture clearly teaches that God cannot fail to accomplish His plan. What trips people up is not the idea of predestination—planning, but the idea of God's sovereignty—the fact that God will necessarily accomplish His plan.

The idea that God will actually accomplish His plan for the world is not a difficult idea to understand. A lot of people think that it contradicts human free will. If people have free will, and if God truly loves us, then He cannot force people to do what *He* wants against their will, because genuine love does not force compliance. Thus, the animating problem people have with the idea of God's predestination is that they think that it contradicts their free will. Can people really be free if they cannot fail to ultimately conform to God's will? The problem is not with God, nor with the idea of predestination, nor with God's sovereignty. The problem is human pride. It is our problem, not God's.

People get confused because they don't understand how God can control every little thing down to the level of quantum mechanics. But such an idea is not necessary at all. All God needs is a comprehensive understanding of human nature, and from that He can accurately predict how things will turn out. God's sovereignty doesn't need to be rocket science, when the simple ability to understand people will suffice. God knows what will happen because He knows what people do with their freedom.

Not only that, but does *love* really mean that compliance cannot be forced? Do parents force children to comply to various rules that are in place for the good and health of the children? Of course they do. Does this mean that the parents do not love their children? Or that the children do not love their parents? Not at all! Does it mean that their children don't have free will? Of course not. Rather, the parents enforce compliance to various rules precisely because they love their children. And the children bend their free will in compliance to their parents because they love their parents. This is another way to explain God's sovereignty and human freedom.

Another is that human free will is an illusion because people are enslaved to sin. They are not enslaved by force but by their own wants and desires. People love sin. Satan has convinced people that doing what they naturally want to do is an exercise of free will, when it is actually compliance and slavery to sin. In this case, real freedom—escape from slavery to sin—is accomplished by doing God's will, not our own. Here, genuine freedom means conformity to God's will because it is God's will that people be free from sin in order to be in relationship to Him. Slaves to sin cannot conform to God's will.

Historic theologians have twisted themselves inside out trying to establish and maintain individual free will and God's sovereignty (predestination). However, such intellectual gymnastics are not necessary, and the effort to maintain historical continuity with such nonsense must end. Rather, we must see through the subtle effort to hold on to what God commands us to let go of in the name of individual freedom.

Indeed, complete individual freedom always requires the denial of God's sovereignty because the only area of jurisdiction regarding individual freedom is personal conscience. And if God is not sovereign over personal conscience, then there are no limitations or boundaries of conscience. And without limits the idea of conscience evaporates. The elimination of limitations or boundaries for conscience amounts to the elimination of conscience itself. A conscience without limitations is a recipe for behavior without conscience. Human freedom is not absolute freedom because life itself requires conformity to cyclical patters of behavior.

Human beings are creatures of habit. And abandonment of such conformity undermines life and leads to death. Genuine human freedom is always freedom within limits. The only issue is the determination of the limits. How much conformity is required? How much variation can be tolerated? What is the standard toward which conformity strives? And who is authorized to determine the standard?

COVENANT

This brings us to covenant theology because God's predestining method involves His covenant. God's plan is to bless obedience and curse disobedience (Deuteronomy 28). This is God's covenantal plan and this plan includes every human being. The history of the Old Testament has conclusively demonstrated that human beings as conceived in Adam cannot live in obedience to God's law, not even when God provides explicit instructions for everything—worship, culture, law, family, etc. That is the central lesson of the Old Testament. Human beings are simply unable to live faithfully apart from Christ. We are all cursed, including Israel—perhaps *especially* Israel because Israel has had a special dispensation of the law, which only served to demonstrate all the more clearly that the law cannot save. It reveals human sin.

However, the revelation of human sin provides the necessary prelude for salvation because coming to grips with the reality of our sin sends us into confession of sin and abandonment of our own plans and desires, neither of which are positive or encouraging to the flesh, to Adam. The initial message about our salvation is the message of our sinfulness, of our need and our inability. The initial message is about our guilt and damnation as a race, as a people who have been created in Adam. The necessary prelude to the message of Jesus Christ is the impending death (extinction) of the human race because of the curse of God's judgment. Without this backstory of sin and failure, the gospel falls flat because it makes no sense.

God is working to perfect—mature—the human race. We are imperfect—immature, and that imperfection is a consequence of Adam's sin. In Adam the wrong fork in the road was taken. The goodness of the world and the goodness of humanity are insufficient to the demands of perfection.[1] Remember that Adam is the natural human archetype. Therefore, in Adam the human race is doomed to extinction because of our inability to live a perfectly and eternally sustainable existence. The given purpose for humanity on earth is dominion, or responsibility for the care and maintenance of the earth—stewardship of it as a function of our worship of God-in-Christ (*Yahweh Elohim*).

God relishes in the obedience of Jesus Christ and in all who follow in His stead. God can trust that those who follow Christ will abide in Christ because they are held in abidance by the power and strength of God-in-Christ through regeneration by the Holy Spirit, not by the frailty of our own human promises. Christians participate in the divinity of Jesus Christ (1 Corinthians 10:16) without the heresy of identification with God, but rather through the orthodoxy of union with Christ. However, this union comes about only through the death of Adam in baptism and regeneration[2] in Christ. It begins as individuals renounce Adam and embrace Christ, and eventually the archetype of Adam and Adam's god, Sin,[3] will be forgotten (overcome) as sin is progressively eliminated from humanity. That day will be a great Day indeed!

ALL THINGS

God "works *all things* (πᾶς) according to the counsel of his will" (v. 11). The Greek word is usually translated simply as *all*, without the *things*, and is subject to the usual confusion regarding the word *all*

---

1 Genesis 1:31, even very good (מאד טוב) is not perfect (תמים). We can especially see this if we use alternative translations of very *agreeable* vs. *complete*. The creation of man was very good, but not complete. Its completion did not begin until Christ came, and will be completed as He returns.

2 This term does not mean that regeneration is the result of the ceremony of baptism. Rather, it suggests the reality of spiritual baptism that produces a change in character that is described as *regeneration*.

3 Sin or Nanna was the god of the moon in the Mesopotamian mythology of Akkad, Assyria, and Babylonia. Nanna is a Sumerian deity, the son of Enlil and Ninlil, and became identified with the Semitic god, Sin. The two chief seats of Nanna's (or Sin's) worship were Ur in the south of Mesopotamia and Harran in the north. Source: http://en.wikipedia.org/wiki/Sin_(mythology).When *Sin* is capitalized in this book it refers to the god, Sin. Ross, Phillip A. *Peter's Vision of The End in Second Peter*, Pilgrim Platform, Marietta, Ohio, Chapter 9: *Lot's Lessons*, section *Sodom*.

that is found throughout Paul's writings. Does the word mean *every single instance* or *some of every class* or what? Let me suggest that the word should be understood as *wholeness* rather than quantitatively inclusive.

Wholeness is a construct of perception that can be applied to all sorts of things. While a whole body consists of all of its constituent parts, we can also refer to a whole arm, a whole leg, a whole ear, etc. An automobile is a whole car, but is made of all sorts of whole parts, as well. There is a wholeness of the transmission, the tires, etc. Wholeness seems to have a kind of arbitrariness or floating assignability to it, and yet it isn't arbitrary at all.

The idea of wholeness is always related to purpose. It is a teleological concept. The wholeness of a thing is always defined by the purpose of the thing. Purpose and wholeness always have context. For the purpose of illustration we can consider this book currently in your hands to be whole, assuming that you are not reading a digital copy and that the book in your hands is not missing some pages. Nonetheless, the wholeness of the book cannot be considered apart from the table of contents, the footnotes, the appendix, etc. And each of these parts refer to other parts and materials to help complete the ideas in the book. In addition, the text of this book makes all sorts of references to things and people who are not physically part of this particular book. And yet, this particular book cannot be understood in its wholeness apart from its various references and allusions to things that are not physically connected to it. Thus, some parts of the book are not bound within its pages, but can be considered to be separate things, depending on the purpose we have for including or excluding them with regard to our consideration of the wholeness of the book.

The idea of wholeness is relative to the context of its use. *Whole* is an adjective not a noun. It describes something. And to understand its context requires understanding what it describes. The idea of wholeness is like the ideas of perfection or infinity, in that it can be used in either a relative or an absolute sense. And apart from knowing the context of its use, confusion can result.

From this perspective, then, we can understand Paul's phrase to mean something like: *God works according to the wholeness of the counsel of His will and then predestines (plans) things according to His purpose.* God's Trinitarian character is the source of all wholeness, and wholeness, like the sum of its parts variously conceived, exists in an entirely different order of existence from the individual parts themselves. *Whole* and *part* are different orders of magnitude (measurement). In addition, different purposes will employ different conceptions of wholeness. For instance, sometimes an individual shoe can be considered a whole shoe, and sometimes the whole is considered to be a pair of shoes. At other times, a truckload of shoes can be considered to be a whole order delivered to a shoe store. In each case the wholeness is composed of a different *ordinal*, though in each case the subject is a single whole, a *cardinal*.[4]

Forehope

God predestined or planned all of this, Paul tells us, "so that we who were the first to hope in Christ..." (v. 12) would do something. Before discussing what these people would do, we need to determine who they are. The idea of being the first to hope in Christ has provided much confusion. Some commentators argue that Paul was talking about the Jews, others argue that he was referring to the Apostles. Both can be considered to be the first to hope in Christ.

The confusion arises because of the Greek word translated as "who first trusted" (προελπίζω, *Authorized Version,* v. 12). The word literally means to hope in advance of confirmation, and might be also translated as *forehope*. We are familiar with the word *foreknowledge* (προγινώσκω), and the Greek construction is similar.

A better translation of the actual meaning is found in *God's Word Version,*

> "He planned all of this so that we who had already focused our hope (or forehoped) on Christ would praise him and give him glory."

It includes the Jews, the Apostles, and all people who forehope in Christ, those whose hope precedes their knowledge or experience or understanding of Christ. In a sense the idea of forehoping is similar to desire in the sense that forehoping is wanting the object of hope (Christ) before the hope is clearly articulated, experienced, understood, or completely manifest.

---

4   The world of mathematics, in particular Set Theory, provides some interesting and necessary analogies. Suffice it to say here that purpose determines usage and usage determines perception. *Wholeness* involves Set Theory because it is composed of parts. *Ordinal* is taxonomic and requires a specific order and classification of a set, while *cardinal* refers to the raw number of parts in a set. They are different kinds of measurement. See Appendix, p. 406.

GOD'S JUDGMENT

Paul said here that the reason that things happen as they do pertains to "the praise of his (God's) glory" (v. 12). This phrase is pregnant with meaning that will surprise us because we are used to hearing and using such terms in particular ways and in particular contexts—prayer and Sunday morning worship. But there is a sense in which our habitual patterns of worship, regardless of what they are, have obscured certain meanings of these words—*praise* and *glory*—from us.

For example, the Greek word translated *praise* (ἔπαινος) is composed of two words (ἐπί and αἰνέω). ἐπί suggests a superimposition of time, place, or order. And αἰνέω is the verb form of the noun αἶνος, which means *story*. So ἔπαινος involves the use of storytelling as a way of commendation and approval. Thus, the praising of God is not something that happens subjectively as one feels a kind of personal passion or appreciation for God, but is the verbal telling and sharing of the stories of God in a positive and appreciative light or character. Such praise is not an individual activity but a social activity. To praise is to recommend something to someone else.

The other word, *glory* (δόξα), is the noun form of the verb δοκέω, which literally means to think, surmise, seem, suppose, etc. It involves a judgment or assessment, and the implication is that it points to and even engages God's judgment or assessment. Thus, God's glory is His assessment of things, His view and understanding of the world in which we live, His evaluation and judgment of it. Thus, praise is provided in story form throughout the Bible. God's *glory* is the meaning and importance (gravity) of His story, and God's *praise* is the telling of that story.

Glory is not a thing like a rock, or a character quality like mercy, or a feeling or emotion like love. *Glory* (כבד) literally means weight or burden. It's a commitment, a concern. According to the dictionary, *weight* is a measurement related to gravity, or it can refer to the relative importance of something. Gold is among the heaviest of the metals, and important things are significant and valuable. Thus, *heavy* or *gravity* can be used analogically to convey the sense of importance or value. God's glory is His gravitas. Thus, God's glory also indicates His position or role as the universal and ultimate referent of everything.

The "praise of his glory" (v. 12), then, involves telling the stories of God's involvement in the world from His perspective. Yes, this involves worship liturgy, but it is not exhausted by worship liturgy because both *worship* and *liturgy* include far more than people normally think. People tend to think of only one aspect of worship—the corporate aspect, and neglect the personal aspect.

WORSHIP

There are two classic forms, elements, or modes of worship. We can call them corporate and personal, formal and informal, gathered and scattered, or public and private. Each word pair points to the same realities and the same differences. People often call the corporate expression *worship* and the personal expression *devotion*, but both are actually biblical forms of worship. Devotion is a level of passion, not a kind of worship.

The first, the corporate element, describes worship on Sunday mornings at church. The second, the individual element, describes worship as the attitude or orientation of ordinary Christians. How Christians live their lives is the practice of worship. Worship is the context, attitude, and orientation of Christian living. Worship is not simply something that we do. It is not simply going to church or reading the Bible. It is not simply an activity or behavior, but it involves our orientation to the context in which we live. That orientation, then, informs and defines our activities, behaviors, preferences, attitudes, etc.

The second aspect, which is individual, personal, and private, is too often neglected. That neglect also undermines the meaning, experience, and exercise of Sunday morning worship, and the serious or genuine engagement of Christianity in general. Indeed, the church, who are the people of God, is currently in the midst of a crisis of worship because public worship provides an accurate expression of our personal worship in the sense that it issues out of and is built upon the pale and frail personal or private worship practices of too many Christians.

True worship is having the proper attitude when we go to church or read the Bible—or when we do anything. If we only have the proper attitude or orientation when we are at church or when we are reading the Bible, then we do not have the proper attitude because the proper attitude of worship is a twenty-four-seven kind of thing. The proper attitude of worship must be a constant companion. It must guide everything that we do.

PRIME HOPE

The *English Standard Version* translates προελπίζω as "the first to hope" (v. 12). As previously mentioned, the word can be understood as *forehope*, which often carries the sense of *first* or *before*. But in this case it doesn't indicate time as much as priority. It is not pointing to the Apostles as being the first people in history to hope in Christ, nor that there is some sort of historic precursor to Christian hope in the Old Testament. Rather, it emphasizes the primacy of hope in Christ, that Christ as the object of hope is and must always be the first, prime, central, and most important element of life.

This prime hope in Christ is the engine of personal worship in that it provides interest and enthusiasm for Christ in the lives of Christians. This hope in Christ, this interest and enthusiasm is always in the forefront of the believer's mind twenty-four-seven. It is never forgotten, ignored, or denied because its primacy form informs and reforms the lives of Christians increasingly into the likeness of Christ. As that likeness increases, so Christ's righteousness grows in the lives of believers such that all of life becomes an arena of worship.

The development of this righteousness is the practice of worship. Worship is the fruit of Christ's righteousness in the lives of believers, but it is also the engine or seed of righteousness. And in the same way Christ's righteousness is the fruit of worship in the lives of believers, but righteousness is also the engine or seed of worship. *Worship* and *righteousness* are different words that describe different aspects of the same thing—the way of life in Christ.

Thus, true worship is living in the righteousness of Jesus Christ. It is living by the directives of Jesus Christ, and/or living in the light of Jesus Christ. True worship is Christ living through His people.

7. Sealed In Christ

In him you also, when you heard the word of truth, the gospel of your salvation, and believed in him, were sealed with the promised Holy Spirit, who is the guarantee of our inheritance until we acquire possession of it, to the praise of his glory. —Ephesians 1:13-14

There are several key ideas in these verses. First, all of this stuff happens *in Christ*. The point is crucial because it doesn't happen apart from Him. There is also the idea of hearing the Word of truth, of hearing the gospel of Christ, the message of salvation in Christ. Then there are the ideas of believing in Christ, of being sealed with the Holy Spirit as promised, of the guarantee, and of the inheritance. And the idea of taking possession of the inheritance—the gifts. Finally, we see that all of this happens as the manifestation of praise to God's glory.

Paul was writing to the church, the *you or ye (ὑμεῖς)* in the *Authorized Version* is plural. This was not a message to an individual, but to the plurality of Christ's people. The fact that they were at Ephesus is circumstantial, which means that it is a message directed, not simply at all individual Christians, but in some sense at Christian wholeness. Salvation involves the restoration of human wholeness in Christ. We could also call it the foundation of human wholeness in Christ because it is only complete when all of Christ's people are living in unity in Him—and that day[1] is still in the future. But it has also begun, and its beginning was real.

---

1 Also called the Eighth Day (Exodus 22:30; Leviticus 9:1; 12:3; 14:10,23; 15:14,29; 22:27; 23:36,39; Numbers 6:10; 7:54; 29:35; 1 Kings 8:66; 12:32,33; 2 Chronicles 7:9; 29:17; Nehemiah 8:18; Ezekiel 43:27; Luke 1:59; Acts 7:8; Philippians 3:5).

These verses are about the integrity and veracity of the gospel as a means of establishing the reality of Christian life on earth. Christian life only happens in Christ, and the fullest explanation of being in Christ is found in the gospel of John. We find it at the end of John in this summary statement:

> "these (signs) are written so that you may believe that Jesus is the Christ, the Son of God, and that by believing you may have life in his name" (John 20:31).

What signs? The Greek word (σημεῖον) refers to events that have meaning, and usually the meaning points to the veracity or truth of God (Matthew 12:38, 16:1, 24:3; Luke 2:12; John 3:2, 6:30, 20:30, etc.). Thus, there are signs that, as we become aware of them and believe them to be true, not only point to, but actually provide life in Jesus Christ.

This chain of events can be understood in at least two ways. The most obvious is that life in Christ is related to believing certain events to be true, most notably His resurrection from death. While I don't want to deny this simple understanding of the facts to be true, it is also important to delve behind the appearances for deeper truths. We don't actually know what causes some people to believe these certain events to be true when others fail to believe them. All we know is that some people trust God and some don't. The only real issue is whether I (you) do or don't.

This brings us to the nature versus nurture question about why people are the way they are. Are people born with a kind of genetic programming that causes them to be one way or another? Or are people born neutral and shaped by their upbringing and education? Another alternative is that people can reject both their nature and their nurture, and freely choose to be what kind of people they want to be. Another option is that God's sovereignty trumps nature, nurture, and human freedom. While much ink has been spent discussing these various options, Scripture simply says that the story of God-in-Christ has been written and shared so that believers may have life in the name of Jesus Christ.

Ninety-five percent of the time that the phrase *in Christ* is used in the New Testament it belongs to Paul. And Paul was simply assuming the reality of John's testimony because he believed it.

> Whoever feeds on my flesh and drinks my blood abides in me, and I in him (John 6:56).

> Abide in me, and I in you. As the branch cannot bear fruit by it-
> self, unless it abides in the vine, neither can you, unless you abide
> in me. I am the vine; you are the branches. Whoever abides in me
> and I in him, he it is that bears much fruit, for apart from me you
> can do nothing. If anyone does not abide in me he is thrown
> away like a branch and withers; and the branches are gathered,
> thrown into the fire, and burned (John 15:4-6).

> I do not ask for these only, but also for those who will believe in
> me through their word, that they may all be one, just as you, Fa-
> ther, are in me, and I in you, that they also may be in us, so that
> the world may believe that you have sent me. The glory that you
> have given me I have given to them, that they may be one even as
> we are one, I in them and you in me, that they may become per-
> fectly one, so that the world may know that you sent me and
> loved them even as you loved me (John 17:20-23).

Paul speaks of believing, living, and doing everything in the
name of Jesus Christ. Is there a difference between simply believing in
Jesus and believing in the *name* of Jesus?

Name

When Scripture speaks of the name of God or the name of Jesus
it refers to the character of God-in-Christ. The names of things in the
Bible are associated with the nature or character of the things that
they name. And when the names are associated with people (or God)
the association refers to the character and/or characteristics of the individual so named. Believing, living, and doing things in Jesus' name
refers to adopting, copying, or imitating the character of Jesus Christ.
Those who invoke the name of Jesus invoke His characteristics so that
they can adopt, copy, and imitate those characteristics in their own
lives. This is the function of the name of Jesus. It serves as a kind of
character archetype.

This also involves the moral dimension of Christianity. Where
morality in general is concerned with principles of right and wrong
or conforming to some standard of behavior based on those principles. Christian morality is concerned with conforming to the character of Jesus Christ, or adopting, copying and imitating the character
of God-in-Christ.

There are physical aspects of such participation in Christ, as well
as moral or spiritual aspects. Human being or human identity is composed of three realities or overlapping wholes. Each of these realities

function as a whole. They function holistically in the sense that each involves a kind of sum or totality of their various parts. Individual bodies are whole, individual spirits or identities are whole, and humanity as a species is a whole. In Christ these wholes are combined and experienced in combination such that the individual is aware of 1) the wholeness of his own body, 2) the wholeness of his spirit or identity, and the relationship between body and spirit, and 3) of his place and role in human society. In addition, this sense of wholeness is found in Christ alone[2] because Christ brings each of these individual realities or wholes into a greater wholeness—an ultimate wholeness, or a wholeness of a different order. Christ or Messiah is the alpha and omega of human wholeness in all of its various aspects.

WHOLENESS & SOULNESS

Of course, Jesus Christ is also a unique human being, which means that people don't *become* Christ. Christians are not merged into His greater wholeness like a drop of water is merged into the sea, because such a merger destroys the uniqueness of individuality—personhood. The wholeness of human individuals is light-years more complex than a drop of water, and that complexity doesn't simply dissolve, even at death. Human identity is cumulative and the wholeness of the accumulation exists in a different realm or dimension than the individual parts. The separate parts can dissolve without the dissolution of the wholeness. Each individual is a perfectly unique being whose wholeness is both precious and eternal. It is valued by others and by God. Each individual person contributes to the wholeness of humanity in a unique way, and that unique contribution is never lost, even though it may be forgotten by others. Individual wholeness persists in the wholeness of humanity, in its unique contribution to the wholeness of humanity. And that individual wholeness is the entity referred to in the Bible as *soul* (Hebrew: נֶפֶשׁ, Greek: ψυχή). It is not that people *have* souls, but that people *are* souls. We *have* bodies.

While it can be said that every individual *has* wholeness, it is better said that individuals *are* whole because wholeness is not a possession, but is a characteristic of being. Yet, we must also acknowledge that individual wholeness involves more than the mere aggregate of individuals because humanity is a social being. Human wholeness al-

---

2   Ross, Phillip A. *Colossians—Christos Singularis*, Pilgrim Platform, Marietta, Ohio, 2009.

ways involves other people because individual human beings are not designed to exist independently.

However, simply pointing out this linguistic concern accentuates the reality that human wholeness is currently not fully whole or complete—not individually, not historically, not spiritually, and not corporately. Thus, it is better to describe the current state of human wholeness as *incomplete* or *becoming*. We are unfinished. We can also think of wholeness temporally in the sense that as the seed is, so is the plant. An acorn is a whole acorn, and when it is planted and grows and becomes a whole tree, it is whole at every stage of its growth. Yet, over time it becomes more whole, but is never other than itself. Wholeness is not static, it's dynamic. It is not a condition but a trajectory over time. It exists in time. It grows, and yet wholeness never becomes something other than what it has always potentially been. It is completed or most whole—perfect—in the fullness of its maturity.

But more importantly, human wholeness is found only in Christ because of Christ's archetypal and historical position as the Son of God and son of man. Human wholeness is the divine character of Jesus Christ that gives, allows, accounts for, and completes human wholeness in all of its various individual and corporate elements and stages. God's Holy Spirit has been engrafted into the heart of His new humanity-in-Christ. Christ provides for the wholeness of the various elements of human identity, both individually and corporately through the power of regeneration by the Holy Spirit. This means that Christ provides for individual wholeness, spiritual wholeness, and the wholeness of humanity. Human wholeness is not complete apart from Christ because He was also a human being. Therefore, individual wholeness cannot be complete until the wholeness of all humanity is complete. This is the *perfection* (τέλειος) that Scripture speaks of in Matthew 5:48. It is a call to completeness in terms of growth, morality, and maturity.

The establishment and manifestation of this wholeness in Christ is the purpose for which God sent Jesus Christ to dwell in flesh, and constitutes the idea of human salvation. And His dwelling in human flesh is absolutely necessary for the manifestation of this wholeness because human beings exist as individuals. Thus, the infinitude of God's wholeness is packed into Christ's humanity as a kind of seed or singularity, where the unity of the singularity does not destroy the diverse individuality of being human, nor of humanity in Christ. The perfection of the reality of God-in-Christ exists eternally in the individuality of Jesus Christ. The uniqueness of the individual known in history as Jesus Christ is essential to the wholeness of humanity. His manifestation as an ordinary human being was/is essential to the fulfillment of human wholeness, both individually and corporately.

Because Christians live and move and have their being in Christ, all individual, personal uniqueness is eternally maintained in Christ. Individual Christians do not lose their uniqueness or individuality in Christ, but rather their individuality becomes even more unique in Christ than it could ever be apart from Christ. Apart from Christ there is no participation in the living eternality of human identity. Those who reject Jesus Christ actually reject the fullness of their own own humanity because of Christ's central role in the wholeness of humanity.

Heard and Believed

It is impossible to believe what one has not first heard, and yet the hearing about the wholeness of humanity in Jesus Christ also requires having some idea that there actually is such a reality as this wholeness, and that it (the wholeness) comes to us as an inheritance through participation in Jesus Christ, who serves as the prime archetype with regard to the maturity and perfection (τέλειος) of humanity.

The idea of human wholeness was planted in human culture by God in the very beginning, at creation. We could say that it was part of what God created when He created *Adam* (אָדָם—Man or humanity) in His likeness. However, human wholeness can't really be considered to be a *part* of humanity. Wholeness cannot be the addition of an element or part, but must necessarily be the interrelated totality of all of the various parts that exist. In addition, wholeness exists and is perceived in a different dimension or order than its various parts. For instance, the wholeness of a human hand is more than the totality of its fingers. Fingers alone cannot be a hand because there is more to a hand than mere fingers. The wholeness of the hand is not found anywhere in the hand. Rather, it is found in the use or purpose of the hand. Similarly, human wholeness is the totality of the self, and is nothing other than the self, but is found in the proper use or purpose of humanity.

Just as an individual human baby is completely whole at birth (but not self-sufficient), that same wholeness grows and develops into what God conceived him/her to be at his/her creation. We are whole and complete in ourselves, but are never self-sufficient. Babies only grow in their full potential in Christ because God designed things this way. God designed the human body to be insufficient in itself, to depend upon others—but more importantly to depend upon Him, upon His Holy Spirit. While our individual wholeness is never less than completely whole, it never becomes completely whole apart from Christ through regeneration. Only through regeneration can we become whole, complete, or *perfect* (אֲדָם, τέλειος). The perfection to which Jesus has called His people is not the perfection of some abstract form of Gnosticism or Greek philosophy, nor the perfection of science, mathematics, or imagination, but the perfection or completeness of history and human maturity *in Christ*, where being in Christ means having one's identity tied to Christ. It means seeing things in the light of Christ, or defining things in the orbit of Christ, or living in the gravity of Christ.

SEALED

Being *sealed* (σφραγίζω) with or by the message, announcement, and promise of the Holy Spirit provides a binding mark of identification and commitment. Being sealed is like wearing a uniform in that it announces team, gang, or peer membership, which includes participation, cooperation, and common ownership. Like the wax seal that bears the image of the king's signet ring identified the authenticity of a letter or document, so being sealed by the promise of the Holy Spirit provides the authenticity of the position of individual Christians as being *in Christ*.

Being sealed also has a specific legal meaning that helps us understand its biblical meaning. A sealed agreement or document in law means that the obligation on the part of the signers of the agreement is binding. It is as if our response to Christ, in this case—belief (v. 14), is a kind of signature on God's covenant, a sign of complicity and agreement with God. Similarly, disbelief is also a kind of response, and equally constitutes our signature, our disagreement with God. The function and purpose of sealing is to bind together the parties of the agreement or covenant, and the result of sealing is the activation of the obligation of the signers to the covenant.

The language of sealing is decidedly legal. And here Paul speaks of being "sealed with the promised Holy Spirit" (v. 14), which means that the sealing in this case binds the Holy Spirit to the church. The Holy Spirit has inked the covenant with Christ's blood. The *you* (ὑμεῖς) to which Paul spoke is plural, and refers to the church. The Holy Spirit is therefore bound to the church as a whole and to the individual members thereof in unity. Individual believers are bound together with other individual believers with the Holy Spirit *in Christ* through or as the church.

Because the believer's response to the gospel is belief rather than unbelief, believers are sealed with or into the positive side of God's covenant—the dispensation of the Holy Spirit into the lives of believers. Unbelievers are similarly sealed into the negative side of God's covenant—life without the Holy Spirit. The negative side of God's promise pertains to God's judgment and wrath, and the absence of the Holy Spirit from unbelievers (Deuteronomy 28). God's covenant functions as the glue of human wholeness. It also grows and matures over time, which means that the covenant is always whole, always the same, yet it grows and matures.

And this negative aspect of the covenant cannot be charged against God, as if God *causes* unbelievers to *not* have the Holy Spirit. Rather, unbelievers don't have the Holy Spirit because they don't want Him. It is their own failure to accept the gift of the Holy Spirit that constitutes unbelief. Unbelievers actively, consciously, willingly, and voluntarily reject God and His covenant by their unbelief. It is like the judge who passes sentence upon a convicted murderer: the judge did not cause the murder because he upholds the law. Yet, without the judge passing sentence, the murderer would not be punished for his crime. The murderer may accuse the judge of all sorts of things, but the judge is innocent of all such accusations.

This sealing constitutes the *earnest* (ἀῤῥαβών) or down-payment on God's promise. It is Christ's down-payment for His people, not theirs for Him. Paul refers to it as "the guarantee of our inheritance until we acquire possession of it" (v. 14). This promised inheritance is the "eternal blessedness of the consummated kingdom of God which is to be expected after the visible return of Christ."[3] But it is more than a psychological state, more than assurance of faith, more than mere belief or assent to various ideas. This inheritance constitutes a kind of wealth that has actual value that is recognized and trusted by others, not money but wealth.

This verse raises two questions: 1) exactly what is the inheritance Paul speaks of? And 2) when and how it is acquired? The answer to

---

3   Francis Brown, Samuel Rolles Driver, Charles Augustus Briggs. *Brown-Driver-Higgs Hebrew Dictionary*, 1906, public domain.

the first question is that God's promise(s) of the Old Testament is inherited by the New Testament. The promise is the fulfillment of God's covenant, which in terms of Deuteronomy 28 would be the fulfillment of both blessings and curses. However, the covenantal fulfillment on God's part, as on our own, is more ongoing than some specific event. God's promise is given to both individual people and to His people as a whole (group, nation, culture, or people). It is described in Deuteronomy 28 in the sense that things either go well or poorly for those involved.

We might think of this inheritance of God's promise(s) as a kind of tool that facilitates the praise of God's glory. Again, to praise means to tell a story. This inheritance will aid in the telling of the story of God's glory, God's view, perspective, opinion, and judgment. We might also think of God's glory as God's personal preferences. The very things that contemporary culture encourages us to abandon—personal opinions, values, perspectives, and judgments—are the very things of our inheritance in Christ. In Christ we are to think God's thoughts after Him. We are to make God's values, thoughts, ideas, and instructions our own. We are to own God's opinions, values, perspectives, and judgments and share them widely. This is what Paul means when he says, "to the praise of his glory" (v. 14).

8. Public Faith

*For this reason, because I have heard of your faith in the
Lord Jesus and your love toward all the saints, I do not cease
to give thanks for you, remembering you in my prayers, that
the God of our Lord Jesus Christ, the Father of glory, may
give you the Spirit of wisdom and of revelation in the
knowledge of him, having the eyes of your hearts enlightened, that you may know what is the hope to which he has
called you, what are the riches of his glorious inheritance in
the saints, and what is the immeasurable greatness of his
power toward us who believe, according to the working of
his great might that he worked in Christ when he raised him
from the dead and seated him at his right hand in the heavenly places, far above all rule and authority and power and
dominion, and above every name that is named, not only in
this age but also in the one to come. And he put all things
under his feet and gave him as head over all things to the
church, which is his body, the fullness of him who fills all in
all.*   —*Ephesians 1:15-21*

Paul goes on to tell the Ephesians saints that the story of their
faith in Jesus Christ was circulating publicly. Because Paul had
heard testimonies of their faith in Christ from others (v. 15), he
could trust that it was true. It was not simply them talking about
themselves or their own faith. Nor was their faith a secret. It was not
something that anyone was hiding. It was common knowledge. And
because of the public testimony of their faith by others he *eucharized*
(εὐχαριστέω) them. He was thankful that their faith in Christ was
common knowledge, public knowledge. This thankfulness that Paul

then demonstrated with his words is the very heart of faithfulness. Being faithful to Christ and being thankful for Christ and His people are
the same things.

To better understand that thankfulness and faithfulness are the
same things, Christians might begin using the word *Eucharist* as a
verb. To *eucharize* is to express Christ-centered thankfulness. Unlike
Charlie Brown, the cartoon character who is known for saying
"Good grief!" out of feelings of frustration and exasperation, Christians need to be known for saying "Good grace!" out of feelings of
love and joy. Living in this good grace or eucharist of God-in-Christ
is the central sacrament of life in Christ. To eucharize Christ is to live
in thankfulness for Him. Such eucharizing of Christ is to be free and
open, not constrained and hidden. It is to be public, not merely private. Such eucharizing is to be unrestrained by law, fear, intimidation,
threat, or regulation because it is of the Spirit. "So it is with everyone
who is born of the Spirit" (John 3:8), because "against such things
there is no law" (Galatians 5:23).

Paul repeated the same idea in verse 16: "I do not cease to give
thanks for you, remembering you in my prayers." Notice that Paul
did not simply give thanks for them, but did not *cease* to give thanks
for them. His thanksgiving or eucharizing was a continuous activity,
not a one time thing or event. Nor was he thanking them for something that they had done. He was talking about them when he wasn't
with them. He continuously spoke thankfully about them. The *you* in
the verse is, of course, plural. He was not simply thankful for any one
of them in particular, but for them as a group, as a whole. He was
thankful for their wholeness in Christ.

Paul prayed for them beginning in verse 17 with a prayer that
runs through the end of the chapter. He began by specifying the God
he was praying to: "the God of our Lord Jesus Christ," who is also
"the Father of glory." And being the Father of glory, God is also the
source of glory, as He is the source of everything.

Saying that God is the source of everything is not simply a statement about creation, that God created everything. It is saying that
God is necessarily and ultimately at the heart or center of everything,
and particularly at the heart and center of all human experience. God
is the lens or filter through which all human experience and understanding flow, whether particular individuals acknowledge God or
not. The acknowledgment of reality is not what makes reality real. It's
real whether you acknowledge it or not.

This God-infused reality of being human is real because it shapes and impacts all human perception. Because all human history points to the fact that humanity emerged into consciousness from a religious context of one kind or another, human consciousness provides the context from which individual consciousness has arisen. The history of human consciousness fades into religious history. Or we could say that all ancient history is religious history. Regardless of what particular individuals may think about God, their thinking has arisen out of some sort of historic, social, God-inspired context. And all human thinking must be understood in its religio-historical context, regardless of how far people may think they are from such context.

This means that simply positing secularism does not make it a reality. To say that something is secular means that it rejects all religious considerations. But if the history of human consciousness is rooted in religion, then secularism is not a function of truth, but of denial. It only announces one's own spiritual blindness, one's blindness to the context of human consciousness and wholeness.

Wisdom Order

Paul prayed that God would give the Ephesian church "the Spirit of wisdom and of revelation in the knowledge of" (v. 17) God. Note the order of things here. We usually think that knowledge reveals wisdom, or that facts reveal truth (wisdom). So we think that the way to get wisdom is to pursue knowledge. But Paul reversed the order by suggesting that the Spirit of wisdom (truth) reveals the knowledge of God. Here Paul said that truth (wisdom) reveals knowledge or God-infused facts.

As I have said many times, the human mind both receives information (structure) and projects information (structure). It both perceives and analyzes its environment, and it projects and contextualizes it. The process of understanding always imposes a particular context upon the things to be understood, and apart from some context nothing is able to make any sense. In addition, the context of things is not *in* the things themselves, but is necessarily *above* (*meta*) them. So the context of humanity is necessarily above (outside or apart from) humanity, and the context of the world is necessarily above the world, as well. Spirituality is as ordinary as breathing air, and equally essential. We spend day and night breathing, but rarely think about air. And when we do think about it, our questions go mostly unanswered. We can't see and seldom feel air, yet it is essential for life.

We usually think that revelation provides wisdom, that wisdom is the result of revelation. But Paul reversed the order. He put wisdom before revelation. Maybe this order means nothing, but we need to examine it because it is there. When we take the words in Paul's order, we can wonder if Paul was suggesting that revelation is the result of wisdom, that revelation issues from wisdom. Whereas, we usually think that wisdom issues from revelation. Granted, they are related, but which is the cause and which is the effect?

The *Geneva Bible* translated the last phrase of v. 17 as "through the acknowledging of him," which has a great appeal because the verb structure suggests that both wisdom and revelation are acquired in an active, positive way—by acknowledging Jesus Christ for who He actually is. This reading suggests that the cause of both wisdom and revelation is the acknowledgment of Jesus Christ as Lord and Savior, that He causes or provides both knowledge and wisdom. Here the mystery is removed from the way that they are acquired, and is reserved for the content of the experience. The mystery is not in how they are acquired, but in the content of the acquisition.

Verse 18 begins with the Greek word ἵνα, which literally means *in order that*. It provides the sense of purpose. It communicates the idea that what follows is the purpose of what has come before. Here it leads us to the idea that the wisdom and knowledge that come from acknowledging Christ causes the "the eyes of your hearts (to be) enlightened" (v. 18). But what exactly does "the eyes of your hearts" mean? Being the purpose for which wisdom and knowledge are provided, it is important to understand what this odd phrase means.

First, the Greek word διάνοια (*heart*) does not mean the fleshly muscle that beats in human chests. And the older versions (*Geneva Bible* and the *Authorized Version*) acknowledge this by translating the word as *understanding*, which better matches the context of wisdom and knowledge that Paul has been discussing. The "eyes of your *understanding*" means nothing other than how we (note the plural because he was writing to the church) understand something. And the subject of our understanding here is the context or the *spirit* (πνεῦμα, literally *air*) of "wisdom and of revelation in the knowledge of" (v. 17) Christ. Paul was writing about the *eyes* of the Holy Spirit. But again the Greek word ὀφθαλμός (eyes) does not simply mean *eyes* when the context is not about the organs in the head. Rather, it suggests an analogy for *vision*.

Thus, Paul was speaking about the vision of the Holy Spirit. And by this he meant both our understanding of the Holy Spirit and the Holy Spirit's experience of vision through our eyes. And what he said was that this vision was *being enlightened* (φωτίζω). The idea here is that this vision of the Holy Spirit provided a source of light, that it was causing Christians to see things—the world—better, more clearly, more fully. The idea is that *in Christ* the world can be better seen, better understood, because of the context that the acknowledgment of Jesus Christ as Lord and Savior provides. Making that acknowledgment provides a perspective that cannot otherwise be seen or known. It puts one's own life in a different context. And that context is the story of humanity provided by the Bible and Christ's role in that story.

PURPOSE

Next, Paul provided the purpose for all of this: "that you may know what is the hope to which he has called you" (v. 18). Having some sense of generic hope is not enough. Even Satan has hope. So, Paul calls Christians to know the object of their hope. Apart from the acknowledgment of Christ's role in the world, and also in one's own life, life is hopeless. There is no hope without Christ because Christ is synonymous with truth, and without truth there can be no real, substantial reason for anything.

With the acknowledgment of Christ comes wisdom, knowledge, revelation, vision, and enlightenment. Of course, these things do not and cannot exist apart from their source, Jesus Christ. But *in Christ* they do exist and they exist abundantly. Therefore, all who are *in Christ* will eventually be overwhelmed by these things, these ideas. And this (being overwhelmed by wisdom, knowledge, revelation, vision, and enlightenment) is the hope of which Paul spoke. Into this hope God has called His people. And apart from Christ, this hope does not exist.

Paul goes on to describe this hope as "the riches of his glorious inheritance in the saints" (v. 18). The Greek word (πλοῦτος) does mean riches and wealth. But because Paul has been speaking analogously we must not think that he literally means money. Rather, in the context of hope Paul means the assurance of one's own personal well-being that accompanies those who have sufficient wealth to care for them in the future. That kind of well-being and satisfaction relieves people of their fear of the unknown, or the fear of not having a secure future. In the modern world we call this kind of fear *anxiety* or *angst*. Knowledge of this hope provides a cure for anxiety.

The riches that Paul spoke of are not earned, rather they are inherited. They are received as a gift, but not a random gift. Rather, they are received because of who we are. They belong to the family, not to the individual. That's what the word *inheritance* suggests. The Greek word here (αὐτός) suggests a kind of self-reference. The word can be transliterated into English as *auto*, which is used as a prefix for many words, i. e., automatic, autobiography, autonomic, etc. It suggests a kind of self-inclusion that might be better translated here as *one's*, as in "the riches of *one's* glorious inheritance in the saints" (v. 18).

To suggest that this inheritance exists *in* the saints makes it seem like the inheritance is a thing or object rather than a quality. The Greek word ἐν denotes a position, instrumentality, or relation. So, a better translation here might be *among*, as in "the riches of *one's* glorious inheritance *among* the saints" (v. 18). The inheritance is the sense of and commitment to contentment in God that exists among believers.

The next purpose of all of this is that we may also know "the immeasurable greatness of his power toward us who believe" (v. 19). This is not a different purpose, but is an aspect of the same purpose previously mentioned, with a different emphasis. The two Greek words ὑπερβάλλον μέγεθος literally mean *hyperbolic magnitude*, or greatness beyond both measure and comprehension. Paul was speaking of God's power (δύναμις) inherent in Christ, and by this he meant God's strength, power, and ability to bring about change—and not just random change, but change for the better according to God's intent and purpose.

POWER

That power includes the power needed to perform miracles, the power to create and mature moral excellence, the power and influence that belong to riches and wealth, the power and resources that arise from mass agreement and popularity (culture), and the power of military might. We might be tempted to think of this as exaggeration and hyperbole. But it is not because of the actual greatness of the corresponding reality. We usually think of hyperbole as overstatement, but in this case it is understatement. God's power actually is much greater than any words can convey.

This mighty power shines both in and through believers according to the vitality or measure that God works through them. This power resides in believers inasmuch as believers reside *in Christ*, but it is not manipulable by them. We are not in control of this power, but rather It is in control of us. Those who think that they can control or direct It are severely mistaken. It is in believers like ocean water gets in a sailing ship. Similarly, believers are in It (the reality of God's power) in the same way that a sailing ship is in the ocean. The ship cannot manipulate or direct the ocean. Rather, the ocean directs the ship because it has, for all practical purposes, infinitely more power.

Paul then compared this with the power of God "that he worked in Christ when he raised him from the dead and seated him at his right hand in the heavenly places" (v. 20). The power at work in believers is the same power that raised Christ from the dead in both its extent and purpose. The extent of God's power is life-giving. No other power in the known universe has the ability to create life. Both science and science fiction wax hyperbolically, believing and hoping that such power is potentially ours. But there is a woeful lack of evidence to back up this idea.

God wields the greatest power in the universe, and with regard to humanity God's purpose is the renewal, revivification, regeneration, and recreation of humanity in the likeness of His Son, Jesus Christ. This regeneration *in Christ* is no less significant than God's previous generation *in Adam*, and inasmuch as Adam was the creation of a new species of life on earth, so is Christ. Again, the importance of this fact cannot be overestimated. It may seem like exaggeration and hyperbole, but it is very real. And humanity is only at the dawn of this realization and its importance for the world.

God's power resurrected Jesus Christ from death and established Him as the Chief Ruler of the world (Matthew 28:18). With Christ now on the world throne, the political race for world domination should be obsolete, and the valuable resources consumed in that arena should be put to better use. Imagine a world where the money that is currently used for war, defense, and political contests would be used for socially redeeming purposes, like education, social services, cultural enrichment, etc. It is curious that those who want political power to correct the problems of the world end up being the very people who cause the problems of the world because their sinful desires are significantly magnified by the power they acquire.

Most translations say that Jesus is seated in *heavenly places* or *heavenlies*. The Greek word (ἐπουράνιος) is a compound of ἐπί and οὐρανός. The latter is usually translated as *heaven* and the former modifies the latter by suggesting a different order of being. It's like the difference between cardinal numbers and ordinal numbers—the difference between *three* and *third*, or *one* and *first*. ἐπί points to an order or magnitude rather than to something quantitative. It is also interesting that the whole word (ἐπουράνιος) does not function as a noun, but as an adjective. Thus, it does not point to a place, but to a quality or attribute, to the order, composition, or arrangement of something.

The point is that Christ was seated in an order, not simply a place. The point is that Christ holds the highest authority in the heavenly order, which means that He also holds the highest authority on earth, among governments, and rulers of every kind. The point is not the mere fact of Christ's being seated at God's right hand, but the many implications for the authorities who govern this world.

High Places

A better translation here might be "*highest* heaven." It is so translated in the *Authorized Version,* Ephesians 6:12:

> "For we wrestle not against flesh and blood, but against principalities, against powers, against the rulers of the darkness of this world, against spiritual wickedness in *high* places."

It is the same word, but here the translators did not use *heaven* because the emphasis of the verse is on the places of high political power in this world. If the word can suggest the highest places of political power in this world in Ephesians 6:12, it can and does mean the same thing in Ephesians 1:20 because the contexts are similar. Paul just mentioned God's power in *this* world, not in some nether realm of Gnostic imagination.

The point of verse 20 is that God raised Jesus from the dead and seated or established Him in the place of highest honor and authority in *this* world, in the same place referred to in Ephesians 6:12 as "high places." The suggestion that this verse is about heaven rather than the seat of worldly power in this world, has gutted the verse of its central significance—that Christ is Lord of this world right now. The point is not that Christ is seated next to God in heaven, though He most certainly is. Rather, the point is that God has raised Jesus from death to the highest seat of worldly power.

Verse 21 continues this theme by adding to the description of Christ's worldly power. Again, the verse is about this world, not heaven. But the assumption that Paul was talking about heaven caused the translators to write the idea of an abstract heaven into verse 20, and the idea is then carried into verse 21. The verses do have a common theme. But again, Paul was not talking about some Gnostic, mint-julep sipping, American, Fundamentalist version of heaven. He was talking about Christ's role and reign in *this* world.

While it may be true that God's heaven is *far above* (ὑπεράνω) the earth, that was not what Paul intended to suggest. *Far above* is not a wrong translation of the word, but it doesn't fit the context, and it channels our thoughts toward heaven. Again, thinking about heaven is not a bad thing, but that is not what Paul intended here. A better translation might be *greatly higher* in the sense of rank, position, authority, and power. The larger context of this section of Ephesians 1 concerns the power of God. And God's power raised Jesus Christ from death and established Him as the highest authority, far greater than all earthly powers. And by *earthly powers* Paul meant to suggest political and governmental power in the world. Christ's power and authority trumps all political and worldly power and authority.

God's power trumps everything. Paul mentioned that it was higher or far superior than all "rule and authority and power and dominion" (v. 21) or "principality, and power, and might, and dominion" in the *Authorized Version*. The idea is that God's power exceeds every kind of power we can think of, including principles, laws, and human intention—will. The application of these verses pertains to worldly power and government, not heaven.

Paul was very much aware that Jesus Christ was a transitional figure in history. Paul taught about the end of the old age and the advent of the new. So, it comes as no surprise that he said that this was true at the time that he said it, but that it would also be true for all time, into the next age, the age that Christ inaugurated. That next age was not some other worldly Platonic realm of ideas, or some Fundamentalist, Gnostic idea of heaven, but was the beginning of what we call Western Civilization. We know this because of the forces that would later restart the clock of history at the birth of Christ. What was the *next age* for Paul is *this age* for us.

FULL-BODIED

Continuing to describe the this worldly power of Jesus Christ, Paul said,

> "And he put all things under his feet and gave him as head over all things to the church, which is his body, the fullness of him who fills all in all" (vs. 22-23).

The act of *putting things under* is also called *subordination*. We see a further refinement of the idea of worldly order and rank rather than an emphasis on the location of the heavenly abode. As Christ is put into the superior position everything else assumes a subordinate position. There is no question that this is true in heaven, but Paul was saying that it is also true on earth. Chris has come! Christ has risen! The world belongs to Christ!

Our forerunners in the faith were not as stupid or colloquial as we like to think. Those who wrote Scripture did not have any sort of three-tiered understanding of the physical universe, as is often portrayed by the enemies of Christianity. While they do sometimes employ language that suggests levels of power and effectiveness, they did not use it literally. Rather, they used it analogously. It is a curiosity that those who accuse Christian authors of such nonsense are themselves reading Scripture literally—woodenly, while refusing to move beyond such a narrow-minded interpretation themselves. They assume that there is no more to Scripture than a literal interpretation, and then accuse the faithful of the ignorance of literalism. They set up a biblical straw man of wooden literalism, and then demonstrate their prowess to defeat him.

For instance, Paul said that God put all things under Christ's *feet* (πούς). No one takes this literally in Greek or English. The *putting under foot* is an analogy for submission, where the inferior defers to the authority of the superior. Again, we note that the idea is one of *position* rather than *location*. The common assumption was that heaven ruled earth, and no one thought any differently, though there were different gods who were thought to issue different orders, especially in the Greek Pantheon. Nonetheless, the overarching truth Paul was communicating was the superiority of heavenly power and authority and the inferiority of earthly power and authority. Thus, all use and discussion of *heaven* was about order, rank, and position rather than location. It is about ordinality rather than cardinality, if I may borrow a mathematical analogy. I'm not suggesting that ancient people knew everything that we know today, but I am suggesting that they knew the difference between rank and place, and that God's place always involves the highest rank. When we read *heaven* in Scripture we should think of rank and authority rather than the location of some disembodied mint julep bar.

Not only did God give Christ "as head over all things to the church" (v. 22), but in doing so God gave Christ *headship over all the church*. Note that the first translation suggests that the church is the caretaker of Christ's headship, while the latter suggests that Christ is the caretaker of the church. The first reading is episcopal, while the latter is congregational. The difference between these two readings is significant and longstanding. And both have to do with rank and order, and neither with the location of the heavenly abode.

THE CHURCH

Verse 23 then identifies Christ with His body, the church. Paul wrote much about this concern,[1] but here he said that Christ's body is "the fullness of him who fills all in all" (v. 23). Calvin said of this verse:

> "This is the highest honor of the Church, that, until He is united to us, the Son of God reckons himself in some measure imperfect. What consolation is it for us to learn, that, not until we are along with him, does he possess all his parts, or wish to be regarded as complete!"[2]

The wholeness of Christ grows as His church grows. Paul's reference to "all in all" hearkens to John 14:20: "In that day you will know that I am in my Father, and you in me, and I in you." The implications of this are vast and significant.

Whatever else verse 23 means, it should call the commonly understood, modern idea and definition of *the church* into question. What exactly is Christ's church? Is it the 501(c)(3) corporation down the street? Is it composed only of those who occupy the pews on Sunday mornings? Does it exist Monday through Saturday? And if so, how so? This is the topic of this book on Ephesians. Assuming that the church is the body of Christ, how does it manifest and reflect the character of Christ? How is the church like the second Person of the Trinity, Jesus Christ? What does this imply about church members

---

1   See 1 Corinthians 10-12, and the relevant chapters in *Arsy Varsy—Reclaiming the Gospel in Fist Corinthians*, by Phillip A. Ross, Pilgrim Platform, Marietta, Ohio, 2008.

2   Calvin, John. *Calvin's Commentaries*, public domain, Ephesians 1:23.

and church membership? Is there such a thing as church membership roles? What constitutes church membership? When Paul said *church* did he mean what we mean today?

Jesus said, "For where two or three are gathered in my name, there am I among them" (Matthew 18:20). Does this mean that the body of Christ is an institution, a movement, or every grouping of believers? What does "gathered in my name" mean? Does it mean that the church is limited to the organizations that we call churches today? Is our definition, idea, understanding, and expression of the church as the body of Christ adequate to the reality given by Scripture? Do our modern institutions interfere with or undermine the actual church? If unity or union with Christ puts us *in Christ*, and puts Christ in us, and all of that unity is then *in God*, what does this imply about the church? Can any human institution authentically embody all of Christ's church? If so, how so? And If not, why not?

I understand that the church has become an institution in the world today, and I am not questioning the validity of that. Though it must also be said that some churches are more faithful than others. Just by raising the faithfulness issue, we can note the difference between Christ's church (as a whole) and Christ's church*es* (individually considered).

The Greek word for *church* (ἐκκλησία) means *called out*. But it doesn't simply refer to a group of people who are supposed to get out of one place in order to gather in another. Rather, it refers to the particular place and the people from which the call issues. The *church* is "an assembly of the people convened at the public place of the council for the purpose of deliberating."[3]

We might better translate ἐκκλησία as *leaders*, but because the context is biblical we would need to understand it to be *Christian leaders*. And again, it is not simply that the church is the gathering of those who lead Christians, but the church is the gathering of public leaders who are Christian. It refers to people gathered together as a group, not to an assembly of disparate individuals. Prior to and contemporaneously to its New Testament use, it referred to Greek or local government, to those who gathered to discuss and adjudicate the concerns of the community, town, or city. It is a governmental word. And it is a democratic word in that the Greeks invented democracy.

The biblical idea of government involves ruling, and ruling involves rules, laws, and/or principles. All ruling involves decision-mak-

3   Thayer, Jospeh. *Thayer's Greek Definitions*, public domain, 1889.

ing on the basis of some standard for judgment, and the story of the Bible is the story of the establishment of a universal standard—Jesus Christ. Government is about rules, standards, principles, authority, and submission.

In the contemporary world we have confused ourselves by thinking that the central concern about authority always lies with the highest authority. And because we are so resistant to authority ourselves, we think that all authority must issue from the highest authority because our resistance will cause us to only obey the highest authority, usually under duress or threat. And as a matter of expediency and practicality we begin with the highest authority in order to stave off the inevitable resistance.

But this approach has proven to be very harmful because it tends to undermine and destroy the various mediating authorities. And without mediating authorities we must all deal with the highest authority. And dealing with the highest authority for the vast majority of Christians concerns is like drinking from a fire hose. Thus, the contemporary world finds that all government inevitably tends toward totalitarianism because we tend to appeal to the highest authority for everything.

The way out of this drift into totalitarianism is to strengthen the mediating authorities by not resisting them ourselves. We each must be more responsive and obedient to all levels of authority, not just to the highest authority.

9. From Wrath To Mercy

And you were dead in the trespasses and sins in which you once walked, following the course of this world, following the prince of the power of the air, the spirit that is now at work in the sons of disobedience—among whom we all once lived in the passions of our flesh, carrying out the desires of the body and the mind, and were by nature children of wrath, like the rest of mankind. But God, being rich in mercy, because of the great love with which he loved us, even when we were dead in our trespasses, made us alive to-gether with Christ—by grace you have been saved—and raised us up with him and seated us with him in the heavenly places in Christ Jesus, so that in the coming ages he might show the immeasurable riches of his grace in kindness to-ward us in Christ Jesus. —*Ephesians 2:1-7*

The essential question regarding the Old Testament and the New Testament is about what changed. The simple fact that the Bible comes in two testaments suggests that something substantial changed, and it did! But discerning and understanding that change are much more difficult than simply acknowledging it. Paul deals with this question in this section.

The Bible divides people into two groups. We see this in the stories of Cain and Abel, Jacob and Esau, Jews and Gentiles and in the New Testament: Christians and not-Christians. In the Old Testament we see the two groups divided by blood feud. In the New Testament, those in the new group have been changed. They used to belong to the old group—*not-Christian*, but were changed and now belong to the new group—*Christian*. And the difference between the two groups is stark. It is like the difference between life and death.

The old group followed "the prince of the power of the air" (v. 2). This is not about an actual prince. The word *prince* (ἄρχων) doesn't point to a particular person or office, but to what we call *civil leaders* as a group. Matthew Henry wrote about "the power of the air" (v. 2) in the early 1700s:

> "The air is represented as the seat of his kingdom: and it was the opinion of both Jews and heathens that the air is full of spirits, and that there they exercise and exert themselves. The devil seems to have some power (by God's permission) in the lower region of the air; there he is at hand to tempt men, and to do as much mischief to the world as he can."[1]

Let me suggest an alternative but not a different understanding. The Greek word ἀήρ means *air*, but then as now the idea of a *prince of the power of the air* makes no literal sense. Therefore, the phrase was likely an idiom referring to civil rulers whose speech was carried by the air. The *prince of the power of the air* pointed to rulers who ruled by the power of their speech—which traveled through the air. Think of it as the power of their spoken orders. Their words were law, as opposed to being ruled by God's Word. They ruled by their own whims. This idea fits well with Henry's understanding, though expressed differently, and it fits with our own modern understanding of Paul's point.

The two groups that Paul was talking about were: 1) those who were consumed with anger, vengeance, wrath, and disobedience to God, and 2) those who were consumed with forgiveness, love, mercy, and obedience to Jesus Christ. Until Christ's resurrection the whole world was subsumed under the first group.

Also remember that Paul was talking to both Jews and Gentiles. But in the light of Christ, Paul put the Jews in the same category as the Gentiles, which would have been a horrific affront to Jews. Paul ignored historic Jewish differentiation by saying that some Jews were believers and some were not. Nonetheless, Paul said here that prior to Christ everyone had been captive to the spirit of ungodliness, and particularly to vengeance. The spirit of vengeance often masquerades

---

1 Henry, Matthew. *Commentary On The Whole Bible*, public domain, 1710, Ephesians 2:1-3, public domain.

as the spirit of justice, where talk about justice hides the deeper desire for revenge against some perceived affront.

This is very much related to Old Testament theology, where an animal was sacrificed to atone for sin, for something that offended God. Because we become or emulate what we worship, it is understandable that people also wanted their offended feelings to be atoned for—righted or revenged. The worst offenses required blood sacrifice. This Old Testament model of atonement carried the day until the final atonement by Jesus Christ and His resurrection, which served to prove the acceptability of His sacrifice.

This ultimate sacrifice by Jesus Christ of Himself satisfied God's blood lust, and unleashed God's forgiveness and mercy. In fact, it was Christ's forgiveness and mercy that led Him to the cross. He modeled forgiveness and mercy in the face of God's blood lust, and His mercy trumped God's blood lust by satisfying it, which then put an end to it.

Prior to Christ's modeling of forgiveness and mercy, the whole world was "dead in trespasses and sins" (v. 1). Humanity was locked in a self-replicating pattern of sin and revenge, understood religiously as the expression of God's justice. Like the infamous Hatfields and McCoys of American folklore, the squabble had been going on so long, and there had been so many infractions on all sides that justice would not be satisfied until all offending parties were dead.

"But God, being rich in mercy" (v. 4) provided another way through Jesus Christ. All of the Ephesian Christians had known the power of God's blood lust because they had been caught up in it. They could not drop the pattern of revenge without offending the religious sensitivities of their own families and communities, who were dominated by the Old Religion. Their exercise of vengeance only guaranteed the return of vengeance against themselves.

God Himself modeled forgiveness and mercy through His Son. But it wasn't enough to just forgive others. Christ had to maintain the spirit of forgiveness and mercy in the face of the worst possible offense. He had to prove and establish a model of forgiveness that could not fail and could not be outmoded. Anyone who adopted Christ's model of forgiveness and mercy, to the extent that Christ did, would break the pattern of revenge against himself. Christ's model could not be surpassed.

The Change

God caused this change by sending Jesus Christ to model it. Paul said that God "made us alive" (v. 5), which is the translation of συζωοποιέω. This word is composed of two parts: σύν, which means *union*, and ζωοποιέω, which means *to make alive, birth* or *vitalize*. This vitalization brings people into union with Christ. The whole phrase reads, "make us alive together with Christ" (v. 5). The fix is to be in union *together* with Christ. To emphasize that it is caused by God Paul interjected: "by grace you have been saved" (v. 5).

This idea of *being made alive together in Christ* can also be called *salvation* (σώζω). It literally means to be preserved from destruction, and yet there is more to salvation than not being dead. Paul said that God "raised us up with him (Christ, who was resurrected) and seated with him in the heavenly places in Christ Jesus" (v. 6). Christ's resurrection was not His return to heaven. That would happen later (Acts 1:9-11). Rather, Christ's resurrection was His return to life. He had been dead and was brought back to life. That's resurrection, and first and foremost it has nothing to do with going to heaven. Christ was resurrected from death in this world to life in this world. It's about life here and now, which is why Paul tied it together with God's making us alive together with Christ. Just as Christ had been resurrected from death, Christians are resurrected from being dead in their trespasses and sins here on earth, to life *in Christ* on earth. None of this pertains to heaven. It's about earth. It's about what we also call *regeneration*.

Paul said that we are seated with Christ in "heavenly places" (v. 6), which is the translation of ἐπουράνιος, and can also be translated as *high places* or *that which is over us*. Heaven is the place that God rules. The word referred to God's government or God's rule, which originates in heaven and is enforced by heavenly power. Thus, to be seated in heavenly places is an allusion to participating in God's government, God's rule. To be seated with God suggests familiarity with God. A citizen of heaven would stand in the presence of God, but an ambassador of God would need to sit down and discuss things in order to understand God, in order to represent Him to foreigners.

Heaven is surely part of the biblical story, and it is related to resurrection and various Christian doctrines. But the goal of the Bible is not to get believers into heaven, but to get heaven into believers. The final goal of the Bible is the renewal of heaven and earth (Revelation 21:2). Too many Christians are trying to escape earth by getting to heaven, but Christ is trying to bring heaven to earth. Thus, the Bible ends where it began—but in a renewed city in a renewed garden. It began with Adam and ends with a great city.

THE BEGINNING

"In the beginning, God created the heavens and the earth" (Genesis 1:1). Before God "created" light, He created the heavens and the earth. Think about that for a moment. This point is little recognized and universally ignored. It conflicts with the ideas of evolution and of the blending of evolutionary theories with Christianity. If we examine the first few verses of the Bible, we will find that they do not speak about creation *ex nihilo* in the Gnostic, Greek way of understanding it. God did not create light and then coalesce everything else from light.

Exactly what did God create? We know that God is the creative source of life. And *life* is defined by eating and reproducing. Only things that eat and reproduce are alive. "God created the great sea creatures and every living creature that moves" (Genesis 1:21). And "God created man in his own image, in the image of God he created him; male and female he created them" (Genesis 1:27). But the Bible does not say that God *created* light. "God said, 'Let there be light,' and there was light" (Genesis 1:3). The word *create* (בּרא) is not in the sentence. This word was used in Genesis 1:1, so it could have been used here in reference to light, but it was not. So, something different happened regarding light.

Genesis 1:1 is not a logical conclusion. It is an axiom, a premise or starting point of reasoning. *Axiom, postulate,* and *assumption* may be used interchangeably. Human origins are simply not available for scientific or logical examination. The truth is that we must assume some sort of origin, and the ancient religions provide various alternatives. The biblical account of our human origin simply must be accepted in order to understand the rest of the biblical story. If it is not accepted, the rest of the story will not make sense. If it is, the rest of the story will prove or establish the veracity of the axiom.

Assume Genesis 1:1 to be true. Again, exactly what did God create? The Hebrew word בּרא can also be translated as *shape, form, make,* and sometimes to *cut down* or *cut out*. None of the meanings imply *ex nihilo* creation. *Ex niliho* creation cannot make any sense to a human being because we have absolutely no experience or evidence of any such thing. I'm not saying that God couldn't do or didn't do it. I'm simply acknowledging that such a thing is beyond human under-

standing or proof. But neither can it be proven that it did not happen.
It is either believed by assumption or denied by assumption.

God created a *habitat*—heaven(s) and earth, a place from which
we can look down and see the earth below our feet and look up and
see the sky above our heads. God created an environment, or a place
where human life can exist. We know know that such a place is quite
rare in the galaxy. In the light of modern science we can say that God
created a habitable planet (earth) in a planetary environment (heaven)
or solar system which supports life. All life forms require cycles or systems. Life only exists in systems. Such cycles include two states. We
can call them sleeping and waking, work and rest, night and day, inclusion and exclusion, on and off, etc. Life oscillates. The first oscillation was night and day.

Firmament

The firmament (רקיע) was essential to God's creation (Genesis
1:6-7). And what was the firmament? There has been a lot of speculation. Christian theology followed the Medieval idea of a three-tiered
world of sky, land, and sea. Augustine wrote that too much learning
had been expended on the nature of the firmament.

> "We may understand this name as given to indicate not that it is
> motionless but that it is solid."[2]

Saint Basil argued for a fluid firmament. According to St. Thomas
Aquinas, the firmament had a solid nature and stood above a "region
of fire, wherein all vapor must be consumed."[3]

The Copernican Revolution of the sixteenth century led to reconsideration of these matters. In 1554, John Calvin proposed that
firmament be interpreted as *clouds.*

> "[N]othing is here treated of but the physical form of the world.
> He who would learn astronomy and other recondite arts, let him
> go elsewhere,"[4]

wrote Calvin. Genesis had to conform to popular understandings of
cosmology, or it would not have been accepted. "As it (Genesis) be-

---

2   Grant, Edward, *Planets, Stars, And Orbs: The Medieval Cosmos*, 1200-1687, Cam-
     bridge University Press, 1996, p. 335.

3   Saint Thomas Aquinas, *Summa Theologica*, "Whether there are waters above the
     firmament?" (1274).

4   Glover, Gordon J. *Beyond the Firmament: Understanding Science and the Theol-
     ogy of Creation*, Watertree Press, 2007, p. 90.

came a theologian, he (Moses) had to respect us rather than the stars," Calvin wrote. Calvin's doctrine of accommodation allowed Protestants to accept the findings of science without rejecting the authority of Scripture. According to many today, the Bible simply reflects the cosmological ideas that were prevalent at the time it was written. And, of course, that is true, but it does not exhaust the truth of the Bible.

Much ink has been spilled over defining the firmament. But the most simple explanation is that the firmament is *land*. Land appeared in the sea and the land separated "the waters from the waters" (Genesis 1:6), that is to say that the land separated the seas.[5] Land also separated the waters above (clouds) from the waters below (sea). The ancient belief was that land floated on the sea, but did not float as high as the clouds. Thus, land satisfies the idea from the biblical narrative regarding the firmament. And the land is *terra firma*, dry land.

Much of this early creation narrative provides an explanation of life as we find and experience it through the eyes or from the perspective of God. The purpose of the Bible generally and of the creation narrative specifically is to provide a thought structure or system that explains the world and our purpose and role in it. God began with the creation of this system (heaven and earth), both the actual physical and biological elements, and the intellectual, mental, and moral elements, and wove them into a whole or a universe.[6] And the point of the universe is that it is all one unified system that has physical, biological, intellectual, mental, and moral elements that exist in harmony to provide for sustainable life.

God created a whole system for life, a universe. And a universe is most assuredly not simply the material or physical stuff of experience, but it is also the unified "verse" or story that enlightens and informs our relationship to the stuff of experience. The Bible begins with the creation or establishment of this system (Genesis 1:1), and ends with the renewal of the system (Revelation 21:1), and its enhancement to

---

5   Consider the modern theory of Pangea, http://en.wikipedia.org/wiki/Pangaea. One of the potential flaws in this theory is that the size and orbit of the earth has remained constant during the continental drift.

6   Universe: "The universe is commonly defined as the totality of existence, including planets, stars, galaxies, the contents of intergalactic space, and all matter and energy" (http://en.wikipedia.org/wiki/Universe). But note that this definition ignores the subjectivity of human existence, which is composed of thoughts, ideas, passions, feelings, and life habits. Surely these things are included in the "totality of existence."

accommodate large populations (a city). It is crucial that we understand exactly what God created in order to understand what is being renewed and enhanced in Christ. Commentators have fixated on the physical elements of the new heaven and earth depicted in Revelation, thinking that God is either going to bring a new planet "online" and/or transport humanity to a new universe.

But what if God's endgame is more modest? What if God is simply going to provide a new and better story about the same universe, such that humanity will see, understand, and relate to the universe in a new way? God's plan is not to change the dirt and stars of the solar system, but to change the hearts and minds of those who dwell on earth, and that story is still very much in process.

THE OLD, OLD STORY

Before we leave this train of thought, let's look at Revelation 21:1,

> "Then I saw a new heaven and a new earth, for the first heaven and the first earth had passed away, and the sea was no more."

Based on what has been said above, the first or old system will pass away, or is passing away, or has past away, depending on our historic vantage point. The old story is giving way to the new story. Paul wrote of the death of the Old Man (Roman 6:6, Ephesians 4:22) and the birth of the New Man (Ephesians 2:15, 4:24).

We understand this change to be both regeneration and recreation. Without a doubt individuals are in the process of being regenerated or born again (John 3:3-5). But the process involves much more than mere individuals because individuals are being saved out of the world and into the church. The story is about the human habitat as much as it is about the people because people require a habitat.

The birth, life, and death of Jesus Christ is the fulcrum or crux of the new thing that God has done and is doing on earth. And the story of Christ is the new story of the New Testament. The coming of Jesus Christ to earth is the leading edge of God's new story, His new heaven and new earth—a new habitat—in Christ. That story began with Christ's advent and will conclude with Christ's return in glory. To properly understand what changed between the testaments, we need to understand what God first created (Adam and a human habitat) and what God's recreation in Christ created (Christ and a new human habitat, or a new way of being human).

We currently live between these two historic markers, Christ's birth in humility and Christ's return in glory. In a sense we can understand this to be the spread and acceptance of the new story or new habitat in Christ as it moves across the globe to be established in every nation. God's goal is the renewal of humanity as a whole, not just a random collection of renewed individuals. The body of Christ is ordered, it is composed of gifted parts that work together. Of course, the renewal of the whole requires the renewal of the parts, but the mere renewal of the parts cannot constitute the renewal of the whole. And it is the renewal of the whole of humanity that constitutes Christ's return in glory, or that constitutes the ground for the return of Christ in glory.

The church as we know it in history is, then, a temporary stage or embryonic entity that has fed and nurtured this new humanity in Christ as it grows through its period of gestation. And at a certain point in time/history we will find that what has fed and sustained the developing embryo must be abandoned at the birth of the wholeness of the entity. At birth the entity can no longer feed upon the historic placenta that has faithfully nurtured it during its gestation. And the effort to remain connected to the placenta of history will poison the new entity in Christ.

The analogy of birth is everywhere in the New Testament, and we must engage it faithfully and fully. What sustained the fetus cannot sustain the infant, and what sustains the infant cannot adequately sustain the adult. According to Paul, the birth of Christ represents the birth of a new humanity in Christ. And the umbilical cord that connected Christ to Israel had to be cut in order to sustain the life of the new entity.

Paul then spoke of feeding Christians milk (1 Corinthians 3:2). Carrying on with this analogy, the new entity requires milk for a period of time, before it is weaned from milk and introduced to a solid diet. Let me suggest that Christ's birth does indeed provide the first historic marker of the development of a new humanity in Christ, and further that Christ's return in glory will mark the freedom from dependence upon the milk of the Word, when the new entity becomes whole in its own right. And further, this time is upon the whole world right now! We are closer to it than any previous generation, and modern science and technology have been born and have utterly changed the world.

The Old Testament church is the placenta that has fed and nurtured Christianity. The historic church is the mother whose milk has fed and nurtured the growth of the contemporary or traditional understanding of the church. Thus, at a certain point the church must abandon the precious placenta that has fed and sustained her, and must be weaned from the milk of the historical church, the early church. At a certain point the growing church must begin feeding on more than milk if she is to grow into a dynamic wholeness suited for humanity at large.

This is not to suggest that the placenta (the Old Testament) or the milk of the early church is wrong, evil, or bad in any way. It most certainly is not! The milk of Christian history, however, has provided temporary nurture for the life or history of humanity, which in the fullness of time must be transcended in order for the new humanity to live life to her full potential, if we are to employ the allusion to human birth. And while these things are to be transcended in human maturity, they are not to be abandoned, discredited, or ignored.

Rather, the path of transcendence is the path *through* them, not *around* them. Both the placenta of the Old Testament and the milk of the early church must be honored in order for them to continue providing the way of growth and maturity into the fullness of humanity in Christ. However, the roles that these things play in maturity are not the same roles that they play in gestation and infancy. Individuals will continue to engage them as they engage Christ. Individuals will continue to be born and to be born again in Christ, and in order to nurture and guide new individuals, they will need the nurture of placenta and milk. But maturing a Christian cannot continue to feed like a fetus or an infant.

WAKE UP IN UNION

Paul said that God has "raised us up with him and seated us with him in the heavenly places in Christ Jesus" (v. 6). The *Authorized Version* translated συνεγείρω as "raised us up *together*" and the literal meaning is to raise together. The Greek word is composed of two words σύν, which means union, and ἐγείρω, which means to arouse from sleep. The meaning is that God has woken us up to the fact that we are in union with Him. As believers come to an increased state of wakefulness, we find ourselves *in Christ*. We don't put ourselves there. We don't work ourselves into union with Christ. We simply find ourselves already there, once we are awake.

Furthermore, we find ourselves *seated* with Christ, not standing. People who are seated together enjoy conversation. They are in relationship because of their proximity. Actually, the word *places* is added to the English; it is not in the Greek. The Greek literally reads *heaven*. But this section of Scripture is not about life after physical death. It's about regeneration, about being born again in Christ. It's about this world, not some Gnostic, phantasmagoric nether-world for departed spirits. Yet, it reads *heaven*, which therefore must refer to something in *this* world.

I submit that it refers to the context of this world in the same way that the solar system is the context for the planet Earth. Further, if we can suggest that earth refers to the materialistic world of matter, then the context of that world includes not only stars, but it includes all of the stuff previously discussed that is involved in the universe—the biological, intellectual, mental, and moral elements that exist in harmony to provide for sustainable human life. We might also think of the earth as the physical hardware and heaven as the controlling software.

God did this so "that in the coming ages he might show the immeasurable riches of his grace in kindness toward us in Christ Jesus" (v. 7). The "coming ages" that Paul referred to here is the contemporary age in which we currently live. Paul was pointing to an unknown future when everything would be different than it was for him. That day has arrived. Not every human being on earth knows this or shares in this new age yet. But the majority of humanity knows about the difference that modernity makes, though they mistakenly think of it as an American or Western thing rather than a biblical thing.

I'm not suggesting that modernity is the kingdom of God. Rather, I'm saying that the modern industrial revolution and the more recent information revolution provide useful tools for understanding Paul's allusion to the "coming ages." Unfortunately, the wholeness of the new humanity promised in Christ is still in the future. It is unfortunate for us because while the tools of the kingdom are currently in our hands, our (humanity's) hands are still infantile and stained with sin. We have misused those tools for sinful and selfish ends. While those tools have allowed sin to prosper in the short run, sin will run its course of death, devastation, and destruction. Evil will implode upon itself to its own destruction, and only then will the whole world understand the need for God's righteousness for the handling of those tools.

Similarly, the tools of surgery are a blessing in the hands of a skilled surgeon, but a curse in the hands of ignorant children. And God's great kindness toward us regarding those tools is the dispensation of the righteousness of Christ broadly across the face of the globe. Of course, the tools themselves would have been discovered with or without Christ because they—science and technology—are constituent to the structure of the world. But the righteousness needed to handle them properly and well comes only from God-in-Christ. And this is God's great gift to the world that constitutes "the immeasurable riches of his grace" (v. 7).

10. Working By Grace Through Faith

For by grace you have been saved through faith. And this is not your own doing; it is the gift of God, not a result of works, so that no one may boast. For we are his workmanship, created in Christ Jesus for good works, which God prepared beforehand, that we should walk in them.

—Ephesians 2:8-10

We are so used to hearing verse 8 that we don't pay attention to it. In order to hear it afresh, we need to hear it in a new way. So, allow me to restate it: *Because of God's grace you have already been made whole by the habit of faithfulness* ... (notice the ellipsis). There are three things mentioned here—grace, salvation, and faith.

Grace (χάρις) is a characteristic of God. He is graceful, which means that He is merciful, kind, and generous. And salvation is dependent upon God's grace. If God should ever stop being graceful, salvation would not be available because the only way that we get it is that He gives it.

The Greek word translated as *saved* (σώζω) is also translated as *made well* or *whole* (*Authorized Version*) in Matthew 9:21.[1] The word has a variety of meanings depending on its use, but none of them suggest some sort of guaranteed entry into an otherworldly plane of existence. They all pertain to this world and suggest the well-being and continuation of life as opposed to death and destruction. The word literally means to be kept safe and sound, rescued

---

1   And also in Matthew 9:22; Mark 5:28, 34, 6:56, 10:52; Luke 8:48, 50, 17:19; Acts 4:9.

from danger and destruction, or delivered—transferred from one condition to a better or more complete condition.

At this point we need to ask about who this refers to. Again, Paul was writing to the Ephesians, but not to everyone in Ephesus. He was writing to the *Christians* in Ephesus. The word ἐστέ is the second person plural of *to be*. There are two ways to read this: 1) Paul was writing to each individual in the church, and 2) he was writing to the church as a whole. Both are true, and so both must be considered. Of course, the totality of the parts do make up the whole. But the whole is more and/or different than the sum of the parts. There is something different about the whole that cannot be accessed through a consideration of the parts. And this something different is easily overlooked and ignored. But because the word under consideration (σώζω) pertains to wholeness, this aspect must be examined if we are to understand it. In fact, the consideration of wholeness is the very heart of Christian salvation.

Faith (πίστις) is the personal conviction of the truth of something. I called it the *habit of faithfulness* because convictions are the foundation of habits in the same way that beliefs are the foundation of doctrine. When we speak about beliefs we are thinking of ideas, but when we speak about habits we are thinking of behavior. Too many Christians think of faith only in doctrinal terms, as if Paul was talking about ideas divorced from behaviors. Defining faith in terms of habits does not exclude doctrinal ideas or the joy of theology, but it insists that more than mere ideas are involved. Habits touch our most basic activities of life, and this is exactly what Paul meant.

...AND MORE

There is no punctuation in the Greek, so it is left to the translators to supply it. The *Authorized Version* put a semicolon at the end of verse 1, where the ASV has a new sentence. Regardless, verse 2 is part of the idea of verse 1: "And this is not your own doing; it is the gift of God...." In order to emphasize the graciousness of salvation Paul repeated the fact of its graciousness. Salvation is not something that we do for ourselves, but is something that God does for us. We cannot cause ourselves to be saved any more than we can cause ourselves to be born. Salvation is an assignment, not a self-selection. And yet, there is a clear moral imperative involved.

It helps to think of it militarily. God has commanded humanity to conquer the enemy—Satan, and because He has assigned General Jesus to command the troops He is assured of His victory. This does not mean that every Christian will be an infantryman on the front lines of battle. But it does mean that every Christian has a necessary role to play, whether it be support services or troops on the ground. God's people are drafted. Sure, some argue that they volunteered, but their willingness does not negate God's command. Nor does volunteering make one a better soldier than being drafted. While draftees are tempted to do less than they are commanded, volunteers are temped to do more—and both temptations constitute violations of orders.

The salvation that produces faithfulness is not of our own doing. And yet the resulting faithfulness is our doing—in Christ, of course. What is not our doing is the salvation that produces faithfulness. We are saved for service that begins here in this world at this time—right now. The purpose of salvation has God's new heaven and new earth (Revelation 21:1) in mind, but that doesn't mean that the new heaven and new earth are to be manifest somewhere else.

God is in the process of bringing heaven here, not abandoning this world to Satan. God's intention is to destroy Satan and his works, not the world. God's intention is the destruction of evil and the maintenance of good, according to His definitions of good and evil (Genesis 2:9). God's plan is not to destroy the dirt and the stars of this world and replace them with new dirt and new stars. Rather, God's intention is renewal. Sin will be destroyed, not life. It is Satan's understanding of the world that God will destroy. And He will destroy it by replacing it with His understanding of the world.

It is God's will, God's power, God's plan, God's way, God's provision, and God's idea—not ours. And that is why Paul can say that Christian salvation is "not a result of works, so that no one may boast" (v. 9). Salvation is not *of us*, but is *of Christ* alone. It is not the result of believing the right things, or belonging to the right church, or teaching the right doctrine, or doing the right liturgy, or making the right decisions. None of that! All of that produces grounds for boasting. If we are saved because we believe the right things, then our salvation is the result of our beliefs—and we can boast in that. If we are saved because we belong to the right church, then our salvation is the result of our church membership—and we can boast in that. If we are saved because we have been taught the right doctrine, then our salvation is the result of our excellent teachers—and we can boast in that. If we are saved by doing the right liturgy, then our salvation is the result of our liturgical observance—and we can boast in that. If we are saved because we have made a decision for Christ, then our salvation is the result of our decision—and we can boast in that. If we are saved by our care for the poor, then our salvation is the result of our charity —and we can boast in that. But Paul said that no one may boast of their salvation because it is a gift of God.

We cannot boast about our salvation in Christ because "we are his workmanship" (ποίημα, v. 10). We are God's pottery, we are not the potter (Jeremiah 18:6). We are fashioned, we do not do the fashioning. We are made, we are not the Maker. We are the result, not the cause.

And our salvation is not the end of the story, it is the beginning of a new story! The beginning of our story in Christ involves the end of our story in Adam. In order for the new story to begin, the old story must end.[2] The period of time in which we currently live is the time between the end of the old story in Adam and the fulfillment of the new story in Christ. The new story has begun in history, and is in the process of taking dominion of the earth in Christ.

This dominion is not like any sort of one world government that humanity can imagine because it is not *of humanity*. It is *of Christ*. And in Christ it is not a one world government, but a God's government world. But not a theocracy. Theocracies are run by people. It is not a matter of the Christian establishment of government in every nation, but is a matter of God's establishment of trinitarian Christianity in every heart. It is not that Christianity is to dominate the world, but that Christ is to inhabit every soul. And while those who don't know Christ will not see any difference between these two things, those who know Christ best know the difference between *domination*, which is not Christ's way (Matthew 20:25-26), and *dominion* (or lordship through service), which is.

In addition, it is not we who are to convert others, but it is Christ who converts all because conversion is a product of salvation, and salvation is God's gift, that no one may boast. "So faith comes from hearing, and hearing through the word of Christ" (Romans 10:17). The only boasting point that Christians have is Christ. We may boast or glory in Christ. We may assist in the hearing, of course, but our involvement is more like turning on the radio than being the D. J. Another way to say or understand this is to examine Christ's role in Christianity versus the role of individual Christians in Christianity.

---

2   For a discussion of this point, see Ross, Phillip A. *Peter's Vision of Christ's Purpose in First Peter*, Pilgrim Platform, Marietta, Ohio, 2011, p. 86-ff.

GOOD WORKS

Notice that the essential element of this new humanity is its situation or context, its *sitz im leben*, which is *in Christ*. Christ is the context or the *whole* of Christianity, the model which functions as a self-similar[3] aleph-null.[4] He is that which is more than the sum of the parts of Christianity. He is that which gives Christianity purpose. He is the end of humanity as Adam represents it, and the purpose of humanity as Christ represents it. In Adam we may have been *homo sapiens*, but in Christ we are *homo Christus*, a new kind of being in the world. God has done all of this for love and fellowship.

A problem arose when Satan tricked Adam and Eve into acting on their own assumptions about good and evil, rather than depending on God's judgment, God's Word. From that point forward Adam and Eve pursued what God calls *evil* because it seemed to be good to them. And doing so led to broken fellowship with God because their decisions and actions serve death, because they ultimately lead to the ultimate extinction of humanity.

One of God's functions is to serve as a kind of governor on the engine of human creativity, where the function of the governor on an engine is to limit fuel intake. Otherwise the engine will run faster than it is capable of, and destroy itself. Science and technology are necessary for the sustainability of large populations on earth, but they also have the capability of destroying the human habitat.

When Adam abandoned relationship with God, he abandoned the protective care of God's values, God's understanding of good and evil. Having been created in God's creative image, humanity is also creative. We are not governed by instinct, but by habits that can be changed. Our conscious choices and creativity can trump our instinctive feelings. We can create a bomb large enough to destroy our human habitat, as we now know. And misusing the energy we need to maintain large populations can poison and undermine the habitat we require for life.

God knew when He created the world that the human use of science and technology would do all the things that it is doing today. God has known this all along. The Bible has always been a message for the future from the past. While it has taken many thousands of years for humanity to discover and develop these things, God has

---

3 See footnote 9, p. 29.
4 See Appendix, p. 407.

known about them all along. We need to read Scripture with this in mind because we now know that God has known it all along.[5] It is important to know this because it helps us see the world through God's eyes, God's perspective.

The new heaven and earth of Revelation 21:1 that was prophesied to replace the old heaven and earth of Genesis 1:1 is a product of the world of science and technology, but not science and technology alone. Rather, the new heaven and earth is a world of science and technology *in Christ*, with Christ as the governor. Prophecy suggests two manifestations of this new world: one that respects God's values and lives in Christ's governance (heaven), and one that doesn't (hell). One leads to eternal life with God-in-Christ, and the other leads to eternal life with Satan, apart from God. One serves the values of life, and the other serves the values of death. The One has come to replace the other.

Thus, the ultimate religious question pertains to the limits of human freedom and ingenuity. It is not that we are free to do and be whatever we want, without regard for God or Jesus Christ, but that we are we free to do and be what God wants us do and be *in Christ*. The ultimate issue here is both moral and existential (or behavioral and ontological), in that it is about who we are, about our identity and being. We are all God's people and are morally bound to God.

God's covenant is still in force. God blesses those who honor Him, and curses those who don't. However, God covenants with *people*—tribes, nations, cultures—not mere individuals. And while those people groups are composed of families and individuals, we cannot know for sure that every faithful family or individual will experience what they would call *God's blessing*. God's blessings and curses are not in a one-to-one correspondence with families and individuals. Sometimes individuals and families experience hardship, like Job did. Our understanding of God's blessings and curses are more Quantum than Newtonian, in that they describe trends rather than hard facts. They are more statistical than arithmetic, more general than specific.

God's purpose, the purpose of God's law and of God's grace—and even the purpose of the interaction between law and grace—is the betterment and maturity of humanity for the glory of God. Or per-

---

5   Unbelievers will doubt this (1 Corinthians 2:14). But if God is who He says He is, His knowledge of science, technology, and the future are necessary and undeniable.

haps it is more accurate to say that God's purpose is *the regeneration of humanity*, of human society, human culture in a *sustainable* way. Indeed, eternal life has perfected sustainability—and that's the point!

BEFOREHAND

God prepared *good* (ἀγαθός) *works* (ἔργον) before hand (v. 10). The word means work—employment, and the idea suggests work that is valuable, beneficial, constructive, helpful, positive, etc.

When Adam was in the Garden, the first thing that God gave him was a job—work. Adam was a taxonomist. His job was to name and classify the animals, and by implication his whole environment. Adam was a scientist because definition and classification are the prerequisites of science. God knew what He was doing. He knew about reality, about science and biology, about astronomy and physics. He knew how reality works, mathematically and scientifically. God knows the physics of reality. And He knew that we would discover all of this and develop it. God also knew that it would take a certain kind of culture to rightly produce and sustain science and technology.

This verse is about more than simply caring for the poor, though it includes that. It is about the engagement of human labor and capital in ways that contribute to the sustainability of humanity over long periods of time, even approaching eternity. Part and parcel of these good works involves what we might call *working good* or *doing work righteously* or *rightly*—with honesty, honor, and integrity. Indeed, honest work, or the application of honesty and righteousness to human labor, contributes significantly to the goodness and sustainability of work. This is how we are to walk in the good work that God has prepared beforehand.

The fact that God prepared it beforehand (προετοιμάζω) suggests that God is purposeful, and that we, having been created in God's image, are also purposeful beings. And indeed, working purposefully is not only quite satisfying, but it also increases the effectiveness of our work. This idea was reinforced by Jesus in a parable:

> "Whoever does not bear his own cross and come after me cannot be my disciple. For which of you, desiring to build a tower, does not first sit down and count the cost, whether he has enough to complete it? Otherwise, when he has laid a foundation and is not able to finish, all who see it begin to mock him, saying, 'This man began to build and was not able to finish'" (Luke 14:27-30).

Planning is essential to work, and even more so for *good* work. Planning and then working with honesty, honor, and integrity is the secret of the success of the ancient Jews, and of the value of the Christian work ethic. It is the secret sauce of American Exceptionalism, the secular wake of Christ's splash into human culture. But to call it American Exceptionalism is both unfortunate and wrong. It is not about America, nor is it exceptional. A better name would be Christian Common Sense because it issues out of Christianity and it is intended to be quite ordinary or common. In fact, the only way that it works as it is intended is for the majority of the population to be actively engaged in ordinary Christianity. It is about Christ's church.

Christ's church is more than an organization. It is an organism in that it is alive, ordered, and dynamic. It is a way of life, a way of living, a society. And because of this it is more than the official gathering on Sunday mornings that we usually call *church*. It is that, of course, but it is much more than that because it involves a way of life or lifestyle. It is life lived from a particular perspective or with a particular set of values and principles. And even more than this, it is like living with a friend who participates in everything we do, who never goes away or leaves us alone.

Church (ἐκκλησία) literally means *called out of*, and by implication it means *called into*. The church is called out of sin and into righteousness, out of worldliness and into godliness, out of self-centeredness and into community service. But it is not the abandonment or denial of self, as in Buddhism or mysticism. Rather, it involves the clarification of self in the context of community.

The Greeks used the word to denote the gathering of citizens called out from their homes into some public place, an assembly for the purpose of deliberation of some public matter. Today we might call it a *town meeting* or *town council* because it dealt with public issues or public policy. This might call into question the idea of the separation of church and state, as Americans currently understand it. However, it means neither the separation of public concerns from private concerns, nor does it mean the merging of civil affairs and church affairs. Both of these ideas involve false dichotomies. Neither religious nor civil matters can be divided into public and private concerns because many legitimate community concerns overlap the public and private delimiters. But neither can religious and civil concerns be merged because they involve different areas of jurisdiction.

WALKING

God has done all of this, revealed these things in order "that we should walk (περιπατέω) in them" (v. 10). The Greek means to make one's way, to progress, or make due use of opportunities. While the literal Greek does suggest walking down a path, the analogy suggests much more. To *make your way* in the world suggests a career path more than it does a trip to Europe. To *make progress* or *to progress* suggests the development of a life skill, which usually points more to career and vocation than to vacation. And *making use of opportunities* usually suggests employment and career advancement more than buying a lottery ticket.

Keep in mind also that Paul was not simply writing to individuals but to the church at Ephesus. This suggests that the walk or work he was writing about also has a corporate aspect. The work was not merely an individual thing—though it most certainly has serious individual implications, responsibilities, and duties. But being a church-wide or corporate thing also has cultural implications, responsibilities, and duties.

The walk (περιπατέω)—or work, activity, occupation, calling and activity—of Christians, individually and corporately, involves following Christ's model of honesty and integrity in all things. But mostly it involves imitating Christ's love of God and His willingness to put aside His own will in order to do the will of God. And when sufficient numbers of people walk and work in honesty, integrity, and industry regarding all things, truth is advanced in such a way as to increase the sustainability of humanity on earth. This is accomplished by increasing the level of personal morality in the light of Jesus Christ, which produces genuine intelligence about the actual world, and in turn serves the development and maintenance of sustainable science and technology.

We need to understand Paul's use of the word *walk*, as an analogy for the way that one lives life, one's central *occupation*. Paul did not have in mind the word *occupation* as it is used today. While Paul would not be opposed to translating it as *occupation*, he had more in mind than one's job. He would be more inclined to agree with Martin Luther's idea that every Christian has a *calling*, which involves employment and work, but is not limited to the modern nine-to-five mindset. Christ calls people into every kind of work, to engage and mature one's natural skills and abilities, which increases the various skills associated with the division of labor.

One's calling is that which provides purpose, meaning, and ful-fillment to one's life. Being called by Christ does not simply mean go-ing into ministry as an occupation, or for a paycheck. It can mean that, but truth is obscured when the paycheck becomes the central el-ement or guiding factor for being involved in overt Christian min-istry. When pastors and missionaries become dependent upon a salary provided by the group they minister to, they become dependent upon those they serve rather than being dependent upon Christ. This kind of dependency can be easily manipulated by those they serve or by themselves in order to ward off manipulation by others. Pastors and missionaries can be coerced by others or self-coerced to serve the ex-pectations of others or themselves rather than the expectations of God. And this is particularly tempting when God's truth is not wel-come or appreciated for whatever reasons.

Such a situation is not the kind of walking that Paul called for.

11. REMEMBER

Therefore remember that at one time you Gentiles in the flesh, called "the uncircumcision" by what is called the circumcision, which is made in the flesh by hands—remember that you were at that time separated from Christ, alienated from the commonwealth of Israel and strangers to the covenants of promise, having no hope and without God in the world. But now in Christ Jesus you who once were far off have been brought near by the blood of Christ.
—Ephesians 2:11-13

Verses 11-12 set up a contrast between the faithful and the faithless by way of circumcision. Originally circumcision was given to Abraham in order to separate or distinguish faithfulness from faithlessness, and historically to distinguish Jews from Gentiles. It is a very curious religious ritual in that it suggests a relationship between sex and God, the commonality between them being covenants—promise keeping. And because human generation is the product of sexual relations, it suggests a relationship between birth or life and God.

Through the Old Testament ritual of circumcision God inserted Himself into human sexuality. By putting His mark on the implement and symbol of human sexuality, God has claimed ownership of human reproduction. Of course, God has always been involved in sexuality, in the generation of species, but through Abraham God claimed an active role in family life and the sexuality that brings it about.

The significance of this has been lost in modern, pagan, and Christian culture. Since the advent of birth control pills and related technologies there has been an escalating effort to deny and remove the connection between sex and God that was inherited through the Christian churches in America and the West more generally. In short, that connection is marriage. That is, sex should only occur in marriage. But there is much more to this relationship than limiting sexuality activity to traditional marriage.[1]

However, Paul's concern here is not sex or sexuality but faithfulness. When God instituted circumcision He institutionalized the distinction between faithfulness and faithlessness, and that distinction has been at the heart of much strife and conflict ever since. The Old Testament is the story of that distinction in human history. And the conclusion of the Old Testament, coming in A.D. 70, was the destruction of Jerusalem and the Jewish Temple.

Christ had come to bridge that distinction by bringing Gentiles into direct relationship with God through Jesus Christ. God's purpose for sending Christ was the healing of the breach that had brought an end to the Jewish nation. All through the Old Testament the Jews identified themselves as the people of God, and stood opposed to everyone else. It is not difficult to understand that this claim and its opposition has caused much trouble in the world because it implied, not only that the Jews were right about God, but that everyone else was wrong. And people don't like to think of themselves as being wrong, particularly when it is suggests that their errors and false beliefs are evil and satanic.

Nonetheless, these are the implications of the Old Testament. It's not that God introduced strife and war to humanity. Not at all! Clans have fought from time immemorial. It seems to have begun with Cain and Abel. What God did was to focus the conflict on one particular clan—the line of Abraham—in order to provide a case study that would bring history to a head by highlighting the central concern, which is group membership. Part of our humanity involves group membership—corporateness. Human beings are necessarily social and derive both identity and existence from social connections. The parts of human identity are individual identity, social identity, and union with or unity in Christ. Human wholeness requires the wholeness of all three parts, such that they are one, yet distinct.[2]

---

1   For more on this issue, see Beecher, Edward, D. D. & Ross, Phillip A., Editor. *Concord Of Ages, Or The Individual And Organic Harmony Of God And Man*, Pilgrim Platform, Marietta, Ohio, 2013, Index: "sexual relations."

2   A "unit" of humanity is not an individual, but a heterosexual couple. See: Ross, Phillip A. *Arsy Varsy—Reclaiming The Gospel in First Corinthians*, Pilgrim Plat-

Paul made a point to say that the Gentiles were called *uncircumcised* by the Jews, who called themselves *circumcised.* The Jews defined their group by circumcision, which implied that the uncircumcised were not members of their group. The very thing that God gave the Jews to serve as a sign of their covenant with God became the thing that divided humanity. God caused this division, and yet most people think of God and religion as being unitive rather than divisive.

Division

Division is a necessary element of creation. God's original creation was not one thing, but two—"heaven and earth" (Genesis 1:1). In the beginning heaven and earth were separated. Then, once light was brought to bear on the earth, "God separated the light from the darkness" (Genesis 1:4). Then God put "an expanse in the midst of the waters," and "separate(d) the waters from the waters" (Genesis 1:6). Then God "separated the waters that were under the expanse from the waters that were above the expanse" (Genesis 1:7). When God created man, He did so by separating a rib from the man to make the woman, thus humanity itself is divided into male and female (Genesis 1:27).

The process of creation itself seems to involve separation and reintegration by God. We grow by the process of cell division, which produces an economy of the human body based upon the division of function, purpose, and labor. Almost everything about individuals is divided or bipolar. We have two eyes, two ears, two arms, two legs, etc. Even our brains are divided into hemispheres. Perhaps these divisions allow us to see things from alternate perspectives. And indeed, life and maturity are all about being able to understand various perspectives. All of human history can be seen as a kind of oscillation between division and reintegration. And the Bible itself teaches that the divisions of history will ultimately be reintegrated in Christ through the unity of the Godhead.

We each and all must remember that we are currently or have been at some time in the past separated from Christ. Human individuality is always separative because each individual is both unique and whole. We have many similarities and commonalities, but we are not all identical. While no two individuals are identical, our very existence as individuals is utterly dependent upon human sociality. Humanity is a species, a particular kind of being that is necessarily both

---

form, Marietta, Ohio, 2008, p. 192.

individual and social. Both of these poles of our existence are necessary for life. Human social integration is the goal of both Scripture
and history. In the beginning the wholeness of humanity was broken
by sin, by Satan's deception. The consideration of whether that brokenness was real or perceived leads directly into the character and reality of sin itself.

When people believe in the brokenness of sin and act on that belief, that very action reinforces the actuality of sin. The consistency of
belief and action intrudes the false belief of sin into the social construction of human reality. What may be mere subjectivity to an individual becomes increasingly objective as it is manifested socially.
Nonetheless, the goal of God in history is the reintegration of human
wholeness, which involves the dissolution and reintegration of both
individual and corporate identity in Christ.

The dissolution involves the acknowledgment of the reality of
sin, and the reintegration involves the acknowledgment of the reality
of God-in-Christ, the three-in-oneness of God's character and our
similarity with God in this regard. The point is that the integration
cannot occur in conscious awareness without the awareness of the
prior division. The idea of integration assumes a prior division.

CIRCUMDIVISION

God set up circumcision in the history of Israel as a kind of division of this kind, dividing those in covenant obedience from those in
covenant disobedience. Note that both groups are under God's
covenant because God's covenant originally applied to Adam and his
posterity, or all humanity. Through Adam all humanity sinned (Romans 5:12-19). God's covenant with Israel served as a model of God's
covenant with humanity.

The practice of circumcision is intensely personal or individual in
that it effects the most personal and private aspect of man, the organ
of reproduction. But as circumcision is practiced in the family upon
newly born infant males, the subjectivity of its privacy becomes a social institution through family practice and social ritual. What is private becomes a public institution. That is, it becomes increasingly
objective as more and more families engage the practice. Similarly,
the institutionalization of morality grows objectively the more it is
practiced subjectively—individually. What is a matter of personal
morality becomes public moral standards as more people practice it.

Circumcision is about group membership or inclusion. It provides a distinctive mark of inclusion and exclusion. This most personal practice divides humanity, and sets up the opportunity for social reintegration, which is the basic structure of the biblical story as a whole. Group membership, then, provides for the play between subjectivity and objectivity, or individuality and corporality (or sociality —the corporate character of human identity).

And all of this is a reflection or image of God's Trinitarian character in that God is the union of three persons—Father, Son, and Holy Spirit. We can also say that God is the union of three roles—Father, Son, and Holy Spirit. But we acknowledge them as *persons* rather than *roles* because their individual characters are more than the roles they play. A *role* suggests a generic pattern of behavior or relationship, whereas a *person* refers to a specific individual or character. In order to emphasize the reality of God in the world, we refer to the Trinitarianism of God the Person, and the diverse character of His Personhood.

ALIEN

By the simple fact of establishing the commonwealth of Israel, God both gathered a community together and divided the larger community. Those on the inside became members and citizens, and those on the outside became aliens. Members were bound to the covenant by their obedience. A *lien* is a kind of binding agreement of the first order. *Alien,* composed of *a* meaning *not* and *lien* meaning *bound,* describes someone who is not bound by a common covenant, or a foreigner. Aliens believe themselves not to be bound to the common covenant of those with whom they reside, so they disregard it, or disobey it. Thus, the two groups are covenant keepers and covenant breakers.

Covenant keepers are "children of promise" (Galatians 4:28) because they inherit the riches and blessings of God, while covenant breakers are "strangers to the covenants of promise, having no hope and (are) without God in the world" (v. 12). Covenant breakers are without God because Adam and Eve turned their backs on God by rejecting God's counsel and fellowship. They believed the Serpent and tried to hide from God. So, God sent them out from the Garden to live by their own wits and resources, because they would not trust God's guidance. Adam and Eve gave birth to Cain and Abel. And "in the course of time Cain brought to the LORD an offering of the fruit of the ground" (Genesis 4:3). It was Cain's idea to bring an offering to the Lord, not God's. Scripture does not say that God initiated it. Abel then followed suit. Abel brought a different offering. Cain had initiated the offering idea. Cain was the elder brother and leader, and had a rebellious heart. But Abel was a follower. He followed Cain's lead, and had a follower's heart. God could use Abel's followership as a model. But God would need to redirect Abel to a better model to follow. So, God accepted Abel's offering, and rejected Cain's.

But Now...

The "But now..." pertains to the "in Christ" (v. 13). Paul declared that the old way was gone, and the new way is *in Christ*. Those who had been far away were brought near by the blood of Jesus Christ. That which had been divided by circumcision (humanity) was reintegrated in Christ. The breach had been healed, the division mended. It was a done deal. It had been completed by Jesus Christ, who had dug a new channel for the flow of history. And yet history still needed to flow in the new channel. The reality of the channel in Christ set the course of history, but, though the course was set, the process still involved the actual flowing of history through the course in Christ. We are today in the midst of the flow of that process.

This is not an argument for Universalism, not in the classic Universalist sense that teaches that every human being will ultimately be saved. But it is in the sense that God's program for the renewal of humanity will ultimately succeed with the salvation of the human genome, the human kind or species *in Christ*. Adam's sin threatened to destroy humanity as a species because humanity is not sustainable apart from God. Christ's repair of the divine/human relationship makes humanity as a species ultimately sustainable, but only *in Christ*.

The old way was to follow in Adam's sin of disregarding God's guidance, God's definitions of good and evil. And the new way is to follow Christ's example of righteous living in the light of God's definitions of good and evil. The difference between these ways of living is so stark as to establish a new species of humanity in Christ.

12. COMITY

*For he himself is our peace, who has made us both one and
has broken down in his flesh the dividing wall of hostility by
abolishing the law of commandments expressed in ordinances, that he might create in himself one new man in place
of the two, so making peace, and might reconcile us both to
God in one body through the cross, thereby killing the hostility. And he came and preached peace to you who were far
off and peace to those who were near.   —Ephesians 2:14-17*

Understanding how Christ accomplished the propitiation of
God on the cross requires knowledge of the Old Testament
because Christ fulfilled its demands regarding the law of
God. And for such an understanding to be real, the actual history of
the Old Testament, the story of God's law in this world, needed to
play out in failure. Were salvation, or living within the boundaries of
God's law, possible on the basis of the natural merits and abilities of
humanity, Christ's sacrifice and presence would not be necessary, nor
the reality of the Holy Spirit. People could just do it by force of moral
will.

Paul had just previously been writing about circumcision, which
had become an important Jewish social custom, to the point of playing a determinative role in Jewish identity that separated the Jewish
community from all other people. Circumcision had become a mark
of Jewish identity because it had been tied to covenantal faithfulness.
But over time what was intended to be a *sign* of covenantal faithfulness had become a *replacement* for covenantal faithfulness. The sign
had become a substitute for the thing it signified.

This problem was rampant during Jesus' time on earth such that Jesus encountered a Jewish community awash in the sin of misplaced devotion, a devotion for the practice of circumcision that was divorced from the actual practice of covenantal faithfulness. Judaism had circled its wagons to protect its self-centered understanding of God's love, rather than making every effort to export God's love to the whole of humanity. Christ had come to fix this problem, to restore actual covenantal faithfulness and to remove the confusion of the sign for the thing signified by opening up the gospel to the Gentiles.

Perhaps it will be helpful to begin with what Paul does *not* mean because this section is easily misunderstood and divorced from its larger context. Paul did *not* mean that God was removing or loosening the requirements of God's law. God cannot do this and remain God because God's demand for the removal of sin from humanity is not the whimsical demand of an Oriental Potentate, but is the necessary requirement of His purity, which is the central aspect of His perfection and His own eternal sustainability. If God ever compromises His purity, His own longevity will be threatened. The compromise of purity leads to contamination, pollution, rot, and death.

Life as we know it is a dance with death, but that is not how God knows life or how He lives it. God is outside of time, we are inside. Human beings are beings of humus—rot or putrefaction. The process of digestion produces refuse—rot, waste, or humus, sometimes called *dirt*. Life is a magnetic, chemical, and molecular dance with decomposition. As uncomfortable as this idea may make you, it is a simple fact of life. And exposing the truth of Scripture involves the exposition of various life facts.

ORDINANCES

If Paul did not intend to eliminate, remove, or diminish God's law, what did he mean when he said that Christ

> "has broken down in his flesh the dividing wall of hostility by abolishing the law of commandments expressed in ordinances" (v. 14).

Or in the *Authorized Version,*

> "abolished in his flesh the enmity, even the law of commandments contained in ordinances; for to make in himself of twain one new man."

These translations are okay as long as they are properly understood. However, the *International Standard Version* (ISV) which translates it as

> "rendered the Law inoperative, along with its commandments and regulations, thus creating in himself one new humanity from the two,"

has gone beyond Paul's meaning.

The difference between these translations is that the ISV had rendered the entire law of God inoperative, presumably because it is opposed to God's grace. And such a supposition is untenable! Grace and law are not in opposition, but in harmony. They do not play the same notes, but they conform to the same tune. Paul's intention was not to put an end to the whole law (Romans 10:4),[1] but to end or alter various *ordinances* of the law. Paul was saying that Christ's fulfillment of the law changed some aspects of the law, some of its ordinances— rules, regulations, and practices. Historically, Christians have understood Paul to be talking about the ordinance of circumcision. But we must not export and apply this verse or this idea too broadly, lest we end in antinomianism. Historically, Christians have also understood baptism to be a replacement ordinance for circumcision. While Christian churches disagree about the mode and subjects of baptism, there is nearly universal agreement that baptism has replaced circumcision as an ordinance of the church.[2]

ONE NEW MAN

Christ's purpose here is to "create in himself one new man in place of the two" (v. 15). There are at least three things to notice about this: 1) that it is an act of creation, 2) where the new creation resides, and 3) that the new creation involves a new kind or species of humanity.

The Greek word translated *create* (κτίζω) is also used in Mark 13:19 to refer to the Genesis creation, in Romans 1:25 to refer to the Creator, and in 1 Corinthians 11:9 to refer to the creation of Adam. It should also be noted that the literal meaning of the word is *to make habitable*. Every creature requires a habitation. In fact, there can be no

---

1   *End* (τέλος) should be understood as *ultimate purpose*. Christ is the ultimate purpose of the law.

2   Christ changed various ordinances or practices. See: Ross, Phillip A. *Rock Mountain Creed—The Sermon on the Mount*, Pilgrim Platform, Marietta, Ohio, 2011.

creatures without appropriate habitations for them. Thus, the use of *create* or *creature* necessarily implies a corresponding habitation. A habitation can exist without a creature, but a creature cannot exist without a habitation.

God was creating a particular kind of being in Christ, a particular character, a particular way of being human in the world, a particular pattern of behavior. We might call it a way of thinking, a way of understanding the world, or a way of living in the world.

The new man being created in Christ is first and foremost a new way of understanding the world, a new kind of human response to the world, a new way of thinking (Romans 12:2). It is a new human archetype that exists first in Jesus Christ, the man, and then in Christ's church as a people. It is a way of living, a way of understanding the world, a way of responding to others and to the world. The New Testament speaks much of this everywhere.

To inquire about the existence of this new creature is to inquire about human character. Paul said that it exists *in Christ*, which has historically been understood to mean that it exists in the church or Christ's body (Colossians 1:18). Thus, it exists in individual Christians, but not merely so because it also exists as the corporate body of the church. It exists both individually and corporately, without loss or confusion of either aspect.

This apparent dichotomy brings us to Christ, who is not dichotomous but trichotomous. It lands us in the Trinity. And because we have been created in the image of God, who is trichotomous in His essential character, so are we who are in His image. Of course our trinitarianism is a feint shadow or image of God's, but it is nonetheless a real shadow or image. The Trinitarian God created a trinitarian people to inhabit a trinitarian world.

God's Trinity includes Father, Son, and Holy Spirit. Similarly, man's trinity includes species, individual, and Holy Spirit. We are connected to God's Trinity through the Holy Spirit. Thus, various characteristics of God can be communicated to humanity (individually and corporately) through the Holy Spirit. Individual Christians are united in Christ through the church by the Holy Spirit.

Finally, the newness of the "one new man" (v. 15) in Christ is the new humanity of the church. The new species of humanity that is the church is the new species in Christ that is replacing the old species in Adam. The old species in Adam is destined for extinction because they cannot let go of sin. Sin leads to death, and to cling to sin is to cling to death and extinction. But the new species in Christ is destined for eternal life because they have let go of sin. Righteousness leads to life, and to cling to righteousness is to cling to life.

When Christ broke down the dividing wall of hostility between these two groups, He made it possible for individuals in one group to go with the other group. And while Christ's purpose is for those who belong to the old humanity to become part of the new humanity, the reverse is also possible. Some professing Christians will fall away from being in Christ (Matthew 13:3-9). Nonetheless, while some individuals who are self-affiliated with Christ will loose that affiliation (Matthew 7:21-ff), the general growth and success of Christ's church generally will eventually take dominion as the new humanity becomes the overwhelming majority of the human population.

According to Revelation, someday Christ will return, gather up the church together for delivery to God. And at that point, the dividing wall of separation that keeps sin from contaminating God's purity will be reestablished as the sheep are separated from the goats. This is a central theme of the Bible and must not be neglected. People will eventually come to see that the destruction of evil is a good thing even when it is personally painful.

PEACE

Peace is not the absence of conflict. The Greek word translated as *peace* (εἰρήνη) literally means *to join*, which fits right into the larger context of eliminating the wall of division between the circumcised and the uncircumcised. Peace comes when humanity pursues the same purpose. And this can only happen in Christ because it requires a bona fide miracle.

The existing history of the world has been contaminated by sin. It's a dance that Adam began on the wrong foot. Yes, Jesus has come to end sin and establish a new world. But this project has proven to be more difficult than traditionally expected, and is taking longer than most people have expected. It is moving forward, but cannot be complete until this world is ready to let go of its history. This does not mean forgetting history, but transcending it.

There are two religious forces in this world—revenge and forgiveness. The religions of the old world are driven by revenge. The old world adherents call it *justice*, but the justice they want is revenge for the wrongs done to them by others. They don't want to live by God's justice themselves because that would mean their own destruc-

tion and damnation apart from Christ, apart from their refusal to forgive. Their commitments to the old religions of vengeance bar them
from embracing Jesus Christ. Embracing Christ requires people to
leave the old ways behind, to abandon the tit-for-tat "justice" that
punishes those who harm or offend them. Christ provides forgiveness,
but stipulates that God will "forgive us our debts, as we also have forgiven our debtors" (Matthew 6:12). In case that isn't clear enough, Jesus elaborated,

> "For if you forgive others their trespasses, your heavenly Father
> will also forgive you, but if you do not forgive others their tres-
> passes, neither will your Father forgive your trespasses" (Matthew
> 6:14-15).

The solution to the cycle of offense and revenge is forgiveness.
And God has taken the lead by sending His Son to provide forgiveness—not merely to offer forgiveness, but to provide everything that
is needed to make it real. God promised that forgiveness would one
day rule this world, and God's promises are not empty or void. Christ,
who is forgiveness personified, has been appointed the ruler of this
world, and His kingdom is growing. Of course, it is not complete,
but it is more complete than ever before. While both the wheat and
the tares are still growing, it is a field of wheat, not a field of tares.

And peace will come, not merely as the wall of division is removed, but as the whole world finds true meaning in the purpose of
Christ, or as the whole world finds purpose in the true meaning of
Christ. Christ is the destiny of the world, and that destiny will rest in
the peace of Christ.

In One

Peace comes from joining, and Paul's context of circumcision
suggests the rejoining of humanity without the distinction imposed
by circumcision, which can be accomplished by removing the ordinance of religious circumcision imposed by the Old Testament. The
idea is that circumcision created a special class of human beings that
were separated from the uncircumcised. The solution to the problem
of division is to remove the imposed institution of circumcision.

This is part of what Paul meant. Just as Paul was removing the
institution of circumcision, he was establishing the institution of baptism as a replacement. But whatever was gained regarding the unity
of humanity by the removal of circumcision would be lost by the im-

position of baptism. If the purpose of removing circumcision was the undiscerning unification of humanity, then the imposition of baptism simply redivided humanity again, though in a different way.

Consequently, we cannot assume that Paul's intention was the simple reunification of all humanity, but was a reconfiguration of humanity on some other basis. Paul was not removing the distinctions between good and evil, or between the sacred and the secular, or between the saved and the lost, nor the holy and the hollow. Paul was not undoing thousands of years of progress that had been made by the Old Testament. Nor was Paul eliminating the value or use of Old Testament law. Rather, Paul was clarifying what Jesus had reconfigured by dying on the cross, by propitiating God, by fulfilling the Law and the Prophets.

Several times Paul addressed two groups when he was preaching. For instance,

> "Paul stood up, and motioning with his hand said: 'Men of Israel and you who fear God, listen'" (Acts 13:16).

Two groups: Israelites and God-fearers. The God-fearers were a class of non-Jewish sympathizers who appreciated the God of the Jews and were involved in various religious activities. The Bible recognizes some monotheistic non-Jewish worship as being directed to *Yahweh* (Psalm 115:11). This idea was developed in later rabbinical writings into the concept of uncircumcised Noahides, Gentiles who followed the Seven Laws[3] which rabbinical writings assigned to Noah, on the basis that Genesis records Noah distinguishing clean and unclean foods before the covenant of circumcision with Abraham and the regulations of the Law of Moses.

The God-fearers were neither completely Jewish nor completely Gentile, but were not ethnic Jews. Nonetheless, they favored and feared the God of the Bible, but were not circumcised. The God-fearers subscribed to the Noahic Seven Laws, rather than the Ten Commandments.

Both the Jews and the God-fearers could be reconciled because they believed and practiced many of the same things. But those who had no respect or fear of God could not be reconciled with believers

---

3   The Seven Laws listed by the *Tosefta* and the *Talmud* are: 1) Prohibition of Idolatry, 2) Prohibition of Murder, 3) Prohibition of Theft, 4) Prohibition of Sexual immorality, 5) Prohibition of Blasphemy, 6) Prohibition of eating flesh taken from an animal while it is still alive, 7) Establishment of courts of law.

because they had no common ground for reconciliation. This is not to suggest that unbelievers could not become God-fearers—they could and many have done so over millennia. But note the ancient character of the God-fearers. It is older than the Moses tradition. Note also the character of Prohibition 6, forbidding the eating of flesh taken from an animal while it is still alive. The fact that such a prohibition exists suggests a degree of human savagery that has been long forgotten. And this suggests the progressive improvement of human character instituted by God over time. The progressive development of human character under the guidance of the Bible has been a good, positive thing. The progressive lessening of sin does not mean that sin has been overcome, or can be overcome by anything other than the propitiation of Christ on the cross.

ONE BODY

Paul believed that Jesus Christ was working to

> "reconcile us both to God in one body (σῶμα) through the cross, thereby killing the hostility" (v. 16).

Jesus was reconciling the two parties by joining them into one body. For millennia mystics have taught that this reconciliation is a mystical process related to God's Trinity in the physical body of Jesus Christ. And while there is an element of truth to this idea, it is not what Paul was talking about because the Greek word translated as *body* here is σῶμα (*soma*) not σάρξ (*sarx*).[4]

Paul understood Christ to be creating one body of believers, who would have similar beliefs and commitments that would be unifiable in Christ. Again, believers and unbelievers would not have the requisite commonalities to forge a unified body, but Jewish believers and Gentile believers (God-fearers) would. God was expanding the size and scope of believers in the world, but not yet unifying the whole of humanity. That part of God's plan will have to wait for Christ's return in glory.

Many unbelievers today want nothing to do with the love, grace, glory, or gifts of God-in-Christ. Other unbelievers are willing to consider the progressive revelation of Jesus Christ in history,[5] willing to engage openly and intelligently in an exploration of Christianity.

---

4   For a discussion of *body* see: Ross, Phillip A. *Arsy Varsy—Reclaiming The Gospel in First Corinthians*, Pilgrim Platform, Marietta, Ohio, 2008.

5   See footnote 5, p. iii.

We're not there yet, but like every believer in every age we can say that Christ's kingdom has grown and expanded more than any previous age has seen.

Hostility

While much hostility has been eliminated by the removal of the wall of separation that was created by circumcision, all hostility has not been removed. Nor did Paul suggest that the removal of the necessity of circumcision would eliminate all hostility. Rather, it eliminated the hostility between the Jewish believers and the Gentile believers, particularly with regard to circumcision. And that tended to relieve tension in other areas of belief and practice, especially as these groups began to focus on Christ rather than on their past disagreements. Christ provided the spirit of the future, of forgiveness. And that forgiveness could be extended backwards to cover the various sins and disagreements of the past, and passed forward to become a beacon of hope for the future.

Some hostility remains between believers and unbelievers. But it is generated by unbelievers because all genuine believers are captive to the spirit of forgiveness and reconciliation in Christ. If it appears that believers are filled with hostility toward anyone, if Christians are communicating hostility toward others, then their captivity and commitment to the forgiveness and reconciliation of Christ must be doubted. One cannot be filled with the love and forgiveness of Jesus Christ and be hostile toward others at the same time. Of course, hostility toward principalities and powers—ideas and social structures—is not the same thing as hostility toward other people. Christ's hostility toward the Pharisees was not directed at them personally, but at the abuse of their office.

Hostility toward others is bred by fear and the desire for revenge. Some call it *justice*, but again, if it is real justice it must be God's justice, for there is no other. And unbelievers will always be driven away from Christ by Christ's insistence that they trade in their desire for revenge and justice for His desire for love and forgiveness. Of course, no one can do this of their own will because our wills have been bent by Adam to seek the justice of revenge. Only Christ's Holy Spirit has the power and access to human character to overcome and straighten out that bend *in Christ*.

Preaching Peace

Preaching has fallen on bad times. It is perhaps the most unappreciated and poorly performed method of communication in the world today. Sure, there are a few good communicators, but only a small percentage of those who preach. People hate preaching today. Compare older definitions of the word *preach* to contemporary definitions to see how far things have deteriorated.

The Greek word used in verse 17 is εὐαγγελίζω, and literally means to bring good news, to announce glad tidings of any kind, but especially of the joyful tidings of God's kindness and graciousness, and in particular, the messianic blessings of Jesus Christ. Note that there is not a bad bone or tone to be found anywhere in the biblical definition.

The contemporary sense of the word suggests religious or moral instruction, especially in a tedious—tiresome, boring, slow and dull—manner. True gospel preaching can only be defined in such terms by people who don't understand it or who don't want anything to do with God—unbelievers. There may be hope for those who don't understand, if they are willing to try to understand. But most unbelievers are without hope—not because God withholds it, but because they don't want it. The god they don't want, however, is a god of their own imaginations, not the biblical God who has come in the flesh.

Paul said that Christ "came and preached peace to you who were far off and peace to those who were near" (v. 17). Note that He preached to two groups. We will extend our analogy and suggest that those two groups were composed of Gentile believers and Jewish believers. Both groups had ears to hear.[6] And those who don't have ears to hear can't hear—again, not because God withholds hearing, but because unbelievers plug their ears with foolishness.

---

6   Matthew 11:15, 13:9, 13:15, 13:16, 13:43; Mark 4:9, 4:23, 7:16, 8:18; Luke 8:8, 14:35; Acts 28:27.

13. ACCESS

For through him we both have access in one Spirit to the Father. So then you are no longer strangers and aliens, but you are fellow citizens with the saints and members of the household of God, built on the foundation of the apostles and prophets, Christ Jesus himself being the cornerstone, in whom the whole structure, being joined together, grows into a holy temple in the Lord. In him you also are being built together into a dwelling place for God by the Spirit.
—Ephesians 2:18-22

Both Jews and Gentiles have access to God through Christ, but not *all* Jews and Gentiles—only *believing* Jews and Gentiles. Again, believers and unbelievers do not have common access because faith is the mode of access. Yet, it is not the faith itself that provides access. It is the object of faith—Jesus Christ. Everyone has faith in something, but only believers have faith in Jesus Christ. And all who have faith in Jesus Christ, both Jews and Gentiles, have common access.

The object of this access is the Father, and the means of this access is the Spirit. The Spirit provides access to the Father through the Son. The Spirit who provides access for the Jews is the same Spirit who provides access for the Gentiles, the God-fearers. The Spirit provides access to the Father through Christ the mediator. Note the role of the Trinity here. Without the Trinity there could be no access, and the commonality between the Jews and the Gentiles is the one Spirit that they share.

Paul has been arguing that the believing Gentiles are brought into union with the believing Jews by the power and presence of the

Holy Spirit, which is a function of regeneration. His argument has been that the Gentiles are grafted into the heritage of the Jews through Christ. The believing Gentiles are "no longer strangers and aliens" (v. 19) but are "fellow citizens" (πολίτης) with the believing Jews. Both groups have common citizenship.

FOUNDATIONAL FELLOWSHIP

The word πολίτης is not spiritual, but political. It refers to a city or nation, not mere residence in an area, but membership in the common governance structures. Of course this had more to do with paying taxes than with active participation in the political process. But at the time, the involvement of most citizens was their contribution to the tax base. We might be tempted to think that Paul was giving the Gentiles membership in the Jewish nation at this point. But that's not quite what he was doing. He doesn't call it the *Jewish nation* or *Israel*, but "the household of God" (v. 19), an *economic* (οἰκεῖος) unit or group.

Verse 20 then takes up the argument from the other end. Here Paul argues, not that the Gentiles are grafted into the stock of the Jews, but that the Jews are grafted into the stock of the Gentiles. The household of God is not built on the foundation of Moses, as is the Old Testament, but is "built on the foundation of the apostles and prophets" (v. 20). The foundation of the citizenship (πολίτης) is not Moses or the Ten Commandments, but the apostles and prophets. The apostles were Jesus' first disciples.

The church at Ephesus had been pushed off its earliest understanding of the gospel by false prophets. Revelation 2:2 tells us that the Ephesian church had been invaded by false teachers, false apostles and prophets who had diluted the truth and distracted the faithful. Thus, the Ephesians had abandoned their first love (Revelation 2:4) and were called to "do the works (they) did at first" (Revelation 2:5). They had lost sight of the truth. Paul knew this and called them back to the foundation of the apostles.

Paul didn't clarify the reference concerning *prophets* because he assumed that his immediate readers understood what he meant, who he referenced. And no doubt they did, but we don't. So, we have to speculate. And as we do, we need to cast our speculations as broadly as possible because we cannot be sure. Certainly Paul referred to the Old Testament prophets. The mention of *prophets* in the Bible surely includes this group. And since the only Bible available at the time that

Paul wrote was the Old Testament, we can rest assured in this specu-lation.

But Paul also said that prophets were active in the church of the New Testament, as well (1 Corinthians 14, Ephesians 3:5). The role of prophets in the New Testament would be the same as their role in the Old Testament, which was to clarify the Word of God. Today we might call them *preachers*, but every preacher today is not a prophet. Nor was every expositor of God's Word in the Old Testament. The distinguishing factor of the prophets was their commitment to truth. Prophets clarify the Word of God truthfully not falsely, wholly not partially. They did in the Old Testament, they did in the New Testament, and they still do today. The voice of the prophets has not ceased, and in the light of Jesus Christ that voice cannot cease—ever. The voice of true prophecy will continue to speak God's truth 'til kingdom come, and then some.

Paul's reference to the foundation of the prophets pointed to the eternal truth that the prophets clarified, both Old Testament and New Testament. And we can extend the application of this into Christian history as many preachers have continued to proclaim, reclaim, and clarify God's truth. Thus, Paul fused the foundation of the Old Testament with the New Testament, which was part of the grafting that he was talking about.

When Paul called Jesus the *cornerstone* (v. 20) of the household of God he alluded to Christ's role as the eternal archetype of human-ity, in that the archetype of Jesus Christ is the common structure, the self-similar[1] pattern or way of life in which Jews and Gentiles are united. Of course, we must remember and honor the fact that this common structure, pattern, or way is a divine Person and not a mere principle. In particular, it is the Person of the Holy Spirit, who pro-vides both access to the Father and unity in the Son, Jesus Christ, who is both the principal of the church and the principle of Christianity.

CHURCH

The word οἰκοδομή occurs eighteen times in the New Testa-ment, and half the time it is translated as *building* and half the time as a variant of *edify* (edification, edifying), which means that we must understand the translation *building* as a verb. The *English Standard Version* translation, "the whole structure, being joined together" (v. 21) provides a nice turn of phrase, as long as we think of *structure* as a

---

1   See footnote 9, p. 29.

verb, too, as in *the arranging of various parts*. The *Authorized Version* does a nice job, too: "all the building fitly framed together," as long as we understand *building* as a verb and *frame* as the action of organization rather than a supporting lattice. Of course, the common understanding of this phrase is more noun than verb, which turns Paul's idea of the household of God into a lifeless wooden object, a mere building, a thing.

We also know this because the process of building and edifying, of structuring and framing, "grows into a holy temple in the Lord" (v. 21). It is a living, growing entity, this holy temple, because it exists *in the Lord* or *in Christ*. It is dynamic, not static, alive, not dead. And Paul specifies how much of it to include: *all* of it!

> "All the building fitly framed together groweth unto an holy temple in the Lord" (v. 21, *Authorized Version*).

Paul specified *all* of the building, and didn't just assume it. He wanted to be sure that nothing was left out of the process. And the very thing that is most easily left out is in this case the most important. It is the wholeness of the process of building, edifying, structuring, and framing, where wholeness is defined by purpose. The purpose of a thing or process circumscribes and undergirds its wholeness. Wholeness is a teleological[2] concept.

The wholeness is easily forgotten or ignored because it isn't a specific *part* of the process, but is the process *as a whole*.[3] The whole actually exists in a different dimension or plane of consideration than the parts. However, this fact has nothing to do with the surreal, ephemeral, or spiritual stuff of classical mysticism. Rather, it is very real, ordinary, and commonly accessible. But it has been hidden in plain sight by the rampant acceptance of Gnosticism in and out of the church(es). The popular preference for the mysteries and intriguing abstractions of Gnosticism blind people to the ordinary reality of holistic thinking.

The structuring, building, edifying, and framing cannot be complete without consideration of the wholeness or purpose for which it

---

2   Teleology: 1) the doctrine that there is evidence of purpose or design in the universe, and especially that this provides proof of the existence of a Designer; 2) the belief that certain phenomena are best explained in terms of purpose rather than cause; 3) the final cause the systematic study of such phenomena; 4) in biology: the belief that natural phenomena have a predetermined purpose and are not determined by mechanical laws.

3   See Appendix I, Membership & Set Theory, p. 405.

exists. The wholeness of a thing or process is defined by its purpose because the accomplishment of the purpose defines its completion. When human beings build or create anything, they begin with a desired purpose. The purpose then "pulls" the thing or process into existence as if the thing or process is attached to an invisible string that draws the thing or process from the future idea of the completion of its purpose. This is not simply an abstract concept, but is a concrete reality. This idea of causality, contrary to popular opinion, is a force anchored in the future that is pulling the present forward, rather than pushing the present into the future from the past. The cause is the future accomplishment of the purpose of its wholeness—its completion, not the past momentum of historical events or partial fulfillments.

The fact that this "holy temple" (v. 21) exists in the Lord is of great importance because it establishes the reality of the process that Paul is talking about. We know that God exists outside of time, that God straddles the past, the present, and the future all at once. He exists simultaneously in the past, in the present, and in the future. Consequently, only God is able to pull history forward toward the accomplishment of His purpose because only God knows and presently exists in the future.

We human beings can only know the past and the present abstractly. And we can concoct all sorts of speculations and rationalizations about causality, thinking that a thing or process is what it is because of its past. We tend to think that the past pushes the present into the future, probably because we only have access to the past and the present. But God, having access to the future knows the purpose of all things and processes. God doesn't have to guess about the cause, He sees it clearly through the accomplishment of its purpose, even though the reality of that accomplishment exists in the future.

In short, God is pulling this present world into the future that He purposed for it. Here's an analogy: We vainly try to push a string of some reality through the hole of the present. But God works from the other side, from the future, like a vacuum cleaner drawing the string forward. God is able to suck the various strings of reality through the hole of the present, such that all of the strings pass through the hole and accomplish the purpose He has given them.

ALTOGETHER NOW!

All of this takes place *in Christ*. The "holy temple" is "in whom" (v. 21), in the Lord or in Christ. And yet, at the same time this holy temple is "being built together into a dwelling place for God" (v. 22) Himself. As I said previously, the Spirit provides access to the Father through Christ. Taking Scripture seriously takes us into a dimension of the world that is more Quantum than Newtonian—and it has always been.

More than mere access is provided. In fact, Paul said that this access to the Father opens the way for God to dwell or reside with the believer *in Christ.* It gets a little confusing because we learn that each Person of the Trinity dwells and resides in each of the other Persons of the Trinity. It plays havoc with our common (Newtonian) understandings of time and space—and that is exactly Paul's intention. God is not bound by time and space as we are, which means that God's wholeness is not found in the same place or in the same way as the various parts of His body. And because Christ is God and the church is the body of Christ, God's existence is different than the existence of individual Christians. Human personhood is a dim reflection of God's Personhood.

All of this means that God's identity or character is Trinitarian in a unique way, while the identity or character of man (humanity) is trinitarian in a common way, common to other people. And the identity and character of Christians is both unique and common because it is united with Christ's identity and character. Thus, the union of humanity and God-in-Christ preserves the uniqueness of God's identity, the uniqueness of each Christian's identity, and simultaneously fulfills or completes the wholeness of each in Christ.[4] The point is that human identity is completed or made whole only in Christ, which has serious implications regarding both the moral and ontological aspects of humanity that must be reconsidered in the progressively unfolding light of Christ.

This "dwelling place for God" (v. 22) is Christ's church or body, the location of which is, like the issues of identity, more Quantum than Newtonian.

---

4   This all sounds very complicated and even mystical, but it is more akin to the reality of math and set theory. Reality is far more complex than previously considered. And God has always known about it, from the first word of Genesis forward. See Appendix I, p. 405.

14. Mystery Revealed

For this reason I, Paul, a prisoner for Christ Jesus on behalf of
you Gentiles—assuming that you have heard of the steward-
ship of God's grace that was given to me for you, how the
mystery was made known to me by revelation, as I have
written briefly.   *—Ephesians 3:1-3*

Paul said, "For this reason..." (v. 1). As it is translated in the *English Standard Version* and other versions it is an incomplete idea. Some versions have added the word *am*, *For this reason I, Paul, **am** a prisoner for Christ Jesus....* The reason Paul mentioned was that a dwelling place or habitation for God was/is being built.

Speaking of himself as a prisoner is an odd way to talk about the great freedom of the gospel of grace that Paul is known for. It can be read to simply mean that Paul actually was a Roman prisoner when he wrote this letter, which is true. And no doubt that's part of what Paul referred to. But it isn't all that he referred to because Paul was forever bound to Christ whether or not he was a Roman prisoner. Paul's bondage to Christ is an essential part of the freedom of the gospel that Paul preached.

Freedom in Christ is much more significant than the simple personal freedom to do whatever you want. The self-satisfaction of this kind of personal freedom is what the Bible calls *slavery to sin* (John 8:34). Freedom in Christ is the freedom to do what God wants you to do, and God wants all of His people to be like His Son, Jesus Christ. It means taking on the character of Christ by living a life of love and service to humanity according to the values and plans provided in the Bible. It means freely producing the fruit of the spirit—"love, joy,

peace, patience, kindness, goodness, faithfulness, gentleness, self-control" (Galatians 5:23). Freedom in Christ means being a slave to the
fruit of the Spirit.

STEWARDSHIP OF GRACE

Paul was known as the missionary to the Gentiles, which is curious because Peter became the leader of the Jerusalem church, which
was mostly Jewish at the time. But over time, Peter became the Patri-
arch of the Roman See, which became the largest branch of the Gentile church. Such are the curiosities of history.

Nonetheless, here in verses 1-2 Paul claims to be the leader of the
Gentile church because he was given the *stewardship* (οἰκονομία) of
grace to the Gentiles. The *Authorized Version* translated the word as
dispensation, but the literal meaning is *economy*, and the best translation in the contemporary vernacular would be *management*. Paul was
given an understanding of Christ's role in history.

To understand Paul's gift we must understand God's plan for the
world, not His plan for this or that individual, but His plan for the
whole world.[1] And to understand God's plan we must begin at the
beginning, where God's grace began. "In the beginning, God created
the heavens and the earth" (Genesis 1:1).

We are so accustomed to thinking of creation *ex nihilo* that we
have trouble thinking of the verse in any other way. It is difficult to
see past our own presuppositions. Nonetheless, imagine for a moment
that Genesis 1:1 is not about the *ex nihilo* creation of the physical
universe of science. Imagine those who first read the verse, long before the advent of modern science. In those days, the world as we
know it—through the eyes of science—did not exist. And this idea—
that the world of science did not exist—perfectly illustrates the point.

Understanding this verse, not through God's eyes, but through
the eyes of those who first read it means going back, not to the moment of some imagined *ex niliho* creation, but to the time of the first
compilation of Scripture. For our purposes it doesn't matter who
wrote or complied it because the point is simply that the moment of
the original creation was already long past. The verse simply offers an
explanation of how things came to be as they are, or as they were before the development of modern science and technology—certainly
before the Flood. And clearly, things were quite different then than

---

1   *God's Great Plan for the World—The Biblical Story of Creation and Redemption*,
    Phillip A. Ross, Pilgrim Platform Books, Marietta, Ohio, 2019.

they are now. We live in a very different world today—and that is exactly the point of Genesis 1:1. It was a very different world back then.

Scholars today know that the Genesis account provides a very different creation story from the other creation stories of the same period. The other stories shared a common evolutionary framework, and were not creation *ex nihilo* stories. The biblical story is unique in the sense that it simply stated creation as being an act of God, without further explanation. *In the beginning God created.* He just did it, and the biblical story begins from there. The Bible is not concerned about how God did it. It's concern is *that* He did it.

Again, *what* exactly did God create? He created heaven (השמים) and earth (הארץ), or most literally *sky* or *high place* and *ground*. We impose our scientific understanding on the verse when we think it means the reality of the Milky Way and beyond. There is no indication of this in the text, and no instructions to do so. A better approach may be to see it in its context, and its context is the Bible. Furthermore, our concern here is not to understand it as those who first read it understood it, but to understand it as those who gave us the completed Bible understood it. Seeing it in its biblical context allows for its fullest meaning and significance to be revealed. And it was this revelation of its fullest meaning and significance that Paul mentioned in his reference to the revealed mystery of (and for) the gentiles.

We are better served to try to understand it as God sees it than as those who originally read it saw it. Their world is not our world, and it is insane to think that we can or should forget what has happened historically since that time. We cannot forget what we know, nor does history flow backward. The traditional understanding is that God authored the Bible and God transcends time. Therefore, the biblical message also transcends time and speaks to us now, illuminating our current understanding of things. This is how faithful saints read and understand the Bible. It is a living document.

Paul was shaping the New Testament in the light of Christ. He was helping the world see Christ in the light of the Old Testament, so that we can see the Old Testament in the light of Christ. First, we accept Christ as the fulfillment of the Old Testament. Then, when we go back and read the Old Testament knowing Christ's role in its fulfillment, we are able to see things previously unseen and understand it much more fully. This is the mystery that was revealed to Paul, and which Paul shared in his New Testament writings. This is the mystery that Paul alluded to.

Paul was alluding to the habitation that God created, the place for human life to flourish. We must not revert to materialism at this point and assume that the essence of God's creation was the material world. The essence of life is not the material world. We are so accustomed to thinking in material terms that it is difficult to get beyond it. We modern people have been schooled in materialism since our earliest experiences. But God is not a materialist!

I'm not arguing for the precedence or preference of a spiritual reading either. That is the Gnostic error. Rather, I'm arguing for a biblical reading, a reading of physicality and spirituality, of material and idea, of matter and energy, all existing as one interrelated system. The world as we know it is a system, a whole. It is now and it was then, during Paul's day and during the time of the first writing and reading of Genesis 1:1. The wholeness of the world is both dynamic and systematic. Life is a dance of energy and matter, idea and material, spiritual and physical. Both feet are necessary to dance the dance.

Habitat

In the beginning God created a habitat for life, and that habitat was whole, complete, and sufficient for life to dance. We must ask whether the original habitat of Genesis 1:1 was different than the habitat of 2013. We don't live in the same world that people lived in six thousand years ago, or two thousand years ago. The world is quite different now than it was then. And this goes to the heart of the mystery revealed to Paul about the Gentiles.

God created a habitat for life. It was not merely a habitat for humanity abstractly considered. Rather, humanity requires all that God created. The human race cannot exist independently of the earth or apart from heaven, our habitat and its context. Human life is embedded into the system or the wholeness of the world, as the earth is embedded into the solar system, and the solar system into the Milky Way. Humanity is the crown of creation.

Paul's argument about the mystery revealed to him and which he has endeavored to reveal to us, is that the Genesis creation of humanity was still in process. God was creating a habitat for Himself *in Christ* (Ephesians 2:22). Just as man is intertwined with the rest of creation, so God is intertwined with Christ in this world (John 17:21). The kingdom of God is coming to earth because the Son of God has inaugurated the family of God-in-Christ through the body of Christ, the church. This is simply a reflection of the reality of the Trinity. The Trinity is not simply a doctrine, it reflects the nature of reality.

Does the Father *need* the Son? Do the Father and the Son *need* the Holy Spirit? Does the Godhead *need* all of His Persons? These questions are anthropomorphic. A better question would be whether the world needs God. Is the created world dependent upon the Creator? God didn't *need* to create the world. He did so simply because He *wanted* to. But now that He has, the world *needs* God to sustain it. And if God wants to sustain it, then He will continue to do so.

God created the world and He sustains it; without God's contribution there would be no world. But God contributes even more. God exists in the wholeness and holiness of the world,[2] yet wholeness is not a contribution. Neither wholeness nor holiness are *things* added. Nor are they parts. They can't be, by definition. Wholeness is not in the world, rather the world is part of its wholeness. And while holiness is often thought of as being otherworldly, it is not something abstract. Rather, it is a characteristic or quality that is coming into this world. Wholeness is both systemic and conclusive. Wholeness is teleological—purposeful. It's the fulfillment of purpose. The purpose of the world is the life of God-in-Christ, or the habitation of God. This is the mystery that was revealed to Paul, and the mystery that Paul revealed through his letters and life.

---

2 See Appendix: Whole & Holy, p. 405.

15. Now Playing

*When you read this, you can perceive my insight into the
mystery of Christ, which was not made known to the sons of
men in other generations as it has now been revealed to his
holy apostles and prophets by the Spirit. This mystery is that
the Gentiles are fellow heirs, members of the same body, and
partakers of the promise in Christ Jesus through the gospel.*
—Ephesians 3:4-6

Paul had been a world class scholar as a Pharisee, so he knew
what he was talking about. He knew that he was in the midst
of revealing God in a way that had been previously unknown
in history. And he knew that what he was writing was sufficient to
accomplish what he said he was doing. He understood the Old Testament better, deeper, and more extensively than the other Apostles. He
was the only Pharisee (religious professional) among them. And his
was the only post resurrection conversion among them.

Paul was not suggesting that the mystery had been revealed to
him alone, nor that he alone was revealing it to others. Rather, the
Spirit was revealing the mystery of Jesus Christ to all of the apostles,
and they were all involved in revealing it to others. The mystery was
too grand to be contained or adequately expressed by any one man. It
would require the whole Christian community, and as we have
learned through the successive ages, it requires the whole of Christian
history to unfold.

Christianity is an historical religion. The revelation of Christ requires sustained reflection upon history. Christianity is not merely
spiritual, nor merely doctrinal, nor merely historical in the sense that
it is a function of historic literature. Rather, Christianity is reality it-

self, unencumbered with the superstitions of ancient religions or the social customs of current speculations. And in the contemporary world it is also unencumbered with various superstitions of science or the blinders of the political secularism that masquerades as benevolent enlightenment.

REPENTANCE RELOADED

This reflection on history is also called *repentance* (μετάνοια). The Greek word is composed of two words: μετά and νοιέω. We are used to thinking of repentance as turning around or going in another direction. And this is not wrong, but it is inadequate to the literal meaning. Μετά literally refers to a higher order. Thus, metaphysics is the consideration of a higher order physics, or a physics that is beyond the usual considerations. And νοιέω is the exercise of the mind —thinking, considering, etc. And when they are put together they indicate a higher order of thinking or meta-thinking, thinking beyond our ordinary daily kind of thinking. For instance, multiplication is a kind of μετάνοια of addition, and division is a kind of μετάνοια of subtraction, and algebra is a μετάνοια of math. The μετάνοια is a higher order function.

The result of repentance (μετάνοια) often involves a turning around or a change of direction, but the change of direction is the result, not the process. And while the result is highly valuable, it cannot be acquired apart from the process. Diminution of the process produces a diminutive result. To get the genuine product of repentance, the genuine process must be engaged. Shortcuts will produce shortsightedness and will fall short of God's intended result.

To repent is to think again or to rethink, but not to simply repeat the thoughts of the past. It is to reflect upon the past in the light of Christ, to see the past in the light of Christ, to shine the light of Christ upon the past and see it with new eyes, with the eyes of Christ. And to see with the eyes of Christ is to see trinitarianily, if I can coin a word. To see through the eyes of the Father and the Son and Holy Spirit, which not only means seeing historically, but biblically. It is to see history through the lens of Scripture, to understand the world in the light of (or in terms of) Jesus Christ, who is the fulcrum of history, in that all judgment (evaluation) has been given to Him (Matthew 28:18).

Repentance is not something static, but is dynamic because it reflects on life, which is in a constant state of flux and change. Repentance is not something that can be done once and then be done with. No! It is dynamic. As life grows and develops over time, so repentance grows and develops as it reflects upon the vicissitudes of life and history in the light of Christ. It it not something that can be done once, but must itself become a way of life.

Nor is it simply applied to one's own life. Of course, it must first be applied to one's own life. Christians must reflect upon their own individual histories in the light of Christ and make various course adjustments. And because course adjustments continually need to be made, so repentance must be continually engaged. But individual course adjustments are not the end or goal of repentance, but provide for entry into the larger considerations regarding family, church, and society (or the larger civil order).

As Evangelicalism narrowed its concerns as a result of its captivity to modern individualism, it has either abandoned or twisted the jurisdictions of family, church, and society to whatever concerns and interests that arise in the absence of the light of Christ. While it is true that Christian salvation requires the salvation of individuals, it cannot be limited to individual considerations. Humanity is a social organism, and all of our individual considerations exist in various webs of social interactions. And those webs or systems of social interaction communicate meta-values and meta-attitudes that infect, affect, and impact individuals in many ways.

Thus, Christian repentance must also include the rethinking all of those webs of social interaction in which individuals exist. And this is exactly what the New Testament teaches. Christianity is not merely about beliefs and doctrines about God and Jesus Christ, but about how people relate to one another. Christianity without Christian morality is no different than Gnosticism—perhaps worse because it masquerades as God's truth.

Jesus said that He would be wherever two or three are gathered in His name (Matthew 18:20). This statement reflects the social and moral aspects of Christianity that are produced by genuine repentance. And its converse is also true: wherever people gather apart from the social and moral considerations of the Bible in the light of Christ, He is *not* with them, regardless of whether they call themselves a church or not. The definitive measure of the Christian church is not whether it is called a church. It is not whether it is officially recognized by the Internal Revenue Service as a 501(c)(3) organization, nor whether it is affiliated with some other group that calls itself a church.

Rather, the definitive measure of a Christian church is the actual existence and recognition of social and moral webs of interaction that are informed, reformed, and performed in the light of Christ by those directly and immediately involved.

THE MYSTERY

The mystery is the unity of the body of believers—Jews and Gentiles. This does not mean that all Jews and all Gentiles have unity in the body of Christ or in the life of God on earth. Only believers can have such unity. There is still division between unbelievers and believers, between unbelieving Jews and believing Jews, between unbelieving Gentiles and believing Gentiles.

Of course, Jesus Christ will unite all extant humanity one day in glory, at the end of the fulfillment of time. But that day is a long way off, and it is important to understand that it is a long way off, and that it will be a long way off for a long time. We must not try to shortcut God's timetable or get ahead of the Lord regarding this unity. When we do, we pronounce unity prematurely and encourage disunity and division because our spiritless efforts try to conflate purity and impurity.

New human beings are born every day, and they are not automatically brought into unity with God-in-Christ. Each individual must intentionally and intelligently consent to the unity, not simply by reciting some creed, but by their actual practice and behavior. Of course, this behavior is not a ticket to enter into unity, but is a fruit of the unity they confess. And because the unity between believers is moral rather than merely doctrinal, grounded more in behavior than in beliefs, more in action than understanding, it involves both learning and practice. It is not mystical in the sense of being magical or unknowable. Rather, it is mystical in the sense of being unknown until it is learned, real-ized (made real). And it is not really learned until it is put into practice daily.

Paul said that believers are

"fellow heirs, members of the same body, and partakers of the
promise in Christ Jesus through the gospel" (v. 6).

He actually said that *Gentiles* are these things, but he did not mean *all* Gentiles. He meant *believing* Gentiles, not just those who repeat creeds but those who live creedal lives. This is an instance where we need to apply repentance to Scripture in order to understand it more fully; understanding the Bible requires putting what we know into practice. Paul said *Gentiles*, and because of our own repentance we understand him to mean *believing Gentiles*. We know this, not merely because of the context of the verse, but because of the context of our own lives as believers. To fail to read our own repentance into Scripture, or to fail to read Scripture with the eyes of repentance, is to misunderstand, understate, and under-evaluate the role of the Holy Spirit in the reading of Scripture.

We know this because Paul said that all believers are "members of the same body" (v. 6)—*members* (μέλος). The word almost always refers to body parts—arms, legs, ears, feet, etc. To be a member of Christ's church is to be a member of His body. Christians are Christ's arms, legs, ears, feet, etc., in the world. We are *parts*, He is the *whole*. We *participate* in His *whole*ness such that His wholeness is enhanced by the participation of all of His parts, His members. And this means that His wholeness will be complete when all of His members are harmoniously participating in His bodily functions, His life in the world.

Of course, Christ has already accomplished this unity in that it is the inevitable conclusion of His life and death on earth because it is the central mission of God. And God's mission cannot be thwarted. However, the world is still in the process of manifesting that conclusion. Thus, it is simply a matter of time.

PARTAKING

Believers partake "of the promise in Christ Jesus through the gospel" (v. 6). *Partaking* here means actively sharing the unity of Christ.

We are so familiar with our own definitions of the word *gospel* that we hardly understand its original meaning. Of course it means good news, but but to understand it, the information (news) must be presented accurately. If the information is poorly communicated, it will be poorly received, which will degrade the communication, and interfere with our understanding of the content. If it is poorly presented as being genuinely good, it may be poorly received and misunderstood to be not so good. In order for it to be truly good news it must be genuinely good content that is communicated accurately.

This concern is lifted up because Paul said that Christians partake in the promise through the gospel. Because the gospel is the vehicle through which we participate, we are agents of gospel communication. It means that the gospel must be communicated through us, through our lives and not just our Sunday worship. We can't communicate what we don't know, so to communicate the gospel we must know it—not merely participate in the blessings of inheritance, but actually know the source of the blessings in such a way as to reveal the connection between the Source and the blessings through the character of our own lives. And if those blessings are not personally on display in our own lives, the believability of the message will be compromised. The brightness of its goodness will dim apart from a community fully engaged in Christ.

Thus, the good news of the gospel of Jesus Christ is not simply about us. It's not simply about *our* salvation or *our* conversion, though both are indeed good news. Rather, Jesus Christ Himself is the object of the good news of the gospel. It is *His* news in that He is both the object and the bringer of it. He is the One who makes it happen. The gospel is about Jesus Christ. He is the message we are to proclaim in both word and life. The good news is not how or when *we* got saved. The good news is the saving power of God through Jesus Christ for repentant sinners. The difference is important.

When I tell the story of my own salvation, repentance, and/or conversion, I'm not sharing the gospel, because the story of *my* salvation will not save anyone else. The gospel is Christ's story, not mine. I'm *not* saying that our personal stories are *not* important, or that we should not share them. They are, and we should! Rather, I'm saying that our personal stories are not the gospel. When we are called to witness, we are not called to witness to our own story. Rather, witnesses are called to attest to someone else's story, or some observation of the facts, the truth of something that has happened. Our testimony as witnesses is not to be about ourselves, it is to be about Jesus Christ, about His story. The good news is that Jesus saves, not that I, wretched sinner that I am, got saved. The difference is crucial.

To partake "through the gospel" (v. 6) means that we participate in the good news. The good news is the message or content of the Jesus story. And our participation in that story means that we play a role in the story, that we are involved in the story of Jesus Christ (Revelation 12:11). It means much more than telling or sharing the story of Jesus verbally, though it includes the telling of the story. It means that we have a role to play in the story, an active role in His story (history).

INFORMATION

The gospel is a story—information. Saying that we are saved by the gospel, or by hearing the gospel, is to say that we are saved by information, by a story. Understanding this from the perspective of our Information Age society provides a new and interesting way to understand salvation, and enhances the implications and applications of the gospel.

Information is defined as knowledge that is derived from study, experience, or instruction. News is information, so good news is good information. It does not mean that the knowledge transferred is always pleasant. *Good* does not always mean pleasant. *Good* means beneficial, and sometimes beneficial things come from unpleasant experiences. The initial response to good news is not necessarily joy and gladness. In fact, joy and gladness have little to do with the determination of whether news is good or bad.

In our Information Age we now acknowledge that there is a mechanical aspect to information, in that computers can process information. But computers do not experience joy or gladness, nor do they study or have experience as we know it. But they can receive instruction. For computers, instruction is usually in the form of a logical conditional $(p \rightarrow q)$. Computing involves a series of electrical switches that are either on or off. We can think of it as a kind of causality, where p causes q, or q is caused by p. This kind of mechanical information is causal. And where the mechanics are all functioning properly, it becomes a connection of necessity.

This applies to the good news of Jesus Christ because the good news of Jesus Christ issues from God's sovereignty, God's power to accomplish His purposes. And Scripture teaches that God will complete what He has begun (Philippians 1:6). The ultimate success of Jesus' mission to save the world is, therefore, a sure thing, a necessity. The only disputable issue is its timing and content. God's purpose in Christ will be fulfilled because His Word does not return void (Isaiah 55:11).

We are saved by the reception of this information because of its ultimate reliability. We are able to trust it because it is a necessary consequence of God's sovereignty. Sure, it is possible to doubt God's sovereignty, but not if God is correctly understood. If God is who He is depicted to be in the Bible, then He is sovereign. And if He is sovereign, He will accomplish His purposes. Trusting in this scheme of things is, therefore, logically valid.

The only objection that is logically possible needs to be aimed at God's character. If God is not who the Bible reveals Him to be in Jesus Christ, then and only then does all of this fall apart. Of course people can misunderstand or misinterpret what the Bible teaches about God. But when people correctly and consistently interpret and understand God as He is revealed in the Bible through Jesus Christ, the conclusion of God's sovereignty and the ultimate salvation of humanity cannot be in doubt.

I suppose that people can doubt the timing by withholding their assent or agreement with God. And the only way to do that is to doubt that one's own self will be included in the salvation of humanity, to contradict God's grace and mercy by clinging to one's own sin. And the only reason to cling to sin is the belief that we are defined by our sins, that the most important thing in the world is ourselves—our own thoughts and personal desires, that what we want for ourselves is more important than what God wants for the world.

16. MYSTERIOUS POWER

Of this gospel I was made a minister according to the gift of God's grace, which was given me by the working of his power. To me, though I am the very least of all the saints, this grace was given, to preach to the Gentiles the unsearchable riches of Christ, and to bring to light for everyone what is the plan of the mystery hidden for ages in God who created all things, so that through the church the manifold wisdom of God might now be made known to the rulers and authorities in the heavenly places. —Ephesians 3:7-10

Paul's gifting was not random, mystical, or magical. He brought many gifts to Christ that he had acquired while he was a Pharisee. He had achieved a high national office among the Pharisees, which means that he had studied long and hard, and had a lot of experience and expertise to bring to his job of Christian prosecution and enforcement prior to his conversion on the Damascus Road (Acts 9). He brought skills in scholarship, law, and some sort of police work, not to mention politics, public speaking, and writing.

Having brought such gifts to Christ from his previous life, and understanding God's grace from the perspective of a believer, he was able to make the connection between what some people call God's *prevenient grace* and the needs of the young Christian church. Looking back he could see God's guiding hand in his life, even prior to his salvation. And isn't that how it works! God doesn't just have control when we allow Him to have control. He has control of our lives long before we are even aware of His existence or His guidance. And we should be very thankful that He does. Left to our own resources we will make a mess of life every time. That's what sin does.

God's power had been working in Paul's life long before he was converted, so that after his conversion he would be able to do what he did. Paul taught us how Christianity is tied to the Old Testament. Others could have done it, and many have assisted in the project since then, but God gave Paul the initial job because he brought the requisite skills with him. This is how God's grace works. God doesn't give Christians gifts that are unrelated to their own natural, pre-conversion gifts, talents, and skills. Rather, He empowers, aligns, and enhances the gifts, talents, and skills that people bring to their conversion so that they can be used for His purposes.

LEAST?

For more than two thousand years Paul has stood at the head of the line of proficient Christian theologians. Paul stands head and shoulders above the many commentators who have filled libraries with their thoughts and ideas. And a good part of those thoughts and ideas are about what Paul said. It seems that Paul would be at the head of the line, not at the rear. How can Paul call himself "the very least of all the saints" (v. 8)? The phrase is the translation of one Greek word: ἐλαχιστότερος. It literally means the least of the least, or the smallest of the small, or the worst of the bad, etc.

How could Paul, who brought all of the skills and abilities previously discussed, think of himself as being least, smallest, or worst of the slew of humble, uneducated Christians, most of whom probably couldn't even read, or couldn't read much? Was Paul simply belittling himself to sufficiently cover the massive pride that dominated his previous life? How could Paul have been sincere in his self-deprecation?

First, we must assume that Paul's assessment was both genuine and honest, that it was not a pretense to hide his pride. The Bible is true and it can be trusted to convey the truth. Allow me to compare my own situation with Paul's in the hope that my experience might illuminate his.

Like Paul, my full conversion to Christianity came late. I was in my mid-thirties, and like Paul, I was not a stranger to religion because I had been interested in it since I was quite young. I grew up in a mainline Christian church and had an active interest in it ever since I can remember. My earliest Christian experience came in my early adolescent years. My earliest interests tended toward the philosophical. In college I majored in Philosophy, and studied various Eastern religions, which were popular at the time. In seminary I studied a couple of new religious movements close up. And by the time I found myself reborn in Christ, I had a lot of religious baggage and false ideas that needed to be straightened out. My conversion experience in the 1980s took several years to unfold. But eventually I came to understand how foolish I had been, looking for God in all the wrong places. I had a lot of false ideas that I had to unwind in order to understand and enjoy the simplicity of genuine Christianity.

Like Paul, I found that my studies and tangential religious rabbit hole hopping had been worse than a waste of time because I had to backtrack or undo so much of my previous thinking. It is in this sense that I can resonate with Paul's comment about being the worst of the worst saints. Real Christianity or genuine faithfulness is not about all of the philosophical and theological complexity that clutters the annals of Christian history. Genuine faithfulness is more simple than Zen Buddhism because it is not trying to empty the mind, but is simply allowing the mind to be what it was created to be in the light of Christ.

True Christianity is not mysterious, it is ordinary. Sure, there are a lot of things that we don't know, and there are a lot of things to learn, and we cannot ever perfectly understand everything. But we can trust what we do understand in the light of Christ, be it great or meager. In Christ our humanity and our individuality are completely fulfilled and complemented in and by the holiness and wholeness of Jesus Christ. And we can rest in that realization, that relationship.

Paul meant that all of his highfalutin education and his position and experience, his Phariseeism, had been in the way. It provided an obstacle to overcome that put him farther behind than those who did not need to overcome the stench of so much dung (Philippians 3:8).

GENTILES

Why was Paul the evangelist to the Gentiles? Surely, some of the others could have done that job? John, for instance, since John's gospel is more philosophical than the others, more tuned into Greek sensitivities and preferences. Paul would have been more suited to the Jews, since he had been a Jew of the highest religious order, and probably knew more about Jewish theology and religious customs than anyone else. But that's not the way it happened. Paul became the acknowledged Gentile evangelist.

One reason may be *because* Paul had been a high ranking Jew, the Jews would have found him to be a traitor, and unworthy to engage in conversation. It could have been that their hatred of Paul kept Paul from being an effective evangelist among them. The Old Testament Jews had been very much caught up in the old religion of vengeance, and had even put out a contract on Paul's life. The Jews saw Paul as a traitor of the worse kind, so he was not able to evangelize them.

But the Gentiles didn't know Paul. They were not prejudiced against him from the start. Paul was able to engage them in conversation. And because Paul was highly educated he could speak intelligently to other educated people, educated Gentiles. Sure, they would find the gospel to be ultimately foolish (1 Corinthians 1), but they would listen to Paul because of his education. Educated Gentiles would be less likely to listen to ignorant peasants. But they listened to Paul because he was both educated and was professing something new—Jesus Christ (Acts 17).

Unsearchable

Are God's judgments really unsearchable and his ways inscrutable (v. 8, Romans 11:33)? The Greek word translated as *unsearchable* (ἀνεξιχνίαστος) is a complex word that literally means something like *of unknown origin and ultimate destination*. It does not mean that the character of God cannot be known. Jesus came to demonstrate the character of God and to interpose Himself as the mediator between man and God precisely so that God's character *can* be known. The unsearchableness of God has to do with God's origin and destination, and by implication, the origin and destination of humanity, as well.

The distant past and the distant future are simply unavailable to us. Rather, God calls us to be what He has created us to be here and now. Dealing with the present is more than enough to fill our plates for more than a lifetime. We are called to live this life, not to speculate about previous or future times that are so far beyond this life as to qualify for alien status of the Star Trek variety.

Fellowship of Riches

Paul was not speaking here merely of the unsearchableness of God, but the "unsearchable riches of Christ" (v. 8). Just as we cannot know the distant past or future, the origins and destination of Christ's riches cannot be known either. Paul's statement begs the question about the definition of Christ's riches.

By speaking of Christ's *unsearchable* riches rather than simply His *riches*, Paul called attention to the origin and ultimate destiny of Christ's riches, their source and destination. He was not talking about their actual, physical presence in the moment, but about their availability and use. Thus, Paul was not simply providing investment advice regarding current assets, nor about the golden eggs one already has in the clutch, but about the location and preservation of the proverbial hen who laid them. Paul's concern was not the wealth that one has, but about the character of the one who has it—and of course, that determines the character of the wealth that one has, as well.

Christ's riches are not merely the bobbles and bangles of material wealth acquisition. Rather, Christ's riches include the character that understands and encourages the social realities of honesty, integrity, and industry that undergird the kind of society that can sustain the blessings of wealth and prosperity over large populations for long periods of time. Indeed, this message is truly good news that Paul was preaching to the Gentiles. There is no one for whom this news is not good.

The *English Standard Version* translates κοινωνία as *everyone* in verse 9:

> "to bring to light for *everyone* what is the plan of the mystery hidden for ages in God who created all things."

The *Authorized Version* translates verse 9 as:

> "to make all men see what is the fellowship of the mystery, which from the beginning of the world hath been hid in God, who created all things by Jesus Christ,"

and is preferred. The *English Standard Version* loses the sense of κοινωνία, the idea that fellowship in Christ is essential to the process. In the *English Standard Version* the good news becomes an abstract, mysterious plan that has been intentionally hidden, rather than the announcement of an active fellowship that calls people into the enjoyment and sharing of Christ's riches.

Indeed, more important than the material aspects of Christ's riches are their enjoyment and sharing. The enjoyment and sharing are not secondary concerns, but are themselves the source of the riches. The riches of Christ are possessions of the fellowship, not merely possessions of the individual. This is not to suggest a communistic or socialist understanding of material possessions, but to suggest the personal character that underlies the generosity and genuine social concern of those who acquire and possess material wealth.

Communism and socialism are governmental structures that are imposed upon societies, whereas Christianity is not a governmental imposition but a voluntary engagement. Much more than the kind of voluntary association involved in various clubs and groups, Christianity involves the kind of love and passion that cannot be denied or withdrawn in the face of personal pain and difficulty. Nor is it a matter of simply signing a register. Rather, great personal cost and difficulties only increase the love and commitment that are expressed through generosity and concern. Christian love is not only love that endures suffering, but it is love that flowers in the midst of suffering.

This does not and must not suggest that suffering needs to be increased in order to bring Christianity to flower. Not at all! There is plenty of sin and suffering in the world without intentionally creating more in some misguided ideal of "serving" Christ by causing suffering. Heaven forbid! Rather, Christian love eschews sin and endures suffering. And this develops the character of generosity and social concern of Christian fellowship that grows and sustains Christ's riches.

THROUGH THE CHURCH

In today's world Christians too often want to impose Christian values upon the leaders of society. We see this in our politics as various groups work to impose their own understanding of *good* upon others through politics, law, and policy. Both sides, both the Right and the Left understand themselves to be working for the betterment of humanity through their various efforts. And both are partially right, and partially wrong. Both focus on some particular aspect of society that needs improvement, on some emphasis that they deem to be a kind of social driver for other things they understand to be socially good.

Liberals tend to focus on resource sharing, and Conservatives tend to focus on personal responsibility. Both are important, but neither can be legislated to the satisfaction of all. Nonetheless, both sides work feverishly to pass legislation that will further their cause, either resource sharing or personal responsibility. But both also see the work of the other side as undermining their own efforts to "help" society. Too much gratuitous resource sharing can undermine personal responsibility, and too much emphasis on personal responsibility can stunt needed resource sharing.

And as long as each side believes that the only or the best way to advance its cause is to impose its values on society through legislation, each side does in fact undermine the efforts of the other. The values of both sides are indeed socially good and important, but neither can be legislated because they are moral values not mere behaviors. Legislation addresses behaviors, but cannot accomplish what the various sides want to accomplish, a change or augmentation of moral values.

The old saying is that morality cannot be legislated. And while all legislation issues from moral sensitivity and imposes some sort of moral behavior, no legislation can create genuine, personal, willing moral sensitivity. For instance, love cannot be legislated because legislated behavior is imposed, not voluntary. And for love to be love it must be voluntary. Sure, some people will engage the legislated behavior whether it is legislated or not, but others will only submit to it under duress.

The problem is that moral instruction is not under the jurisdiction of the state according to the Bible. The state has the jurisdiction of the sword, of the imposition of justice regarding perpetrated crimes. The state deals with the consequences of immorality. The church, on the other hand, has the jurisdiction of the Word, of the teaching and instruction of God's morality, because there isn't any other kind that is as moral. And God's biblical morality has a wholeness that includes the concerns of both conservatives and liberals because it is truly and wholly moral.

Looking to the state or civil secular government to inculcate moral values through legislation is like trying to get blood from a proverbial turnip. The state cannot give what it does not have, it cannot teach what it does not know. It can only give and teach false imitations of moral truths because it accesses and uses the tools and processes of enforcement. It cannot handle or process both the fine granularity or the inclusive wholeness of genuine biblical morality because it is committed to codifying everything within its grasp. And biblical truth is only partially codifiable. Only the grosser moral truths of Scripture can be processed into general principles. And the common view of biblical principles tends to be myopic—shortsighted. Biblical truth must be processed personally not principally, and wholly not partially. Biblical morality is not the mere application of biblical principles as if they are cold, calculated algorithms of some process, but requires a personal applicability that is beyond the sensitivities of mere algorithmic application. Morality is necessarily religious because it must be both personal and whole, and any morality that is not religious cannot be moral in the fullest sense of the word because it denies or lacks part of what is required for wholeness—religion, in the best sense of the word. Any wholeness that ignores God cannot be whole.

In contrast to this governmental or principled approach to morality, Paul commends that Christian morality happens "through the church" (v. 10). The church is not only the appropriate vehicle for the inculcation of morality, but is the only vehicle that is truly able to do so because the church, properly functioning, engages Scripture personally through the regenerate eyes of the Spirit and wholly in fellowship with the community of believers. All true Christians are regenerate, and all truly regenerate people are Christian. Thus, the regenerate are personally involved in Christ and involved in His body—the church.

INSTRUCTION

Notice also that the church is to provide instruction to the "rulers and authorities" (v. 10). The *Authorized Version* reads, "principalities and powers," which suggests the governments of this world. However, Paul added the phrase "in the heavenly places" (v. 10), which makes it sound like the church is to inform heaven about Godly wisdom. No matter how it is interpreted, it is oddly phrased.

There are three pieces of verse 10:

> "so that through the church the manifold wisdom of God might
> now be made known to the rulers and authorities in the heavenly
> places."

They are: 1) the church, 2) the wisdom of God, and 3) the rulers and authorities. The action of the verse involves making God's wisdom known. Is Paul saying that the church is to make God's wisdom known to the rulers and authorities? Or that the rulers and authorities are to make God's wisdom known through the church? Does the church inform the rulers and authorities? Or do the rulers and authorities inform the church? There is no simple answer, in that this involves the long-standing conflict between church and state that has simmered since long before Jesus' arrival on the scene. Ideally, there is to be harmony between church and state.

The mission of Scripture is to reveal God's will and way to this wayward world. Regardless of who informs whom, the crux of the matter is that the correct information about God's wisdom and will is to be successfully conveyed. When the church falls into corruption, the state must convey God's wisdom. And when the state falls into corruption, the church must convey God's wisdom. Ideally, church and state both work together to convey God's wisdom and eliminate corruption by restricting themselves to their distinct jurisdictions.

The model is for the state to exercise the ministry of the sword (justice or consequence), and the church to exercise the ministry of the Word (fellowship or instruction). The fullness of God's wisdom speaks to both concerns, and when the church functions correctly, it diminishes the role of the state because there is less injustice to prosecute. When the state functions correctly, it encourages willing sensitivity to moral instruction because of the fear of just consequences.

Nonetheless, the ordinary model is for the church to embody the values and ways of God's wisdom, whereas the state provides corrective measures for the sin of the abandonment of God's wisdom. Thus, the state has no modeling or instructive function regarding God's wisdom. The great temptation in every age is for the state to do all that it can to promote and encourage God's wisdom—which is a good thing. But the only tools the state has are tools of imposition. And so the state begins to encroach upon the job of the church with the tools of imposition. And the success of such an effort ends up engaging the Fascist tools of oppression.

It is very difficult to allow God's grace and justice to unfold in God's time, regardless of whether the state fails to exercise its role of justice correctly, according to God's Word in the light of Christ. The great temptation is to get ahead of God, by trying to be more holy than God, or more righteous than God requires. The temptation is to try to short-circuit the ordinary consequences of sin by imposing the instruction of grace apart from regeneration. Grace is wonderful on the receiving end, but much more difficult to dispense to others. People love to receive God's grace, but have great difficulty being truly graceful to others. Regardless, the church is to model God's grace by being gracious. If any errors are to be made, it is better for both church and state to err on the side of grace and mercy than wrath and vengeance.

Heavenly Places

If heaven is the place where God's will reigns, then why does the "manifold wisdom of God" need to "be made known to the rulers and authorities *in the heavenly places*" (v. 10)? Again, both the phrasing and interpretation of this verse are odd. Perhaps the heavenly authorities would like to know when we are doing things "on earth as it is in heaven" (Matthew 6:10), though one would think that we wouldn't need to apprise them of this, either. If God is all-knowing, then He'd just know.

Regardless, we know that God's plan is to bring His heavenly administration to this planet through Jesus Christ, at which time there will be coordination and harmony between heaven and earth. A free flow of information between heaven and earth will be established, such that communication will travel in both directions, on earth as it is in heaven. Not only will God know, but we will know as as well.

In this verse *heavenly places* is the translation of one word: ἐπουράνιος. It refers to that which is imposed upon high places. Remember that *heaven* means *sky* or *high place,* and *earth* means *ground.* Let me also suggest that there is a relationship in both Testaments between the many Old Testament references to *high places* and *heaven,* in the sense that the original meanings of both words referred to *high ground* and all of the military and strategic advantages that high ground holds for military operations, and the power and wealth associated therewith.

This relationship is not linguistic, but is associational, thematic, and analogical. Everything about the ideas of *heaven, high places,* and *high ground* suggests power, wealth, and influence. And at some level the theological or other worldly idea of heaven and God's ultimate purpose of bringing His will to earth means that His will, His values and purposes, are to dominate the worldly centers of power, wealth, and influence.

However, true Godly dominance is not imposed upon unwilling people! That's just not the way that God works. Godly dominance cannot be imposed upon anyone and remain Godly because the exercise of coercion cannot produce or bring about Godly values or purposes. All of God's people must willingly embrace God's ways, values, and purposes. And any suggestion to the contrary cannot be a biblical expression of Godly ways, values, or purposes.

17. Purpose & Glory

This was according to the eternal purpose that he has real-
ized in Christ Jesus our Lord, in whom we have boldness and
access with confidence through our faith in him. So I ask you
not to lose heart over what I am suffering for you, which is
your glory.   —*Ephesians 3:11-13*

Paul is still talking about the mystery of Christ that was given or explained to him so he could preach it to the Gentiles, to those unfamiliar with the Old Testament. And the phrase *eternal purpose* points to the Old Testament where God has laid the foundation for Christ's manifestation in this world. But the mystery of Christ is not something that baffles our understanding because it cannot be adequately explained. Rather, the mystery of Christ can only be adequately explained through the story of the Old Testament, which was unknown or inadequately known by the Gentiles.

The mystery is the whole story of Jesus Christ, which began before Genesis 1:1. And the truth is that neither the Gentiles nor the Jews knew the mystery. The Gentiles did not know it because they did not know the Old Testament, and the Jews did not know it because they did not know or recognize Christ as the fulfillment of the Old Testament.

Christ's fulfillment of the Old Testament story brought that story to an end or conclusion. But the end of that story does not mean that the teachings of the Old Testament are now defunct. It does not mean that what the Old Testament teaches is no longer useful, or that all the laws of the Old Testament are no longer valid or helpful. Rather, the completion of the story of the Old Testament reveals the validity of the laws and usefulness of the Old story in the light of its conclusion, of its end—it's purpose, in the light of Christ.

The light of Christ changes the story of the Old Testament by revealing its purpose (or end—τέλος). That purpose is then brought to bear upon all of the details of the Old Testament. And once the manifestation of Jesus Christ is understood as the central purpose of the Old Testament, we can go back and see how the details of the Old Testament point to the manifestation of Jesus Christ as the anticipated Messiah. If we think of the process of physical birth, we can see that the fetus (Christ) was first dependent upon the mother (Old Testament), and that once birth occurred, that dependency changed.

The umbilical cord was cut and the placenta (ceremonial law) discarded. That which once provided nourishment and purification was abandoned, and at the same time other sources of nourishment and purification were adopted (nursing and diapers). These phases of growth were known as the Early Church, and they, too, have been long abandoned. The church today is long past its nursing and diaper stages, though many Christians and denominations are intent on maintaining them.

The mystery of Christ that Paul acknowledged continues to grow and develop in history. The eternality of Christ means that the development and maturity of His story is also eternal. Thus, the development of modernity and the various issues of the current times are also part of Christ's story of maturity. And because God is omniscient, He has always been aware of the realities and issues of life that so dominate us today, and of the science and technology that drive them.

Access

The fact of the reality of this mystery gives believers access to Christ through faith, which encourages boldness and confidence. It is important to notice that the verse and the access, like the personal relationship we have with Christ, is multifaceted. It's a church thing, which means that it is both individual and corporate, not one or the other, but both are necessary. While the Person of Jesus manifested the *whole* of Christ, the people of Christ each manifest a *part* of Christ, some particular gift or function of the body (an ear, hand, finger, foot, etc.). After Christ's ascension, His bodily wholeness became corporate in the same way that the wholeness of a type is manifest in the archetype. That which serves as a model is the perfection of what emulates it.

This relationship of part to whole, or example to model, is the divine or mystical aspect of the relationship, in that eternity is cast into time (or infinity into finitude, or the ultimate into the proximate). In one sense, such a relationship is absurd and impossible. Yet in another, it is so ordinary as to be merely mundane. In the same sense in which God Himself, eternal and omnipotent, manifests in the human flesh of Jesus Christ, so Jesus Christ Himself, also eternal and omnipotent, manifests in the human flesh of His church, His bodily parts.

Yet, just as the Father remains the Father and the Son remains the Son, so church members do not become Christ, but remain themselves. And just as the Father is glorified by the Son and the Son by the Father, so church members actively glorify Christ and are glorified by His presence in their midst.

Whose Faith?

Where the *English Standard Version* reads "through our faith in him" (v. 11), the *Authorized Version* reads "by the faith of him." The difference is huge in that the one is about our faith and the other is about Christ's faith. And this difference illustrates a major theme of modernity: the loss of objectivity, and/or the rise of subjectivity. This theme has played out in Evangelicalism as the increased role of the individual and the diminished role of Christ Himself with regard to the efficacy of salvation.[1] We are not saved by our faith in Christ, but by trusting Christ's faith in God. It is not that Christ has faith that we will make the right decision, but rather that the faith of Christ is being reproduced in us. Christ has faith in God, not in humanity. Whatever faith we have is not our own, it originates in Christ. Christ has given His faith to us because ours is inadequate.

Christians do not and cannot pull themselves up by the bootstraps of their own faithfulness. No matter how hard we try, all our trying amounts only to works-righteousness. But to have the slightest amount of Christ's faith given to us is always more than adequate to accomplish all of God's purposes because the smallest amount of Christ's faith is infinite, where the greatest amount of ours is finite.

---

1   This issue is illustrated in a series of articles by David Brand in *The Christian Observer* (2012): http://christianobserver.org/series/shall-their-unbelief-make-the-faith-of-god-without-effect/.

There has been a great shift over the centuries away from the un-derstanding that the faith that Christians have is Christ's faith, to the understanding that the faith that Christians have is their own faith in Christ. It is understandable in that every Christian must own the covenant for him- or herself. Every Christian must be personally and actively involved in relationship with Christ. There must be an em-phasis upon individual personal faithfulness. However, this emphasis goes too far when it ignores or diminishes the idea that we are saved by Christ, and not by our own exercise of faithfulness. The exercise of faithfulness is a response to the gift of faith.

Christ has done more than throw a life preserver in the direction of the mass of drowning people, leaving them with the burden of grabbing hold and hanging on. People who are dead in their tres-passes and sins are not able to grab or hold anything. Furthering this analogy, those whom Christ saves are already unconscious in the wa-ter. So He must extricate them and resuscitate them. And only then can they exercise any faithfulness of their own. Yes, of course, they must engage the faith personally. But that is what the Bible calls *sanc-tification*.

Glorious Suffering

Paul not only suffered for the gospel, but he suffered for the Eph-esian Christians. His suffering for the gospel was on their behalf. He was doing it for them. However, he was not suffering in their stead, as if his suffering would spare them from suffering themselves. That's not what he was doing.

All Christians are called to suffer. Jesus told His disciples, "If they persecuted me, they will also persecute you" (John 15:20). Paul knew this. Christ's suffering was not intended to spare others from suffer-ing. Rather, Christ was modeling how to suffer graciously, and Paul was imitating the model. Paul knew that Scripture forbids both com-plaining and vengeance, and teaches forgiveness. In the face of suffer-ing, especially when one is being persecuted, Christians are to endure the pain and suffering of persecution with grace and poise by extend-ing forgiveness and reconciliation. Paul was modeling such suffering for the Ephesians, and all other Christians.

There are only two responses to suffering: 1) complaining and swearing vengeance, or 2) forgiveness. The first response will perpet-uate conflict in a tit for tat round of vengeance for vengeance. Only forgiveness will stop the cycle. Those who are caught up in the throes of vengeance most often think of themselves as seeking justice rather than vengeance. But when both parties feel themselves to have been wronged by the other, the justice of one only foments further offense in the other. The exaction of personal justice, of taking the law into one's own hands to any degree, or the defense of one's own honor, always perpetuates the conflict.

Even when legitimate courts are involved in the exercise of justice, grudges will continue unless genuine forgiveness is engaged. Anything that attempts to restore offended honor only contributes to the pride and self-justification of the offended person. In fact, every attempt to defend one's own honor is nothing more than veiled pride. Real honor is always other-directed.

We cannot give honor to ourselves. Rather, true honor means being held in high esteem *by others*. Sure, we can act honorably, but doing so does not guarantee that others will see our actions as honorable. Genuine honor comes from the voluntary deference or regard of others. The definition and use of honor is necessarily communal. It issues out of shared values, and is exampled by the epitome of those values. But when values are not communally shared, honor is not possible. The condition of opposing social values is inherently dishonorable, unless people act in service to values that are trans-cultural, values that are of a higher order than the values of one's own society. The only context in which honor is meaningful is the context of shared values. And where values are not shared, no honor is possible.

The loss of honor causes great personal suffering because it attacks and undermines one's sense of personal identity. Meaning and value are functions of identity, and the loss of meaning and value generate personal angst and personal unrest. The loss of honor means that the person loosing it sees him- or herself as having lost social esteem, as being valued less by others. Taken to the extreme, the loss of honor and value can lead to depression, poverty, and even death. Again, individuals cannot give themselves social esteem apart from increasing pride, which is a major sin.

In the Old Testament the word translated as *honor* (כבד, *kabad*) can also be translated as *glory*. Honor and glory are aspects of the same thing in the Old Testament. Thus, we give God glory by honoring Him, by giving Him esteem and praise. Doing this is true worship, yet true worship is not mere doing. True worship is more being than doing. It's more an attitude than an action, more a way of life than simple church attendance. Truly honoring God issues out of personal identity, not mere behavior or action. One cannot honor God without believing God's Word to be true. And one does not truly believe God's Word apart from trusting and living as if it is true. Regardless of what one does liturgically, the failure to honor God in this way leads to false worship. Therefore, true worship is not a function of liturgical activity, but of personal identity. The implications of this determination are legion.

In addition, we must take care that our outward actions and words of praise, glory, and honor reflect and augment our personal identity, for our worship is worse than nothing if our subjective values and attitudes do not correspond to our true identity *in Christ* (Matthew 15:8). While outward liturgical worship is a good thing and must be encouraged by all of God's people, the mere absence from church attendance of itself does not reduce or diminish our identity in Christ.

There are many circumstances that prevent or preclude one's participation in public worship—illness, necessities involving work and family, travel, etc. In addition, not all liturgical worship honors God. False prophets and false teaching have been dogging God's people for millennia. Because true worship issues out of personal emulation of the characteristics of Jesus Christ, the best protection against false or wrong worship liturgy is the personal emulation of the characteristics of Jesus Christ. Thus, false worship can be avoided as long as one worships in Christ's name by actually emulating Christ's character qualities in one's own life.

True worship that honors God-in-Christ will often cause the suffering involved in the loss of social honor because God-in-Christ is not universally valued or held in high esteem. Honoring God often involves the loss of social honor when society at large does not honor God. And the usual consequences of such loss of honor tend to bring both social scorn and increased poverty (lost friends and opportunities). Social persecution through ostracism often leads to job difficulties and loss, or a reduction in business opportunities.

> "Count it all joy, my brothers, when you meet trials of various
> kinds, for you know that the testing of your faith produces stead-
> fastness" (James 1:2-3).

18. All Filled

*For this reason I bow my knees before the Father, from
whom every family in heaven and on earth is named, that
according to the riches of his glory he may grant you to be
strengthened with power through his Spirit in your inner
being, so that Christ may dwell in your hearts through faith
—that you, being rooted and grounded in love, may have
strength to comprehend with all the saints what is the
breadth and length and height and depth, and to know the
love of Christ that surpasses knowledge, that you may be
filled with all the fullness of God.* —Ephesians 3:14-19

Let's remind ourselves of the reason that Paul alludes to: *suffering fuels the gospel.* He feels the pain and anguish of his suffering, and his loss of honor. But because it serves the gospel of Jesus Christ, it brings him joy—not happiness, but joy. Happiness means being appropriately adapted to one's present circumstance. Tears at a funeral can be an expression of happiness for having known the deceased person, or for knowing how much the deceased person will be missed.

But joy is a matter of being appropriately adapted regardless of one's present circumstance. Joy defies its circumstances and sings in the face of suffering and death. Christian joy cannot be defeated because it is rooted in hope, rooted in the future fulfillment of God's plan. And this is the reason that Paul spoke of here. His gracious suffering reminded him of who he is in Christ, and encouraged his attitude of worship.

Bowing the knees is an allusion to worship. Notice that he bows his knees apart from being in church. He was not at a public worship event, but was in the midst of writing this letter when he bowed his knees to the Father. *Bowed* it is a literary reference to an internal reality or attitude toward God. It is likely that he was writing when he began praising God in his mind, maybe even vocalizing the honor he felt, as he was glorifying God. He may even have actually knelt in prayer and thanksgiving in that moment.

Every Family

Verse 15 points to the Creation story, and how all of humanity stands in the lineage of Adam. The logic is simple. God created Adam, and Adam fathered humanity. All people are God's people. This is not part of an argument for Universalism or universal salvation but is simply the plain reading of Paul's words.

Genesis goes on to tell us about Adam's first two sons, Cain and Abel. Cain and Abel were very different. Cain worked the ground, and Abel tended sheep. Both brought God offerings from their work. Cain brought fruit, and Abel brought the firstborn of his flock. Scripture indicates that some time had passed before Cain brought "an offering" (Genesis 4:3), which suggests that Cain's offering was not from the initial firstfruit, but was more a seasonal frirstfruit.

Scripture also mentions that Abel brought "of the firstborn" (Genesis 4:4), and that God preferred Abel's offering over Cain's. The allusion is that Abel honored God more than Cain because his offering of the firstborn suggests the preeminence of God in Abel's mind, where God was more of an afterthought to Cain. In addition, Abel's offering was used as a model for the sacrificial system that God would give to Israel.

The story of Cain and Abel is first and foremost a story, and stories provide lessons. The lesson drawn here honors God and sets up the Old Testament theme of two different kinds of worship, two different approaches of worship, issuing from Adam. We might call them obedience and disobedience, or covenant keeping and covenant breaking. One puts God first, the other treats God as an afterthought. However, the reality is that "all have sinned and fall short of the glory of God" (Romans 3:23). Nonetheless, the various stories of the Bible teach the value of conformity to biblical ideals and principles.

This theme of conformity—the blessings of obedience and the cursings of disobedience—continues throughout the Old Testament in the struggles between Jacob and Esau and culminates in the contrast between Saul and David. Nonetheless, the conclusion of the Old

Testament, found in the New Testament, comes with the arrival of the long-awaited Messiah, Jesus Christ, and the failure of the mission of God's own special people, Israel, to bring the gospel of salvation to humanity at large. Paul's point was that all people are God's people. To which we might add that the abundance of human sin has not affected the character of God. God and Sin[2] are completely opposed to one another. So, any thought that God may be the cause of human sin is wide of the mark.

HEAVENLY FAMILIES

The story of Adam and Eve is the story of earthly families. But Paul wrote of heavenly and earthly families. Again, we are so accustomed to thinking of *heaven* in celestial terms that we are blind to any other meaning the word may convey. It means that God is the Creator all life, wherever heaven may reside. It means that God continues to be God when people go to heaven, to extend the analogy to the heavenly realm. But we might also consider it to mean heavenly-minded earthly families.

If we are to understand *heaven* as an analogy to the Old Testament *high places*, as previously discussed, then we must conclude that God's authority applies to both the lower, earthly things and the higher, heavenly things. Here it provides another reference to the idea that all people are God's people, which extends and supports this major biblical theme.

Here we see that "every family in heaven and on earth is named" (v. 15) after the Father of Jesus Christ. There is a family likeness between Father and children. The children are patterned after the Father. But the character of the Father is so immense (divine) that it has difficulty fitting into the limitations of individual human beings. In fact, God's character is so immense in human terms that it fills three divine Persons—Father, Son, and Holy Spirit. It should be no surprise that God's character does not fit into any individual human being. Even Jesus Christ is only one member of the Godhead. Yet, Jesus is both fully divine and fully human.

So, the likeness or image of God in which human beings are created is a divided likeness (Acts 2:3). We might also call it a diverse likeness, where the multiplicity of individuals holds in tension both the unity of the Spirit and the diversity of various aspects of the divine image, various aspects of the fullness of God's character.

---

2   See footnote 3, p. 57.

Lest we think too little of the human image of God-in-Christ because it is divided and diversely appropriated among human beings, we must understand that the reality and math of the infinite is different than the reality and math of finite. The math is important because it provides an intelligent description of the realities of God's divinity conceived of as something infinite. The "divine spark" that exists in human individuals functions like the aleph-null in set theory.[3]

Therefore, the fact that human beings are created in God's image —which, whatever else that image may be, is infinite—means that there exists in every human individual a "spark" of God, a spark of infinity. However, this does not mean that human individuals are gods, nor that they are themselves infinite, nor that all people will be saved. But it does mean that God considers them each infinitely valuable. And it also means that each human individual participates in the infinite, in eternity—though the participation of each individual is not the same.

GLORIOUS RICHES

The measure of God's blessings for His people is "according to the riches of his glory" (v. 16). To see how wealth is related to glory and honor, consider that the root (*hon*) of *honor* is the same for *honest*. Second, understand that God is honorable because He is righteous. He is truth itself. Honesty cannot manifest apart from God and His righteousness. And anyone who says that it can is misinformed or a liar because such a statement denies the true character of God.

Now imagine the economy of a nation, any nation, any economy. Imagine how that economy would perform if all dishonesty, graft, and corruption as defined in Scripture were eliminated. This is not an argument for efficiency, but for the simple honesty and righteousness of financial transactions using honest money.[4]

The same principle of the elimination of dishonesty, graft, and corruption applied to the areas of science and technology would also greatly benefit their advancement. Neither science nor technology can be maintained, much less advanced, when the data streams and

---

3   See Appendix, p. 407. I have already alluded to this idea on page 157, where I said, "the smallest amount of Christ's faith is infinite, where the greatest amount of ours is finite." The application of this insight is that infinity can be divided without loosing its infinite character. Think of this as an allusion to the generation of biblical kinds.

4   See Hoffman, Michael. *Usury in Christendom: The Mortal Sin that Was and Now is Not*, Independent History and Research, 2012.

maintenance procedures are infected with dishonesty, graft, and corruption. Rather, the development and maintenance of science and technology require the disciplines of righteousness—honesty, integrity, consistency, and industry.

Imagine a society dedicated to the use of honest money and righteous science and technology. All we can do at this time is to imagine the fruit of such a society and the blessings that would accrue to its people because the current state of affairs is so far from such an ideal. But we can imagine the blessings of such an idea. Such are the riches of God's glory—and we haven't even addressed the spiritual riches yet!

God's intention is to "grant you to be strengthened with power through his Spirit" (v. 16), according to the measure of the riches of God's glory, said Paul. We need to be strengthened with the power of Christ in order to cope with God's blessings. Such blessings are not available to unrighteous people, nor can they be maintained in the presence of dishonesty, graft, greed, and corruption. Only a righteous society can harness true Christian capitalism[5] for the development of true science and technology for the true benefit of all of God's people.

Paul said that this strengthening or development needs to take place in our "inner being" (v. 16), which is also called the *soul* or *conscience*. Conscience is the first element of self-government, not that the self writes its own rules, but in that the self is the most effective officer of the law to be encountered (so to speak). Self-government means self-direction, not in the sense that we each choose our own direction, but in the sense that we are each charged to know the right path and to keep ourselves on it, God willing.

Christian conscience is that voice that is awakened through regeneration. It is the voice that convicts the self of sin, not the voice that justifies the sin of the self. The difference between these two voices is not distinguishable by the unregenerate because the unregenerate have yet to hear the true voice of the Holy Spirit, who speaks of God's righteousness. The thing that differentiates the regenerate conscience from the unregenerate conscience is the way that the regenerate conscience convicts the self of sin. In addition, the regenerate conscience in one person will recognize the regenerate conscience in another person by their common understanding and

---

5   By *Christian capitalism* I simply mean capitalism with much less sin, or capitalism governed by Christian virtue, as opposed to libertarian capitalism that is infused with self-interest.

agreement with the definition of sin and the sinfulness of the various sins discussed in the Bible (Galatians 5:19-21). This agreement contributes to the foundation of Christian unity.

WHY SUFFER?

Paul was explaining that his suffering for Christ and for the Ephesians served a great purpose. And serving that purpose provided much more joy than could be annulled by the pain of suffering. The purpose was "so that Christ may dwell in your hearts through faith" (v. 17). Here we see Paul's incarnational theology.

He didn't say that the purpose was for the ideas, principles, or morals of Christ to dwell in their hearts, but for Christ Himself to do so. The actual Person of Christ can actually dwell in the heart (the soul or mind, as it is the fountain and seat of the thoughts, passions, desires, appetites, affections, purposes, and endeavors) of another only through the indwelling of the Holy Spirit. And because God is Triune, the wholeness of God is fully contained in each of the Trinitarian Persons of the Godhead.

The actual Person of Christ is necessary because apart from the Personhood of the Godhead, God is nothing more than an idea or a mechanical algorithm. The dynamic vitality of life requires a vital, dynamic God. This does not mean that God Himself changes. His character doesn't change. But the circumstances of life change, and as they change various other heretofore unrealized characteristics of God are revealed to meet the newly discovered demands of life. This dynamic revelation of God-in-Christ over time can sometimes look like God changes to His time-bound creatures, but He does not.

Jesus Christ is the fullness of the Godhead manifesting in history, and the Bible is fully adequate to communicate that fullness. But God's fullness is not communicated all at once. Rather, it unfolds in history, in time. As history continues, it creates a longer time-line for reflection, which reveals the character of God in greater detail and depth.

God is most fully known through the power and presence of the Holy Spirit through regeneration. Regeneration then produces a perspective that knows God personally. Knowing God personally then reveals the fact that other people also know God personally, and their knowledge of God is both similar and different than one's own. Thus, God is known more fully by knowing these similarities and differences. And these are known by knowing both Scripture and God's people, through whom He manifests various of His character qualities.

Through Faith

Faith is the means through which God dwells in the hearts of believers. Another word for *faith* is *confidence*. The faithful are confident in God and in God's understanding and expression of truth—His Word. Biblical faith is a trusted pathway to the highest desire of the soul. Biblical faith functions like a gyroscope that maintains an upright position in constant balance.

The fact that the Person of Christ dwells in the hearts of believers does not mean that Christ's Person is therefore devoid of the ideas, principles, or morals of Christ. Far from it! Rather, the presence of the Person of Christ insures that His ideas, principles, and morals are both adequately and correctly applied to the exigencies of life. For apart from the actual presence of the Person of Christ through the Holy Spirit the ideas, principles, and morals of Christ can be too easily misapplied and/or diluted to the point that they are not efficacious.

The presence and power of the Holy Spirit in the lives of believers through regeneration protects believers from the delusions of *mere* ideas, principles, and morals that are devoid of real life, even though their words may appear to be true. Real truth must always be holistic—fully dimensional—because apart from the greater reality of the whole, the mere sum of the parts cannot operate with unity of purpose. The holiness (wholeness) of God must include the reality of all of the Persons of the Trinity, which reaches into humanity. Anything less than this cannot be whole, by definition.

Faithful Christians are fiduciaries of God-in-Christ. A fiduciary is bound to act as a trustee for the benefit of another. Jesus Christ acted for the benefit of all believers through His propitiation on the cross, and He established believers as fiduciaries of His estate until He returns. Faithful Christians act on behalf of Christ, whose concern was for the blessings of faithfulness for all of His people.

Why, Again?

Paul was sharing all of this information so that Christians

"may have strength to comprehend with all the saints what is the breadth and length and height and depth" (v. 18)

of Christ's love. Length, height, and depth are odd measures of love. It sounds as if Paul was talking about the three-dimensional Cartesian coordinate system that can be graphed as *x, y,* and *z* axes.

However, *length* or *breadth* (πλάτος) can be interpreted as either one of those axes or as suggesting great extent. *Height* (ὕψος) can equally be interpreted as a Cartesian axis or as suggesting high rank, station, or regard. And *depth* (βάθος) can mean one of the axes or as suggesting profundity. They likely mean the great extent, high rank, and profundity of Christ's love.

I have maintained the idea of the Cartesian coordinate system in this discussion in order to give Paul's intended meaning the widest extent, the highest rank, and the most profundity possible. While Paul had no idea of the Cartesian coordinate system himself, he was well acquainted with the materiality of physical reality. By using terms that describe the three dimensions of materiality, Paul was also insisting that the love of Christ not be understood merely in intellectual or abstract philosophical terms, so that Christ's love cannot be separated from His physical body, as the Gnostics were prone to do. Using these three terms captured the philosophical aspects of Christ's love and underscored Paul's incarnational theology.

Note also the plurality involved in this discussion: "to comprehend with all the saints" (v. 18). This plural reference is not just a reference to the multitude of saints—their number, but to their wholeness, as well. Full comprehension of Christ's love for the saints requires the involvement of all of the saints, all those who are the various objects of Christ's love. Because Christ loves all of His people individually, they all must be individually included for a full understanding to be held.

This plural reference also serves Paul's incarnational theology. Christ was not merely incarnated in His body as the First Century individual, Jesus Christ, but by the power and presence of the Holy Spirit through regeneration Christ is also incarnate in/as His church body today. Christ is incarnate in each individual believer in part, and in the wholeness and purpose of His whole body as His church.

Paul then underscored again the point about not separating the Person of Christ from a philosophical or religious understanding of Christ when he said that we are "to know the love of Christ that surpasses knowledge" (v. 19). He did not say that we should avoid or deny knowledge, but that the love of Christ is greater than knowledge. It is greater in the ways that we have been talking about. The love of Christ includes the presence of His Person by the power of the Holy Spirit. He is alive through His resurrection! Christ was resurrected so

"that you may be filled with all the fullness of God" (v. 19).

Whoever reads Paul's letter with understanding is to be filled—*all* who so read it. Paul was not talking about simply filling our heads with knowledge. Yet, he was not denying the beauty or usefulness of knowledge, either. Knowledge is a beautiful and helpful thing. But God wants to fill more than our heads, more than our minds, more than our thinking. God also wants our bodies to be overflowing with Christ's life!

Of course Paul wanted Christians to think like Christians, but he also wanted us to do more than think. When our heads are full of Christ we think like Christians, and when our bodies are full of Christ we live like Christians. We must do both. In the same way that Christian communion requires more than prayer and liturgy—we must actually eat the bread and drink the wine. Christian living means more than thinking, even more than praying. Just as the neglect of our own bodily needs can bring about individual illness, so the neglect of the body life of Christ's church brings about various social ills.

19. CHURCHLY GLORY

*Now to him who is able to do far more abundantly than all
that we ask or think, according to the power at work within
us, to him be glory in the church and in Christ Jesus
throughout all generations, forever and ever. Amen.*

—Ephesians 3:20-21

The first phrase of verse 20 refers to the "fullness of God" in verse 19. Remember that the original Greek manuscripts have no punctuation, section breaks, or chapter breaks. In addition, the word translated as *now* (δέ) is not expressed in English. It is a continuative conjunction like *and,* whose function is to tie two words or ideas together. *To him who is able* is the translation of one Greek word: δύναμαι, and might be more accurately translated simply as *is able.* The idea here is that the fullness of God is able to do whatever is needed.

Superlative is added to superlative in the effort to describe what the fullness, wholeness, and holiness of God can do. Paul was pointing to the fact that there is much more to God than language. Sure God is the Word who was in the beginning, "and the Word was with God, and the Word was God" (John 1:1). But at the same time God is much more than words. Of course, God's reality is spiritual reality, but much more than mere spiritual reality, too. God is real and material, and the incarnation of God as Jesus Christ as a real, specific, individual human being provided a demonstration that God's reality is also as real as our own. The superlatives were added to suggest that God is more than a mere idea, and can actually do things in the real world. Again, Paul emphasized incarnational theology.

While on the one hand we are encouraged to pray and to ask God for what we need, on the other hand, Paul tells us that God can do and does do even more than we are able to imagine. There are millions of details that must be correctly balanced for our lives to exist as they do, and without the correct balance we would not be able to function as we do. Most of these things operate apart from our awareness, and we don't think about them or pray about them. And the few things that most people do pray about tend to be pretty trivial in the grand scheme of things. Yet, God wants us to pray about them, to talk to Him about them because that conversation is valuable to Him, as well as to us.

The last phrase of verse 20 is odd: "according to the power at work within us." It seems to suggest that God is limited by the power at work within us. One way to understand it is that He blesses us according to the measure of our ability to work with Him. Another way is that the power that makes God able to do these abundantly superlative things is the same power at work in us, but it is limited in us by the level or degree of power it can manifest in us. Thus, God is limited by our ability to cope with or channel His power in our lives. Another way to say it is that God is limited because of our sin. Not that sin trumps the power of God, but that sin interferes with our ability to work with God. This latter idea is preferable because sin is our problem, not God's.

The whole of verse 20 provides clarification regarding God, and serves to identify the God being discussed. Paul was careful not to share God's glory with any idea of God that is unworthy or untrue to the whole character of God-in-Christ.

Limits

The idea that God will provide for His people beyond their ability to imagine encourages a kind of reckless abandon regarding the prayers of Christians. We should not fear asking God for anything, but trust that He is already way ahead of us with regard to the supply of our needs. If there are limits to God's desire or ability to supply our needs, they are beyond our imagination, which means that human beings are not able to rationally or adequately discuss God's limitations, if He has any.

And yet in the very next phrase Paul seems to say that God's limitations are directly correlated to us, "according to the power at work within us" (v. 20), as if the energy output of a battery is limited by its capacity to store energy, or the volume of a glass of water is limited by the size of the glass. While the storage capacity of a battery, or the size of a glass have nothing to do with the actual availability of energy or water, the battery and the glass themselves have limits.

Ancient Christian theology from the early church taught that God is omnipotent or all-powerful. The classical proofs are readily available. However, the fact of God's omnipotence does not necessarily mean that His reality will conform to our ideas of His abilities.

Paul said that God is far beyond our ability to think or imagine, which means that we cannot know the full extent of God's abilities. However, just because God is more powerful than anything we can imagine does not mean that we can definitively say that He is infinitely powerful. He may be, but we have no way of knowing, and less of proving any such thing. Even in Ephesians 1:21 Paul was speaking about earthly power. In today's world of the Hubble telescope we know that the earth is but a very, very small spec in the vast universe. The idea that God is more powerful than anything in the world is not equivalent to saying that God is all-powerful.

The Gnostic, Greek philosophical idea that God has the unlimited power to be able to bring absolutely anything about in this universe in an instant, apart from any apparent means, by the sheer force of His will is simply unknowable and unverifiable. It is not that God may not have such power in the fullness of His being, but that the structure of this universe, the environment, and limitations of nature and humanity, are such that God's power conforms to the limitations of this universe because that's the way God created it. Because God operates on laws and principles in this universe, He limits His power and influence to the means of those laws and principles. He could create other kinds of universes, so His ultimate power is not denied. But this universe appears to operate in a particular way.

Another element of this argument is that the laws and principles that God uses in the operation of this universe are still not clearly know to us, not even to advanced mathematics, science, or technology. While incredible advances have been made, those advances may yet prove to be the mere tip of the proverbial iceberg of what is possible. What we call advancements today may in the future be reclassified as unfruitful rabbit holes of failed effort.

Unfortunately, Christians have long accepted the Greek philosophical idea of God as a philosophical abstraction rather than the biblical (Hebrew and Christian) understanding of God as an actual

Person. Paul has been working hard to establish God as a real Person and not a mere abstraction, not even the actuality of a perfect idea. Paul said that Christ, who is God incarnate,

> "humbled himself by becoming obedient to the point of death, even death on a cross" (Philippians 2:8).

He submitted to His humanity while in the flesh, which means that He shared the limitations of our humanity as well, in order to relate with us. We cannot think beyond our capacity to imagine, nor can we say anything meaningful about what is beyond our imagination. Similar arguments may be presented regarding many of the various characteristics of God set out in the ancient creeds.[6]

GLORY

Because glory and honor are nearly interchangeable, to say, "to him be glory" (v. 21) means that Christ is to be honored. But because the church is the body of Christ, we might also understand it to mean that Christ is to be honored as the church, and the church as Christ. It means that all Christians are to hold all other Christians in honor, not because individual Christians are equivalent to Christ—they emphatically are not! But because the various members of Christ's body share the honor of the wholeness and holiness of Christ, they should be honored as Christ is honored. All Christians should give all other Christians deference, honor, honesty, and respect.

Similarly, to disrespect any part of the body is to disrespect our wholeness as individual persons. For *me* to disrespect any part of my own body is for me to disrespect my whole self. This was the central meaning of 1 Corinthians 12:26:

> "If one member suffers, all suffer together; if one member is honored, all rejoice together."

There is a special connection between the member and the wholeness of the body, both individually and corporately, in the sense that each part serves the purpose of the whole. And it is that service to a common purpose that provides for the unity of the bodily members.

---

6   This is a very large idea. For further discussion see Beecher, Edward: *Conflict of Ages—The Great Debate of the Moral Relations of God and Man*, 1853, 2012, and *Concord Of Ages—The Individual And Organic Harmony Of God And Man*, 1860, 2013, Pilgrim Platform, Marietta, Ohio, Phillip A. Ross, editor. Note my criticisms and corrections of Beecher.

Unity does not mean equality. The different parts of the body are not the same, not equal—except inasmuch as they all need to be equally honored. Their honor is not derived from the job that they do, their function in the body, because each part has a different function, and some functions are more critical, more important than others. The body can continue with the loss of some parts, but not others. Losing a finger or toe is painful and it makes life more difficult. But loosing the heart is deadly. Nonetheless, fingers and toes need just as much honor as the heart. They all serve the overall health of the body. And *health* is just another word for wholeness. To be healthy is to be whole, and *visa versa*, wholeness requires the correct functioning of each part according to the purpose of the whole body.

In The Church

This honor is supposed to manifest in the church (v. 21). Scripture speaks of both *churches*, in the plural, and *the church*, in the singular. And because the church is the body of Christ on earth, we must understand her trinitarianily, as being both one and many at the same time.[7] From this perspective, we see that *churches* are parts and *the church* is the whole. Yet, each church is also a whole of a different measure.

The critical issue here is who speaks or who can speak for the whole. While all of the various parts are united in service to the purpose of the whole, no single part can speak for or dictate that purpose to the other parts, because no single part has the combined perspective of the whole. And yet, it is the obligation of each part to speak directly to and for the whole within the confines of its own individual circumstances and perspective as best as it is able, always being open to correction. For instance, the toe does not normally enter into conscious communication with the brain when it is functioning normally, healthfully. But when the toe has a problem, it speaks directly to the brain in order to direct the attention of various other parts to aid in the resolution of its problem. At that point the brain speaks or allows the toe to speak authoritatively to the other parts. And yet depending on the circumstances, the other parts cannot blindly obey, but must evaluate their own circumstances. For instance, if a soldier stubs his toe in battle, he may not be able to stop and tend the toe until circumstances permit.

---

7   Ross, Phillip A. *Colossians—Christos Singularis*, Pilgrim Platform, Marietta, Ohio, 2010.

Thus, the wholeness or holiness of the church is best found in the role of the Holy Spirit, and that role is ever-present or ongoing in order to express and interact with the dynamic circumstances of the church in real time, in the world. Life is not static. Rather, life flows and adapts to its changing circumstances—seasons, for instance. Individuals are to be in direct relationship with the Holy Spirit through regeneration, while their relationship with the Father is mediated by Christ, and their relationship with Jesus Christ is mediated by the Holy Spirit. The Father spoke to and through Jesus, and Jesus spoke to and through the Holy Spirit, and the Holy Spirit speaks to and through the people of God.

Yet, to understand the nature, character, and extent of the church(es) we must see how Paul used the idea of the church in the context of this verse—

> "to him be glory in the church and in Christ Jesus throughout all generations, forever and ever" (v. 21).

Notice how Paul links the church to Christ Jesus. There is no church apart from Jesus Christ, for the church is His body on earth. There are no non-Christian churches. Churches are inherently Christian, though many groups use the term *church*, they do always not have a biblical church. Whatever biblical churches are (groups of Christians), there are many of them, and they are eternal. Yet, there is also a sense in which the church is single, whole, and complete.[8]

In addition, church(es) are for all generations or ages (γενεά). The Greek word means all successive generations of children. There are at least two meanings of this idea. First, it means that people from every historical time period are to be involved. The church is a per-

---

8   How we measure churches determines how we define them. Larger human populations increase the dimensional field of human interactivity with our environment. More people provide more human interaction with the environment, which in turn impacts science and technology. The essential idea of "fractured" dimensions has a long history in mathematics, but the term itself was brought to the fore by Benoit Mandelbrot based on his 1967 paper on self-similarity in which he discussed fractional dimensions. In that paper, Mandelbrot cited previous work by Lewis Fry Richardson describing the counter-intuitive notion that a coastline's measured length changes with the length of the measuring stick used. In terms of that notion, the fractal dimension of a coastline quantifies how the number of scaled measuring sticks required to measure the coastline changes with the scale applied to the stick. There are several formal mathematical definitions of fractal dimensions that build on this basic concept of change in detail with change in scale. – http://en.wikipedia.org/wiki/Fractal_dimension

manent fixture in human society. It will not pass out of usefulness or evolve into something else.

This does not mean that it will exist in the same form during every generation, though I suspect that church(es) will always be recognizable as church(es). As human society develops, and especially as large populations impact the development of science and technology, churches will continue to grow and mature.

The other way that church(es) are for all generations pertains to the idea of children, parents, and grandparents being involved in the same congregation. Such participation mitigates against generational or age-graded separation that disrupts inter-generational communication. While there is nothing wrong with kids getting together or parents going out together without the kids, there is much to be gained from inter-generational worship, prayer, fellowship, and education. The communication and interactions of children, adults, and the aged are educational and will provide the best possible environment for the growth and maturity of the young, and for the comprehensive development of the wholeness of humanity.

Amen

Paul inserted an *amen* to underscore the eternal glory of Christ in His church that he has been discussing. It had been a Jewish custom to respond with an *amen* from the congregation to prayers, text recitations, and discourses that were particularly appropriate. And this custom transferred from the synagogues to the Christian assemblies. It was a way to make their own the substance of what had been spoken. The word *amen* was transliterated from the Hebrew into the Greek of the New Testament, and then into Latin, English, and many other languages. It is a nearly universal word, and has been called the best known word in human speech.

The word *amen* (Strong's H543) is almost identical to the word for *believe* (Strong's H359), also translated as *faithful*. Thus, it came to mean *sure* or *truly*, and served as an expression of trust and confidence. Paul inserted it because he was sure of what he had said about the eternal glory of Christ and His church. May we follow in Paul's example of assurance. Amen!

20. Hastening

*I therefore, a prisoner for the Lord, urge you to walk in a
manner worthy of the calling to which you have been called,
with all humility and gentleness, with patience, bearing with
one another in love, eager to maintain the unity of the Spirit
in the bond of peace.* —Ephesians 4:1-3

Paul described himself as a *prisoner* or *captive* (δέσμιος) for
Christ, not simply a Roman prisoner, though he was also a Roman prisoner at the time. According to Acts, trouble and unrest broke out everywhere Paul preached. The Jews accused him of
sedition and had even put a contract on his life (Acts 25:3). Paul's case
was much like Jesus' case had been, especially because Paul had taken
up Jesus' cause. Roman soldiers had to intervene to keep the peace,
and Paul eventually sought Roman protection, and insisted on taking
his case to the highest Roman court he could reach, to Felix, the Governor.

Paul also described himself as a servant or slave (δοῦλος) of Christ
elsewhere. Such terms today do not help the cause of Christian evangelism in that people generally don't want to be prisoners, captives,
servants, or slaves of anyone. Nonetheless, Paul's words remain an important reminder of what Christianity really is. Yes, it is freedom—release from unconscious slavery to sin by becoming a conscious slave
to Christ. Christians don't have absolute freedom to do whatever they
want because Christians are people of principle. Christians are moral.
And principled, moral people willingly subject themselves to various
biblical principles and rules. It is important to note that Christians find
their principles and rules in Scripture and not in their own desires.

Christians are not people without customs and rules. One of the purposes of the Bible is the establishment of social norms.

The idea of "walk(ing) in a manner worthy of the calling to which you have been called" (v. 1) is all about conformity and obedience to principles and morals—norms. The *worthy manner* is the morality, and the *calling* assures you that God means for *you* to apply the morality. Morality always means conformity to a standard of behavior.

People today argue about the behavior of the standard, as if Christ did not provide a clear example. The value of the role of Jesus Christ in Christianity is that of a moral archetype or norm. Scripture counsels Christians to imitate the apostles as they were imitating Christ (2 Thessalonians 3:7, 9; Hebrews 13:7; 3 John 1:11). Indeed, character imitation is the primary driver for Christian morality, which is also called *faithfulness*. This imitation is more than obedience to mere principles or some sort of moral algorithm. Rather, it is a matter of regeneration by the power and presence of the Holy Spirit such that the Spirit of God is alive in the life of the believer. Thus, this imitation is first a matter of *being*, and secondarily of *doing*.

Of course, we are not saved by our morality or by our imitation of Christ. Clearly, neither morality nor imitation are the gospel, they are the fruit of the gospel. We are saved by Christ and not by our own efforts. We are saved by Christ's faith, which He gives to believers through regeneration, and not by our own faithfulness. We must take care to understand that our faithfulness is a product of Christ's faith. It is a gift, and is not our own.

In today's world various counter ideas or forces have come to oppose the idea of Christ providing a moral norm for humanity. Championing the cause of dethroning Jesus Christ as the human norm, Queer Theory[9] has taken the lead. The concern of the queer theorists is that conformity to social norms tends to limit human creativity by restricting behavior and experimentation. They argue that the development of unfettered human creativity requires the elimination of restrictive, moral social norms—and especially any sort of traditional understanding of biblical norms.

> "Queer is by definition whatever is at odds with the normal, the
> legitimate, the dominant. There is nothing in particular to which

---

9   It is important to understand that Queer Theory is a major contributor to the rejection of biblical Christianity. See: http://en.wikipedia.org/wiki/Queer_theory.

it necessarily refers. It is an identity without an essence. 'Queer' then, demarcates not a positivity but a positionality vis-à-vis the normative."[10]

At the heart of Queer Theory is the refusal and rejection of any sort of human norm in the hope of expanding creativity by defying all expectations of conformity. However, no such thing can actually be accomplished in society because when breaking the norm becomes the norm, the new queering of the that norm becomes normative, and social order deteriorates as a result. Maybe it can be said more clearly in terms of popularity: when being unpopular becomes the dominant social norm, it is then popular to be unpopular, and the norm of unpopularity vanishes. Indeed, the queer struggle—the many sorts of personal identity issues prevalent in the homosexual experience—rages *because* the norm must always be foremost in mind in order to contradict it. One can only be truly queer in opposition to all social norms, which is a recipe for identity confusion and social deterioration.

And because the most basic norms are those imposed by God and His Word, God and His Word must be continually rejected, or at least reinterpreted. The current efforts to carve out a kind of Christianity where God encourages or at least does not condemn homosexual behavior must necessarily undermine the efforts and viability of Queer Theory because of the effort to norm homosexuality. At the point that homosexual behavior is successfully normed, it will no longer be queer because of the queer mandate to reject norms. At that point Queer Theory becomes meaningless or it must continue to undermine the norm by becoming even more aberrant.

Because human beings are necessarily social, and because sociability requires norms and morals in order to maintain science and technology—and because large populations require science and technology to exist,[11] the consistent practice of Queer Theory provides a serious impetus for social collapse. Or as Proverbs 8:36 says that "all who hate me (biblical wisdom) love death."

---

10 Halperin. David. *Saint Foucault: Towards a Gay Hagiography*, Oxford University Press, 1997-02-06, p. 62.

11 The current population of the earth requires science and technology to produce adequate food, shelter, and medicine. Without such things the earth would experience a rapid depopulation of biblical proportions. However, this argument is not an endorsement of the current use and abuse of science and technology.

Thus, the "manner worthy of the calling to which you have been called" (v. 1) is conformity to the character of Christ. To be more specific Paul provided both positive and negative patterns of behavior to emulate. Paul listed the negative things to avoid:

> "Now the works of the flesh are evident: sexual immorality, impurity, sensuality, idolatry, sorcery, enmity, strife, jealousy, fits of anger, rivalries, dissensions, divisions, envy, drunkenness, orgies, and things like these. I warn you, as I warned you before, that those who do such things will not inherit the kingdom of God" (Galatians 5:19-21).

And then he listed the positive things to engage:

> "But the fruit of the Spirit is love, joy, peace, patience, kindness, goodness, faithfulness, gentleness, self-control; against such things there is no law. And those who belong to Christ Jesus have crucified the flesh with its passions and desires" (Galatians 5:22-24).

Notice that Paul began this list with sexual immorality. The *Authorized Version* translated the two Greek words here as *adultery* (μοιχεία) and *fornication* (πορνεία), which includes all sexual activity outside of traditional bisexual marriage. The importance of marriage with regard to spiritual maturity cannot be overemphasized.[12] Indeed, the marriage supper of the Lamb (Revelation 19:7-10) is the high point or climax of the entire Bible, reenacted through the Eucharist, and it is no fluke that it is a picture of marriage and requires appropriate sexual role modeling.

Humility

We are to "walk in a manner worthy of the calling to which you have been called, with all humility" (vs. 1-2). The *Authorized Version* translated ταπεινοφροσύνη as *lowliness* because it literally means having a humble opinion of one's self, of thinking of one's self as unworthy and unimportant. We might also call this the acceptance of the idea of sin being at the heart of all human desire. We are humble because we recognize our own propensity to sin. Pride is the opposite of humility and does not recognize sin.

The language of pride has infested our contemporary culture—worldwide. This new language has accompanied the teaching and

---

12 Beecher, Edward, D. D. *Concord Of Ages, Or The Individual And Organic Harmony Of God And Man*, Phillip A. Ross, Editor 2013, p. 71, and "marriage" in the index.

promotion of self-esteem in our schools, where children are taught to have self-respect and pride in themselves. The effort is an attempt to overcome the low self-esteem that in past times seemed to be attached to poverty and failure. I say that it *seemed* to be attached to poverty and failure because both Scripture and truth say otherwise.

Self-esteem or pride produces people who are self-satisfied. They believe that they are okay just as they are and that they will be able to rise to any occasion on the basis of their own personal abilities and/or stature. They will either be able to accomplish whatever they want naturally or they believe others will value them enough to help them accomplish it. They do not have any motivation to consider their own sinfulness.

Contrary to this are people who feel inadequate, people with low self-esteem. I grew up in a nominally Christian home. My family lived across the street from the church we attended, and we all spent a lot of time at the church—weekly worship, Sunday School, youth group, potlucks, meetings, janitorial services, etc. My time in public school preceded the self-esteem craze. I don't know if my sense of self-esteem came from church or school—or if it was just natural to me. I can't say that it was particularly low, but neither was it high. I was an outstandingly ordinary kid. I didn't stand out for any reason.

My experience in the military as a conscientious objector provided a turning point in my life. At that point I decided to stand against the crowd because I thought they were wrong—all of them. I opposed the war in Vietnam, but I also opposed the idea of not serving my country. So, I served my country, but opposed the use of weapons—which put me in a position of opposition to everyone else in the military, except my fellow conscientious objectors.

There were three groups of conscientious objectors: the fearful, the rebellious, and the religious. The fearful didn't want to be near guns because they didn't want to get hurt. The rebellious objected to the war, but had failed to successfully avoid the draft. And the religious tended to be rabidly non-violent. I was opposed to the war, and opposed to running away from service, and I was not a rabid pacifist. So, I didn't fit any category, and made no real friends.

Needless to say, I made no long-term military friends, and have no post-service military buddies. My military service turned me inward—introverted. All of this is to say that my lack of self-esteem caused me to compensate with preparation. Most of the time, my feelings of inadequacy cause me to over prepare in order to make up for my perception of self-deficiency.

Over the years, I have come to see that this is also what the Bible intends for its teaching of humility. Biblical humility is not a matter of thinking lowly of one's self, but of thinking correctly about one's self. Humility causes self-doubt, which leads to caution and preparation. And of course, the truth of us all is that we are unrepentant sinners apart from Christ. We all stand guilty of sin, both cosmic and personal, and we are also subject to God's damnation because of it.

However, our damnation is not a reflection on God's character, but is simply the consequence of His righteous judgment. He demands perfection and we cannot provide it apart from Christ. We are inadequate to meet God's demands on our own. And the natural response to our own sin should be humility. We ought to think lowly of ourselves because the truth is that we are lowly. We ought not to think more lowly of ourselves than we actually are, but that is not our usual temptation. Rather, the temptation that we naturally succumb to is thinking more of ourselves than we ought—pride. Our damnation is a reflection on our own character, not God's.

Thus, Jesus Christ has initiated a program of character change and improvement. This does not mean that we are saved by these things. No! We are saved by Christ, who has dispatched His Holy Spirit to protect us while we are engaged in this program, and to provide for us what we cannot provide for ourselves. We are saved by grace through faith. God has graciously sent Jesus Christ as a propitiation for sin, and the Holy Spirit brings us the sufficiency of Christ's faith so we are not judged on the inadequacy of our own character.

MEEKNESS

> We are to "walk in a manner worthy of the calling to which you have been called, with all humility and gentleness" (vs. 1-2).

The *Authorized Version* translated πρᾳότης as *meekness*. The idea here is that of a mild disposition and a gentle spirit. Meekness toward God means acceptance of His dealings with us as being good, and because of this we are not to dispute His teachings or resist His ways. We are to wholly rely on God—His Son, His salvation, His ways, and His church—rather than on our own strength to defend us against the world's injustice. Thus, meekness requires Christians to suffer the injuries they receive at the hands of evil people because God is using them to accomplish the purification and maturity of all of His people, individually and as a whole.

Such suffering does not mean that we are to do nothing about the injustice of the world. Rather, it means that we are to engage God's tools to fight it, not our own, or those of human manufacture. God's tools are worship and service. We are to actually be the people that God has called us to be in the places that we already are. We are to be the fullness of Christ's church, and that fullness includes the engagement of those things in John's book of Revelation.

The church must undergo the crisis of confrontation with the world, with Satan himself, as John foresaw. The church cannot be perfect—whole, holy, and complete—without passing through that experience. Just as deliverance from personal sin is emotionally and spiritually difficult for individuals, so the deliverance of Christ's church from her corporate sin is also emotionally and spiritually difficult for the church. In fact, the church can only grow and mature so far without a purgation of the likes of Revelation.

The church must pass through such fires because she is composed of people who are still in sin, people who have caused the church to sin. It's like an alcoholic needing to hit bottom before turning around. Bottom is relative. Some bottoms are lower than others, some are easier and some are harder, but all are bottoms—turning around points. Without hitting the bottom, there can be no turnaround. The point of turnaround marks the bottom. The church needs to find a way to deal with her less than perfect history that neither denies it nor is controlled by it. She must quit relying on old, sinful habits. She must learn from her history, not deny it. She must be willing to call a spade a spade, to grow out of her childhood, into adulthood.

And this is why Christ called and modeled suffering for His people. We are called to suffer as Christians—and to suffer joyfully!

> "…we rejoice in our sufferings, knowing that suffering produces endurance, and endurance produces character, and character produces hope, and hope does not put us to shame, because God's love has been poured into our hearts through the Holy Spirit who has been given to us" (Romans 5:3-5).

Paul taught that our suffering, both personally and corporately, has a purpose. It is to be productive suffering that produces endurance, character, and hope. And if these things are being matured in Christ, then we can know that we are on the right track. And if they are not, we must make whatever course corrections are necessary to make our suffering productive of these things.

Productive suffering produces *patience* (ὑπομονή) and the ability to bear with difficulties. The failure to learn patience is more painful than the struggle to learn it. So, if you have any choice, choose to learn and practice patience in all things. Patient people are not turned from God's purposes, even by the greatest trials and sufferings. If there is any trick to learning patience, it is practice. Practice patience in the little things so that you will know how to engage it when the big trials come.

Character, translated as *experience* (δοκιμή) in the *Authorized Version*, is an end product. It indicates the completion of a process, or the learning of a lesson—a person who has been tried and approved, a person of experience. Whatever lessons are to be learned cannot be learned apart from the trial—the difficulties. God's plan is a plan of Christian character maturity through discipleship (discipline).

However, it is at this point that an interesting biblical anomaly must be confronted because the test that God uses measures our response to failure. And if we pass the test, we fail to be defeated by failure. It is only by failing the various tests that we learn how to cope with failure. One who does not fail never learns the lessons of failure. Therefore, God has made the test such that we cannot pass it. We are not able to pass God's testing, God's trials. We are destined to fail. And in our failure, God sends His Helper, the Holy Spirit, who heals our wounds and renews our spirit. The test must necessarily lead to our failure in order to strengthen our humility and lead us to trust God, and not ourselves. Failure is designed to open us to the Holy Spirit.

It is only from our failures that we learn to seek and trust God's Holy Spirit. Indeed, the central lesson of the Bible is that renewal or regeneration comes out of failure, and only out of failure. The Holy Spirit is dispatched only at the end of our resistance, our rebellion. This is the message of the cross. We may not like this idea, and any-one who says that they do like it is lying or self-deceived. It is not our idea. It is not a human idea, that we grow in godliness through failure. Success usually produces pride. Failure alone produces humility. That's just the way it is!

FORBEARANCE

We are to

> "walk in a manner worthy of the calling to which you have been
> called, with all humility and gentleness, with patience" (vs. 1-2).

The *Authorized Version* translated μακροθυμία as *longsuffering*.
Here is a character quality in complete variance with contemporary
people. While it is popular to speak of toleration of others out of concern for political correctness, we tend to use it offensively as an accusation of others in order to encourage *them* to tolerate *us*. Apart from
this use, there is no other area of life for which people are tolerant or
toward which people are encouraged to be tolerant. We have been
captured by the spirit of instant gratification. We want what we want
and we want it now!

We see this in our medical advertisements where every affliction
imaginable—and many are simply contrived—is met with the demand
for drugs. Big Pharma now defines, diagnoses, and prescribes chemi-
cals for every possible discomfort. Consider the flu and the Centers
for Disease Control (CDC). The CDC recommends that everyone
get a flu shot, but never mentions the simple practice of hand washing as a flu avoidance technique. There is no money to be made from
simple hand washing.

Or consider consumer debt spending. Never in the history of the
world have there been more wealthy people (all Americans are
wealthy by world standards) who have been more in debt than contemporary Americans.

In stark contrast to this spirit of instant gratification, stands Jesus
Christ, the suffering servant, who endured the pain of death on the
cross for sin He did not commit in order to save a people plunged in
sin. Jesus suffered the cross because God has longsuffered sin in this
world. And Jesus is the model Christian. We are to be like Him, who
forgave those who crucified Him *while they were doing it*. The
Christian message is not that others must forebear us for our quirky
ways, but that we must forebear the sins of others against us.

LOVE

And if this isn't enough, we are called to do all of this while
"bearing with one another in love" (v. 2). The *Authorized Version*
translated ἀνέχομαι as *forebearing*, which—like *foresight* and *foreknowledge*—means engaging in said behavior *before* any experience,
and not as a reaction to experience. Like God's prevenient grace, we
are to engage in prevenient bearing with one another. We are to lead

with toleration and longevity rather than frustration and disappointment—in everything at all times.

We are called to agape love (ἀγάπη), love that expects nothing in return. We can also translate *agape love* as self-sacrificing service. We might also think of this as prevenient service. We are to model agape love, self-sacrificing service to others, as Jesus modeled it for us.

UNITY

And the heart of our motivation for doing all of this is to be the desire for Christian unity. But note that this unity is not something to be sought, but something to be realized. It is not that we don't already have it, so we must do whatever it takes to get it. No! That's not what Paul said. He said that it is to be *maintained*. That is, it is already in place, so we must take care not to lose it or bruise it. We are to be

> "eager to maintain the unity of the Spirit in the bond of peace" (v. 3).

Paul was writing to the church at Ephesus, to people who were already in the church. He accused the Ephesian church of being unified. Paul knew well that every church is a mixed bag, composed of all sorts of people, some of whom would persevere to the end and be saved, and some who wouldn't. We need to remember that the Ephesian church to whom Paul wrote was the same Ephesian church mentioned by John in his Revelation.

> "To the angel of the church in Ephesus write: 'The words of him who holds the seven stars in his right hand, who walks among the seven golden lampstands. I know your works, your toil and your patient endurance, and how you cannot bear with those who are evil, but have tested those who call themselves apostles and are not, and found them to be false. I know you are enduring patiently and bearing up for my name's sake, and you have not grown weary. But I have this against you, that you have abandoned the love you had at first. Remember therefore from where you have fallen; repent, and do the works you did at first. If not, I will come to you and remove your lampstand from its place, unless you repent'" (Revelation 2:1-5).

False apostles were in her midst, yet Paul called them to *maintain* unity. They had even abandoned their first love, their love of Christ—yet, Paul called them to *maintain* unity! But how could they *maintain* unity in the midst of falsehood, poor commitment, and the loss of their passion for Christ?

Paul's understanding of unity is not the same as ours. The Greek word (ἑνότης) is a conjugation of the idea of oneness. The root of *unity* is *unit*, which is a noun that means

> 1) An individual thing or person regarded as single and complete, esp. for purposes of calculation: "the family unit." 2) Each of the individuals or collocations into which a complex whole may be divided: "large areas of land made up of smaller units."

A unit is a set.[13] A unit is a group of things that is considered to be one thing for some purpose or other. Thus, the idea of church unity is necessarily trinitarian in the various ways I have discussed in several of my books.

But Paul was talking about more than mere unity. He insisted that Christians be *eager* (σπουδάζω) to maintain unity. The *Authorized Version* translated the word as *endeavoring*, suggesting that it requires some effort to maintain it. But again, the effort is to *keep* the unity, not to *achieve* it. The effort is to keep from alienating others, rather than the development of some kind of super theology or polity. It was the false apostles, also called *super-apostles* (υπερ λιαν αποστολων) in 2 Corinthians 11:5 and 12:11, who were working on a super theology in order to institute a super unity out of Gnostic mysteries. The Corinthians were in a different church, but it was the same problem. It has always been the same problem, which can be traced back to the Tower of Babel. We are not to create a unity that serves our own purposes, which usually serves our empires rather than God's kingdom. Rather, we are to gladly and preveniently work to maintain unity according to God's Word.

PEACE

And we are to do all of this "in the bond of peace" (v. 3), without the ravages of war and strife, without theological conflict and opposition, and with a spirit of harmony and camaraderie with our brothers and sisters in Christ.

However, peace is not some super spiritual mindset of quietude and suck-it-up introversion. We are not to become super Gnostic Buddhists in character, deferring our differences or avoiding varia-

---

13   See Appendix: Membership & Set Theory, p. 405

tions of opinion. Rather, Christian peace is a noisy, messy affair—like family.

No one fights like family, but when push comes to shove, family trumps all—our Christian family, that is. Family is where we learn to be individuals, and where we learn the importance of blood kinship. Family is where we learn who we are and Whose we are. And we learn these things by growing and maturing, by going through the various stages of childhood and adolescence. Family is where we try various *personas* on until we find our unique fit. Family is where we are brutally honest and fiercely faithful. Family is where we fight and make up, only to fight about something else—and make up again. This is Christian unity. This is the *unit* called Christianity.

Christian unity is necessarily full of discussion and divergent opinion about all sorts of things, yet the bonds of peace are not to be broken. It is not an agreement to disagree, or other such logical nonsense. Rather, genuine disagreements must be hammered out on the anvil of God's Word until we are able to correctly understand Scripture as God intends it, and accept our brothers' and sisters' divergences, trusting that differences of perspective do not detract from God's truth, but serve to expand it to greater degrees of fullness and maturity. Indeed, the joy of Christian theology is a treasure yet to be discovered, a raw material yet to be mined, and a resource yet to be developed for the true benefit of humanity.

Peace is not to be the purpose of the conflict, won after long battles and worrisome wars. Peace is not the purpose of Christianity that is to be realized only after jihads of self-discipline, self-sacrifice (that end in premature death), or murderous revenge in the name of some aberrant idea of god or some perversion of God's character or purpose. None of that!

Rather, peace is the process, the way, and the life. It is the Christian life itself. We are not to fight for peace because the process of fighting destroys the desired peace. Peace cannot be won, as if it is a prize or the reward of some contest. Christianity is not a contest, nor is salvation a prize for good behavior.

Rather, the engagement of Christian peace must be done wholeheartedly. We must give everything we are, everything we have, to the cause of Christ, the cause of peace, the process of peacefulness. The peace of Christ is full to overflowing—full of various opinions, full of differing positions, full of alternate means and radical diversions. The peace of Christ is like a great feast, where the dining hall is full to the brim with hungry people, noisy people—all kinds of people expressing all kinds of ideas about God's love and care. It is a feast where the wine of God's love flows freely and libatiously, filling people—not with intoxication or confusion, but with the ecstasy of God's love and a clarity of spirit undreamt of by unbelievers.

21. One Of All

There is one body and one Spirit—just as you were called to the one hope that belongs to your call—one Lord, one faith, one baptism, one God and Father of all, who is over all and through all and in all. But grace was given to each one of us according to the measure of Christ's gift. —*Ephesians 4:4-7*

The one body that Paul refers to here is σῶμα (*soma*), not σάρξ (*sarx*). The distinction has to do with the physical body of the flesh of an individual verses the corporate body of believers.[1] This distinction does not suggest the immateriality of the corporate body, but serves to contrast its ordinality with its cardinality.[2] And that contrast serves to suggest that regardless of the number of individual Christians there may be, they all belong to one set. And we may add that all that pertains to set theory pertains to the church of Jesus Christ.

It may be argued that I have imposed modern ideas on the ancient text, which I have.[3] However, everything that is explicit in modern mathematics, which has been developed in the light of the trinitarian nature of the reality in which we live, has always been implicit in the trinitarian nature of the church. Paul was intuiting what modern mathematicians have made more explicit. And because Paul

---

1   Ross, Phillip A. *Arsy Varsy—Reclaiming The Gospel in First Corinthians*, 2008, and *Varsy Arsy—Proclaiming The Gospel in Second Corinthians*, 2009, Pilgrim Platform, Marietta, Ohio.

2   See Appendix, p. 406.

3   Everyone imposes understanding from a particular context upon what they read. It cannot be avoided. See: Ross, Phillip A. *Varsy Arsy—Proclaiming The Gospel in Second Corinthians,* Eisegesis & Exegesis, 2009, Pilgrim Platform, Marietta, Ohio, p. 70.

was writing under the influence of the Holy Spirit, who Himself is a member of the Trinitarian Godhead, the ideas of modern mathematics and of set theory have always been inherent in Christ's church and God's Word.

By also mentioning "one Spirit" (v. 4), Paul equated the unity of the corporate body to the unity of the Holy Spirit. This is a further denial of the Gnostic idea of the separability of the body and spirit that Paul has denied several times already. Body and spirit are one in the same way that individual Christians are one corporate body. There are distinctions and differences that can be observed, but they do not contradict the unity of the whole. Calvin commented on this verse:

> "We are called to one inheritance and one life; and hence it follows, that we cannot obtain eternal life without living in mutual harmony in this world."[4]

Note that Calvin tied the unity of God and God's promise of inheritance with the cooperation of Christians in the church in this world. It is a wonder that so many self-proclaimed Calvinists have failed to understand and practice this teaching. Indeed, Paul was trying to undermine the sinful desire to attack other people as a method of self-actualization. It is so easy to differentiate ourselves from others, and to express superiority by group distinction and tearing others down. It is much more difficult and important to self-actualize one's real and unique identity in the light of Christ, for no other method reveals such fullness, beauty, and uniqueness of character.

PURPOSE

The hope of one's calling is the purpose for which God calls people. The hope is that God's purpose in calling you will be fulfilled—accomplished. And the hope is part of the unity or oneness of the call, and part of the unity and oneness of God's church, which is one in Christ.

God uses one divine call for all of His people. He calls us all to the same thing—repentance, to turn away from what is ungodly, and to turn to Jesus Christ, to receive and embody Christ the Lord. This is a universal call, not that God expects everyone to hear and obey it, but that all who do hear and obey hear the same call to repentance.

---

4   Calvin, John. *Calvin's Complete Commentary*, Ephesians 4:4, public domain.

Though this aspect of God's call is the same for everyone, there is another aspect of His call that is unique to each individual. And that aspect pertains to one's role or place in Christ's church. Each and every Christian is called through repentance to some particular role, place, function, and/or task in the body of Christ. And the role, place, function, and/or task is not something to be completed or abandoned in this life. Rather, it is an ongoing, longer than life-long occupation, and should provide great joy and satisfaction in spite of the difficulties involved. The difficulties add a sense of confidence to the joy because Jesus promised that difficulties would be encountered (John 15:20). When difficulties are not noticed or encountered, we need to reexamine ourselves and our service to Christ because something is amiss if there are no difficulties.

The Greek word translated as *one* (μία), which pertains to *faith,* is a different word than that translated as *one* (εἷς) pertaining to *body, spirit, Lord,* and *baptism.* εἷς is understood numerically as one (1), where μία means *first,* as in order or rank. This distinction is similar to that of cardinal and ordinal numbers, which encourages the analogies and mathematical references to this issue.

God is *of, over, through,* and *in* all (v. 6). The word *all* (πᾶς) has two possible senses: singular and plural. Individually it means *each* and *any.* And collectively it includes *every, all, the whole, everyone, all things,* and *everything* understood as a whole or unit. But the word is also used metaphorically, as when Scripture says that the all the world has gone after Jesus. Of course, *all* the world, understood literally, did not go after Him. We see the same thing when all Judea was baptized by John. Neither *all* Judea, nor *all* Jerusalem, were baptized in the Jordan. The words *world* and *all* are used in some seven or eight senses in Scripture, and very rarely does *all* mean *all individuals,* taken individually. The words are generally used to signify that Christ has redeemed some of all kinds—some Jews, some Gentiles, some rich, some poor, some male, some female, and has not restricted His redemption to any particular kind, class, sex, or nation.

Permeation

The word *of* in "God and Father *of all*" (πᾶς, v. 6) is implied. It means that the *all* referred to are God's children. And *all* means *everyone* descended from Adam. So, how can we reconcile this understanding with John 8:44, "You are of your father the devil, and your will is to do your father's desires"? By acknowledging that a person can have more than one person who plays the role of father.

Children from divorced families can have more than one father, as can children whose mothers have remarried after the death of a husband. And if we understand fathering as a role rather than a family relationship, all sorts of people can act as—and be—fathers to children not biologically their own. In addition, grandfathers and great grandfathers can be considered to be the father of their grandchildren and great grandchildren.

The difference between children of God and children of the devil is about obedience to God's covenant. His obedient children are blessed and His disobedient children are cursed by the authority and jurisdiction of His covenant. God's covenant is universal in that it applies to all of humanity. And apart from its universal jurisdiction, there would be no authority to damn anyone. We know that all authority has been given to Jesus Christ (Matthew 28:18). Jesus has the authority to separate the sheep and the goats (Matthew 25:32-33), and the wheat and the chaff (Matthew 3:12, Luke 3:17).

We know that all people are created by God, so He is Father to *all*. But we also know that Satan's sin has deceived *all*, so the Devil is also father of *all*. And we know that Christ has come to save the world, and that some of every tongue and nation will be saved. Thus, the "God and Father of all" (v. 6) means the God and Father of all Christians.

Over And Above

The God "who is over all" (ἐπί, v. 6) refers to God's superimposition, or the placing of one image on top of another such that both are visible. Thus, the fact that God is over all suggests that God's identity or image is placed upon that of believers—Christians, which then blends the identity or image of God with the identity or image of the believer without confusion. That is, both images are individually discernible though they are combined. Believers remain believers and God remains God. Believers do not become God.

Here we can see that the trinitarian characteristics of the Godhead are reflected in the characteristics of believers, not perfectly but dimly (1 Corinthians 13:12). This implies that God's Trinitarian character is imposed upon believers so that Christians share in the character of God's Trinitarian identity. The Trinity provides the model for Christian character. Each of the Persons of the Trinity serves the other Persons of the Trinity so that each Person's self-concern is facilitated through His concern for the Others, which takes precedence. Similarly, each believer can best take care of him- or herself by caring for other people—not by giving them what they want for themselves, but by giving them what Christ wants for them.

Jesus Christ is the archetypal human being. He's the model, so we cannot be fully human apart from Him. And the link to the Trinity comes from the Holy Spirit, whom God has dispatched to reside with and/or in believers through regeneration.

On Account Of

The God and Father who is "through all" (διά, v. 6) is the God who is the ground or reason by which something is or is not done. The reason, ground, or cause is the initial or original source and impetus for whatever is done. Again, we see that God is the head-water for human activity.

The oneness of God is both specific to the God of the Bible, as He said in the First Commandment, "You shall have no other gods before me" (Exodus 20:3), and all encompassing, in that God is at the source of everything. Indeed, everything has definition and meaning only in reference to Him.

The Wholly

Where The *English Standard Version* translated v. 6 "in all," the *Authorized Version* translated it as "in you all." The literal meaning of the Greek is *in all humanity*, keeping in mind the discussion above. God has ultimate jurisdiction over all humanity, and will admit some into heaven and reject some, leaving them hell-bound. It is both just and merciful to reject unrepentant sinners. It is just because damnation is the right destination for unrepentant sinners. And it is merciful because bringing unrepentant sinners into heaven would contaminate the purity of heaven, and put heaven's residents in unnecessary danger of harm because sinners would exercise their sin in heaven.

Over and again we come up against the issue of whether God intends to save all humanity or only some people, and we must understand that the issue itself is confused because it involves us in a false dichotomy. We cannot expect God or Scripture to correctly and clearly answer questions that issue out of false premises and lead to false dichotomies. Too many people are too ready and willing to challenge God before they sufficiently examine their own presuppositions. We are completely free to ask God anything and to question all biblical doctrines, but because of God's otherness, His holiness, and perfection, we must first hear what He has already said in the Bible.

God has initiated the grace of the gospel because of His radical love for His people. Having provided everything through the propitiating blood of His own son, Jesus Christ, on the cross, God now treats people as they treat Him. He responds to people as they respond to Him. If they refuse to accept His grace and mercy, He refuses to listen to them. And whenever people receive His grace and mercy, He rushes to receive them. And this is terrifically good news!

When God's program of salvation is finally complete, He will have saved the human genome from extinction, and thus will have saved all humanity. But until that time, some will continue to be lost, which brings God great sorrow for the unnecessary waste of genuine opportunity. God's program of salvation will not be complete until either Christ's return, or some other instructions provided by Christ upon His return. We currently live in the time of the growing wheat and tares (Matthew 13:25-30), which means that both good and evil are currently growing, both Christ's people and His enemies are growing. The good is getting better and the bad is getting worse— and this is exactly what we see in our world.

But Grace...

In contrast to all of this oneness and unity of God-in-Christ, we find that each believer has been infused with a specific gift, a giftedness or fitness for a particular role or function in the body of Christ. That gift or role is also called the Christian's *calling*. The engagement of our calling is an expression of Christ's church, His body. And His body, like ours, is composed of both doing and being. Doing without the being becomes mindless slavery, and being without the doing becomes the height of irresponsibility. So, both being and doing are necessary. Being and doing are like the human symmetry of right and left. Though people have two hands, most have a handed preference. They are either right-handed or left-handed. We tend to prefer one and under use the other. Yet, most of the time both hands are needed for full human functionality. And so it is also with being and doing. People may have a preference for one or the other, but both are necessary.

Paul's point in verse 7 is that people do not enjoy the same measure of grace, that God does not distribute grace equally. People are

not equal, not the same. In fact, the joy of life is found in the play between our similarities and our differences. When differences become
too disparate, communication and understanding break down. And
when our similarities become too common, interest wanes. Equality is
an abstraction, an idea. In reality, no two things can ever be perfectly
equal. This truth has serious consequences regarding the dream of
American equality. And the first consequence is the realization that
equality is a dream. The origin of the American dream of equality[5] is
found in Exodus 12:49:

> "There shall be one law for the native and for the stranger who
> sojourns among you."

American equality does not pertain to birth, talent, opportunity,
ability, etc. The only way that it actually makes coherent sense is that
it pertains to equal treatment before the law. The dream is that the
law not treat people differently, that all people are under the same
law. However, Scripture says it much better by emphasizing the unity
and universality of the law, rather than the condition of the people.
By focusing on God (His law), the reality of this hope has enduring
substance. Whereas focusing the idea of equality on people rather
than on law puts the attention on the flux of humanity rather than on
the stability of God. It has created the dream of human equality rather
than the sure hope of the universal applicability of God's law for all.
And the only way that equality can work is for some aspect of the law
to be set forth as ultimate or objective, as God has done with the Ten
Commandments, and not on the flux of human precedent and case
law.

The point is that God's grace or His gifts understood as talents,
abilities, and opportunities are not the same for everyone. Equality
understood in this way is simply impossible. Demonstrating human
differences, Paul will soon mention some of the various roles to be
played in Christ's church (v. 11). This idea of different gifts, roles, and
functions in the church was also discussed in Paul's first letter to the
Corinthians:

> "Now there are varieties of gifts, but the same Spirit; and there are
> varieties of service, but the same Lord; and there are varieties of
> activities, but it is the same God who empowers them all in every-
> one" (1 Corinthians 12:4-6).

---

5   See Appendix: American Dream, p. 410.

Note the play between unity and diversity. Unity and diversity are not opposed to one another, but are measures of the same things on different scales. They are akin to Plato's one and many, and to the idea of the whole and the parts.

22. Speculation

*Therefore it says, "When he ascended on high he led a host
of captives, and he gave gifts to men." (In saying, "He ascended," what does it mean but that he had also descended
into the lower regions, the earth? He who descended is the
one who also ascended far above all the heavens, that he
might fill all things.)* —Ephesians 4:8-10

Paul quoted from Psalm 68:18, which attributed David's king-
ship to the work of God. The idea is that just as God overshad-
owed David's rise to and exercise of power, so God shepherded
Jesus to be the administrator of God's kingdom. Just as God had given
David gifts to lead, both personal gifts and gifts through other people,
God gave similar gifts to Jesus Christ. And just as David had delivered
his people from many dangers, so Jesus would deliver His people to
God. Commentators agree that these verses point to Christ' ascension
(Acts 1:9-11).

Christ's ascension involves a superimposition of one role upon
another, or His installation into the role of human archetype, the
event when Christ officially became something akin to the aleph-
null[6] of His church, the member of the set that bridges the individual
elements of the set to the whole of an infinite set. Christ's ascension
marks His transition from earth to heaven, from the realm of the finite
to the realm of the infinite.

Paul's point was that just as Christ was taken up, He must also
have come down, because of His eternal nature. Christ's descent into
the lower regions does not simply mean that He descended into hell,
which He did, but that He descended into time, and in particular into

---

6   See: Appendix, Aleph-null, p. 407.

time on earth. Thus, Christ is able to ascend into eternity and descend into time. Earth-bound time is defined by the earth's relationship to the solar system. Time has always been determined by the rotation of the earth, though it is unlikely that Paul would have understood it as we do. Paul would have understood it as the movement of the sun across the sky (earth's rotation) and the passage of the seasons (earth's orbit around the sun).

Thus, the allusion found in Acts 1:9-11 simply and clearly suggests that Jesus was taken into a cloud—either into some kind of flight or into space. This is the plain reading of the text. What it means or how we are to understand it are less clear, and will always be understood within the cultural context of those reading it. This was certainly true in the first century, and because this contextual bias will always be true, it must be the intention of the text. In this way the text lends itself to the attribution of being alive. It grows with the history and maturity of the culture(s) in which it has been embedded.

DAVID

When David became king (ascended on high), he brought his followers into power with him. According to 1 Chronicles 12 mighty men of valor followed David, men trained for battle who could handle shield and spear, whose faces were like the faces of lions, and were as swift as gazelles on the mountains. They were impressive soldiers. They were men of courage who had a warrior spirit, who patiently received the training they needed to be mighty warriors, who were skilled in the use of their weapons—skills gained from their training. They had the calm demeanor of men who were confident in God. They were mobile, active men, ready to fight wherever they were needed.

And most importantly, they loved David. David captured the hearts of those he had taken captive in his many battles. He turned captives into followers—and that is the meaning behind the illusive phrase about taking captivity captive. He turned enemies into friends and followers by his commitment to God's truth. And the fact that he trusted those who had once fought against him, against the state or the kingdom of Saul, enabled those who had been enemies to trust him more fully. David became known for his fair treatment of people. When it came time to divvy up the booty, David made it a point to be both fair and generous.

"When David came to Ziklag, he sent part of the spoil to his friends, the elders of Judah, saying, 'Here is a present for you from the spoil of the enemies of the LORD'" (1 Samuel 30:26).

And because Paul was quoting Psalm 68:18, which was in part a remembrance of David's ascension to the throne of Israel, Paul was comparing David and Jesus Christ, in that Christ had ascended to the throne of God's kingdom! In a sense David bought his army with his generosity. And Christ has done likewise, He paid the price for our sin. Paul called the Holy Spirit

"the earnest of our inheritance until the redemption of the purchased possession, unto the praise of his glory" (Ephesians 1:14, *Authorized Version*).

"You ascended on high, leading a host of captives in your train and receiving gifts among men, even among the rebellious, that the LORD God may dwell there" (Psalm 68:18).

Paul's point in part was that God will capture and change the hearts of His enemies so that He may even dwell with them—with His former enemies! God was on a kind of capture and release fishing mission, capturing fish of all kinds from one body of water and releasing them into another body of water—His body. This is what the biblical allusion about capturing captivity is about.

Paul then explained his quote, at least the part about ascending. The word ἀναβαίνω (*ascend*) in verse 9 is the same word used in verse 8, and both refer to עלה (*ascend*) in Psalm 68:18, which has a variety of meanings, all of which convey a sense of upward movement, literal, moral, and spiritual. But his explanation reverses the direction of the movement:

"what does it mean but that he had also descended into the lower regions, the earth" (v. 9).

Paul, knowing well the meaning, drew the conclusion of Christ's prior descent from heaven to earth.

Paul said this because he knew that Jesus Christ was a member of the Godhead, and was therefore eternal. He based an interpretation of a Psalm about David on Christ and expanded it into a greater implication. This is an important hermeneutical insight because it shows Paul's freedom regarding the text. While such use of biblical texts cannot always be defended, it is sometimes appropriate.

Clearly, Paul felt completely justified in applying Old Testament Scripture to Jesus Christ, and speculating about the implications. Of course, Paul was operating in the Spirit, which means that he was *in Christ*, and being in Christ provided him with some freedom and assurance that is not available outside of Christ. And again, Paul was an Apostle, and we are not, so we are to imitate Paul. We are to share in Paul's freedom and assurance in our understanding of Scripture, not perfectly but adequately.

Spirituality

The traditional understanding of Christ's descent into the lower regions of the earth (v. 9) means His descent into hell. The idea of *lower* (κατώτερος) here refers to something inferior. And the idea of an inferior thing here is interesting. The *Authorized Version* translated it as *parts* (μέρος), while it means division or share. Whatever else it is, it is less than a whole. Becoming a man (a part of humanity), Christ gave up His divinity (wholeness) for a time (Philippians 2:7).

The Hebrew word translated *hell* is שׁאוּל, and is derived from the primitive word שׁאל, which carries the connotation of *ask, inquire, request,* and even *demand*. Again, we see that all such inquiries come from a lack or absence of something. We see the idea of something less than whole, something less than holy, remembering the relationship between *whole* and *holy*.[7]

From an earthly perspective heaven includes everything higher with regard to place, quality, or dimensionality. Heaven refers in one way or another to a higher dimension, perhaps even a more refined or more robust dimension, and surely a spiritual dimension.

Dimensions can be measured, like the dimensions of height, length, and depth. Time can be considered a dimension, but is quite different than the first three measures because it involves motion, or intradimensional movement. Spirit(s) can also be measured. They are measured morally, on the basis of good and evil. Assessing spiritual dimension(s) is done with the faculty of discernment, the ability to distinguish good from evil. Indeed, all measurement or determination of good and evil involves spiritual discernment. However, measurement of the spiritual dimension(s) is determined—not simply by knowing the difference (a kind of distance) between good and evil, but by living the difference, going the distance personally. Spiritual

---

7   Appendix: Whole & Holy, p. 405.

dimensions(s) are not simply abstract thoughts or literary descriptions. They are real life realities.

Thus, Paul's speculation about Jesus moving up and down from heaven to earth also means movement between eternity and time, and between wholeness and particularity. Interestingly, such movement is as much about changing perspectives or contexts as it is about particular locomotion. Jesus' ascension is as much about reframing His life spiritually, as it is about relocating His Person. Clearly, both things are involved—and that's the point. We cannot and must not conceive of Christ's ascension as being exclusively about His body mysteriously floating up into the misty clouds. That image stands as an allusion that illuminates a greater truth. We see this understanding expressed in the next verse:

> "He who descended is the one who also ascended far above all the heavens, that he might fill all things" (v. 10).

Here Paul pushed the analogy as far as possible. Jesus Christ has the power to move freely in and out of time and eternity. Similarly, He can move between wholeness and particularity, from the Godhead to Messiah in the flesh. And as He moves in these ways we find that what actually moves is not the fleshly body of Jesus, but His context. We see Him in a greater context, first as the Lord of the universe and then as Messiah in the flesh, or *visa versa*. First as Joseph's son, then as the Son of God—the same man understood in different contexts. What changes is our perspective about Him, for God Himself doesn't change.

This is mysterious and somewhat beyond our usual considerations. We cannot understand it perfectly, ultimately, or completely, but we can understand it adequately. From a practical perspective it is no different than understanding that a man can play different roles in his life—son, brother, father, grandfather, butcher, baker, candlestick maker. The same man can be seen in different contexts, different roles, and from different perspectives. Each reveals the same man, yet what is revealed is genuinely different. The one man can fill many roles, the one man can be seen from many perspectives.

Paul's point was that the same man, the same individual who descended from heaven to be the body and Spirit of Jesus Christ ascended back to the highest heaven, "far above all the heavens" (v. 10). Without taking away from the literal understanding of Jesus ascending into the clouds, we can also understand it as an analogy. But we

must not limit ourselves to the analogical understanding by disbeliev-
ing the literal image because the veracity of the analogy requires the
viability of the reality of the literal perspective. Yet, the more fulfilling
and satisfying meat is the analogy, not the literal image.

FULLNESS

This same idea of a change of perspective or context can be seen
in Paul's next phrase, "that he might fill all things" (v. 10). We all have
a common, practical understanding of *full* and *empty*. But behind the
practicality lies the purpose, because the word *practical* is always related to some purpose. To say that a thing is *practical* implies and requires some purpose that it accomplishes. Practical is a method of
accomplishing something, and what is practical for one purpose is not
for another. Again, the point is that practicality always requires purpose.

For instance, we can ask about the most practical method of traveling. But to answer the question we need to know where the person
is going. If you are just going to the grocery story, jet travel is not
likely to be the most practical. But if you are going to Europe for a
vacation, it probably is.

In addition, *full* and *empty* are words of measure. Something is
full or empty according to some standard. For instance, full to the
nearest gallon will be different than full to the nearest quart. In order
to speak intelligently of something as being full or empty we need to
know the purpose it is being used for and the standard of measure to
be used. In order to say that Christ *fills all things* requires the definition of Christ's purpose and the measure by which to evaluate the
things to be filled. And that brings us to another issue.

All things is the English translation of one Greek word: πᾶς,
which can mean *all, any, every,* and even the *whole* of a thing. The
Greek phrase includes the nominative article τα, which makes πᾶς
definite. A literal translation might be *fill the all*. Because the purpose
of the Bible is to reveal and establish Jesus Christ as the Messiah of
God, and the true archetype of humanity, and because Paul knew this
and was writing specifically about this in all of his letters, we can understand Paul to have meant that Jesus Christ fulfills the purpose of
God in everything. Or to say it differently, *all things find their true
purpose in Christ*, and this is even more true regarding people.

Again, the role of Messiah to humanity is like the role of the
aleph-null to an infinite set in set theory, in that Messiah connects

Christ's church to the God of the Bible in a similar way that the aleph-null connects the members of an infinite set to the wholeness of the set. The point of making this comparison is to establish the reality of the idea of God in a way that conforms to the stringency of mathematical description in order to help people who have rejected traditional ideas about God to better understand reality, which issues from God. Of course, this analogy does not prove God, but it may move the conversation about God in a more productive way.

And by suggesting that reality issues from God, I don't simply mean to support the veracity of the first several chapters of Genesis with regard to creation, but I also mean to assert that nothing in the world can be understood correctly apart from God. God created all things, and the creator of a thing determines the purpose for the thing. Knowing a thing requires knowing its purpose and context. This is particularly true with regard to people.

What constitutes *fullness* depends on the purpose for which the fullness is required. Fullness leads to wholeness and completeness with regard to some purpose or standard. What we find in Scripture is not absolute proof for God, but a story about the development of human character, a system of improving humanity through honesty, integrity, and industry, beginning to end. God is the wholeness and holiness who is in the process of completing the highest moral purposes known to history. This is not an argument for works-righteousness, but it is an argument for Christian fruit.

23. Distribution & Maturity

And he gave the apostles, the prophets, the evangelists, the shepherds and teachers, to equip the saints for the work of ministry, for building up the body of Christ, until we all attain to the unity of the faith and of the knowledge of the Son of God, to mature manhood, to the measure of the stature of the fullness of Christ, so that we may no longer be children, tossed to and fro by the waves and carried about by every wind of doctrine, by human cunning, by craftiness in deceitful schemes. —Ephesians 4:11-14

Here Paul tells us how God provides the wholeness of the church. He does so by providing everything, every gift that the church needs to function. Of course, Paul's list does not name every conceivable gift or role in the church, but it does provide the roles and instructions it needed to begin—and that was Paul's role. We know that Paul intended many more roles and gifts than he named because he alluded to the full maturity of the church. Paul provided a list of the gifts necessary to begin and a vision of the full maturity of the church.

For the most part too many Christians have misunderstood what Paul said in these verses. When we think of ministry, of those who are in the ministry or those who do ministry we think of those Paul named: apostles, prophets, evangelists, shepherds, and teachers. We think of these people as those who are actually engaged in ministry. We think that the work of ministry is doing what apostles, prophets, evangelists, shepherds, and teachers do. But that is *not* what Paul said. Nonetheless, let's begin by examining Paul's list and see what ministry is not.

Apostles (ἀπόστολος) are to be engaged in politics. Strong's says that an apostle is a "delegate; specifically an ambassador of the Gospel; officially a commissioner of Christ." Notice that all of these words— delegate, ambassador, commissioner—describe politicians. Apostles are representatives who are to be engaged in the activities of representative government. And government is concerned with law, so these apostles were what we call *lawyers*. Most politicians are lawyers and all politicians work with law.

Prophets (προφήτης) are inspired speakers, what antiquity called *poets*. In the Old Testament prophets foretold the future, which amounts to speaking on behalf of God about God's decrees and plans. Paul borrowed the term and extended the domain of prophecy to include the manifestation of Jesus Christ, and the New Testament documents. In contemporary language we would call prophets *preachers*, because preachers today are to do what prophets of old did—explicate God's decrees and plans.

Strong's defines *evangelists* (εὐαγγελιστής) as preachers, which is not wrong, but is inadequate—not because of Paul's failure to convey his meaning, but because of our failure as a Christian culture to actually hear him. Our presuppositions, which have shaped our understanding of Christianity, preclude Paul's essential meaning. The *evangel* is the good news that Jesus Christ, the Messiah of God, has come to save the world. And evangelists are those who announce or broadcast this message. This means that evangelists announce and broadcast the good news messages that are formulated by prophets. The role of evangelists is to communicate God's truth and the way of Jesus Christ to others, as determined by the apostles in session. Evangelists deal with those who are outside the church, those who don't yet know Christ.

Shepherds (ποιμήν) care for sheep, Christ's people. Strong's calls them *pastors*. The pastoral role is patterned on the role of the shepherd to his sheep. Shepherds care for the flock. They provide them with adequate food and shelter, and protection from predators and mishaps. They also provide medical care when needed, which includes regular sheering. Unsheered sheep will not be healthy because their coats will become unmanageably long, filthy, and debris laden. Today, we would understand the central role of the pastor to be health related, which would include everything we identify in the healthcare industry—doctors, nurses, surgeons, dietitians, counselors, etc.

Teachers (διδάσκαλος), as Paul understood them, would be involved in what we call today *education*. We tend to think of education in secular terms today, but that is not how Paul thought of it. Nonetheless, teachers would be involved in everything that we know as the education industry today, from preschool to post-graduate education.

The important thing to see at this point is that none of these things were considered by Paul to be ministry. Sure, there is a sense that they are all service related occupations[1] and can be defined as ministry understood as service. Rather, all of these occupations are preparatory to the work of ministry. All of these are involved in training and maintaining ministry, they are not directly involved in ministry as such. Each of these gifts or roles or occupations have been given "to equip the saints for the work of ministry" (v. 12). The *Authorized Version* translated the phrase as "for the perfecting of the saints, for the work of the ministry."

Where the *Authorized Version* added a comma, the *English Standard Version* did not. The addition of the comma makes it seem as if the second clause is simply a restatement of the first, where the absence of the comma makes the second clause the object of the first. Regardless, the idea is that those occupations listed by Paul were to provide and serve those actually engaged in ministry. They are support services that prepare people to do ministry. But before we discuss ministry, we need to understand who is to be involved in it because none of those listed are to be engaged in the primary ministry of the church.

SAINTS

Those involved in ministry are the *saints* (ἅγιος). It is common for Protestants today to think of all Christians as being saints, in contrast to the Catholic idea that saints are canonized by the church. But both of these ideas are inadequate to the reality.

First, not all Christians are adequately prepared for ministry. And their preparation is the task of those who are apostles, prophets, evangelists, shepherds, and teachers. Because their preparation is the task

---

1   The Bible usually translates ἔργον as *works*, which Strong's defines as "business, employment, that which any one is occupied." Thus, it may be useful to rethink what the Bible says about *works* in terms of one's calling or occupation. The traditional opposition of faith and works is based on a false definition, which leads to a false dichotomy.

of these people, we must understand that those who are to be prepared are not yet prepared.

Christians are being prepared to be saints, to be sacred, pure,
morally blameless, religiously and ceremonially consecrated or separated from the sinfulness of the world. Christians are to separate
themselves from sin, not perfectly but adequately enough to begin to
grow in holiness and wholeness. The Christian way of life is different
and apart from the worldly way of life. This is taught everywhere in
the New Testament.

In the beginning we can think of these two ways of life as being
exclusive of one another, clearly separated from one another. But as
Christianity grows and engages the biblical dominion mandate[2] it interacts with the world through ministry and evangelism. And as the
church grows in the world, this interaction increases. What was originally black and white becomes grayed through interaction. Think of
the interaction as the circumference of a small but growing circle inside of a larger circle. As the smaller circle grows, its circumference
(the areas of interaction with the larger circle, the diameter) increases.

Also note that in this image only the circumference of the circle
interacts with what is outside of the circle. The action is always on
the margin. This suggests in a crude way that not all Christians are to
be engaged in evangelism. Rather, the overwhelming majority of
Christians will be involved in ministry, not evangelism. Nonetheless,
all Christians are called to be saints, to be holy, whole, sacred, pure,
morally blameless, religiously and ceremonially consecrated.

But this is not the work of ministry. Rather, it is the work of
preparation for ministry. The job of apostles, prophets, evangelists,
shepherds, and teachers is to help Christians to become increasingly
sanctified (or saint-ified, if I may wax creatively), to grow in faithfulness in preparation for ministry. Being sanctified essentially means
growing in Christian character or manifesting mature Christian fruit
—the fruit of the spirit (Galatians 5:22-23).

Second, I'm not saying that those who have been canonized by
the church are not saints. Rather, I'm saying that their canonization is
not necessary, and is even unbiblical because it creates a group of su-
per-saints. Nowhere in Scripture do we find any such practice. In
fact, we find that Paul calls such a practice *Gnostic* (2 Corinthians
11:5). While there is nothing wrong with studying and imitating
those who accede to the highest and most faithful lives of Christian

---

2   In Christ, the Genesis 1:28 mandate is given to Christ, Matthew 28:18-20.

character, we must always understand that Christ alone is the model Christian. He is the archetype of the new humanity-in-Christ, which we are to emulate every day, in every way. To lose sight of Christ as our model leads to the degradation of Christianity and the loss of its effectiveness in the world. We are not to emulate one another—not even the best and brightest. Rather, we must keep our eyes on Jesus Christ as the author and finisher of our faith (Hebrews 12:2).

MINISTRY

The function of ministry (διακονία), the central occupation of Christ's church is *attendance*—not like a fan attending a baseball game, but like a servant or a waiter waiting a table. To *attend* also suggests benevolent aid, and official service, service as an official. It is also historically related to teaching and the duties of the diaconate. Christians are to serve Jesus Christ first and foremost. And one's work is the primary channel of service. The modern idea of voluntary work and service creates another false dichotomy. Church work is not to be understood as the professional management of the church organization, or as voluntary work by the laity for the church organization. Rather, church work is the ordinary labor associated with one's calling, occupation, and/or employment.

Ministry does not mean what we call *church attendance* or *church involvement*. Rather, church involvement today is more related to the work of apostles, prophets, evangelists, shepherds, and teachers. And church attendance is more like a weekly pep rally or Bible study. For the most part we correctly understand ministry to be related to worship, but we mistakenly think that worship is no more than what happens in church on Sunday mornings.

We have confused the idea of *attendance*, meaning "to work for or be a servant to," with the idea of *attendance*, meaning "presence at an event." While there is nothing wrong with attending worship services at your local church, that's not what Paul was suggesting here. What we think of as the local church—the building down the street—was not in existence at the time. Sure, Paul was familiar with local synagogues, and they provided the model for Christian churches, but Paul was not growing a social organization called the *church*. He was growing the organism of Christ's body in the world. God's intention from the beginning has been to own human culture by eliminating all forms of culture that oppose Him. And this is the central idea that has driven cultural conflict wherever Christianity has spread. God's ultimate purpose is the elimination of sin and evil from human culture. God has been working to replace the culture of Sin[3] with the culture of Christ. The elimination of sin is actually a good thing!

We know that *liturgy* is defined as the work of the people, and we understand liturgy to be what happens in the church service on Sundays. We think that *liturgy* means the order of the Sunday worship service. Of course, it has come to mean that over time—and it is true to an extent. But there is so much more to real worship than what happens on Sundays. The Sunday service is only the tip of the worship iceberg. Understanding Christian worship correctly and fully (holistically) will seriously impact our understanding and definition of the Christian *church*. We need to understand these various terms biblically, and not rely upon our common usage because common usage obscured the biblical definitions eons ago. Common usage blinds us to the biblical meaning because the common usage has deteriorated the true biblical meaning.

This is only to say that over time language becomes a reflection of common usage rather than original intent. Such deterioration is a common consequent of human sin and of sin's god. God's purpose, from His calling of Abraham (Genesis 11:31) through Christ's advent (Matthew 1:1) and the return of Jesus Christ in glory (Revelation 21:1), has been to replace the culture of Sin with the culture of Christ. That purpose has unfolded over time eschatologically, which means that every generation is closer to the culmination of God's purpose than all previous generations.

Church Work

Thus, the work of Christ's church is to attend to Christ in the larger culture. Christians should think of themselves as servants (δοῦλος) of Christ (Romans 1:1). Christians are to run errands for the Master, to do the Lord's bidding, to wait on Christ like a servant, in the midst of whatever we are doing, whether at work, in worship, at home, and during recreation. Again, we are to wait on Christ like a waiter waits a table, and this is to be our central occupation. Is is not that we wait on the Lord in the midst of whatever else we are doing, like we are waiting for a bus. Rather, we are to do nothing else, to do everything for Christ's sake! Serving Christ is to be our central occupation, and everything else we do is to help perfect and complete that

---

3   See footnote 3, p. 57.

service. Christians are Christ's servants, and this service to Christ is Christian worship, regardless of place or time.

God's intention is for the body of Christ to become the corporate body of humanity, which then becomes by definition the heart of human culture. Christians are to separate themselves from the evil influences of Sin's culture by replacing those evil influences with the godly influence of Jesus Christ manifest in faithful believers.

Hebrews 10:25 cautions Christians to not neglect to meet together, and while such meetings are central to every church, they are not identical with regard to what we call today *church membership*. Hebrews 10:25 is simply the call to meet regularly with other believers—anywhere, not just at church, and not just with your local church. Jesus encouraged such meetings when He said,

> "For where two or three are gathered in my name, there am I among them" (Matthew 18:20).

The church is manifest wherever Christians meet in the name of Jesus Christ.

To be gathered in Jesus' name means to corporately manifest Jesus' character. Whenever we invoke Jesus' name we ask to be inhabited by His character. Those who meet in the name of Jesus Christ commonly confess their love and submission to Christ. Such meetings are tantamount to the meetings and gatherings of the servants of *Downton Abbey*.[4] The sole purpose of the servants in *Downton Abbey* was to attend to the wishes, well-being, and directions of the Lord of the manor. Similarly, Christians are to attend to the wishes, well-being, and direction of the Lord Jesus Christ, who is the Lord of human culture (Matthew 28:18-20). And the purpose of such meetings is

> "for building up the body of Christ" (v. 12).

Every Christian church is to be engaged in such building up or edifying (οἰκοδομή) of the body of Christ. But no single church or denomination can ever lay claim to being the whole body of Christ— nor the head of the church, for Christ is the Head, and He sent His representative, the Holy Spirit to serve in that role. Every church must avoid thinking and acting as if it alone is the whole body of Christ or the Head of the church. Rather, each Christian congrega-

---

4   The British period drama television series by the same name created by Julian Fellowes, which first aired in Great Britain in 2010 and in the United States in 2011.

tion is a part of the body in the same way that each individual member of a church is a part of that local church. Individual Christians are the living stones (1 Peter 1:5) of a local church, and each local church can be thought of as being a living wall, floor, window, door, etc., a part of Christ's whole body. Every part of the body is required to be what it is in order that the body may be whole. And no part is the whole, rather the whole manifests in, through, or as a different measure than the parts.

However, it is important that we don't think that Paul's understanding of church work is limited to working with what we call churches today. Rather, a fuller understanding includes what we call work—jobs—as being whatever we do to occupy our time. The work of Christ's church is to care for Christ's people, which includes business, medicine, education, production, manufacturing, research, etc. The things that develop the economy are the things that provide for God's people. And these things are also the work of ministry.

EDIFY

The work of the ministry is the building up or edification (οἰκοδομή) of the body of Christ (v. 12), the people of God. One English definition of edify is "make understand." Thus understood, the work of ministry is the effort to make the body of Christ a blessing to everyone everywhere at all times and in all places.

The Greek word οἰκοδομή (*edifying*) is composed of two words: οἶκος, which can mean *dwelling* or *household*, and δῶμα, which means *to build a roof*. The idea is to build households into the body of Christ. And households in Paul's day were also centers of business, production, manufacturing, research, etc.

> "And he gave the apostles, the prophets, the evangelists, the shepherds and teachers, to equip the saints for the work of ministry, for building up the body of Christ …" (v. 11-12).

We can now understand this verse to say that apostles, prophets, evangelists, pastors, and teachers are to prepare Christians to grow in spiritual maturity so that they can be attentive to Jesus Christ both personally and corporately in order to build (establish) such households into the body of Christ—all for the purpose of blessing others.

Individual Christians are called to manifest and develop their gifts in the world, which means the world of home, work, and leisure. This ministry is the calling and vocation of all Christians. Just as

Adam was given work to do in the garden—he was a taxonomist, so each individual has been given a job for which s/he has been gifted to engage for Christ. Some jobs and their requisite giftings are enjoyable and plush, and some aren't. Most are quite ordinary. All involve work. And all are necessary for the wholeness of the body.

Bodies grow, and during that growth they are always whole, at every stage. Infants are whole people, as are children and adults. This means that whatever wholeness is, it continues to be whole throughout the process of growth and maturation, which involves massive and dramatic bodily changes. And yet, human wholeness can be broken—and has been broken by sin. Sin, which is essentially the denial of God, amounts to the denial of one's own wholeness. Wholeness is like truth in the sense that the denial of truth doesn't make truth untrue. Nor does the denial of wholeness make wholeness unwhole. But denial of truth does effect human behavior, in that those who deny God and/or wholeness, cease to act on the basis of God and/or wholeness. Rather, they act on the basis of self. They act selfishly or self-centered rather than God-centered or centered in wholeness.

Individual Christians are called to ministry outside of what we currently think of as the church, in the larger culture in order to redeem the world. It is Christ's job to redeem the world, and He does it through the church—His people, who act as His body in the world. The redemption of the world is accomplished through liturgy, but not just the liturgy of the church during worship. That's important, sure. But it's just the tip of the liturgy iceberg. The bulk of Christian liturgy involves the work of the people through their calling, their vocation, including homemaking. In fact, homemaking (or household management—οἰκουρός) is at the heart of it.

Individual Christians are front line soldiers for Christ, not that they are all actively engaged in evangelism *per se* (spiritual combat). Most soldiers actually serve in support positions behind the lines, apart from combat. Similarly, most Christians provide support services for the body of Christ. Most Christians are to be actively engaged in the world, in the culture in which they live, in order to apply Christianity to the culture through their work (v. 12. ἔργον) and relationships. This is done by actually being faithful Christians twenty-four-seven. And the most important and effective field of evangelism is one's own home, and second is one's work.

In fact, no Christian can avoid this responsibility. We either do it well or we do it poorly, but our lives, our jobs, and our families pro-

vide testimony every day to the larger culture about the veracity of
Jesus Christ. It is not evangelism programs that move the gospel forward, it is ordinary Christians living, working, and playing for Christ
in the midst of ordinary living. And it is exactly here that Christianity
is losing the cultural war. It is not evangelistic tours by great evangelists that move the gospel forward, it is ordinary Christians who truly
love Jesus Christ in the midst of their ordinary lives, and who are
content to live quite lives for Christ (1 Timothy 2:2).

Super Christians (1 Corinthians 11:5, 12:11) tend to testify about
themselves, about their super accomplishments and exploits. It's not
always done explicitly, but is often done implicitly. Ordinary Christians don't need to speak about themselves when they live in simple
faithfulness. In fact, speaking about one's self brings attention to one's
self rather than to Christ. God loves it when we love Jesus in obedience to His commands and desires, even—especially—when no one is
watching, when no one cares. That makes a far better impression because its real, because it happens in the midst of ordinary life, because
it is not a performance for entertainment or self-aggrandizement.
This work (ἔργον) is done

> "for building up (or edification of) the body of Christ" (v. 12).

It is important to know who the recipients of this edification are,
who are being edified. Or stated negatively, if we don't know who is
to be edified, we can't possibly get the job done. And to get the job
done fully and completely, we must know who they *all* are.

TIME

Before we can consider the wholeness of the body of Christ we
must discuss *time* and the effects of time on the world and on the
things in the world. Most theologies do not consider time and the effects of time and maturity upon people or societies. People and societies grow, change, and mature. Individuals and societies do not need
to discard or ignore their original characteristics and/or values during
growth and maturity. Yet, those characteristics and values can change
considerably during the process—and yet remain the same. An old
man is the same person as he was as an infant, and yet he is quite different in every measure. The difference between the seed and the
plant pertains to both wholeness and time. The seed is the potential of
the plant, and the plant is the realization of the seed. And the transition from potential to realization happens in time. Growth involves

change, yet the thing that grows remains the same in some fundamental sense.

Time has one of two possible effects in the world, and those effects can be categorized in a variety of ways: life/death, light/dark, good/evil, etc. Time introduces and develops process.[5] Life grows things and death decays them. Both are processes in the world in which we actually live. Both are active and both happen in time.

The church or body of Christ is the primary object for edification, and edification is a process that takes time. To edify the church means to make Christians understand the Bible, Christ, Christianity, the Gospel, the Holy Spirit, etc. The job of apostles, prophets, evangelists, pastors, and teachers is to make the church understand all of these things. And the church is then to take that understanding to the world by building on it through their work, the liturgy of life in Christ. Non-Christians will ideally then see the difference that the church makes in the lives of her people, and want what they have— faith in Christ. Those people will then come to the church because they want to learn about Christ. The model is pretty simple—attract unbelievers to the goodness, beauty, and truth of God-in-Christ.

UNTIL

Christians are to engage in this edification

"until we all attain to the unity (ἑνότης) of the faith" (v. 13).

Attain makes it sound like unity is something that we have to achieve. And while that is a popular idea, it is wrong. Christian unity is God-given, not humanly attained, though it manifests cumulatively over time. Unity grows because populations increase. Unity is the state of wholeness, and wholeness is not the responsibility of the parts to attain, but is the reality in which parts cohere. The meaning of the parts is found only in the whole. What is part cannot become whole in and of itself. Even though all of the parts are necessary for wholeness, the

---

5   Process philosophy is implied, but not in its established forms (A.N. Whitehead, Charles Hartshorne, etc.). Process philosophy to date has been more influenced by Greek Philosophy and evolutionary science than biblical Christianity. Nonetheless, the point is that time plays a very important role in the world and must not be denied. Process philosophy tries to account for change and development. Following Plato, philosophers have posited true reality as being *timeless*, based on permanent substances unaffected by time, which remain the same regardless of time or place. This view has crept into Christianity through the influence of Greek philosophy. However, the process of time is real and must be taken into account. Conversely, the denial of the reality of the impact of time is a form of Gnosticism.

whole is greater than the sum of the parts. It exists in a different order, by a different measure.

While the Greek word καταντάω is translated as *attain* (*English Standard Version*) and *come* (*Authorized Version*), it is composed of two words: κατά, which suggests various kinds of joining together, and a derivative of ἀντί (anti), which means *opposite*. The idea is that opposites (or different faces) come together (or face one another). Their unity is the fact of their togetherness, their facing one another, their conversation—not their agreement. Though *unity* and *wholeness* are different words, they share the common idea of oneness, accord, and harmony—and that's the general idea conveyed here. Harmony and accord don't mean that everyone plays the same note at the same time. The unity of the church is a unity of what sometimes seems like opposing or different ways of understanding. It is the unity of opposites or opposition. Actually, the unity is refined and established through the process of opposition, discussion, and resolution. Thus, real unity is not possible without the inclusion of opposition (1 Corinthians 11:19).

Faithful Christians need opposition in order to shape and strengthen their faith. Without opposition there is no personal, felt need to dig deeper into the Scriptures to discover what Scripture actually says. Oppositionless faith produces weak Christianity, which quickly becomes something other than or less than true Christianity. Anyone who has grown in their faith knows what it is like to grow out of one kind of belief structure and into another. Paul pressed this argument to the Corinthians.

> "For, in the first place, when you come together as a church, I hear that there are divisions among you. And I believe it in part, there must be factions among you in order that those who are genuine among you may be recognized" (1 Corinthians 11:18-19).

All Christians tend to grow out of and into various sorts of factions. Factions are necessarily based on partial truth, by definition. Factions always dissent from the majority opinion. Factions work to produce clarity and maturity as the dominant opinion is shaped in its response to the particular issues brought into conflict by the factions. Time brings fluidity and dynamism into the mix. Thus, the kind of unity that Paul wrote about is not simple descriptive unanimity. It is not cookie-cutter Christianity where everyone parrots the same ideas and explanations. Rather, Paul's understanding of unity is dynamic and multifaceted. It is Proverbs 27:17 unity where "iron sharpens iron, and one man sharpens another." It is possible to describe the same truth in different ways, from different perspectives.

In the midst of this kind of unity there is doctrinal sword wielding combat. Sparks fly in the process, which produce smoke and heat as well as light. This kind of unity is not simple doctrinal agreement. Rather, it is characterized by deep commitment to principles and bold defense of God's truth. Yet, the commitment to God's truth must be so strong and faithful that it is able to recognize both the importance and inclusion of weaker brothers who believe differently, and stronger sisters who provide better expressions of God's truth. All believers must make necessary adjustments to their biblical principles in order to be better aligned with the weaker brother and the greater truth of the stronger sister. Faithfulness to God's truth accommodates superior arguments from improved lighting (in the light of Christ). Faithfulness to God adjusts the principles of God's truth when better light is made available. And God's people come to understand that such adjustments are necessary to stay on course, to stay on the path (Acts 24:14) in the dynamic world of time.

Truth existing in time is dynamic, not static. Truth doesn't change, but people who exist in time grow and mature. The whole truth itself doesn't change. Rather, our understanding of truth in time follows a path of maturity that is true to God's original decree, true to God's initial hope and plan for the world. Truth in time is like a cannon ball in motion, following a trajectory to its intended target. Truth in time can also be like a rocket to Mars that uses the gravity of another body, like the moon or the sun, to slingshot to its destination. The trajectory is always true to its aim, its intended end, target, or goal, though dynamic in its course. The reality of truth in time is far more complex than previously imagined, and beyond what is imaginable today. Truth in time is the path that actually gets you to God's intended destination. And variation from that path is always an error.

Our understanding of truth is refined in time by wrestling with those who oppose our best personal understandings of truth. Whatever you or I think can be no more than a faction (or fraction) of the whole truth. Similarly, no individual Christian can fully comprehend the magnificence of the whole of God's truth. Our understanding is enhanced and expanded through the challenge of wrestling with opposing ideas, descriptions, and explanations. But our wrestling must be engaged in love with honesty, integrity, and industry in order to maintain the connections that are required by the whole. This is part of the practice of holiness or whole-iness.

KNOWLEDGE OF THE SON OF GOD

There's more. Unity apart from knowing God is futile. So Paul also insisted on knowing God personally. Notice however, that knowing God personally is not enough, not sufficient. Our knowledge of God must also lead to unity,

> "until we all attain to the unity ... of the knowledge of the Son of God" (v. 13).

It's not so much that we are all to know the same things in the same ways, but that we are all to know the same Person—Jesus Christ. And as with all persons, no two individuals have exactly the same experience of the same person. Sure, we know the same person in similar ways, but we also know different things that are learned from different experiences of the person. Even when people experience something together in the same place and at the same time, there are differences in their perspectives. Yet, Christians are to be in unity of some sort.

The Gnostics were right, in that knowledge is involved in the process of salvation. But they were wrong about its source and where it comes in the process. Knowledge is a product of perception, and perception is a product of perspective. A thing can be perceived (seen) from different perspectives, from different people, positions, or locations. Knowledge comes from analysis of what is perceived or seen, and differing perspectives yield different results, different evaluations. Yet, the object of knowledge is often the same for the varying perspectives.

Thus, knowledge alone does not help us see or understand the world better. Rather, better knowledge is the *result* of seeing the world from a better perspective. Better knowledge about our perspective does not provide us with a better perspective, though it can clarify our existing perspective. Rather, a better perspective provides us with more knowledge. While knowledge does increase from seeing a thing from a variety of perspectives, we must have a standard in order to measure and analyze the target of our perception. It is the comparison of the standard with the experience or perception that allows the knowledge to increase.

PERSPECTIVE

In the physical world we can think of perspective as a function of location. Changing one's location provides a different perspective. But there is a deeper sense where one's perspective is a function of worldview—values and presuppositions. Our values and presuppositions (morals and beliefs) shape the way we see things.

The classic face or vase optical illusion provides an illustration. Looking at the black we see a vase. But when we look at the white within the box we see two faces looking at each other. While there is no change of location on our part, there is a change of perspective that illustrates how presuppositions or values shape what we see. When we focus on the black we see the black as substance and the white as empty space. But when we focus on the white we see the white as substance and the black as empty space. In one we value or believe in the substantial reality of the black and in the other we value or believe in the substantial reality of the white. This simple, two-dimensional example suggests how what we value can effect us in more significant ways.

Again, knowledge alone cannot provide us with a different or expanded perspective because knowledge is the analysis of our perspective. Knowledge can increase our understanding of our perspective, but it cannot provide us with a different perspective. To get a different perspective in the more significant sense of the term, we must transcend and/or expand the limitations of our own perspective. And this is like pulling ourselves up by our own bootstraps—it cannot be done. Rather, it can only be done with outside help. We cannot do it to ourselves by ourselves.

Thus, the expansion, growth, and/or change of perspective requires an other, someone who's perspective is different than one's own. This is true on an individual basis, and on a social, corporate, or human basis, as well. Interaction with other people can expand our perspectives, values, and worldviews. And this is a good thing. However, interaction with others cannot reveal truth because social interaction cannot get us beyond a human-centric perspective. Other people only provide other opinions, other perspectives, not objective truth. To get beyond a human-centric perspective we must communicate with a superior perspective, and the mode of that communication must be receptive. For instance, we cannot express something that is greater (more intelligent, more sublime, more whole, etc.) than we are. But we can receive an expression of something greater than we are.

Real growth and maturity that results in a more objective perspective requires the reception of communication from outside of ourselves. And, by the same logic, from a corporate perspective, it requires the reception of communication from outside of humanity.[6] Yet, there must be a human receptor in order to receive and complete the communication circuit that comes from outside of humanity. Thus, we receive the best possible communication (defined as the most whole or holy) from God through Christ via the Holy Spirit, but only through Christ because only Christ is both fully divine and fully human. The sinlessness of Christ is required for the undiluted and unpolluted reception of the purity of God's truth (the content of His communication).

We can think of this communication (communion) as trinitarian because it comes from the Trinitarian God. There are three necessary facets for communication to be complete: sender, receiver, and conduit The meaning, message, or information exists at a different level or measure. God is the sender, Christ is the receiver, and the Holy Spirit is the conduit of the communication. The Holy Spirit makes contact with people; His form inhabits them. God satisfies the condition of otherness because He is perfectly and uniquely holy (whole). Christ, being a member of the Trinity Himself, alone qualifies as a worthy receiver of God's truth because His worthiness issues from His purity, His sinlessness, which guarantees that sin will not contaminate God's message. Christ alone can receive God's message without the contamination of sin. Christ's reception of God's message (or perspective) insures that the message is received by humanity because Christ is fully human.

The Holy Spirit, being the conduit of God's message, is in contact with God through Christ to individual believers, and thus provides for the transmission of God's truth (or perspective) in real time, in history, in the dynamic present—not completely or perfectly, but adequately. Christ sends the Holy Spirit to dwell with and inform His

---

6   Once life is started, it converts energy from its environment, the sun, other forms of life, etc., into energy for sustenance and growth. But because all life is biogenetic or self-creating, the first instance of life must have been exceptional. The energy or information necessary for life must have come from somewhere outside of the natural world(s), because non-living matter cannot beget life, as we understand it.

people, both individually and corporately, to provide God's truth (or perspective) as Christ's people engage their own various spiritual gifts within the resurrected (living) body of Christ, also known as His church. This is the knowledge of the Son of God that Paul spoke about.

In addition, we can now see that Christ's church involves and includes all of the various giftings or bodily functions necessary for His life in this world. The wholeness of Christ's body cannot possibly be contained in any single denomination, nor even within what we call *churches* today. The word *denomination* necessarily signifies a subclass or faction, by definition. Christ's body includes far more than what has been traditionally or currently thought of by any denomination. In fact, God has been creating Christ's body in history, and His body will not be complete or fully mature until God's end purpose is achieved, when Christ delivers the kingdom to God (1 Corinthians 15:24). This delivery constitutes a bestowal or investiture of a new being or way of being for humanity that is sanctioned by God, and therefore, is indefinitely sustainable on earth.

MATURE MANHOOD

We are to continue in this vein

> "until we all attain ... to mature manhood" (v.13). The Authorized Version translates it as "unto a perfect man."

The Greek word translated as *mature* or *perfect* is τέλειος, which, as we know, means *end purpose*. Because our trinitarian identity in Christ includes both our individuality and our corporality, there are two senses or meanings here.

There is the sense of our individual maturity, which means our personal maturity *in Christ*. This maturity involves the mastery of (or by) the fruit of the spirit that Paul named in Galatians 5:22-23:

> "love, joy, peace, patience, kindness, goodness, faithfulness, gentleness, self-control," and generalized in Ephesians 5:9: "for the fruit of light is found in all that is good and right and true."

The maturity that Paul alluded to is Christian maturity or mastery of (through submission to) biblical morality in the light of Christ. This must not be confused with displays of pious preening and/or the pretense of superiority that is too often found among too many peo-

ple of various sorts, and whom Christ warned against in His parable
in Luke 18:9-14:

> "He also told this parable to some who trusted in themselves that
> they were righteous, and treated others with contempt: 'Two men
> went up into the temple to pray, one a Pharisee and the other a
> tax collector. The Pharisee, standing by himself, prayed thus:
> "God, I thank you that I am not like other men, extortioners, un-
> just, adulterers, or even like this tax collector. I fast twice a week; I
> give tithes of all that I get." But the tax collector, standing far off,
> would not even lift up his eyes to heaven, but beat his breast, say-
> ing, "God, be merciful to me, a sinner!" I tell you, this man went
> down to his house justified, rather than the other. For everyone
> who exalts himself will be humbled, but the one who humbles
> himself will be exalted.'"

The second sense of this maturity applies to the body of Christ as
a whole and involves, not mere institutional maturity regarding the
coordinated function of the body of Christ as a whole, but also includes the institutionalization of the fruit of the spirit in human culture, such that all of the individuals involved function maturely
through the generous manifestation of Christian fruit.

And just in case there is any doubt about how far Paul thinks this
maturity ought to go, he added:

> "until we all attain ... to the measure of the stature of the fullness
> of Christ" (v. 13).

While Christians do not become God or Christ as the result of union
with Christ, that union brings us as close as possible to Christ-likeness
without obscuring our own individual identity or uniqueness. It
means that we are to follow Christ, not to the cross on which He
died, but to the life He would live had He not died and was in our
shoes today. This doesn't mean that Christians have to do the very
same things that Christ did, but that Christians are to respond to their
own unique circumstances, challenges, and opportunities as Christ
would. We are to replicate His character, not His actions.

Asking "What would Jesus do?" is a very appropriate way to live
in Christ, as long as we answer the question biblically and then actually do what Jesus would do. However, Jesus would not need to wear
a bracelet with WWJD emblazoned on it in order to remind Himself
of this obligation. In fact, Jesus would likely reject such a vain display
on the basis that wearing such a thing is an expression of false piety

because it issues out of pride, in the sense that it either can give the impression of faithfulness without actually engaging in faithfulness, or that its purpose is to give others the impression of one's spiritual superiority.

Asking what Jesus would do in such and such a situation is a function of prayer, and Jesus directed us to

> "go into your room and shut the door and pray to your Father who is in secret. And your Father who sees in secret will reward you" (Matthew 6:6).

Actually following Jesus is never a function of popularity, where popularity means thinking alike, acting alike, or looking alike, because every Christian has been gifted differently for different callings, different functions in the body of Christ. And the different members of a body don't perform the same function. They don't act alike or look alike, though they function harmoniously.

Why?

Paul hoped "that we may no longer be children" (v. 14) as a result of maintaining unity, that we might grow up. Implicit in this hope is his accusation that the Ephesians were in fact children at the time, and that all who have not completed this process are still children in the faith. This necessarily stands as an accusation of the whole church of Jesus Christ until all Christians have attained to this measure. And because Christians are always being born and born again, this is an eternal concern, and an ongoing process.

The point is that Christians begin as children because they have been born again in Christ. Infants begin life feeding on milk and are weened to solid food over time. Paul understood himself to be feeding new Christians with milk (1 Corinthians 3:2). He was not suggesting that milk is bad. It's not. It is necessary—and so is graduating to solid food. Just as Paul was concerned that the Corinthian church was not growing properly, evidenced by its addiction to spiritual milk, he was concerned in the same way with the Ephesian church, as is evidenced here.

It should also be noted that Paul counted himself as a child here: "so that *we* may no longer be children" (v. 14). Paul understood the relationship between individual Christians and the wholeness of the church. He knew that the maturity of individual Christians is related to the maturity of the church as a whole. Individual parts don't grow beyond the character of the whole. While he may have considered himself to be more mature than most at the time, he also realized that the church as a whole would mature through history and surpass whatever level of maturity he had personally attained. This does not mean that the church would one day outgrow its need for Paul—not at all! Rather, because new Christians would always be coming into the church, they would always need to reference Paul's historic place and teachings as an Apostle. Christians must always follow in the historical trajectory of God's plan for the world.

TOSSED

Paul looked forward to the day when Christians would not be

> "tossed to and fro by the waves and carried about by every wind of doctrine" (v. 14).

Again, this phrase suggests that Paul found this to be a common problem in the churches of his day. He was well aware of the struggle to establish orthodox doctrine. We know this because Paul was constantly arguing with various false apostles, not just misinformed Christians or theologians, but people who had usurped the highest echelons of Christian leadership (2 Corinthians 11:5, 12:11).

The early church was not a bastion of faithful orthodoxy and orthopraxy, but was a cauldron of strife and struggle—as the church has always been. The entire history of Christianity is the expression of birth pangs (Galatians 4:19, Revelation 12:2). The teachings of Paul and the Apostles contradicted both tradition and common sense among the ancient Jews, Greeks, and Romans. The teachings of the church disturbed common ideas about truth and reality. They challenged and upset social, religious, academic, and governmental ideas, practices, and policies. Christians were thought to be atheists by the religious standards that were most common at the time because the Christians believed the usual gods of Greek and Roman culture to be false gods.

Paul was aware of all of this, and looked forward to a day when the church would grow beyond these kinds of childish concerns. It is not that childishness is a bad thing. It is not! But if children do not continue to grow to maturity, their childishness becomes a problem. Children are necessarily childish, but childish adults are problematic on several levels.

Part of our maturity must include growth in doctrine (διδαχή). *Doctrine* means the substance of the teaching or the lesson. But this is not the form of the word used here. Paul used διδασκαλία, which points to the process of teaching or the instructor. The various *winds of doctrine* refers more to the various instructors than to the content of their teaching. While every instructor may intend to teach the same doctrine, each will come at it from a particular perspective and emphasize different elements. The phrase means that we are to distinguish between the essential doctrine and the individual emphasis of the instructors who teach it. The different parts of doctrine that are emphasized by different instructors are not as important as the parts of doctrine that the instructors agree on. Not all instructors will agree, so there is a concern about orthodox doctrine. We are to focus on the commonalities not the differences.

We are not to get carried away with doctrinal differences, but are to remain grounded on the true doctrinal commonalities. The issue here is unity, and unity is maintained by holding to what we have in common, and not dividing over our every difference. It is not that we are to ignore our differences or try to meld them into a common idea. No, our differences are what make life interesting. Our differences drive the pursuit for clarity, compassion, and comprehension. We need to discuss and evaluate our differences, but not divide over them. By remaining in unity (Paul called us to *maintain* it, Ephesians 4:3) while defending our differences, we set up a kind of creative tension in the church that drives biblical research and development. The purpose of Christian unity is not to have all Christians thinking the same things in the same ways. Rather, it is to have Christians from different perspectives contributing to a common trajectory or body of thought. Christian unity is the commitment to remain together in spite of our differences.

Of course there are limits to Christian unity. Heresy is real and apostasy is a constant danger. However, the determination and/or accusation of heresy and apostasy are not the responsibility or jurisdiction of individual believers. Time and again, Paul assigned those responsibilities to church elders. It is incumbent upon us to give that responsibility to our church elders and to support their conclusions and processes. I'm not saying that ordinary Christians should refrain from doctrinal discussion. Rather, I'm saying that ordinary Christians should feel free to discuss and defend doctrine with all of their abilities. But at the end of the argument, they must not break fellowship unless explicitly instructed to do so by their own elders.

When iron sharpens iron (Proverbs 27:17) sparks fly and the iron gets dented. In the process of sharpening the iron can get hot and even smoke at times. The dents, the smoke, and the heat are all part of the sharpening process. The discipline of Christian unity is not getting all Christians to think alike, but is the steadfast refusal to break fellowship with those with whom one disagrees. Unity is more moral commitment than doctrinal agreement. And this is the difficulty of unity. It takes patience, endurance, love, forgiveness, and understanding. None of these character qualities are advanced by only talking with those who agree with you.

Cunning Schemes

We can also be carried away by "human cunning" (v. 14), or "cunning craftiness" in the *Authorized Version*. These words translate the single Greek word πανουργία, which is made of up of two words: παν (*all*) and ουργία (a conjugation of *work*). Strong defines it as adroitness, trickery, or sophistry. We can think of it as work that is all about humanity, or work that is centered in humanity, or humanism. Think of Satan in the Garden of Eden, who "was more *crafty* than any other beast of the field that the LORD God had made" (Genesis 3:1). This is the craft of human cunning, or human-centered thinking.

Part of this cunning is further specified in Paul's next phrase, where he cautions Christians not to get caught "by craftiness in deceitful schemes" (v. 14). The *Authorized Version* reads, "whereby they lie in wait to deceive." We understand this as an ambush, but the Greek carries the sense of fraud, where something false or of lesser value is substituted for something true or of greater value. Fraud is exactly what the false apostles were doing, which means that the church was at best tempted to believe lies, and at worst had already swallowed too many lies.

The root meaning of the Greek word μεθοδεία (*deceive*, v. 14) is *method*, a way of doing something, or a system. Paul was not opposed to systems *per se*, but to fraudulent (πλάνη) systems. The problem is not having a system, but having the wrong or faulty system. The problem with humanism is that it leaves the biblical God out of its system, or we might say that it substitutes its system for God.

Verses 13 and 14 compose a complete idea of the purpose for building up the body of Christ, which is the establishment of Christianity, both God's grace and the work of the church. The work of the church is the growth and maintenance of unity. Fighting and arguing is easy, and they have a long tradition in the world. Disunity is like water in that it naturally runs downhill. It requires no effort for it to naturally follow gravity.

Grace & Work

Neither Scripture generally nor Paul specifically set grace and work in opposition to one another. Sure, they are quite different ideas and it is useful to contrast them, but both are necessary for a complete understanding of the gospel. Let me suggest that the interpreters may have erred by translating ἔργον as *works*, in the plural. To put it in the plural makes it into a noun, and it's a verb. While there has been a lot of good, and much clarification that has resulted from the idea of *works* and its opposition to *grace*, there has also been a lot of harm and confusion that have resulted from it. It might be helpful to return to the original meaning of *work* as a verb rather than a noun, and see what comes of it as we rethink some of the classic verses and related historical conflicts.

Think of *work* as one's calling, occupation, vocation, or one's place and function in the body of Christ. In this way, work is not done in order to justify one's faith, nor to garner entrance into the church, nor to impress God or anyone else in any way. Just as Adam was in the Garden to work, so Christ is in the world to work. Work is essential to human identity, health, and longevity. God has a purpose for the world, and the work of His people contributes to the fulfillment of that purpose.

The unity of the church is a gift of God's grace that is undeserved, unwarranted, unlimited, and too often undervalued. Nonetheless, the maintenance of the unity of the church is part of the work of the church. The work of the church is to work together harmoniously. And it's hard work! It augers against the natural gravity of human relationships by applying the supernatural glory of God's grace. The gift is free, its maintenance is hard work. The gift requires no effort to receive, but its maintenance requires more effort than we alone can muster. The help of the Holy Spirit is needed. In addition, it requires the full array of Godly disciplines—contemplation, fasting, study, prayer, worship, rest, silence, solitude, and service. And it manifests the full harvest of spiritual fruit—love, joy, peace, patience, kindness, goodness, faithfulness, gentleness, self-control, etc. Where church unity exists, you will find these disciplines and fruits, and where it doesn't, you won't. We will indeed know Christ's disciples by their fruit. However, it takes one to know one.

The "deceitful schemes" (v. 14) that Paul had in mind involve fraudulent methods that substitute one thing for another in the language of the church. The problem with deceit is that it is difficult to detect unless one knows the truth that the deceit intends to hide. For instance, when Paul wrote that we are

> "saved through faith; and that not of yourselves: it is the gift of
> God" (Ephesians 2:8),

he did not mean that we are saved by our own faith. Rather, we are saved by the faith of Jesus Christ, the faith that led Christ to the cross. That faith, Christ's faith, is then given to believers as a gift of God.

Of course other verses do suggest that people are saved by their own faith. For instance,

> "he said to the woman, 'Your faith has saved you; go in peace'"
> (Luke 7:50).

Yet, the actual faith of the woman was her belief that Christ's faith or faithfulness was the cause of her salvation. She was not saved because she believed in Christ. Rather, she was saved by the faith of Jesus Christ that God would redeem His people as a result of Christ's propitiation. Because she had faith that God would redeem His people, she received the gift of faith *in Christ* because Christ was the vehicle through which God would save His people.

The fraudulent schemes regarding faith include the idea that people can be saved because they have the personal strength of character *in themselves* to conjure up enough faith to convince God to save them. The fraud substitutes *their own faith* for *the faith of Jesus Christ*. The faith of Jesus Christ involves everything involved in His fulfillment of the Old Testament prophesy about the Messiah. The fraud is believing that we have the character in ourselves to believe in Jesus, which gives us the ability in ourselves to decide what is true and what is not. The fraud is that we can believe in Jesus without believing that the whole Bible is completely trustworthy, that we can decide what is true and what is not, apart from God and His Word.

Lord, deliver the church from such delusion!

24. WHOLE LOVE

Rather, speaking the truth in love, we are to grow up in every way into him who is the head, into Christ, from whom the whole body, joined and held together by every joint with which it is equipped, when each part is working properly, makes the body grow so that it builds itself up in love.
—Ephesians 4:15-16

Speaking the truth is difficult, especially in the contemporary world where science and technology have so changed everything previously understood, and have forever changed the way that people live in the world. Science has shown us that things are far more complex than our ancestors could imagine, more complex that we can still imagine. There are no simple truths for contemporary people. There never actually were, but when life was more simple (natural, or without the aid of modern science), people were less aware of and dependent upon scientific complexities.

In addition, love as Christ has expounded it is difficult. Christ calls us to love our enemies. We cannot ignore them, nor can we expect them to love us. We have to find ways to love them, which means that we must understand them to a degree in order to communicate with them. It is difficult enough to communicate with people we love and trust, as anyone who is married can attest. Love and communication with enemies demands great patience and special grace.

Here Paul calls us to speak the truth in love, which means the exercise of that patience and reliance upon that special grace. The Greek word (αληθεύ) translated *speaking the truth,* is actually a negative word because it contains the prefix ἀ, which means *not.* The rest of the word refers to something that has been hidden, even unwittingly hidden. The word means *not hidden, not ignored.* And the love (ἀγάπη) in which we are to speak the truth is agape love, unconditional love that is expressed in action as service. Agape love is love that is not hidden, diminished, or muted.

Paul's message was that we are not to hide the truth in love, or *with* love. Christian love, expressed as service or help, is not to hide the truth. Of course, we are to speak lovingly—kindly. But our kindness must not cover over or hide the truth. And all truth is God's truth. People usually understand this to mean that we are to speak the hard truths with kindness, and this is true. But it also means that we are not to ignore or hide doctrinal truth with love and acts of mercy. We are to do acts of mercy *and* speak words of truth.

To grow (αὐξάνω) is to increase. Growing children get bigger, growing adults get wiser. To *grow up* means to increase in maturity and wisdom. To grow up *into* Christ means to use Christ as the model for our maturity. We are to model Christ, and Paul provided the example (1 Corinthians 4:16, 11:1). In order to grow in maturity in Christ we must imitate Paul and the Apostles with increasing accuracy. We must follow more closely, not the actions of the Apostles, but their character qualities.

Every Way

We are to grow up into Christ in *every* way! The *Authorized Version* translated πᾶς as "in all things" (v. 15). The word simply means *all, any, every,* or *whole,* and here it suggests the extent of our salvation. We could say that *for the Christian* there is no area of life that is exempt from Christ's Lordship. But if we exclude non-Christians by suggesting that they are exempt from the Lordship of Christ, that would mean that there are some areas or lives (those of non-Christians) that are exempt from Christ's Lordship. But there are not! God is sovereign over *all* creation, and God has given Christ *all* authority. So, there are no people, nor any areas of life that are exempt from Christ's Lordship.

But, you might object, *what about unbelievers who reject Christ?* Most people think that before any such decision is made, people are simply neutral, neither bound for heaven nor for hell. But that is not what the Bible teaches! The Bible teaches that sin poisoned the world and the minds of men long before Jesus came along. And that Jesus came along *because* the whole world had been poisoned by sin.

The truth is that sin has already poisoned the minds of everyone born since Adam and destined humanity to hell and damnation. We do not begin life in a neutral position. We begin on the train to hell.

Christ has come with a plan to stop the train. It is not just that He provides a way for individuals who agree with His plan to get off the train. There is some truth to this idea, but the whole truth is that His plan is to stop the train that threatens humanity with death and destruction. And to accomplish that plan He will need His people on the train. If all of the Christians get off the train, who will stop it? The right answer is that Christ Himself will stop it, but He will stop it as He does everything else—through His people. The Christian calling is not to get off the train, but to stop it from landing in hell. Christianity is not an escapist option for cowards, but is a call to action for everyone.

This fact then suggests the extent of the salvation that Christ offers. There is a long-standing discussion about whether the efficacy of the cross extends to all people, or just to believers. The problem with this discussion is that it ignores the effects of *time* by pretending that time makes no difference.

Scripture teaches that God intends to save humanity from eternal destruction, extinction. And it teaches that *only* believers will be saved. We reconcile these teachings by considering the impact of time. Christ came to save all of humanity, but He first came to a small group of people in Palestine a long time ago. He came to save a group in every age. So, while He began a long time ago with a small group of people, when His purpose is finally accomplished in the future, all who survive to the end will believe. But in the unfolding process of time and history, many people will not believe and will be lost to damnation.

And their damnation has been authorized by Jesus Christ because He has been given all authority. Christ's role in the world is both unitary and divisive. He unites believers by sequestering them from unbelievers. He authorizes believers to work for the salvation of all of His people, and agrees with God that the unrepentant have no inheritance in the kingdom.

The bottom line is that the group of believers, known as the church, began small, and has grown through the centuries, and will one day not only dominate the whole world, but will include every extant human being. That's a long way off, and it will not occur until Christ returns in glory. But at that point *all* humanity (say ninety to ninety-nine percent) will be believers of some sort. This does not mean that absolutely every individual will believe perfectly—of course not. The point is that the church began with a small group of people and will one day include all but a tiny sliver of humanity. But it takes time. And furthermore, it means that the mechanism of salvation is the church and the target for salvation is not just random individuals but the culture or the whole of human culture. The culture will be turned toward Christ as the majority of individuals become active, involved and faithful Christians in their society and follow Christ in every way.

Head

Without question, Christ is the head of the church, the source. But because the church is called to be leaven for the culture, and to impact culture in every way, we must also come to understand that Christ is the head and source of the culture, too—the whole culture—because He has been given all authority (Matthew 28:18).

Many people will not understand how this can be true, especially in a culture like ours that openly rejects Christ. Well, the rejection of Christ does not mean that Christ is not sovereign. In fact, all who reject Christ continue on to hell and damnation, and do so by the authority of Christ. However, the situation is *not* that Christ sends innocent people to hell. Rather, Christ agrees with God that unrepentant sinners have no place in heaven, and when they refuse to take the opportunity to repent, to rethink their lives and habits in the light of Christ, when they reject the help that Christ alone provides, that rejection means that they would rather continue on their journey to hell.

Paul championed Christ's headship in Ephesians 1:22 when he said that God

> "put all things under his feet and gave him (Christ) as head over all things to the church."

Paul used the same word for *all things* (πᾶς) in Ephesians 4:15. Note that everything is subjugated to God, and Christ's headship over all things has been given to the church. Christ's headship over all things means that Christ can direct all things, like the head directs the body. And in the same way, the head of the church directs the body of the church. The head and body, though different, are not separated. They function together in unity in order to fulfill Genesis 1:28, the dominion mandate:

> "And God blessed them. And God said to them, 'Be fruitful and
> multiply and fill the earth and subdue it, and have dominion over
> the fish of the sea and over the birds of the heavens and over every
> living thing that moves on the earth'" (Genesis 1:28).

Under the leadership and direction of Christ, the church or body of Christ has dominion over all things. And indeed, we find that in the current era, science and technology have given humanity such dominion. Obviously, this does not mean that what we call churches have political dominion over all human culture, nor that they should have. Rather, we must understand that what we usually call churches and what the Bible means by the term *church* are not the same things. The differences are many and significant.

Nonetheless, humanity as a whole does currently have (or nearly so) the kind of dominion over the earth as is suggested in Genesis 1:28. The only thing left to accomplish in order to complete that task now is the dominion of humanity by Christ, the head of the church. However, we must not conclude along with the Roman Catholics that such headship belongs to the Pope or to any other human being. It belongs to Jesus Christ by the power and presence of the Holy Spirit through the regeneration of humanity as a whole.

The usurpation of Christ's archetypal role in the lives of His people is a common and serious error of judgment. People are too quick to use Christianity for their own purposes, whether the codification of belief or the regulation of behavior in ways that exceed what God has provided in Christ. Codification and regulation tend to diminish reliance upon the Holy Spirit. And such reliance is necessary to cope with the dynamics of change involved in population growth and maturity in this world.

What works in one place and time does not necessarily work in all places and times. What works for a city of five thousand does not work for a city of five million. Policies and programs issue out of Phariseeism. However, the Christian character traits modeled and taught by Jesus Christ do, in fact, work everywhere. Christianity is about character not public policy, except that public policy must not discourage the development of Christian character.

If Christ is the human archetype that has replaced Adam in his original archetypal role, then Christ's role as archetype applies to all humanity. And the Bible clearly teaches that Christ is the new human norm or archetype. Sure, there will be some individual deviation from the norm, but humanity has been created to function best when individuals operate within the bounds of Christian norms, the archetype of Jesus Christ. A norm does not require one hundred percent compliance in order to be a norm, neither do minor deviations from the norm make the model not a norm.

JOINTS JOINED

Paul goes on to say that each joint of the body in union with the head supplies its particular function to the whole body. The Greek word translated *body* here is σῶμα (*sōma*), not σάρξ (*sarx*).[1] The difference is that *sōma* refers more to a corporate body and *sarx* refers to the flesh of an individual body. The same differences pertain to the English word *body*. Paul was talking about the church as the body of Christ. The whole body of the church is held together by the various joints (ἀφή), and each part is joined to the direction or leadership of the head. Sometimes that direction is explicit, as it is here, as Paul provides it for the Ephesians. And at other times it is automatic, like the beating of our hearts or our breathing. Because the analogy is body related, we must engage the fullness of bodily language to fully understand it, including autonomic systems.

The idea is that the various parts of the church are both united in wholeness to the head and held together by the ligaments that join them, such that the body of Christ is able to function in the world. The church is equipped for worldly service by its wholeness manifest by the harmonic functioning of its various parts.

It may be useful for modern people to begin by saying what does *not* qualify or define church membership. Without a doubt those who are not members themselves cannot determine qualifications or set definitions for church membership. Those who are not part of Christ's church cannot make such determinations. This idea has profound implications for contemporary churches.

At issue is whether the Internal Revenue Service (IRS) has the jurisdiction to determine the qualifications or definitions of church structure and membership. If we argue *yes*, then we must also argue that the IRS is a legitimate part of the Christian church—which would end the idea of the separation of church and state, and would contra-

---

1   See footnote 1, p. 193.

dict the founding and constitution of the United States and the IRS—
and the Bible.

If we argue *no*, then we must rebuke and deny all such attempts
by the IRS to define the church because it has neither the qualifications nor the jurisdiction to do so. If this is the case, then the IRS
should be sued by the churches for overstepping its jurisdiction. Note
that in either case, the implications require serious changes in U. S.
governance. Church and state must either be joined or separated, but
the current practice of IRS meddling in the rules of incorporation for
churches must end.

Because the church belongs to Jesus Christ who is the head of the
church, membership qualifications and definitions belong to Him
alone, remembering God's Trinitarian character. Note that this does
not mean that no one other than Jesus Christ is involved. Rather, we
understand that Christ Himself is a member of the Godhead, whose
definition is Trinitarian—Father, Son, and Holy Spirit. There are
huge implications that issue from the reality of the Trinity. Christ's
Trinitarian character is both individual and corporate,

> "recognized in two natures, without confusion, without change,
> without division, without separation; the distinction of natures
> being in no way annulled by the union, but rather the characteris-
> tics of each nature being preserved and coming together to form
> one person and subsistence, not as parted or separated into two
> persons, but one and the same Son and Only-begotten God the
> Word, Lord Jesus Christ"[2]

There are two important implications of this: 1) Because the
Holy Spirit is the author of Scripture, both Testaments are necessary
for the proclamation of the whole truth of Christ Jesus. And 2) Because Christians are brought into Christ by the power and presence of
the Holy Spirit through regeneration, the church as the body of
Christ participates in Christ through the reflection of Christ in the
character of individual Christians, which were created in God's image. Thus, the qualifications and definitions for church membership
and church functioning are determined by both Testaments in the
light of Christ, and embraced by all persons involved—Father, Son,
Holy Spirit, individual regenerate believers and the corporate body of
the church.

---

2   Council of Chalcedon, 451.

Note that there are five roles involved. *Persons³* were historically understood to have a role in the king's court, and were distinguished from *serfs*, who did not. Thus, those who have a role in the King's court are: 1) the Father—God, the King, 2) the Son—Jesus Christ, 3) the Holy Spirit, 4) individual, regenerate believers, and 5) the corporate church as the wholeness of the body of Christ, speaking through various ages and perspectives with one voice.

Grow

Paul said that the proper working of each part "makes the body grow" (v. 16) or live. Or to put it negatively, when the parts are not working properly, the body does not grow. Evangelism brings new Christians into the fold of the church, but for the church to grow as it should, more than evangelism is required. Each part must exercise the gifts that have been provided in order to bloom where God planted it. God does what the Father does. Jesus does what the Son does. The Holy Spirit does what the Spirit does, "blows where it wishes" (John 3:8). Individual believers must exercise faithfulness where God has planted them. And the church must learn how to speak with one voice, though that voice has trinitarian characteristics in order to say all that needs to be said.

No one person can speak for all. Rather, each person must speak for all, for the wholeness of the church. Thus, inclusion in Christ's church is by confession, where all persons in Christ admit to the reality of the wholeness of God in thought, word, and deed. Admission into Christ's church is self-admission, but only in the sense of this holistic understanding of self, as being composed of these five persons who function in unity. The purpose of all of these sixteen verses is then presented:

> "so that it (the church) builds itself up in love" (v. 16).

The purpose is the edification (οἰκοδομή) of humanity by the church. Christians are to edify themselves through self-discipline and sanctification, to edify the world through evangelism, and to edify one another through fellowship. However, it is an error to think of edification only in emotional terms, as encouragement. Edification is to be encouraging, of course, but it also has an intellectual compo-

---

3   It is essential to understand what persons are. See: Smith, Christian. *What Is A Person? Rethinking Humanity, Social Life, and The Moral Good from the Person Up,* The University of Chicago Press, Chicago, Illinois, 2010.

nent. To encourage another is to offer uplifting wisdom and honest intelligence. It is not merely emotional commendation, but must also reflect the best understanding of the wholeness of God, as well. It is not mere cheer leading, but is more like personal instruction or coaching, explaining the theory, and demonstrating its many applications.

People can edify themselves by giving themselves a good pep talk, and that might be needed sometimes. But most of the time such things are more in service of pride than faithfulness. The more fruitful option is to trust God, to trust that God is good, that God actually loves us and wants what is best for us, and that God's Word is completely reliable. A lot of people think that trusting God means blind faith, but nothing could be farther from the truth. God doesn't want blind faith. God is the light of truth, and opposes every kind of blindness. Blind faith kills curiosity, and God loves curiosity because curiosity is the engine of creativity. God cures blindness!

When people read the Bible they too often respond, "That's impossible! That can't possibly be true." But such an approach to the Bible is fundamentally flawed because it allows doubt and distrust of God and His Word to lead our thinking. It is much more productive to respond, "That's weird! How can that be true? What would reality be like if that were true?" We can doubt ourselves, but we must not doubt God.

Genuine truth is always uplifting, even when we don't understand all of it, or like it. Intelligence is defined as having our thinking in harmony with genuine truth. To know truth is to be intelligent, even when we don't know everything there is to know about the whole truth. Of course, the most important truth to know is the living truth, or truth about life. And living truth is dynamic, not static. Static truth is dead, not living, because life itself is dynamic.

Thus, knowing truth is not like knowing a fact about something. Facts are static. Facts are truth's footprints in time. To know the truth is to know something alive, something growing, something dynamic. It's not that God grows or changes, but we grow and change. And as we do, our understanding of God grows and changes. But the fact that it grows and changes does not mean that what it used to be is now untrue. It's just that it is more true now. For instance, I am today the same person I used to be when I was a little boy. Yet, I have grown so much that it is true to say that I'm not the person I used to be. Except I am! It sometimes seems confusing, but it's not. It's really quite simple.

In Love

All of this functions together

"so that it (the church) builds itself up in love" (v. 16).

Agape love is the instrument used to edify the church. And here we see that other people are absolutely necessary for the process. One cannot build up one's self in love, because love requires an object, an other. Of course, Christians are to love themselves, but love that is not focused on others is a far cry from genuine Christian love. Agape love is love with legs. It is not just words or feelings of love, but is the action of love—service. To love another person is to work for what is best for him or her. And agape love is to do so without any expectation of reward or return. Agape love is other directed.

And in the fullness of the Godhead each Person involved can be other-directed: the Father serves the Son and the Spirit, the Son serves the Father and the Spirit, and the Spirit serves the Father and the Son. Similarly, in the church each Christian serves the wholeness of the body by serving others, and the wholeness of the body (other members) serves each individual Christian as each acts on the wholeness of the church. The foot serves the wholeness of the body by doing what feet do. And the wholeness of the body, the other parts, serve the feet by caring for them, not just emotionally but physically. The eyes watch them, the hands clean them, the mouth feeds them, the heart sends them blood, etc. All contribute to the well-being of the whole.

Agape—love without expectations, working in service to God's desires for other people—drives edification. Agape is the engine of edification. Agape wants what is best for others—not necessarily what they want for themselves, but what God wants for them. Agape is the engine of Christian maturity.

25. No More!

*Now this I say and testify in the Lord, that you must no
longer walk as the Gentiles do, in the futility of their minds.
They are darkened in their understanding, alienated from the
life of God because of the ignorance that is in them, due to
their hardness of heart. They have become callous and have
given themselves up to sensuality, greedy to practice every
kind of impurity.* —Ephesians 4:17-19

The *English Standard Version* translates the word οὖν as *now*,
which overlooks its meaning as a conclusion. It is translated
therefore in the *Authorized Version*. Nonetheless, the whole
phrase, "Now this I say and testify in the Lord" (v. 17) serves to un-
derline that what follows is an undeniable conclusion from what has
preceded. And Paul's conclusion is that Christians must not walk—
that is think, act, behave, believe, or worship—like Gentiles, or non-
Christians. We *must not* be like them.

The conclusion is unavoidable, stark, and divisive. Yet, it does
not weigh against Paul's argument for Christian unity. Rather, it en-
forces it by clarifying that Christian unity is *Christian* unity, and not
the promiscuous unity of all humanity—not until all humanity is
Christian. Of course, Paul hoped that one day Christianity would include all humanity, but not on their terms—on Jesus' terms. Paul intended, hoped for, and planned for the success of Christ's mission in
the world to someday include the whole world.

This perspective, known as *postmillennialism* or *triumphalism*,
has fallen on hard times for the past century or so. It first stumbled
during the American Civil War, which was really a religious or
worldview war. The North represented the unitarian aspirations or

the Liberalism of state unification through uniformitarian policies of a strong central government driven by Washington D. C. The Unitarian Controversy (early 1800s) had recently swept through the Northeast and claimed a good number of Congregational and Presbyterian churches, and infected many others with its anti-trinitarian doctrines.

In contrast, the South represented Trinitarian Calvinism or the Conservative idea of small central government with checks and balances that would allow stronger state governments. The issue was whether the primary power would lie with a centralized national government, or with the various states in federation.

Christian triumphalism took another hit during the War of 1812, and another during WWI and WWII. The vision of Christ's triumphal victory and dominance in the world, like Humpty Dumpty's fall, has been irreparably broken. The vision for a Christian government of an American Constitutional form will not recover. However, it is necessary to understand that what was broken was a false view of Christ's triumphalism, not its reality. What was broken was the Great Awakening vision of Christianity, which was itself an historical anomaly that was built on various flawed ideas that had also shaped the U. S. Constitution. And what triumphed was the unitarian/universalist, Liberal ideas of multiculturalism that have produced the current state of affairs in the world.

As good a document as the Constitution is, it is not perfect. The intention of the Constitution was to bring two opposing religious and political factions together through compromise for the sake of the nation. Those opposing factions were essentially composed of those who support traditional American Christianity and those who do not. The American Christianity in view is the Puritanism of the early American colonies prior to the First Great Awakening. Unfortunately, the Puritans imposed the same sort of religious monopoly upon the colonies that they fled from in England. The central difference was that now *they* were in charge. The corruption involved in the pursuit of power has never been tamed. Notice that the compromise served the purposes of the new nation, not the purposes of Jesus Christ. This is a hard idea to accept because the American experiment has had so many fantastic successes in so many different areas over such a long period of time, and Christians have always thanked God for those successes. While the cultural apparatus was in the hands of Christians during the early years of the new nation, the nation appeared to be Christian. But as the cultural apparatus changed hands over the centuries, the nation has appeared to be less and less Christian, less Puritan.

Indeed, the American experiment is still in the process of bringing to just about every nation on earth a kind of salvation from poverty into the many blessings of Western Civilization, fueled by science and technology. I don't want to disparage the tremendous successes of this endeavor. I am very grateful! But neither do I want to neglect my prior commitments and claims by God-in-Christ to be a citizen of His kingdom on earth.

At the very time that the American experiment began to be seriously exported around the world following the Civil and World Wars, America also began to divest herself of her inherited Christian commitments, traditions and values. Thus, Western Culture was not exported as the fruit of Christianity, but as the fruit of the American experiment, and over time sans Christianity. At the very time that the fruit of Christian civilization began to be exported across the globe, it was also being divested of its true Christian roots, heritage, and character. It has been much easier to export the Godless fruit abroad, and more difficult to expunge Christianity from the home front. Nonetheless, much success has been made on both fronts, to the shame of Christ's glory.

What is difficult for Christians to realize today is that those Christian commitments, traditions, and values that have been and are under attack by non-Christians and those outside the churches are under attack in part because they are flawed. The Christianity under attack is seriously flawed, and can be improved. The Lord is forcing His people to reconsider, reevaluate, and reformulate some of the most basic Christian commitments, traditions, and values in the greater light of Christ that continues to unfold.[1] This is nothing new, it has happened all through history as the church faced new people, new situations, and new developments. However, this is not an argument for Liberalism, far from it! It is an argument for reconsideration, for rethinking, and repentance *by the church*! The church must lead with public repentance and real change that truly reflects genuine biblical truth, honesty, integrity, and compassion.

The greatest danger for Christians in the midst of our current situation is the desire for retrenchment and retreat into the past, to call on old solutions to solve new problems. This is a serious danger because it is so attractive and easy to do. It is also a serious danger be-

---

1   See footnote 1, p. iii.

cause Christians are actually still in the cultural driver's seat. The problem is not that Christians don't have jurisdiction or control, the problem is that Christians have a lack of vision. We need a vision that is greater than our problems. We cannot expect unbelievers to have true answers for real problems because their unbelief constitutes the denial of the greatest truth available to humanity—Jesus Christ. By the same token, Christians must not deny the reality of the failure of traditional answers to the questions and problems uncovered by scientific and technological advancements.

This does not mean that previous understandings of Christian orthodoxy and orthopraxy are wrong. It means that Christianity is a living tradition. Christianity itself grows and matures because it is alive. It means that old answers, like old clothes, no longer fit a growing body. However, the church must not abandon her past, nor should she become less faithful to God's Word over time. Rather, she needs to grow and mature in genuine faithfulness. She needs to grow in grace and mercy, of course, but also in righteousness.

Change

Paul said

> "that you must no longer walk as the Gentiles do, in the futility of their minds" (v. 17).

Note the imperative. This is not an option. Christians must not do things like the Gentiles do them. The Greek word ἔθνος (*ethnos*) points to the nations or ethnicities. We are not to be like them or do things like they do. We can understand Paul to be opposed to the worldviews, cultures, beliefs, gods, and godless practices of the various cultures of the nations and ethnicities—their religious beliefs, practices, and cultures. This view is completely opposed to what we know as multiculturalism and diversity because they celebrate the very things that Paul opposed.

However, neither Paul nor the Bible are opposed to the various nations, nationalities, or ethnicities of the world. It is not the color of skin or the place where one grew up that Paul opposed. The church was founded in Acts 2 on racial or ethnic diversity. Christians are called to love and serve all people, even their enemies (Matthew 5:44). Paul was not opposed to people of any kind, but he was opposed to what is false and everything that is opposed to God-in-Christ.

The term *gentile* is a carryover from the Old Testament, and refers to all who are not Jewish. Paul then adapted the term to mean all who are not Christian. Paul meant that Christians should not do things like those who are not Christian do them. We must not follow the world. We must not succumb to popular thinking or practices that originate in the world or in worldly thinking. And this is a particular problem whenever the church becomes influenced by the world, which has been a recurring problem in Christian history. It is a continuing struggle for the church because new believers are always coming into the church, and those same new believers are coming out of the world.

Paul also meant that we are not to follow the thinking of Greek philosophy, which was dominant in the world at the time. The Romans had defeated the Greeks and absorbed the best of Greek philosophy into Roman culture. This should be obvious, but what we find in Christian history is that Christian theology merged with Greek philosophy as various outstanding intellectuals of the day began interacting with the church. Greek philosophy has always been identified with intelligence and culture in Western civilization, and the church has generally capitulated by using Greek philosophical categories for its understanding and expression of biblical theology.

Paul's opposition to the world means that worldly thinking, especially Greek philosophy, is futile and vain because it is completely unaware of Jesus Christ, who is wisdom personified, and because it is based in Godless, abstract speculation and imagination.[2] The Greek word that Paul used is ματαιότης, and means thinking that is devoid of truth, full of perversion and depravity. It means thinking that is frail and lacks vigor or commitment to life in Christ. It means short term thinking, thinking that is unsustainable practically.

When Paul said *walk*, he meant *do*. And when he said *futility of mind*, he meant *frivolous thought that is devoid of truth*. We can understand Paul to have been concerned about eternity or sustainability. As Christians, both our activities and our thoughts are to be focused on what is eternal, what is sustainable, on the long run not the short run. He meant that we must abandon all forms of dishonesty, graft,

---

2 "All of Western philosophy is but a footnote to Plato" (A. N. Whitehead). The Thomistic effort to use Greek philosophy to understand Christianity—genius though it is—is misguided because it uses Aristotelian categories of analysis. It analyzes truth with errant categories, human categories.

greed, and corruption. We must abandon the values and practices of Sin.[3]

This, of course, is much easier said than done. It cannot ever be completely finished this side of glory. Thus, the process continues today. In our day we find that the forces that have exported the American experiment all over the globe over the past fifty or so years are increasingly opposed to traditional Christianity. America is currently being purged of its Christian history and influence. As the values of multiculturalism and diversity have taken their place in American culture, people are increasingly discovering that these new values are opposed to traditional Christianity. And of course, Christianity has always been opposed to the values of multiculturalism and diversity as defined in contemporary society, as we see from Paul.

This conflict of values has been fueling what several contemporary authors have called the *culture wars*.[4] This war or struggle between conflicting cultures can be traced all the way back to Abraham leaving Ur—and earlier. Abraham didn't just up and leave. He left as the culmination of a longstanding struggle. His leaving Ur was as much the conclusion of a process as the beginning of a journey. Abraham's departure from Ur, and from his father's god, Sin, was simultaneously the beginning of the Judeo-Christian culture that has culminated in Western civilization.

History

The point to note is that Christianity has not followed Paul's leadership and instructions to not "walk as the Gentiles do" (v. 17) as well as it should have. Many Greek, Gentile, and worldly ideas and practices have been adopted by various versions of Christianity over the eons. Nor did the Reformation completely cleanse Protestantism from the acculturation of worldliness. This is not a perfect world, which means that we always live in the midst of compromise and confusion. The Reformation made many improvements in its recovery of biblical Christianity, but has also fallen right back into many of the same difficulties that it first corrected.[5]

Many Protestants hoped that they could found a new beginning for Christianity in America, and they immigrated in order to do just

---

3   See footnote 2, p. 6.

4   http://en.wikipedia.org/wiki/Culture_war.

5   Edward Beecher discusses this. See footnote 12, p. 182.

that. The Mayflower Compact,[6] the first governing document of Ply-
mouth Colony, was written in 1620 by the Separatists who became
Congregationalists. New England was originally planted as colonies
of churches. The oldest settlements were churches engaged in civil
matters. Of course, not everyone in New England lived in a church
colony, but those with power and authority did.

"The state was constituted practically, by a union of churches."[7]

Originally, there was no separation of church and state. The church
dominated the state because only church members could vote, and the
governing meetings were church meetings. Thus, Christians dominated civil government concerns.

Over time, secularism (the rejection of religion and religious
considerations) grew and Christian dominance was increasingly questioned. Congregational churches were widely established in the Ply-
mouth Colony, the Massachusetts Bay Colony and New England.
The model of Congregational churches was carried by migrating set-
tlers from New England into New York State and then into the
North-West Territory, which became the states of Illinois, Indiana,
Michigan, Ohio, Wisconsin, and a small portion of Minnesota. With
their insistence on independent local bodies, Congregationalism became a key player in many social reform movements.

Over time non-Christians (non-church members) were given the
vote. And at that time, that vote pertained to both church and civil

---

6   The Mayflower Compact reads: "In the name of God, Amen. We, whose names
     are underwritten, the loyal subjects of our dread Sovereign Lord King James, by
     the Grace of God, of Great Britain, France, and Ireland, King, defender of the
     Faith, etc.

          Having undertaken, for the Glory of God, and advancements of the Christian
     faith and honor of our King and Country, a voyage to plant the first colony in the
     Northern parts of Virginia, do by these presents, solemnly and mutually, in the
     presence of God, and one another, covenant and combine ourselves together into a
     civil body politic; for our better ordering, and preservation and furtherance of the
     ends aforesaid; and by virtue hereof to enact, constitute, and frame, such just and
     equal laws, ordinances, acts, constitutions, and offices, from time to time, as shall be
     thought most meet and convenient for the general good of the colony; unto which
     we promise all due submission and obedience.

          In witness whereof we have hereunto subscribed our names at Cape Cod the
     11th of November, in the year of the reign of our Sovereign Lord King James, of
     England, France, and Ireland, the eighteenth, and of Scotland the fifty-fourth,
     1620."

7   *The Congregationalist and Boston Recorder*, vol, LXXVI, Thursday, 31 July 1891,
     No. 31, 256.

concerns. In other words, non-Christians were then allowed to vote, not only in civil matters, but in church related matters! And this created more discontent and division that is rooted in the differences between believers and nonbelievers.

To solve this problem religious societies were formed and given control over the churches. However, religious society membership was not identical with church membership, and some Halfway Covenant Christians found that religious society membership could satisfy their desire for religious association without the demands of religious commitment involved in church membership. Over time, the churches grew used to being taken care of by the religious societies, which called pastors, funded ministerial salaries, and paid church expenses. The development of religious societies, then, constituted the first expression of the separation of church and state.

Religious societies understood themselves not to be churches, and often governed themselves by secular means, means not determined by Scripture. Thus, secular governance practices crept into church governance;

> "…it has come to pass that the churches themselves are in many
> things managed after secular methods and by secular men."[8]

Thus, worldliness increasingly crept into the churches, no doubt in the form of financial interests.

The solution to this problem was for churches to incorporate so that church members would have complete control of their churches, to stop non-Christians from running things;

> "…existing churches are rapidly becoming incorporated."[9]

Thus, incorporation became the means for Christians to regain control of their churches. However, incorporation always means that the corporation is a *creature of the state*. In order for Christians to gain control of their own churches, they made them creatures of the state!

This brief history shows the enduring problems and the struggles related to Paul's admonition to

> "no longer walk as the Gentiles do, in the futility of their minds"
> (v. 17)

---

8   Ibid.
9   Ibid.

that have endured into contemporary culture. Paul's admonition is as meaningful and important today as it has ever been. The church has never mastered this concern.

DARKENED

Those who walk as the Gentiles do, suffer from a darkened or obscured (ματαιότης) understanding. Something obscures their thinking. Something veils the truth from them, but they don't realize it. A lot of unbelievers today think that *Christians* are the ones who are blinded by their faith, and that they themselves (unbelievers) are *not* blinded because they reject faith as a criteria for understanding the world objectively. But this is not true, everyone operates from a faith basis. It is impossible to have no faith, just as it is impossible to have no assumptions or presuppositions. Everyone has a particular perspective, everyone makes assumptions on the basis of what they believe to be true about reality, and those who say that they don't or who say that they are objective, are deceived, at best.

One gentleman I recently had an online discussion with said,

> "As for the matter at hand I can understand where you are coming from as that view is certainly what the Bible itself suggests is correct, but living in the 21ˢᵗ century I cannot fully abide by it."[10]

He claimed to have been an active, church attending Christian who understood that the Bible teaches God's sovereignty. He even attended a Bible school with the intention of becoming a pastor. But like most Americans he elevated the sovereignty of the civil government above God, citing the Preamble of the U. S. Constitution as the central authority. He would not describe his position as I have done, but the result is the same. In particular, the supreme sovereign authority he claimed was the constitutional phrase *We The People*. It is also commonly accepted by the U. S. Supreme Court that the authority of government comes from the consent of the governed. And of course, there is an element of truth in this.

Any government that does not have the consent of its people will be tumultuous and short-lived because the people will resist and struggle against it. The situation in America is that American civil government had been understood through the lens and morality of Christianity by the majority of people long before the Constitution.

---

10   Ross, Phillip A. *Buttal & Rebuttal—A Clash of Belief and Unbelief*, Pilgrim Platform, Marietta, Ohio, 2010, unpublished.

The majority of the people, being Christian to some degree, have always imposed Christian categories, values, and understanding upon America and her government. Of course, America has never been completely Christian, and the Constitution created a kind of compromise between Christians and non-Christians at the founding. That compromise has always been in play. But the Christian majority has been popularly dominant—until recently.

The idea of the *American Experiment* was coined by Alexis de Tocqueville in the 1830s:

> "In that land the great experiment was to be made, by civilized man, of the attempt to construct society upon a new basis; and it was there, for the first time, that theories hitherto unknown, or deemed impracticable, were to exhibit a spectacle for which the world had not been prepared by the history of the past."[11]

America has always been the seed of the new world order that has been discussed ever since Tocqueville published his book. The establishment of the United States of America was the founding of that new world order, and it has utterly changed the whole world beyond the wildest imaginations of anyone prior to its founding. As Christians we must acknowledge that God knew about the American continent when He talked with Adam in the Garden of Eden.[12]

CONFLICT

We must also acknowledge that the story of the Bible is a story of conflict between believers and unbelievers, or covenant keepers and covenant breakers. This conflict inhabits every chapter of the Bible, Old Testament and New. Paul referred to this conflict when he said that Christians

> "must no longer walk as the Gentiles" (v. 17).

Believers must not think or act like unbelievers. We must no longer be like those whose minds are darkened by sin and Sin's agents.

The difference between believers and unbelievers is that believers have faith in Christ and unbelievers have faith in something else. The difference is not in the subjectivity of the individuals, but in the object of their faith. Believers are not better than unbelievers. Rather,

---

11 Toqueville, Alexis de. *Democracy In America*, Volume 1, 1835, http://www.gutenberg.org/files/815/815-h/815-h.htm.

12 See footnote 1, p. iii.

the object of faith for believers—Jesus Christ—is superior to the object of faith for unbelievers—themselves, history, humanity, some other god, etc. The difference between believers and unbelievers does not belong to them subjectively. They themselves are not inferior, their idea of God is.

This is widely misunderstood because each individual thinks that *their* group is superior—smarter, holier, more blessed, etc.—than the others. But people are people are people. The difference is not about people, the difference is about the differing objects of faith. The one true God-in-Christ is greater than all of the false gods, multiplied a thousand times over. What is real is superior to imagination.

Of course, ideas have consequences, as does believing in differing objects of faith. Paul notes that one such difference is that unbelievers are

> "alienated from the life of God because of the ignorance that is in them" (v. 18).

Unbelievers are self-alienated. They are not associated with God because *they* don't want to be. They do not like what God likes or value what God values. They prefer to live in the world of their superstitions, where they think they have control, rather than to live in God's world, where they would have to relinquish the illusion of being in control. Their unbelief is their choice. They are free to believe otherwise, but don't.

Paul describes the ignorance of unbelief as ἄγνοια. The Greek word can be best understood as the failure to perceive with the mind, to understand (νοιέω). We need to understand the word *understand* in its original meaning, which was to *stand under*. Unbelievers fail to stand under God, to be submitted to God. Unbelievers refuse to acknowledge God's sovereignty. And this is the issue of dispute that has been woven into the compromise of the U. S. Constitution. Christians have always understood *We The People* as being people under God. But *God* appears in the U. S. Constitution only in the Preamble as "Nature's God." God is also suggested by phrases like "created equal" and "endowed by their Creator." Such phrases allow Christians

to read their Christian understanding into the document, and it allows Deists[13] and unbelievers to disregard Christianity.[14]

Evidence for the reality of this ongoing conflict can be seen in
the story regarding words "under God," which were added to the
Pledge of Allegiance in 1954.[15]

Fixity

Paul said that the Gentiles do what they do

"due to their hardness of heart" (v. 18).

The *Authorized Version* calls it "blindness of heart." The Greek word
(πώρωσις) means callous, stubbornness, obduracy. To understand
what Paul was talking about we need to keep ourselves from slipping
into the habit of thinking that we already know what he was talking
about, because he was talking about this very thing, this habit of taking a fixed position in our analysis. Hardness of heart produces fixity
of opinions.

Because we identify ourselves as Christian we think that we don't
do what Paul accused the Gentiles of doing—but we do! We have
seen how this issue of not being like the Gentiles has continued to be
a problem in the most Christian nation on earth over the centuries as
we have briefly examined some U. S. Constitutional issues and the
ongoing struggle between two groups of Americans. Christians are
by and large guilty of hardness of heart or taking and holding a fixed
belief about reality. Christians pride themselves on this and call it
faithfulness.

The most dedicated Christians work hard to study the Bible in
order to come to a fixed theological position that purports to account
for the whole of the Bible. We do this because we understand the
Bible to be whole, to not contradict itself—and these things are true
and good. We work to develop a system of thinking that accounts for
all of the diverse biblical data, to "get our arms around it," as they say.
Academicians tend to approach the Bible as they approach science:
examining the evidence, and proposing a theorem to account for it.
Over time, science provides more evidence about the Bible in a vari-

---

13 To see the contemporary extremes of the anti-Christian fruit of Deism, see John-
    son. Robert L. "The Bible's Ungodly Origins." http://www.deism.com/bibleori-
    gins.htm.

14 See Appendix: The American Dream, p. 410

15 See Appendix: Under God, p. 413.

ety of ways, and as that evidence is considered, the biblical theorems are adjusted to account for it.

This is not a bad or evil process. It is necessary in order to make sense of the Bible in the light of our own social, scientific, and Christian maturity. The problem comes when people adopt a particular theorem as final, as if it were not subject to criticism or improvement —and then look at all attempts to improve it as heresy, apostasy, and/ or speculation. When people cling to outmoded biblical or theological ideas to the point that they deny the reality or benefit of new data, they suffer from what Paul called "hardness of heart" (v. 18). The problem is that when we can get our arms around God's Word, so to speak, that very process of encompassing it tends to keep us from the growth and maturity that continue to unfold in history, because in order to get our arms around God's Word, we tend to treat our theology as fixed rather than dynamic.

I'm not suggesting that people not develop biblical and theological theorems or positions. Indeed, theology is too important to neglect. The only thing that is worse than clinging to an outmoded position in the face of genuinely new data is not having a position to cling to in the first place. Indeed, this clinging *is* an act of faithfulness. And the art of faithfulness is mastered in the ability to develop what the theologians call *systematics*, but to do so in a dynamic way that conforms to the ongoing flow of history, the development of theology, science, and technology, and the developing maturity of personal and corporate spiritual growth. At the point that a person stops growing in this way s/he is guilty of hardness of heart.

I am not suggesting that Christians do not or should not have an enduring commitment to God. However, the idea that God is immutable is more Greek than Hebrew.[16] Of course, there is a sense in which God doesn't change, but it refers to God's purpose and person. We must always keep God's Trinitarian character in mind, and ask whether God changed when Christ incarnated in human flesh and died on the cross for the propitiation of sin. God's purpose did not change, but His means did—He sent His Son. Of course, He always had this in mind, but when He actually did it, things changed.

---

16 The idea of immutability is more abstraction than substance. For a discussion of the doctrine of immutability see: Beecher, Edward. *Concord Of Ages—The Individual And Organic Harmony Of God And Man*, Phillip A. Ross, Editor, Pilgrim Platform, Marietta, Ohio, 2013.

As history continues to unfold and more and more people get swept into God's kingdom, God Himself does not change, but His kingdom grows. And growth requires change. Again, God's purpose, God's love, and the intent of God's covenant with humanity does not change, though everything else in the world does. God does not change, but people do. People see things differently over time. People grow.

Paul accused the Gentiles of ideological fixity or stubbornness. It's a condition of the mind, a kind of belief that gets stuck in a rut. It stops growing, stops maturing, stops interacting with the data of reality, and imposes an ideological structure or framework upon reality that keeps a person from seeing and/or accepting new or previously unseen data.

Systematic theology is particularly prone to this problem because people work very hard to come to a systematic understanding of Scripture, and the claims of systematic theology are so great—claiming to comprehend the wholeness of the Bible, being able to explain every apparent contradiction by some system. The natural consequence of a systematic structure is calcification, the hardening or fixing of the system as being congruent with God's understanding. Indeed, the hardening or fixing of a system is necessary for its explanation. However, the moment a systematic structure becomes fixed, it ceases to be dynamic. And to associate a fixed systematic position to God is to remove the life from God, because life is dynamic not fixed.

This reality regarding God and fixed theological understandings presents a huge difficulty for serious students of the Bible. Fixed systematic understanding is necessary for communication about God, yet at the same time, fixed systematic understanding of Scripture will always fall short of conveying a true understanding of God's dynamic character. The only option is continual growth and reformation of understanding.

Fixity first shows itself in biblical history with the Serpent in the Garden of Eden—Satan. Not only did Satan plant doubt about God's Word in Eve's heart, but he thought that he knew what God knows.

> "For God knows that when you eat of it your eyes will be opened,
> and you will be like God, knowing good and evil" (Genesis 3:5).

The Serpent believed that he knew what God knew and knew it as God knows it, which means that he thought that he was able to "get his arms around God," to understand God as God understands

Himself. And the only way to do this is to condense God's thoughts into a comprehensive system, a fixed system. While it is true that we must do our best to accomplish this, to understand God to the best of our ability, the fact is that the more we believe we have accomplished this, the less true it will be. It is good to make this effort, to strive to understand the world as God does and to understand God to the best of our ability.

But when we think that we have succeeded, when we believe that there is no better way of understanding God or His world than what we have created, we have at that point fixed or frozen the development of theological systematics in such a way as to exclude any further development. Doing so will always result in a system that falls short of God's reality, and we will be guilty of following Satan rather than God. God is dynamic, alive. When we think we understand Him on the basis of some fixed system, we will always be short of the mark.

Again, this does not mean that the effort to systematize our theological understanding is evil or without merit. It is very useful for spiritual growth, sanctification, and maturity. However, we must always be able and willing to modify our system as the progressive revelation of Jesus Christ in history provides more light. Again, I'm not talking about progressivism, but about the growing manifestation of Christ in history.

Passion

Paul continued his discussion of the Gentiles, whom we are not to emulate, by saying that

"they have become callous" (v. 19).

The *Authorized Version* reads, "who being past feeling." The Greek word (ἀπαλγέω) suggests a lack of connection between thought and feeling, or between idea and emotion. It suggests a bifurcation of reality in the sense that thoughts exist independently of emotions. The idea is Platonic in origin and expression.

Paul argues against this idea by suggesting that the reality is the opposite, that thoughts and ideas are always necessarily fused with emotion, that there is no such thing as pure thought that is devoid of emotion, no such thing as pure human objectivity. He said that Gentiles have become callous to their own feelings, that they deny the necessary connection between thought and emotion.[17]

Those who do not know Christ personally ignore or deny the necessary moral connection between thought and reality that functions through emotion. This can be easily seen in reference to sex. Gentiles, particularly the ancient Greeks, did not believe that there is a connection between love and sex, or between marriage commitment and sexual fidelity. Many ancient Greek men simply did not value marital fidelity. And this understanding of marriage and sex is common today, likely because the development of birth control technologies have broken the relationship between sex and pregnancy for women.

Thus, today women are free to approach sex as men do, that is, without any necessary connection to potential pregnancy. The moral bond between love, marriage, and sex has been broken in the minds of a growing number of contemporary people. Nearly everything in the contemporary world mitigates against the biblical insistence that all sexual expression must be contained to the marriage bed. In our world we see lots of sex and little of pregnancy. More people today find that their personal identity is related to their freedom of sexual expression than with their marriage vows. People have become callous to moral obligations that are not self-determined or that do not consider commitment to one's self to be the highest obligation. Thus, religious morality that is generated by commitment to others or commitment to God has fallen on hard times.

---

17 For a discussion of the relationship between logic and moral feeling see: Beecher, Edward. *Concord of Ages*, Appendix, "Note on Logic."

26. Off And On

But that is not the way you learned Christ!—assuming that you have heard about him and were taught in him, as the truth is in Jesus, to put off your old self, which belongs to your former manner of life and is corrupt through deceitful desires, and to be renewed in the spirit of your minds, and to put on the new self, created after the likeness of God in true righteousness and holiness. —*Ephesians 4:20-24*

The Ephesians had departed from their first understanding of Jesus Christ. John said it this way, "you have abandoned the love you had at first" (Revelation 2:4). Paul was writing to the Ephesians in order to correct them because they had already strayed from his teaching. Like the ancient Israelites who waited for Moses to come down with the Ten Commandments, they were "a stiff-necked people" (Exodus 32:9) who were quick to turn away from God to their old habits of faithlessness.

The Hebrew (קְשֵׁה עֹרֶף, *stiff necked*) means hard, cruel, severe, obstinate, and stubborn. They were not receptive to new ideas. They believed what they believed and they stuck with it. There is a sense in which this can be understood to mean faithfulness. They faithfully clung to their ancient ways, their old traditions, ideas, and customs, which meant that they did not adapt easily to new ideas. They thought that they already understood everything they needed to understand, and rejected everything new, regardless of the source.

They suffered from religious and ideological fixity. To a degree, this is a strength, but beyond that degree it becomes a weakness. It is important to understand and honor the roots of the faith. We should never think that we have outgrown those roots. But neither should we think that there is nothing more to the faith than its roots. The faith itself is a living thing. Like a flower, it would die without its roots, yet it cannot live if it only has roots. Faith grows and matures. It produces flower, seed, and fruit, and yet it is never anything other than a specific kind of plant. It only produces more of the same in the process of its life.

Paul had not written to congratulate them on their harmonious faith, maturity, and unity, but quite the opposite. Had they immediately sprung into mature faithfulness, Paul would not have had to write to them, to present them again with the vision, hope, confidence, and practical instructions regarding Christian faithfulness. But because they needed to hear it, Paul wrote it out in detail.

Babes

We too often think that the first century Christians had it made because they were so close to the source, to Jesus and Paul and the Apostles. We too often think that the future of Christianity involves the return to those days of glory when the first century church(es) had it right. But that is *not* what the testimony of the New Testament teaches. Every New Testament writer wrote to correct problems and give instructions, not because the churches were pristine or bastions of mature faithfulness, but because they were neither.

The first Christians, like Christians ever since, drug their old, godless habits, preconceptions, and superstitions with them into the church in order to baptize those very things in the name of Jesus Christ. It's not that they intended to do so, but they did so unwittingly, because new believers do not yet have the maturity in Christ to discern what they are doing in the light of Christ.

This trend has actually never stopped. It began in the New Testament churches and continues to this day, in part because so many Christians understand Christian faithfulness as returning to some imagined idyllic conditions of the first century. It is a constant temptation and practice of Christians in every age, including ours. Of course, there is a sense in which returning to the "old paths" (Jeremiah 6:6) is exactly what needs to be done. When Christ's people have strayed from the original path, they must return to Christ's way. But once people have engaged Christ's way, the ideal at that point is not to remain as immature babes unweened from their mother's milk, but to begin training for the feast of the meat of mature faithfulness (1 Corinthians 3:2, Hebrews 5:12).

We see the lengths to which people will go to cling to sin most clearly among homosexuals, who are working very hard to make the Bible not condemn the practice of homosexuality as sinful. Homosexuals are very creative and intelligent, and they are using their creativity and intelligence to reinterpret the Bible to make it seem that it does not condemn the sin of homosexuality. For such unrepentant sinners, everything must bend to accommodate their favorite sin, so that they do not have to repent in order to receive God's blessing—or so they hope.

It's not that they can actually change God's Word or God's blessings with their creativity, though that's what they think they are doing. Rather, God is using them to bring to light the many sins and shortcomings of Christ's church today in this world. The church cannot condemn homosexual sin without condemning a host of other sins at the same time. The damnable thing about the homosexual argument is that it brings to light the double standards of the contemporary churches for condemning some sins and turning a blind eye to others. However, the remedy is not to turn a blind eye to all sin, but to insist on the exposure and genuine repentance of all sin. The conflict over homosexuality in the church will feed the spirit of true repentance in the church, God willing. But like all repentance, it will be difficult and painful.

HEARD

Paul questioned the faithfulness of the Ephesian Christians. Because they were acting as they did, he wondered if they had ever actually heard the gospel. He phrased it positively, "assuming that you have heard about him" (v. 21), but his doubt is clear. The *Authorized Version* reads, "If so be that ye have heard him." How could they act and think like Gentiles if they had actually understood the message of Christ? Only those who have actually followed Paul into Christian maturity can even conceive of the question.

Children don't question the immaturity of other children. Children don't question the actions or behaviors of other children until trouble irrupts. But adults understand that one thing leads to another. This provides a great analogy for the contemporary churches because today homosexual actions or behaviors cannot be challenged or questioned by anyone without the threat of reprisal by the political correctness police, and increasingly of litigation. To offend anyone about anything, particularly any legally protected beliefs or behaviors, is to open one's self or one's organization to public scorn and legal liability. Indeed, the homosexual lobby has successfully pitted the state against the church. Obedience to civil law with regard to homosexuality now impedes the development of Christian maturity in the church. Any church that speaks against homosexuality for any reason does so under threat of public scorn and possible civil litigation. Homosexuality has increasingly become the tip of the spear in the church/state conflict.

While the original function of the church was to provide moral and spiritual guidance, that guidance with regard to the sinfulness of homosexuality is being outlawed as the intentional result of the work of those who most blatantly refuse to repent of that particular sin. The asylum has been taken over by the inmates! And because homosexuality was a very common sin among the Greeks, and Ephesus was a Greek city, we can understand Paul to have believed that all who practiced homosexuality had not repented, and the failure to repent amounts to the failure to actually hear the gospel of Jesus Christ.

"If anyone has ears to hear, let him hear" (Mark 4:23).

This does not mean that unrepentant homosexuals have never listened to a condemnatory sermon against homosexuality, or never read the biblical verses that condemn it. It means that they have never accepted or believed that the Bible means what historic Christians understood it to mean ninety-nine percent of the time. They do not believe that their refusal to repent has consequences of any significance. Sure, some people don't like it, but some people don't like a lot of things that don't result in ultimate condemnation by God.

Taught

There are two pieces to Paul's concern here: 1) those who act like Gentiles have not yet heard Christ, and 2), nor "were (they) taught in him" (v. 21). The *Authorized Version* reads, "been taught *by* him." His concern was that they had not been brought into Christ in order to be taught *by* Him directly, in personal relationship with Christ. There is some teaching that needs to be done—and learned.

Gentiles do as they please. Sure, we could say that they follow their gods, but Paul believed that their gods were figments of their own imaginations. Belief in such figmentary gods issues from human imagination. In any case, Gentiles operate out of human imagination —they call it *creativity*. But functioning in Christ or believing in

Christ does not issue from human imagination. Christ must be *taught* because He is beyond imagination.

Of course, it is possible to know about Christ, without actually being obedient to Him. Satan is such a character. Satan believes in Christ, he knows that God is real and that Jesus Christ is His Son. But Satan remains in opposition to God. Satan thinks that he understands God enough to stand in judgment of God.

> "For God knows that when you eat of it your eyes will be opened,
> and you will be like God, knowing good and evil" (Genesis 3:5).

This is Satan's evaluation, not God's. This is what Satan thinks that God believes. God doesn't believe that sin or disobedience will result in the opening of Eve's or Adam's eyes to truth. God is not an idiot who thought that Adam's sin made him somehow equal to God. When Moses wrote,

> "Then the LORD God said, 'Behold, the man has become like one
> of us in knowing good and evil'" (Genesis 3:22),

he had his tongue in his cheek. Sin does not provide knowledge of good and evil. Strong described the Hebrew word הֵן, as a "primitive particle; *lo!* also (as expressing surprise) *if.*" It should read, "*Oy vey*, the man *thinks* he has become...." Adam and Eve *thought* that they could discern good from evil, but God knew that they could not discern life from death.[1]

The whole of the Old Testament teaches that Adam and his progeny got it wrong. Satan and his minions are wrong, but they still believe this sincerely. And that belief amounts to a judgment about God, *against* God. Satan implies that God was not being fair, or forthright. God was not giving humanity all that it deserved. Satan, not God, believes that engaging this disobedience would make them like God, and able to know good and evil in the same way that God knows them—with ultimate certitude. But Satan was mistaken.

There are a lot of things to be taught about Jesus Christ. First and foremost is that His story begins in Genesis 1:1 and runs through Revelation 22:21. It's a long story, and learning it takes time. After you know that story, you still may only know *about* Jesus. Knowing about someone is not the same as knowing someone personally. I know about George Washington, but I don't know him personally. And I know Jim personally, but I don't know everything about him.

---

1   See Appendix: False Dichotomy, p. 415

Knowing Jesus personally is a function of regeneration. Paul's conversion provides a model (Acts 9).[2]

Truth

We usually say that something is true, or that we promise to tell the truth. But we don't say that the truth is *in* someone, except in the case of Jesus Christ. There is no article in the Greek, though it can be implied. Here it would be just as good to say "truth is in Jesus" (v. 21), without the article.

The Greek word translated as *truth* (ἀλήθεια) literally means *not hidden*. It means that nothing is hidden in Christ. Or, we could say that in Christ everything is revealed. Or, that Christ is related to everything. Or, that being in Christ illuminates everything. Or, that nothing is hidden from Christ, or by Christ.

Understanding what this means in its fullest measure requires understanding the concept of wholeness.[3] Christ is the keystone and capstone of human wholeness. No single individual is completely whole in and of him- or herself. Individuals are always necessarily a part of something greater than themselves. An individual in isolation is not a sustainable entity. No individuals in complete isolation have ever existed. Adam had God, and even God is Trinitarian. Individual identity necessarily includes more than the individual because individuals only exist in some context, and their context is necessarily part of their individual identity.

Individuals in reality are like points in Euclidean geometry, in that their identity or location can be defined by two measurements, represented as x (a horizontal axis) and y (a vertical axis). With regard to individuals the x axis refers to one's time and place in history, and the y axis refers to one's nearness to God, who is outside of time and place. The x axis is one dimension, and the y axis is a corresponding but different dimension.[4] And, like a Euclidean point, individual iden-

---

2   Paul is not the only model. The New Testament provides various models through the lives of the Apostles.

3   See Appendix: Wholeness & Holiness, p. 405.

4   In terms of physics, *dimension* refers to the constituent structure of the volume of space and its position in time, as well as the spatial constitution of objects within structures that correlate with both particle and field conceptions. They interact according to relative properties of mass, and are fundamentally mathematical in description. Modern theories tend to be "higher-dimensional" including quantum field and string theories. The state-space of quantum mechanics is infinitely dimensional in theory.

tity is identifiable by its relationship to similar measures. Geometry it-self is an abstract, systematic analysis of the principles that are found in physical reality. Understanding geometry allows for an ordered manipulation of physical reality in ways that are sustainable over time.

We could ask, which is more real: the principles of geometry or the physical reality that makes them true? But the question is mean-ingless because the principles and the reality exist in unity. We might describe them as codependent.

Thus, the wholeness of which Christ is the center involves the unity of three things: 1) the abstract principles, 2) the concrete reality, and 3) the fact of their unity in relationship with one another. This unity of the whole includes the x, y and z axes, which are all necessary for actual physical existence. Each axis represents a completely differ-ent measure or dimension, and contributes to the description of size and location, what is necessary for actual physical existence. Each part or axis can be discerned (measured) individually or independently, but no individual axis actually exists individually or independently. The idea and/or doctrine of the Trinity is an expression of ultimate whole-ness, of which this Euclidean analogy merely points.

Putting Off, Putting On

Paul speaks of putting off the old and putting on the new, as if personal identity is like a cloak, a piece of clothing. He can do this because he is referring to abstract principles that allow us to both un-derstand and manipulate physical reality, and history, which is a sub-set of physical reality. In this case, the principles are analogous to the principles of Sin[5] (or Satan), which Paul refers to as "your old self, which belongs to your former manner of life and is corrupt through deceitful desires" (v. 22), and the principles of God (or Christ) which Paul refers to as "the new self, created after the likeness of God in true righteousness and holiness" (v. 24).

The cloak is an analogy for righteousness, which we are to wear. It is not that we are to pretend to be righteous for show, like we dress up for the opera. We wear clothing in public, so analogously we are to practice righteousness publicly. Righteousness is to characterize what we do in public, our interactions with other people. This would include business interactions, buying and selling at the market, per-formances, politics, etc. Again, it's not that we are to pretend to be

---

5   See footnote 3, p. 57.

righteous, but that we are to act according to the righteousness of Christ as modeled by the character of Christ in the New Testament.

Prior to the historical coming of Christ in the flesh, Christian principles had no actual reality, no fullness of being. Only through the incarnation of Jesus Christ did the principles of Christ enter history where they have been demonstrably used to manipulate human reality, human history. Christ not only changed the history of this world, but since His coming, history itself is measured by His manifestation, in that Western civilization now measures time and character on the basis of Christ's birth and Person. This measure of time is almost universally accepted all over the world, especially in relationship to money and finances. Christ's character is a more subtle measure, but nonetheless real. Christ's righteousness is almost universally accepted today as true righteousness throughout the world.

At the time that Paul wrote, the manifestation of Christ in the flesh had just happened. Paul was a first generation Christian. Prior to Jesus Christ, the principles of Christ were not an option because those principles required the manifestation of true human wholeness in physical reality. This meant that both the Second Person of the Trinity, Jesus Christ, and the Third Person of the Trinity, the Holy Spirit, had to manifest in human flesh in history. The manifestation of Jesus Christ was not sufficient to unite humanity with God, the Father. The manifestation of the Holy Spirit through regeneration in the lives of believers was/is the final leg of the process, which Christ initiated when He sent the Holy Spirit (John 15:26).

Prior to personal regeneration—the fruit of the Spirit, there was no actual option available. All human identity was subsumed in Adam, who had been waylaid into the service of Sin by Satan in the Garden. Satan's occlusion of God's truth developed into various cultures and religions over time as populations migrated over the globe, each of which developed somewhat differently. Yet, none could overcome either God's original stamp of likeness upon humanity or Satan's initial occlusion of God's truth, wholeness, and perfection.

When the Holy Spirit appeared to the Apostles in the Upper Room (Acts 2) the process of the manifestation of the wholeness of God began in humanity, in history through various native languages. And Paul's encounter with Jesus Christ on the Road to Damascus (Acts 9) demonstrated that the manifestation of the Holy Spirit was not just a one time event in history in the life of Jesus, but would be an ongoing process throughout history. Paul and the other Apostles endeavored to document the character of Christ for the new Christians who were coming into Christ through regeneration. While regeneration brought people into Christ, the experience of regeneration alone was not sufficient to guide Christians into mature faithfulness in Christ.

While regeneration originates from outside of time, and is correspondingly described as instantaneous, growth in maturity happens in time and is usually described as a personal struggle over time. Paul knew that this change from the old self to the new self was not instantaneous, that it was hard work and didn't often feel like or produce success (Romans 7:15-22). He recognized that there are two parts involved: 1) the putting off, and 2) the putting on. In that order! In order to change cloaks, the one needs to come off before the other goes on. All of this is what Paul was pointing to when he assumed

> "that you have heard about him and were taught in him, as the truth is in Jesus" (v. 21).

CORRUPTION VS. RIGHTEOUSNESS

The old self represents

> "your former manner of life and is corrupt through deceitful desires" (v. 22),

your life prior to regeneration was your life *in Adam*. It is important to note that the *you* (ὑμᾶς) in this verse is plural, that it does not merely point to the individual. What has been said above about individual identity being a construct is as true about our life in Adam as it is about our life in Christ.

Neither the corruption nor the righteousness are endemic to humanity, nor to human individuals. The order of human development is important. Created "very good" (Genesis 1:31) in God's image, Satan led Adam astray, without any natural ability to escape from Satan's influence of corruption, his false dichotomy. Only another archetype like that of Adam could exert sufficient influence to correct the flaw of Adam's corrupted archetype. God sent His Son to provide what could not otherwise be provided—the righteous archetype of Jesus Christ in the flesh. Adam could not see that the central human conflict was *life versus death*, or *the preservation and sustainability of human life*, not *good versus evil*, or *the preservation and sustainability of a certain group*.

Prior to the advent of Christ there was no actual option other than the corrupted archetype of Adam. And in order to correct the corruption of humanity in Adam, God needed to allow Adam's archetype to play out, to manifest its corruption clearly in history, as a testimony against the corruption of Adam.

That testimony comes in two acts: First, God established a religion for Adam to corrupt. That story is the Old Testament, and it concluded with the third destruction of Jerusalem and the Temple in A.D. 70. That religion was founded upon blood vengeance because the spirit of vengeance dominated the people of Adam, because of Satan's corruption.

The second act began with the advent of Jesus Christ and was built on His teaching of the superior doctrine of grace and forgiveness. And God established the truth of Jesus Christ on the spirit of blood vengeance (the cross) so that the people of Adam could understand and accept Christ (Messiah) as issuing out of God's authority. God spoke in terms they could understand. God demonstrated Christ's superiority by gladly providing forgiveness to those in Christ. While the vengeance of God punished Christ for humanity's sin, the forgiveness of God regenerated (resurrected) Christ, and humanity through the power of the Holy Spirit. God used the life of Christ to paint a picture that vengeance leads to eternal death and forgiveness leads to sustainable life.

Forgiveness is given by the grace of God. God gives it forward in Christ, as a model of how we are to give it forward to others. There are only two basic kinds of religion in the world: the religions of vengeance, and the religion of forgiveness. Christianity, which began in Genesis 1:1, demonstrates how God is changing the one into the other. A lot of people see the God of the Old Testament as a God of vengeance or justice—and He is. But the Old Testament is not the whole story, nor does the vengeance of justice describe the whole character of God, not even in the Old Testament.

To understand God's true character we need to understand the whole truth about God. He didn't begin life as a vengeful God and slowly evolve more loving characteristics—no! Humanity first encountered God in the Garden as Jesus later described Him: kind, loving, graceful, etc. But Satan misunderstood and/or denied God and planted that misunderstanding and denial in Adam and Eve. It was Adam's job to teach Eve about God, but Satan intervened. God had given Adam both the freedom and the responsibility to complete that job, to teach Eve. God had nothing to do with Satan's intervention. It's not that God *allowed* Satan to intervene, but that God allowed Adam the freedom to teach Eve, and Satan encroached upon that freedom.

The Ruse

As history unfolded, Satan's misunderstanding took root, and because it was God whom Satan misunderstood, that root of misunderstanding was religious. God accommodated Himself to that misunderstanding for a time in the Old Testament in order to demonstrate the natural consequence of Satan's misunderstanding to humanity through history. And what we see in the Old Testament is the history of vengeance in the name of God and God's justice. Satan misunderstood God's justice, first as the divine right of kings, and then as if it was a kind of radical equality. Both are humanistic. We see this in Satan's analysis of God:

> "For God knows that when you eat of it your eyes will be opened, and *you will be like God*, knowing good and evil" (Genesis 3:5).

It seems like Satan was suggesting to Eve that God was worried that humanity would become like or equal to God as a consequence of eating the forbidden fruit. Satan suggested that eating the fruit (acting on their own judgment) would indeed accomplish that result, that it would result in equality with God. And while God was trying to keep them from becoming equal, Satan seems to have thought that it would actually be good and helpful to do so. Thus, Satan set out to accomplish his plan of radical human equality with God, first through the divine right of kings, and later through radical equality among all individuals. Satan's idea was that all human individuals should get equal treatment from God because they would be God's equals. That is, that God should not distinguish between good and evil—nor should we. This is not the idea of equal consideration before the law, but is a matter of equal judgment by the law, which is absurd because it nullifies the purpose of the law. If all behavior is equal before the law, then the law cannot judge behavior at all.

Finally, in the name of God's justice God Himself took ultimate vengeance upon His own Son on the cross for the sin of the world. That's the Old Testament story, but it's not the end of the story. The true character of God was revealed on the cross as Jesus Christ forgave even those who put Him there. God then resurrected Jesus Christ from death and installed Him as the new archetype of human health and wholeness.

Many voices today want to cleanse the Old Testament of its vengeance and violence, but doing so would deface the true story by eliminating the awful vengeance that is endemic to the sin that God forgave. It would ignore the fact that God's forgiveness of sin results in the death of Sin. It would diminish the full extent and expression of God's forgiveness by diminishing the degree of human sin to which humanity had fallen. It would diminish the power of God's forgiveness to put an end to the vengeance and violence of sin. Sin's vengeance is the historical reality and prerequisite of God's forgiveness. To diminish the violence of the vengeance diminishes the magnitude of the forgiveness.

Those who want to cleanse the Old Testament of vengeance and violence are motivated by the desire for equal judgment of all people in God's eyes. They think that it is unfair for God to treat people differently, to treat law-abiders and law-breakers differently. The demand for radical equality insists that all people—good and bad, right and wrong, believers and unbelievers—receive the same judgment (forgiveness) from God, that God not discriminate between good and evil. Thus, such a desire finds support and common ground with Satan, and Satan's grand plan of radical human equality with God.

THE DIFFERENCE

God, on the other hand, discerns the difference between good and evil righteously, correctly. God's ultimate purpose (τέλος) is the destruction of evil in the world. And the destruction of evil is a good thing. However, God knows that people themselves are not evil because He created them good. Evil is the consequence of Satan's teaching in the Garden, Satan's program of radical equality.

And this means that God is not out to destroy *people*, but to destroy the false teaching and false understanding of radical equality, and the *ideas* that suggest that the differences between good and evil can be overlooked without consequence. God's target for destruction is not people, not even people who self-identify with evil. Rather, God's target for destruction is ideological. God is after principalities and powers, not those who believe falsely. God's plan is to change people, not to eliminate them. God's plan is not to return people to their pre-Fall blissful innocence and ignorance, nor to get people into some blissful, Gnostic heaven, but to reveal Satan's ideological idiocy, to reveal the consequences of Satan's misunderstanding and false teaching. God's plan is not to evacuate believers into heaven, but to eliminate hell from earth.

27. ONE ANOTHER

Therefore, having put away falsehood, let each one of you
speak the truth with his neighbor, for we are members one
of another. Be angry and do not sin; do not let the sun go
down on your anger, and give no opportunity to the devil.
                                        —*Ephesians 4:25-27*

James Jordan has said somewhere that we Christians need to one-
another one another, using *one-another* as a verb. It's a clever way
to make the point that as Christians we are all in the same camp.
The Greek word ἀλλήλων (*one another*), appears in the New Testament ninety-four times. That's a lot, so it must be important.

It's also important that Paul set a requirement for this one-anothering, namely, putting away falsehood. It's not a requirement in the
moral sense of an injunction like, "you can't go to bed until you brush
your teeth." It's not something that *ought* to be done. Rather, it's
something that *cannot* be done until the requirement is met. It's more
like, "the night won't disappear until the sun rises." There is a necessary condition to it because it is impossible to one-another another
until *after* we stop valuing falsehood. The very act of valuing falsehood stops people from one-anothering one another.

The reason that people don't one-another one another is that
they do not believe that they are in substantial unity with some particular group of other(s). Christianity has been divided up into a
thousand sects. It's impossible to be Christian without belonging to
some particular sect. Yet, each sect mitigates against the unity of
Christianity. With the sect mindset, the very act of belonging destroys unity. What a mess we've made of it! Paul says to us that in order to one-another one another, we must put this falsehood away.

We must embrace the larger and/or prior truth of Christian unity and stop claiming sectarian identity.

Unity is not something that Christians need to build. Common theology will be the result of living in Christian unity, not the cause of it. Trying to build common theology as the precursor of unity cannot happen because the common theology comes from living in faith with one another. We have been approaching it from the wrong end because we believe wrongly. We've got it *arsy varsy*[1]—backwards.

Speaking Truth

Once we put away the falsehood, once we set the ship of Christianity right side up, we can then begin to "speak the truth with his (our) neighbor" (v. 25). But as long as we reverse this critical order—of trusting in order to discover our common theology, rather than endeavoring to find common theology as the prerequisite for trust—we will be locked into our various corners of partisan belief without remedy.

Part and parcel of this process is knowing who our neighbors are. To misidentify our neighbors or to fail to treat them as neighbors is to fail to heed Paul's instructions. Christ came to correct the Jewish error regarding the identification of one's neighbor. The Jews understood *neighbor* (πλησίον) to mean any other person in proximity, or any of our fellow human beings. However, they tended to limit it to any member of the Hebrew nation and commonwealth, to the chosen people. The Jews only considered other Jews to be their neighbors with regard to the various biblical injunctions, which is not what the Bible teaches.

Christ came to correct that understanding, to restore its original intent. Christ's understanding was that one's neighbors were all people in one's proximity, irrespective of nationality or religion. For Christ (and Paul) our neighbors include whoever we live near and all those we chance to meet in our travels.

After several thousand years of Jewish life and culture, the thing which differentiated the Jews from the rest of humanity—being the chosen people of God—became a stumbling stone. It created two mutually exclusive groups of human beings. We could call them Jews and Gentiles, believers and unbelievers, or covenant keepers and

---

1   Ross, Phillip A. *Arsy Varsy—Reclaiming The Gospel in First Corinthians*, Pilgrim Platform, Marietta, Ohio, 2008.

covenant breakers—today we call them Christians and non-Christians. And as true as this division is, it does not reflect the ultimate truth about humanity. The ultimate truth is that all human beings belong to the common race or type or biological classification known as the *human genus* or *Hominidae*. The differences related to genetics, culture, religion, language, etc. have become increasingly insignificant over time and history, when compared to our commonalities. Over time, Western culture, including theology, science and technology, which are fruits of Christianity, have become both explicitly and implicitly increasingly dominant throughout the world. In fact, the size of the current world population depends upon the fruit of Western culture.

REGERMINATION

As this fruit of Christianity is scattered across the globe, we should expect it to ripen and rot, as all fruit does when nothing is done with it. Nonetheless, the process of rotting exposes and prepares the seed of the fruit for regermination. And as that seed regerminates and grows, it grows the Vine that planted the original seed. Again, God is in the process of replacing the religion of vengeance (Sin[2]) with the religion of forgiveness in Christ, replacing the religion(s) of Adam with the religion of Christ. God is replacing the archetype of Adam with the archetype of Christ. That change will alter the structure of humanity, the way of being human in the world.

Those who follow the religion of vengeance are not able to trust others, particularly those who are different than themselves. That lack of trust interferes with the development of the only thing that can overpower the spirit of vengeance—cooperation. The only way to defeat or overcome the religion of vengeance is with a superior religion, the religion of forgiveness in Christ. Trust and cooperation grow out of forgiveness.

But the followers of vengeance cannot be expected to just up and change religions themselves, of their own accord. People are not able to simply change their most fundamental assumptions about themselves and the reality in which they live. People are essentially creatures of habit, and apart from outside interference, habits do not change.

This is why it was necessary to introduce a new religion in order to change or replace an old one. A new religion requires a new God,

---

2   See footnote 3, p. 57.

or at least a new Son of God. So, God arranged it, and the rest is history. The new God is the Son of God, who is God Himself. However, the truth of Jesus Christ is the truth of the Bible, and this means that the New Testament be read as the fulfillment of the Old Testament, and the Old Testament be read in the light of Christ. And cutting any corners regarding the progressive revelation of Jesus Christ through the Bible and history undermines the fullness of that revelation, which cripples the ongoing development of theology, science, and technology.

Christ is truth itself, and as such everything derives its most fundamental definition, meaning, and purpose in the light of Christ, including the development of theology, science, and technology. As theology, science, and technology themselves grow and mature as disciplines, they need to track closely to the arc of truth that God is drawing the world through. In order to do that, the development of science and technology must maintain contact with two points: the point of origin (or the past) and the point of fulfillment (or the future as God has envisioned it)—beginning and end, alpha and omega.

MEMBERS

Paul said, "for (ὅτι) we are members of one another" (v. 25). It can also read "*because* we are members of one another." The verb *we are* (ἐσμέν) is in the indicative, which means that it conveys an objective fact about something, and represents those to whom Paul was writing, to the Christians in Ephesus. Remember that Jesus came to correct the Old Testament understanding of who the neighbors of God's people are. The Jews limited *neighbor* to only include the chosen people of God, but Jesus opened that definition up to include all whom the people of God come in contact with.

This is not an argument for the traditional understanding of universalism, that everyone is or will be saved. No! But it is an argument that Jesus intends to bring His gospel to the entire world, to every living soul. Unfortunately, there will probably always be some who reject the gospel of Jesus Christ to their own damnation. Nonetheless, Jesus' intention is to reach every extant human being as history continues to unfold. And this process will continue as long as new human beings continue to be born. Eventually, Christianity will dominate and only a few naysayers will hold their ground against the universal truth of God.

Consequently, this final phrase of v. 25 is evangelistic in purpose. Paul tells us that our mutual membership in Christ is a given. The wholeness of humanity, which necessarily flows out of Jesus Christ because He is the new archetype of humanity, is simply a fact of reality. It's a done deal in the sense that Christ has already completed it. That's what Jesus died for. It was accomplished by His death and resurrection. He doesn't need our stamp of approval, or our agreement to make it real. God alone is the source of its reality. We who are in Christ are members of one another, and we are charged to treat our neighbors—everyone we come into contact with—as fellow members in Christ. Even if they aren't, yet! Even if they haven't heard of Jesus. Even if they think of themselves as enemies of God or our enemies, for Jesus told us,

> "Love your enemies and pray for those who persecute you, so that you may be sons of your Father who is in heaven. For he makes his sun rise on the evil and on the good, and sends rain on the just and on the unjust" (Matthew 5:44-45).

Loving our enemies and praying for those who persecute us is a function of being Christian. It's not that people are to do this in order to become Christians, but rather, this is what Christians do. Of course, people are not made Christian by our treating them as Christians—but it helps! People are made Christian by Christ. Following Christ, as Paul did, helps us as the people of God to remove obstacles to the faith. When Christians understand themselves to be ordinary, to model Christian human belief and behavior as ordinary belief and behavior, rather than to be the leading edge of some sort of special or super human group, we model the bridging of the gap between believers and unbelievers. When we assume Christ to be who He said He is, we encourage others to do the same.

Most people, when confronted with the truth of Christianity will respond favorably because it actually makes sense. It's only when people have been previously conditioned against the gospel of Jesus Christ or when Christ's truth has not been presented correctly that they find it objectionable. And what is objectionable is not the truth of Christianity, but the various false ideas that oppose Christianity, and the false religion that masquerades as Christianity. Paul pejoratively referred to those who understood themselves to be on the cutting edge of something new that God was doing, those who thought that they were special in the eyes of God, as *super-apostles* (2 Corinthians 11:5, 12:11). Being a super Christian is not a good thing.

The assumption that all human beings are members of one another in Christ greatly facilitates the growth of Christianity. Just as the assumption that humanity itself is divided into two irreconcilable groups—believers and unbelievers, covenant keepers and covenant breakers, or Christian and non-Christian—hinders it. And yet, the Bible teaches both perspectives. How can this be? In a word—*time*.

GROWTH

Immediately following Jesus' crucifixion and resurrection there were very few followers of Christ in the world. At that time it could honestly be said that there was a sharp distinction between the followers of Christ and the rest of the world. And that argument could legitimately be made for centuries because the spirit of Christ that opposed the world was a small minority. But over time, as Christ's influence in the world began to manifest and influence the dominant culture, which at the time was Roman. It could be said that Christ became less opposed to the world over time, as more and more people converted to Christianity.

Of course, this development was not steady, but has continued in fits and starts, two steps forward and one step back. This pattern of Christian growth has continued to dominate the world over millennia. The gospel of Jesus Christ, and its cultural fruit—honesty, integrity, and industry which provide the soil out of which science and technology emerged—have been slowly growing in Western culture, and of late in the other cultures of the world, as well.

The world has been in the most chaotic period of cultural change it has known since the Industrial Revolution. God is reshaping human culture in the light of Christ with the fruit of Christianity. And the Trinitarianism that is unique to Christianity provides the only sustainable path forward. The world has suffered from the failure to properly integrate theology, science, and technology into the ecology of the Earth, because many people continue to reject Christ.

The West has suffered from the cultural monopoly of Western Christianity for a millennium. While the doctrine of the Trinity has been developed in Western Christianity, that development tended to be more Greek than Hebrew, the result of which has been the philosophical dominance of Adam's false dichotomy that has shaped both the life and the problems of the West, which have of late been imported to the world. That false dichotomy pulls in two mutually exclusive and mutually wrong directions.[3]

One impulse tends toward the dominance of monotheism, monopoly, and monoculture, and the other toward the *laissez faire* approach of polytheism, multiculturalism, and anarchy. Various aspects of Western civilization have promoted and supported some version of one or the other of these impulses at various times and in various ways. The result is that these two ideologies are in perpetual war with one another, each blaming the other for the evils of the failure of proper integration. However, the truth is that neither pole of this false dichotomy can provide integration. The one side leads to totalitarianism and the other to anarchy, and neither of these options is viable or sustainable as a form of government.

Trinitarian Christianity proposes, not an option or a third way of compromise, but an entirely different approach to theology that has provided the foundation for the development of science and technology by solving the Platonic dilemma of the one and the many.[4] The proper understanding of the doctrine of the Christian Trinity provides an approach to God and to His world that reveals its truth through the practical experience that has already produced science. Not only is there no conflict between religion properly understood and science, but the two are in the kind of mutual interdependence that is revealed by the doctrine of the Trinity. And while there is a sense in which God does not change, theology, science, and technology most certainly do change because we change. To suggest that people have always been the same is to deny the impact that God has had upon the world.

I'm not arguing for the evolution of humanity. Rather, I'm arguing for the growth and maturity of both individuals and culture over time in the light of the progressive revelation of Jesus Christ through history. We are growing up into God's vision of our maturity in Christ. We don't ever become more than human beings, but we do become increasingly more fully human.

ANGER

Regarding the change of worship of the God of vengeance in Sin to the God of forgiveness in Christ, Paul gives us permission to "be

---

3   See Appendix: False Dichotomy, p. 415.

4   This is a subtle and somewhat complex argument, and a recurring theme in much of my work. Various explanations and references may be found in my other books.

angry" (v. 26). We cannot control our feelings, our emotions. Emotional feelings are similar to other physical senses.[5] When we touch a hot stove, we cannot *not* feel it. The feeling is real. So, Paul tells us not to try to deny our feelings, but to allow them to exist. Feel the anger (ὀργίζω), the violent passion of the mind that is the source of the desire for vengeance. The effort to deny it is unrealistic and amounts to the denial of reality. Paul just told us to "put away falsehood" (v. 25), and the denial of reality is a falsehood. So, feel the anger and deal with it.

But whatever you do with it, "do not sin" (v. 26). Feel it but do not act on the feeling. This phrase is the translation of one Greek word: ἁμαρτάνω. It is one of those negative words like *acapella*, where the *a* means *without*. It could be translated as *be without sin*. However the root word is μέρος, which signifies a *part* of a larger whole. It might be a part of something that is due, or a part that has been assigned to someone, or one of the constituent parts of a whole. It is true that sin lacks wholeness, but the meaning of the word here is more about the wholeness than the sin. Consequently, a better translation would be *do not break the wholeness or unity*, with the implication being that the wholeness refers to humanity or human fellowship. The idea is to feel the anger, but don't let it interfere with or destroy the unity of humanity in Christ.

In order to do this, we must deal with the anger. We must acknowledge its reality, not just to ourselves but to all who are involved —and the sooner the better. Thus, Paul commends us to

"not let the sun go down on your anger" (v. 26).

Deal with it as soon as possible, and don't let it fester over night. If at all possible, we are directed to resolve it right away. If it involves a misunderstanding, correct it. If it involves an offense, find the forgiveness to overcome it, whether the forgiveness is yours or the other person's is of no importance. What is important is the expression and acceptance of the forgiveness.

While the *English Standard Version* reads *angry* and *anger*, the second word in the Greek is quite different. Προργισμός means the indignation and exasperation that develops into wrath or belligerence. The problem with anger is that it is self-justifying. Left alone, anger

---

5   Nevin, John Williamson & Ross, Phillip A. *The True Mystery of The Mystical Presence*, Pilgrim Platform, Marietta, Ohio, 2011, Appendix III: "The Eight Sense of Man."

will always rationalize that the blame or fault belongs to the other person. Anger is incapable of accurate self-analysis, and that's why it must be discussed. By all means, discuss it at the earliest possible opportunity. And if you cannot discuss it with the other people involved, then bring it to God-in-Christ in prayer for forgiveness. But don't let it stew.

Unmitigated anger is one of Satan's favorite tools. Paul understood clearly who motivates the sin of anger. Anger itself is not a sin, but it can easily become a sin if not dealt with. Paul tells us to

"give no opportunity to the devil" (v. 27).

The idea is not to give Satan a foothold in our experience or language. If there is any opportunity for this to happen, it most likely will, because the devil is an opportunist.

In addition, slander (διάβολος) is personified as the devil here, and that's not wrong. But the idea can be conveyed without the personification. The idea is to close out all opportunities for slander and/ or false accusation, either against one's self or by one's self. Slander and accusation feed the beast of vengeance, but the vengeance does not satisfy. Thus, vengeance apart from forgiveness always leads to more vengeance. Religions based on vengeance are self-perpetuating. Humanity well knows the difficulties of overcoming the religion of Sin. God has been working on that project for about five thousand years.

28. STOP!

Let the thief no longer steal, but rather let him labor, doing
honest work with his own hands, so that he may have some-
thing to share with anyone in need. Let no corrupting talk
come out of your mouths, but only such as is good for build-
ing up, as fits the occasion, that it may give grace to those
who hear. And do not grieve the Holy Spirit of God, by
whom you were sealed for the day of redemption.
—Ephesians 4:28-30

In these verses Paul provided several negative injunctions against various ongoing sins that had been brought into the church by new believers. Were none of these things actually going on at Ephesus, Paul would have no incentive to speak about them. But because they were, he did. Paul didn't simply want certain things stopped, he wanted to use these particular things as evangelism tools.

Paul did not set up special evangelistic meetings or develop special techniques or testimonials aimed at anyone in particular. Rather, he tried to integrate evangelism and testimonials into the ongoing life of ordinary Christians. And at that time, ordinary Christians were previous sinners and pagans who had no history of the kind of cultural improvement that we know. Their conversion to Christianity was marked by the strongest contrast between godlessness and godliness. In contrast, today America has enjoyed the cultural effects of some two thousand years of Christianity in the world.

To think that Christianity has not changed the world is just plain silliness. Of course it has! And while the world is a long way from perfection, many social and cultural improvements brought about by Christianity are commonly accepted today as being normal, understanding that science and technology are among the fruits of Christian culture. The process is far from perfect or complete, and in some ways has even deteriorated over the past several decades. Nonetheless, people come into the churches today without as stark a cultural change as they did in Paul's day because modern secular culture enjoys many Christian blessings. The church has influenced world culture today more than people realize, even though the past several decades have worked to undermine that influence. The development of Christianity happens on the social level the same way that it does on the individual level—two steps forward and one back. But over the long run, there has been growth and maturity.

OCCUPATIONAL CHANGE

"Let the thief no longer steal" (v. 28).

Thieves generally turn to thievery in order to avoid work as a means of financial support. Paul was talking about habitual thievery as a lifestyle. Coming to Christ would prohibit certain kinds of work, like doing what is immoral or against the teachings of Christ, and would encourage certain other kinds of work, honest work. Paul had learning a trade in mind, something sustainable that would provide a decent living and provide for a family. But as important as honest work is for an individual, said Paul, the reason for a thief to engage in honest work is not for his own benefit, though he would benefit greatly. Rather, the purpose for a thief to engage in honest work is for him to evangelize and provide help for the needy.

Most thieves steal because they are needy. They are unable or unwilling to work for a living. Thieves generally come from lives of poverty and ignorance. And thieves are usually pretty good at reading people. They have to size up jobs and assess risks, etc. Such are their job skills. Paul was sending repentant thieves to assess and provide for needy people. They would likely be able to correctly assess those who presented themselves as needy, to sort out the scammers. But also to witness to the poor, not simply with words, but with their new lifestyle in Christ.

Repentant thieves would provide a most appropriate witness to the needy, by providing both actual help and an example of the virtue of honest work, which would witness to the reality of regeneration. Notice that these former thieves are to provide sustenance, not just to Christians, but to "anyone in need" (v. 28). Other thieves would generally be able to see through a false testimony, and would tend to keep the repentant thieves more honest about their testimony and their new lives in Christ. The repentant thieves would also be able to appreciate their own lot in life—'ere but for the saving grace of Jesus Christ go I. For without obedience and work, they would be in the same boat as the needy. Everybody would benefit from this simple dictum. The needy would get help and the church would provide a witness.

Corrupt Talk

"Let no corrupting talk come out of your mouths" (v. 29).

It is a wonder today that we need to define corrupt talk, that we don't know what it refers to. This is probably because today nothing is off limits for modern expression. In fact, today the more shockingly rotten the topic, the better the ratings! Younger people will grow up thinking that it's okay to talk about anything, that talk itself has no moral effect. But this is exactly the opposite from what this verse teaches.

How corrupt does something need to be before we should *not* talk about it? Of course we shouldn't talk about the really gross stuff, but who is to say what's gross and what isn't? In our age of permissiveness, one person's definition of gross is another person's definition of pleasure. As long as popularity rules the media—and there is no indication that media is driven by anything else, there will be no solution to the problem of who's to say. As long as all opinions are of equal value, no one can say anything with authority.

But Paul was saying here that Jesus is the One who should set our social standards—norms. Paul was saying that corrupt talk corrupts people, that the very act of discussion exposes people to the contagion of rot. What the world considers to be the maturity to be able to handle such "adult" topics, Paul considers to be, not maturity at all—but poor manners, unacceptable values, and worthless character. No doubt Paul was talking about:

"sexual immorality, impurity, sensuality, idolatry, sorcery, enmity, strife, jealousy, fits of anger, rivalries, dissensions, divisions, envy, drunkenness, orgies, and things like these" (Galatians 5:20).

If modern people eliminated talk about these things, they would find precious little to talk about. And if this is true, then people are being used by the minions of Satan to spread the doctrines of Satan's filth. All of this corrupt talk gets past our moral sensors because it is usually disguised as news, entertainment, and sports. Imagine contemporary media without news, entertainment, or sports as they are currently being done. I'm not suggesting that there is not any real news that is worthy of being broadcast. There is, but much of it isn't being broadcast because truth threatens falsehood. Nor am I suggesting that all entertainment be banned. But if the above things were banned from entertainment, there wouldn't be much left to talk about. Other kinds of entertainment could be created—and it would have to be created because precious little gossipless entertainment exists today. I'm not saying that all sports is bad. It's not! But much of what passes for sports today is nothing more than gossip, gambling, and corrupt talk. Large sports venues are well-known avenues for criminal money laundering.

Paul didn't just recommend what not to do, he went on to tell us what to do, what kind of talk is pleasing to the Lord. That which is

> "good for building up, as fits the occasion, that it may give grace
> to those who hear" (v. 29).

We should *edify* (οἰκοδομή) one another, encourage one another's growth in Christian wisdom, piety, happiness, holiness, and health. The degree that this sounds boring or impractical to you is the degree that you have already been corrupted.

People are quick to associate this kind of thing with the Puritanism that founded America. I don't want to bash the Puritans because they did represent an actual moral upgrade in the history of the morality of the world. But for us to go back to some previous era, pining for some supposedly pristine moral perfection of the past, reveals the degree to which we have failed to understand and practice actual Christianity. All pining for the Golden Age of some past period of history issues out of a failure to understand or value the progressive revelation of Jesus Christ in history. It represents a failure to read the Bible holistically and to appreciate God's purpose and the growing success of His cause in the world.

We can no more go back to some idealized Puritan age than we can go back to an idealized age of the Early Church. We can't even go back to the 1950s. The past is gone. It's over, never to return. Christian hope lies in the future, but not just any future. Our hope lies in the future of God's making. God is building His church out of living stones (1 Peter 2:5), out of extant people in this world, not some imaginary people of the past or the future—not even the best Christians of the past, nor some imaginary people of some abstract, future heaven. God is real, so Godly things are the things of reality in this world.

EDUCATION

This lesson appears to be a hard lesson for Christians to learn. We are sorely tempted to think that our own perspective and analysis are always the *sine qua non* of rational intelligence. It is so difficult to be genuinely self-critical or what the Bible calls *humble*. And this difficulty tends to rise as people become increasingly "educated" in the contemporary sense of the word. To educate means to impart knowledge by formal instruction, to school someone, or to train for some particular purpose or occupation. And the latter sense is increasingly what education does in our contemporary world. Today, education is about job training, not human development.

However, we must understand that all education promotes some particular perspective. There is no such thing as value free or objective education. The values and perspectives that are taught are the values and perspectives of a particular perspective, a particular curriculum, and some particular teachers. In the contemporary world of public and higher education that means that we are educating our children to believe the values and perspectives of secularism, or godlessness. Teaching biblical values is against contemporary educational policy.

The problem is not that our educational policies and practices are failing. Quite the opposite! The problem is that they are very successful. Our educational policies are doing exactly what they are designed to do for the secular world, and until Christians understand this they will continue sending their children to their local slaughter houses of Christianity—public schools. The "objectivity" that they teach is increasingly anti-Christian.

Unfortunately, what passes for Christian education today is not much better. Christian education is usually no more than the indoctrination of students into some partisan expression of Christianity, usually of the fundamentalist variety. We can judge the condition of Christian education by examining the books that stock the shelves at a Christian bookstore. There we find a plethora of books that appeal to popular tastes, and precious few books that have stood the test of time.

The largest Christian publishing companies are not owned by Christians, and are driven by the same concerns that drive secular publishing—sales, not orthodoxy. Paul's concern about corrupt talk begins with the subtle corruption of orthodoxy among those who don't see it themselves, and who don't believe those who do. And not believing those who do, they trust themselves, their own "objective rationality."

Paul said that we are to edify one another, not just other Christians but our neighbors, as well. Those who do understand are to teach those who don't. The means of education really should be in the hands of those who understand. Education should not become a business that is dedicated to the business of education rather than a ministry that is about the Master's work. Thus, the Bible does not put education in the jurisdiction of civil government because civil government has the power to impose law, but not the ability to teach morality.

In opposition, civil government justifies its involvement in education because, it argues, it is the only jurisdiction that can guarantee "objectivity" by forbidding all partisan perspectives. However, the "objectivity" of civil government is the partisan perspective of godlessness, which is then imposed on all equally. In the name of objectivity, civil government teaches both pantheism and atheism in order to not teach some particular form of Christianity. And because federal policies prevail, this perspective has become the dominant perspective across America. As the teaching of children has historically moved from home to church to state, so the curriculum of education has moved from Christ to humanism to godlessness (or secularism). If anything, this demonstrates the effectiveness of federal policy, and not its failure.

Fitly Grace

Paul has two other qualifications regarding our communication with others: that it "fits the occasion," and

> "that it may give grace to those who hear" (v. 29).

The *Authorized Version* translated the first as "that which is good to the use of edifying." The idea is not simply that our communication needs to relate to its immediate circumstances, but that it needs to relate to the purpose of Christ, which is the edification of His church. We need to fit our edification of others into the immediate circumstances of *their* situation. We need to show people how their circumstances fit into the reality of Christ. But not by imposing some pet Christian belief on circumstances that are otherwise not related to Christ. But rather, by revealing Christ in the midst of their own existing circumstances.

There are two methods of such edification: imposition and discovery. Imposition forces Christian interpretative categories upon every situation. Discovery, on the other hand, reveals the truth of Christ in the underlying forces and structures that define a situation. The method of imposition imposes Christ on the situation, whereas the method of discovery clarifies the situation in the reality of Christ. Imposition fits Christ to the occasion, whereas discovery fits the occasion to the reality of Christ. And the difference between them is quite stark, in that imposition tends to shut down free and open discussion, whereas discovery is built on free and open discussion.

The second qualification or guide is to insure that what people hear serves the priorities of God's grace. All communication by Christians should reveal God's grace in one way or another. It should lead people to see His grace and help them freely respond to it. We cannot impose God's grace upon people. Freely was it given and freely must it be received. What makes grace graceful is that it has been freely given *before* people ask for it or respond to it. It is not given as an answer to our request for it. If it comes as an answer to our request, it would not be the kind of radical free grace provided by Jesus Christ.

People don't need to ask Jesus into their hearts, they can simply look and discover Him to be already there. If He is not there, people have nothing to respond to. Responding to God's truth is not a matter of asking God for it. To respond is to see that it is already there, and fall on our knees in thankfulness. The human response to God's grace is always Eucharistic. It's a function of thankfulness, not a request for something we do not have. God gives, we respond.

The other thing to notice is that only those who actually hear (the Lord, the gospel, the truth) are able to respond to God's grace. It is not that God impedes their hearing or keeps anyone from hearing, but that people either fail to listen or close their own ears to God's truth. The failure to hear or connect to God is never God's fault, for Christ's propitiation is sufficient for all humanity. The gospel of God's grace and mercy is extended to all. But all do not respond. This does not mean that God is not omnipotent, it just means that God does not impose grace upon people apart from their personal response. God treasures the love and obedience of a free people, not the mandatory worship of people who would rather be elsewhere.

Grief

We are not to

"grieve the Holy Spirit of God" (v. 30).

There are two sides to this concern. One involves grief that is felt by the Holy Spirit, and the other is grief that is felt by the individual. Both issue from a common source. And before we look at that source, we need to understand what grief is. To grieve is to feel sorrow for loss, usually the loss or death of a relative or friend. And this is exactly what Paul meant.

Paul wrote to those in Ephesus who had some experience with Jesus Christ, to those who knew Christ, who had what we call a personal relationship with Him. The source of grief would be anything that would disturb that relationship, that would strain or harm the relationship, undermine or destroy the trust that such a relationship is built on. Grief is felt upon the loss or death of a relationship, a separation. Anything other than a conscious, loving, responsive, obedient relationship in Christ through the Holy Spirit brings grief, and is advised against.

The Spirit is grieved when we do not act upon the reality of His presence with us, when we treat Him as if He is dead or unreal. When we fail to engage or walk away from the Holy Spirit, He is grieved. In this case, the grief belongs to the Holy Spirit. His wholeiness is harmed by people who deny the reality of His role in human wholeness.

The other side of grief comes when *we* feel it, when we feel like we have been let down by the Spirit, or when we feel like He has not responded as we think He should, or that He has left us. Anytime these kinds of thoughts and feelings are engaged we can trust that they are false because He is never the one who abandons relationship. God never abandons His side of the covenant. He will not let us go—ever. And if we persist in our ignorance or denial of Him, He will bring various sanctions to us in order to move us out of our ignorance and denial.

God's job is not to give us whatever we want, or whatever *we* think would be best. God is not here to meet our perceived needs. Don't get me wrong! God does meet our needs, but He meets *His* understanding of our needs, not ours. Whenever there is abandonment, it does not come from God. We need to pay very close attention when it feels like God is punishing us for something because God does try to correct bad thinking and behavior. But He doesn't do this because He doesn't love us. He does it *because* He loves us.

> "For the Lord disciplines the one he loves, and chastises every son whom he receives" (Hebrews 12:6).

In contrast, only when people prove themselves to be unresponsive to God's nudging, does He let them do whatever they want, whatever they think is right. Not because He doesn't continue to love them, but because He knows that love must be freely given and freely responded to. People are free to respond to God or not. He forces the issue into consciousness, but He does not force the outcome.

> "Claiming to be wise, they became fools…. Therefore God *gave them up in the lusts of their hearts* to impurity" (Romans 1:22-24).

Unbelievers call this *freedom*, believers call it *death*.[1] God doesn't force people into obedience, but allows us the freedom to find various ways to agree with Him on our own. He also gives us the ability to influence and to be influenced by others. There are many ways to influence people, and the most effective involve honor. We influence others by being honorable ourselves, and we are influenced by those we ourselves honor. Honor encourages imitation.

Marked

To be "sealed for the day of redemption" (v. 30) does not mean avoiding contact with the outside world for fear of being infected. Nor does it mean that redemption happens in one day. Rather, it means that Christians have been marked or identified by the Holy Spirit for liberation from captivity or slavery. Redemption (ἀπολύτρωσις) means that our liberation is procured by the payment of a ransom.

When we consider the whole story of the Old Testament as the context of this idea that Jesus Christ has paid a kind of ransom to free humanity from captivity, we find something odd. The Jewish Passover, the central celebration of Judaism, honors the liberation of Israel from Egyptian captivity early in history. The Jews in Jesus' day considered themselves to be a free people because of that liberation.

---

1   See Appendix: False Dichotomy, p. 415.

But apparently, neither God nor Jesus considered the Jews to have been a free people because Jesus came to liberate the captives from sin, which not only included Jews but was focused on them in particular.

Paul said that

"all, both Jews and Greeks, are under sin" (Romans 3:9).

And yet Israel celebrated her freedom from captivity every year during Passover. Were the Israelites free or not? Well, they managed to get free from Egypt, but not from Sin. Their religious atonement rites, as dictated by the Old Testament, did not perform as they expected. Of course the prophets had complained about this for centuries.

> "And the Lord said: 'Because this people draw near with their
> mouth and honor me with their lips, while their hearts are far
> from me, and their fear of me is a commandment taught by men,
> therefore, behold, I will again do wonderful things with this peo-
> ple, with wonder upon wonder; and the wisdom of their wise
> men shall perish, and the discernment of their discerning men
> shall be hidden.'" (Isaiah 29:13-14).

> "Thus says the LORD: 'What wrong did your fathers find in me
> that they went far from me, and went after worthlessness, and be-
> came worthless?'" (Jeremiah 2:5).

> "I hate, I despise your feasts, and I take no delight in your solemn
> assemblies" (Amos 5:21).

For whatever reason(s) Israel remained in captivity or became ensnared again in captivity to Sin, to their own sin rather than to Egypt's. And Jesus was sent to release them, as well as the whole world from Sin's grip. But how are Christians to revere the Old Testament when its teachings and practices were not able to free people from sin?

At best, we must understand that the Old Testament is not adequate for this task of freeing people from Sin, and it never has been, nor was it designed to be adequate in this regard. This, however, does not mean that the Old Testament is useless. Far from it! God's law is an eternal guide, a teacher. Prior to regeneration in Christ, people are under the law and its judicial consequences. God's law convicts everyone. Following regeneration in Christ, the consequences of disobedience are nullified because 1) Jesus paid the price for everyone in

Christ, and 2) true Christian faithfulness does not violate God's law. This does not mean that Christians do not violate God's law, but rather that all such violations issue from unfaithfulness. Thus, in the flow of human history, the Old Testament religious practices of Israel did actually complete the moral and spiritual upgrade that they began.

Following Christ, the Old Testament serves as a guide, a teacher. Following Christ, the role of the Old Testament can be seen more clearly in the history of the redemption of the world. The Old Testament Israelites provided important and significant historical help regarding the progressive revelation of Jesus Christ in history. In the light of Christ the Old Testament can be read more clearly.

Christians understand that Christ was with God at Creation, and has always been with God through His involvement in the Trinity. Thus, the revelation of God's law through Moses served as a kind of historical prefigurement of Jesus Christ. The gospel of Jesus Christ makes no sense apart from the revelation of God's law through Moses. The story from Moses to Christ's birth is the story of the failure of Jewish religion to extricate even the Jews themselves from Sin, much less the rest of the world. It is the story of the failure of religion apart from Jesus Christ, apart from the Trinity.

God In History

The ancient Jews had the best possible religion, one dictated by God Himself. But not even God Himself could extricate humanity from Sin *apart from Jesus Christ* because there is no actual God apart from Jesus Christ. In order for God to be fully God in human history, Jesus Christ must manifest in the fullness of His Person—both human and divine. The Godhead is not whole without Him, nor is God completely real in this world without His actual human manifestation in it. The infinite fullness of the Godhead is enhanced through the manifestation of the Holy Spirit in the lives of believers through regeneration. All of this must be manifest in human history in order for the Godhead to be whole, complete in this world. This is the promise of Christ's return and the New Jerusalem (Revelation 21:2).

This reality reveals the necessity for the advent of Messiah in history in order for God to actually be God in human awareness. God cannot be fully God for us until He is fully manifest in human history, in human awareness. There are three necessary elements for the complete manifestation of God in history. First, the idea of the reality of God must be presented in history. This was accomplished through

Moses' revelation of the law and his initial compilation of Scripture. The book of Scripture conveys the only correct and complete idea of God's actual reality. Second, the reality of the Person of God must manifest in history. Jesus Christ accomplished this. And third, the reality of God-in-history (*in Christ*) must manifest in human consciousness or history, both individually and corporately. The Holy Spirit accomplishes this through regeneration.

All of those in whom this accomplishment exists—through regeneration by the power and presence of the Holy Spirit—comprise Christ's church or body. This personal and social transformation is necessarily conscious. Part of its reality is the personal and corporate awareness of it. People cannot be regenerated without knowing it. They may not know exactly when or how it happened, but they will know *that* it happened, that they are on the other side of it. Like biological birth, to be alive in Christ is to know that you are alive in Christ.

There is also a social reality involved in personal regeneration. Regeneration produces an awareness of the reality of the Holy Spirit. The regenerate are aware of this reality in themselves because the Spirit brings about changes in their thinking, values, and behavior. The regenerate begin to grow in likeness to Jesus Christ. They begin to value Him and His teachings, His character, His Word. And at the same time, they become aware of others who share the same Spirit, the same sort of thinking, values, and behavior. There is a social dimension of regeneration, and it is called *the church*. It includes the definite article because it is a unified whole.

It can manifest as an official organization, an organization with officials (officers), a formal church. Unfortunately, not all organizations that call themselves *Christian* actually embody the thinking, values, and behavior of the Holy Spirit, not completely or correctly. In addition, some groupings of regenerate individuals are not formally involved in official organizations.[2] Nonetheless, the body of Christ or the church includes all individuals and groups who are actually regenerate. There are two aspects or requirements for people to be identified as Christian: 1) they must self-identify as such, and 2) the Holy Spirit must concur. Self-identification is pretty straight forward, but the concurrence of the Holy Spirit is more complex (Matthew 7:21).

---

2   Ross, Phillip A. *Informal Christianity—Refining Christ's Church*, Pilgrim Platform, 2007.

Generally, the way this concurrence works is that the Holy Spirit in me recognizes the Holy Spirit in you. We recognize certain commonalities in thinking, values, and behavior that reflect Scripture among other people who self-identify as Christian. Sometimes the concurrence of the Holy Spirit is part of an official organization, and sometimes it is not. In the same ways that people of the same nationality can recognize one another, so regenerate Christians recognize other regenerate Christians. They speak the same language, so to speak. Another way to say it is that repentant Christians recognize other repentant Christians because genuine repentance leaves a mark. It changes the way that you treat yourself and other people.

The important thing to note about the concurrence of the Holy Spirit is that it cannot be programmed, which means that it cannot be controlled. The Spirit blows where it wishes (John 3:8). Regenerate Christians generally gather together regularly for worship, communion, study, prayer, service, fellowship, etc. However, it is not the paperwork or the organizational structure that defines Christ's church, nor any legal requirements like the IRS 501(c)(3) filing status or any other legally filed paperwork.

For instance, Christ's body may include several people in a neighborhood who gather informally, even though they attend different churches. Such a grouping may even include some people who do not currently attend or belong to any local church. Christ's church or body is much more dynamic and comprehensive than any limitations set by human beings. It must be, because there are times in history when official churches become corrupt and apostate, and attendance or membership in such churches cannot be mandated by the Holy Spirit. Thus, Paul could recommend that faithful Corinthian Christians separate themselves from the apostate Corinthian church (2 Corinthians 6:17). Christianity involves a life of vigilance because life in Christ is dynamic, not static.

29. CARRIED AWAY

Let all bitterness and wrath and anger and clamor and slander
be put away from you, along with all malice. Be kind to one
another, tenderhearted, forgiving one another, as God in
Christ forgave you.   *—Ephesians 4:31-32*

These two verses provide the entire moral teaching of the New Testament. Paul tells us what not to do and what to do in order to live in Christian faithfulness. And it all rests on the forgiveness of God-in-Christ. Ninety percent of the world's problems would disappear if people would simply live in obedience to these two verses, which also means that the presence of the world's problems stands as an accusation of simple Christian unfaithfulness.

There are three pieces involved: 1) what to avoid, 2) what to engage, and 3) the foundation or justification. The things to avoid include: bitterness, wrath, anger, clamor, slander, and malice. Let's look at them one at a time.

Bitterness (πικρία) includes wickedness and hatred. Bitterness is a very common sin. It involves resentment, cynicism, disgust, and distrust. Paul tells us that we have control of this feeling, that we can choose to put it away, to not engage it. And by doing this regularly over time, we can learn to simply ignore it. Imagine your life without any bitterness on your part.

Now, begin living that way.

Wrath (θυμός) involves passion, emotional heat or intensity, anger, and belligerence. Wrath is more pronounced than bitterness, yet it shares many similar traits. Paul said,

> "Be angry and do not sin; do not let the sun go down on your
> anger" (Ephesians 4:26).

All of these feelings do arise. No one is immune from them. The advice is to ignore them, to not pay attention to them, to not let them effect our behavior. We cannot stop them from arising, and denying them only gives them power. This ability, like any talent, improves with practice. So, practice early and often.

Clamor (κραυγή) is the first manifestation of behavior that results from engaging bitterness, wrath, and anger. To clamor is to cry out or croak, to make complaining remarks or noises under one's breath. It is to complain. The ancient Israelites also committed this sin:

> "And the people complained in the hearing of the LORD about
> their misfortunes, and when the LORD heard it, his anger was kin-
> dled, and the fire of the LORD burned among them and consumed
> some outlying parts of the camp. Then the people cried out to
> Moses, and Moses prayed to the LORD, and the fire died down. So
> the name of that place was called Taberah, because the fire of the
> LORD burned among them. Now the rabble that was among them
> had a strong craving. And the people of Israel also wept again and
> said, 'Oh that we had meat to eat! We remember the fish we ate in
> Egypt that cost nothing, the cucumbers, the melons, the leeks, the
> onions, and the garlic. But now our strength is dried up, and there
> is nothing at all but this manna to look at'" (Numbers 11:1-6).

People don't usually understand how serious of a sin this is or the effect it has on our emotional psyche. It is serious because it saps people of patience, kindness, and consideration—and it is contagious! The mentality of crowds is contagious. People get swept up by crowds. Complaining encourages others to join in a round of complaint escalation to see if they can outdo one another with the severity of their complaints, which only increases the problem. Jesus and Paul agreed with Moses that it is unhealthy and is to be avoided.

Slander (βλασφημία), translated as *evil speaking* in the *Authorized Version*, is the next step in the escalation, as complaining turns into blame. The Greek root is where we get the English word *blasphemy*, but here it is not directed toward God, but toward other people. And in the same way that blasphemy demeans the character of God, this kind of blasphemy demeans the character of other people.

Today, for slander to be libelous it must contain some element of falsehood. It is the lack of factuality that makes it libelous, and not merely the fact that the person being attacked doesn't like it. The slanderer may be misinformed about various facts, and not be aware of the falsity of the accusation. But the ignorance of the attacker does not relieve the slanderer of either the guilt or the sin of the slander. Older words that describe the character of slander are *scurrilous* and *calumnious*. The easy way to avoid slander is not to say false or degrading things about others.

Malice (κακία) is the last term in this list, and it refers to malignity, ill-will, and the desire to harm others. It is a kind of wickedness or depravity, and often begins with a disregard for law. It involves wickedness that is not ashamed to break laws, and originates from the disregard of God's law and/or the desire to determine law for one's self. It begins with a self-identity that is full of pride and despises biblical norms. It thinks of itself, not as ordinary, but as unique, contrary to common norms. Malice involves the reversal of values such that evil is valued because it is uncommon, and good is despised because it is common. Of course, the malicious person does not see it like this. Maliciousness values the outlier for its radical diversity from the norm, rather than valuing the commonality of the norm. The malignant person cannot discern and/or does not value subtle differences of character, but prefers a self-identity that is outside of the norm. Such people usually consider themselves to be special and/or more important than others.

This is a difficult concept to convey because so many people today have already traversed a reversal of values, and the current culture now generally honors and promotes this reversal of values as if it is the correct order of values. As maliciousness becomes increasingly popular, it also becomes increasingly thought to be healthy, and the reverse—preference for the time-honored human norms instituted by Jesus Christ—are increasingly thought to be not healthy. Where Christianity works to make Jesus Christ the norm or archetype of humanity, the spirit of malevolence does the opposite.

This is the character of original sin that has issued from Adam's rejection of the idea that only God can determine good and evil. Adam and Eve sought to be like God in this regard, determining good and evil for themselves, at the behest of the Serpent (Genesis 2:17, 3:5). In a fit of pride, Satan thought that he knew God, and God's thoughts and values, well enough to codify them. We see this when the serpent asked Eve, "Did God actually say…" (Genesis 3:1). Eve answered by adding to God's conditions, "neither shall you touch it" (Genesis 3:3). The Serpent then corrected Eve, "God knows that when you eat of it your eyes will be opened, and you will be like God, knowing good and evil" (Genesis 3:5). Again, God knows better than to think that sin can make humanity His equal. It is Satan's assessment of God, and it is short of the reality—and that is the problem. It's a not an accurate assessment of God's understanding. Everything that the Serpent said is in service of this lie.

God said that the critical concern in this world involves the two trees or systems: the tree of life and the tree of the knowledge of good and evil. But the Serpent said that God's concern was only one of the trees, the one that differentiated good and evil. God said that the central concern in this world is between life and death, where the Serpent said that God's central concern was morality—good and evil. God focused Adam on the tree of life, where the Serpent focused him on the tree of the knowledge of good and evil. God said that concerns about morality—good and evil—do not always serve life. Morality is usually understood to be about rules and regulations, and God said that those who concentrate on rules and regulations often tend to choke life.[1]

And this is exactly what Jesus said, "But woe to you Pharisees! For you tithe mint and rue and every herb, and neglect justice and the love of God" (Luke 11:42). The Pharisees were all about rules and regulations, but Jesus was about love and life. The gospel of grace is opposed to the drudgery of rules and pietism. God told Adam that moral knowledge does not necessarily promote eternal life or salvation, when the morality is self-determined. Whereas the Serpent told Eve that moral knowledge does produce eternal life or salvation. The gospel of grace reveals the fact that pietism or legalism can choke life. However, the life that comes by grace produces a genuine love of God's law.

Do This!

Don't grieve the Spirit, don't engage bitterness, wrath, anger, clamor, slander, or malice. After discussing what not to do, Paul began specifying what to do.

"Be kind to one another" (v. 32).

The Greek word χρηστός means *fit* or *useful*, and carries the implication of financial generosity. Kindness means helping one another in difficult times, and while all difficult times do not involve money, many do. Kindness includes the willingness to give or lend money to others in need, remembering that loans among fellow Israelites (be-

---

1   See Appendix: False Dichotomy, p. 415.

lievers) were mandated to be provided at no interest, and better yet—as a gift. We are not to profit from the distress and misfortune of others. A lot of problems would be solved if we stopped such profiteering on the misfortune of others. The current insurance, legal, and medical industries profit from human misfortune and are implicated here.

Interestingly, χρηστός can also be translated as easy.

"For my yoke is *easy*, and my burden is light" (Matthew 11:30).

God's people are yoked with kindness and caring for one another. And it is instructive to see that Jesus Himself yokes people with the burden of kindness and resource sharing. This is not socialism or communism, where the state redistributes resources among citizens. When the state redistributes resources they are taken by force as taxes and given to others. Whereas here resources are freely given or lent to the needy at no interest, no force is involved. Here, those who receive such kindness are encouraged to pay it back and pay it forward, and because interest is forbidden in such cases, those who receive such loans would be much more able to pay it back. Here, the well-off are encouraged to be generous, and the needy are encouraged to be responsible.

Χρηστός is also translated as *good*:

"No one tears a piece from a new garment and puts it on an old garment. If he does, he will tear the new, and the piece from the new will not match the old. And no one puts new wine into old wineskins. If he does, the new wine will burst the skins and it will be spilled, and the skins will be destroyed. But new wine must be put into fresh wineskins. And no one after drinking old wine desires new, for he says, 'The old is *good*'" (Luke 5:36-39).

The old is good or fit because it conforms to God's values. The value of wine improves with age. Wine collectors know this. And from this we understand that true religion or that into which the Spirit is poured also improves with age. It takes time for the benefits of religious values to mature and accrue. An application of this idea can be called the progressive revelation of Jesus Christ in history. Jesus was saying in the parable above that it would take time for the religion He was founding to accrue benefits to society. Or we can understand it to mean that He was saying that it would take time for people to mature individually, to appreciate and understand what He had given them.

Paul calls Christians to be "tenderhearted" (εὔσπλαγχνος, v. 32), or sympathetic toward one another. The world considers this to be a sign of weakness and immaturity, but Paul calls it a sign of Christian strength and maturity. The unsympathetic can also be called *sociopathetic* because they have an undeveloped conscience. The tenderhearted have well-developed consciences that are sensitive, compassionate, and caring, which means that they are easily hurt. Thus, Christians are called to suffer and to bear suffering gladly with joy.[2]

Suffering is mentioned eighty times in the New Testament, and the suffering servant (Isaiah 53:8; 1 Peter 3:18) is a major biblical theme, though it is commonly neglected by most Protestants. People don't like suffering, and don't know how to meet it with joy, so they ignore it and try to avoid it. However, we ignore it at our own peril because we cannot be tenderhearted or enjoy the maturity of being sensitive to God's concerns without suffering the pain that accompanies such sensitivity. The sensitivity increases the potential for pain, and that's just the way this world works! The trick to meeting it with joy is found when the appreciation of the sensitivity is greater than the discomfort of the suffering.

FORGIVENESS

We are also to forgive one another (v. 32). This is the heart of being like Christ. He gave Himself for the forgiveness of the world. To be like Him, we are to give ourselves to the forgiveness of others. And the idea of forgiveness is to *give first*. To forgive is to stop blaming people and absolve them from debt or expectation of return. We are to lead with forgiveness in all of our relationships as a way of modeling Christ's forgiveness of us. Forgiveness can defuse even the most stringent sense of vengeance. The more genuine the forgiveness is, the better it works. Again, replacing the religions of vengeance with the religion of forgiveness is God's long range plan for the world.

Forgiveness is the central teaching of the Bible. The Old Testament Jews sought forgiveness through the sacrifice of animals, through the sacrificial system of the covenant relationship, which God established after He brought His people out of Egypt. Bringing the

---

2   James 1:12; Matthew 5:10-12; Luke 6:22-23; Acts 5:41; Romans 8:17-18, 8:35-37;
     2 Corinthians 12:9-10; Philippians 1:29, 2:17; Colossians 1:24; Hebrews 10:34;
     1 Peter 4:13-16.

sacrifice demonstrated their sense of need. Laying hands on the sacrificial animal symbolized identification of the sinner with the sacrifice, as did the surrender of the life of the animal. Emphasis on an unblemished sacrifice emphasized the perfection of God. God's forgiveness, channeled through the sacrificial offering, was an act of mercy that was freely bestowed by God, not purchased by the one bringing the offering. The whole purpose of the sacrificial system for the ancient Jews was to relieve them of sin.

But it didn't work, and it couldn't work! The ancient Psalmist knew that Israel was on the wrong track when he wrote:

> "For you will not delight in sacrifice, or I would give it; you will not be pleased with a burnt offering" (Psalm 51:16).

As did Isaiah:

> "What to me is the multitude of your sacrifices? says the LORD; I have had enough of burnt offerings of rams and the fat of well-fed beasts; I do not delight in the blood of bulls, or of lambs, or of goats" (Isaiah 1:11).

And Amos:

> "I hate, I despise your feasts, and I take no delight in your solemn assemblies" (Amos 5:21).

It didn't work because the hidden purpose of the sacrificial system was not to forgive sin through the sacrifice of animals, but to set up the coming of Jesus Christ, who alone atoned for sin and provided forgiveness. And the fruit of that forgiveness was God's dispensation of His Holy Spirit upon believers. The Old Testament was not a complete revelation of God, but only the prelude.

Faithful Old Testament saints knew this and longed for the coming of Messiah. The Psalmist knew this:

> "The sacrifices of God are a broken spirit; a broken and contrite heart, O God, you will not despise" (Psalm 51:17).

But the people of the Old Testament often forgot this, and when they did they drifted into more sin. Or rather, they were led into sin by their forgetful priests and kings.

> "Because this people draw near with their mouth and honor me with their lips, while their hearts are far from me, and their fear of me is a commandment taught by men, therefore, behold, I will

again do wonderful things with this people, with wonder upon
wonder; and the wisdom of their wise men shall perish, and the
discernment of their discerning men shall be hidden" (Isaiah
29:13-14).

> "For they are all adulterers, a company of treacherous men. They
> bend their tongue like a bow; falsehood and not truth has grown
> strong in the land; for they proceed from evil to evil, and they do
> not know me, declares the LORD. Let everyone beware of his
> neighbor, and put no trust in any brother, for every brother is a
> deceiver, and every neighbor goes about as a slanderer. Everyone
> deceives his neighbor, and no one speaks the truth; they have
> taught their tongue to speak lies; they weary themselves commit-
> ting iniquity. Heaping oppression upon oppression, and deceit
> upon deceit, they refuse to know me, declares the LORD"
> (Jeremiah 9:2-6).

God knew that the sin of vengeance was considered to be a religious virtue by the god of Sin.[3] Sin seeks vengeance for injustice,
slander, and dishonor as a matter of justice. And every act of
vengeance produces more injustice, slander, and dishonor in the eyes
of those who receive the vengeance. And this means that people cannot stop the cycle of vengeance without divine interference. Because
the god of Sin encourages vengeance in the guise of justice as a godly
virtue, the God of forgiveness needed to act decisively to provide a
model for Godly forgiveness, in order to replace the one with the
other.

God has provided the way, the model of God-in-Christ, and the
power to accomplish all that needs to be accomplished to make this
substitution of the one religion with the other both real and efficacious through the power and presence of the Holy Spirit. Note also
that God's model is Trinitarian—God-in-Christ (v. 32). The Trinitarian model is necessary in order that God may be in Christ, and that
Christ may be in His people, in His church, though His Holy Spirit.

Too often Christians are concerned about getting people into
church, having them attend worship services. Too many Christians
think that faithfulness means attending church services, and that
evangelism means getting other people to attend church services. But
that's not what Scripture teaches. Paul was certainly not opposed to
people attending worship services. He encourages it everywhere. But

---

3   See footnote 2, p. 6.

that was not his primary or his first concern. Rather than working to get people into church, Paul was working to get Christ into people— or more accurately, to *reveal* and increase Christ's presence in people's lives. Thus, our job is not to *put* Christ in people's lives, but to *reveal* His presence in their lives. Revealing God's reality and presence in the world, in history through Jesus Christ and the dispensation of the Holy Spirit, is the condition for the reality of personal regeneration.

30. ORAL SIN

*Therefore be imitators of God, as beloved children. And
walk in love, as Christ loved us and gave himself up for us, a
fragrant offering and sacrifice to God. But sexual immorality
and all impurity or covetousness must not even be named
among you, as is proper among saints. Let there be no filthi-
ness nor foolish talk nor crude joking, which are out of
place, but instead let there be thanksgiving. For you may be
sure of this, that everyone who is sexually immoral or im-
pure, or who is covetous (that is, an idolater), has no inheritance in the kingdom of Christ and God.*

—Ephesians 5:1-5

Christians are called to mimic (μιμητής), imitate, and follow God as a beloved child would do. But this doesn't mean that we should remain immature. Rather, because God's values are the opposite of the world's values, Godly maturity is childlike in that it is innocent, unfeigned, and without pretension. Spiritual maturity means growing in these qualities. Children take things at face value. They don't try to second guess things. They are trusting and transparent. Children are credulous because they lack experience of the world. Christians are to be credulous in spite of their experience of the world.

To imitate God means to incorporate God's character into our own. It is the call to imitate God that makes God's character so important, because to misread God's character is to follow Him wrongly. And to follow wrongly is not to follow at all. God provided the Ten Commandments and the Levitical law in the Old Testament as the means by which to follow Him. But doing so with only the

Old Testament proved to be impossible. No one could follow God's law sufficiently, not even with Levitical help. It was just too different from the Adamic human character that had been defaced by sin. Sin made it seem like there was no difference between justice and vengeance because both were arrayed against perceived evil. Indeed, the character of the Old Testament was captured and contained by the struggle between various perceptions of good and evil.

We can glimpse the character of this struggle by considering the ancient religion of Zoroastrianism, also called Mazdaism and Magianism. Zoroaster's ideas led to a formal religion bearing his name by the sixth century B.C. and have influenced other later religions including Judaism, Gnosticism, Christianity and Islam. Zoroaster simplified the pantheon of early Iranian gods into two opposing forces: Ahura Mazda (*Illuminating Wisdom*) and Angra Mainyu (*Destructive Spirit*) which were in conflict. This ancient Iranian religion was once the state religion of the Achaemenid Empire, under Cyrus the Great (550–529 B.C.) and Darius III (336–330 B.C.). It was also present during the Sassanid Empire, the last pre-Islamic Persian Empire (224-651 A.D.).

Note that Muhammad (610–632 A.D.) lived during the last days of the Sassanid Empire, and that the Islamic Caliphate and civil war (632–750 A.D.) ended by taking over the Sassanid Empire and occupied almost exactly the same area. This suggests that Islam may have been a kind of Zoroastrian revival or adaptation that interpreted and modified Christianity to fit into its religious and philosophical categories.[1]

In contrast, the New Testament provides a clear presentation of the character of God in Jesus Christ, amplified by the Apostles. In Christ we find, not the struggle between good and evil (Genesis 2:9), but the expression and manifestation of the Tree of Life. In Christ we find that the conflict between good and evil is a false dichotomy[2] because both good and evil are erroneously defined by Sin[3] and were adopted by Adam and Eve. Christ came to correct this error and set forth the gospel of eternal life.[4]

---

1   Hoyland, Robert G. *Seeing Islam as Others Saw It: A Survey and Evaluation of Christian, Jewish and Zoroastrian Writings on Early Islam (Studies in Late Antiquity and Early Islam)*, The Darwin Press, Inc., 1998.

2   See Index: False Dichotomy, p. 415.

3   See footnote 3, p. 57.

4   See *Malice*, p. 299.

The Bible teaches that the central conflict in this world is about two trees or systems: 1) the tree of the knowledge of good and evil, and 2) the tree of life. Satan advances a false dichotomy regarding the knowledge of good and evil, and God-in-Christ advances the tree of life. Satan's dichotomy is false because Satan's definitions of good and evil are ignorant of the concerns regarding sustainable life in this world. This does *not* mean that the difference between good and evil is false or illusory, but that Satan's or man's determination of the ultimate categories of good and evil is too narrow to include the wholeness of God or humanity.

Only God can make the true or correct determination of good and evil, and the whole of the Bible presents God's determination. When we (humanity) accept God's value judgments, life is sustainable, and when we (humanity) make those judgments ourselves, apart from God, it is not (Proverbs 8:36). Again, the false dichotomy as Satan promotes it is *good vs. evil*. But the correct dichotomy is *life vs. death*, or *Godless morality vs. the morality of God-in-Christ*.[5] The Old Testament must be understood in the light of Christ, and the New Testament must be understood as the fulfillment of the Old. This same conflict has been raging since Satan deceived Eve, and cannot be resolved apart from the holistic understanding of it through all human history.

Love With Legs

Again, the central religious conflict in the world is between the religions of vengeance and the religion of forgiveness. Satan's central strategy is to confuse the issue such that his erroneous analysis makes sense to sinners (to themselves), and he has been working at this confusion since he first showed up in the Garden of Eden. Satan's strategy is to frame the dichotomy by defining good and evil with human values, by using human sanctity as the ultimate value. God-in-Christ, on the other hand, has framed the dichotomy in terms of God's values, which include human sanctity—but not at the expense of ultimate truth.

Paul solved this dichotomy by commanding that we "walk in love (ἀγάπη, v. 2). To exercise agape is to engage in selfless love of one another without expectation of any return or response. It is to do what is right—not what you or I think is right, but what God thinks is right. God is not opposed to human sanctity. In fact, human sanc-

---

5   See footnote 3, p. 57.

tity is at the heart of God's mission in the world. God wants us to be holy—sanctified, but He also knows the truth about Sin and sin's deceptions. One of the major points of the Bible is to help people see the world and their place in it through God's eyes, from God's perspective, and not simply from their own perspective.

I have made a point of using the term *God-in-Christ* in order to emphasize the Trinitarian unity of the Godhead, and because Christ is our model or archetype. Paul said that we are to engage agape toward one another

> "as Christ loved us and gave himself up for us" (v. 2).

He was willing to die a death of extreme suffering on the cross to make the point. That's the model! However, we are not called to follow Christ by dying on a cross, but by being *willing* to suffer a painful death. That death begins in baptism, and should permeate everything we think, say, and do for the rest of our lives.[6] Christians are not called to martyrdom or to physical death, but to life abundant and eternal—sustainable life.[7] And to gain such life means living without the fear of suffering or physical death. Paul went on to say that Christians are to be

> "a fragrant offering and sacrifice to God" (v. 2).

The *Authorized Version* calls it "a sweetsmelling savor." Our lives are to be pleasantly aromatic as a means of evangelism. Think of the smell of fresh baked bread, or cookies fresh from the oven, or a summer barbecue. People are naturally attracted to such smells, and will tend to follow their noses. Paul made an allusion to Old Testament sacrifices where the sacrificial animals were roasted, and similar smells would fill the sanctuary.

The olfactory sense provides a kind of visceral knowledge. Animals are more sensitive to the kind of knowing related to olfactory memory. It is a deep, vital, basic kind of knowledge, and is quite different than linguistic or visual knowledge. Love includes this olfac-

---

6   Ross, Phillip A. "O Death," *Poet Tree—Root, Branch & Sap*, Pilgrim Platform, Marietta, Ohio, 2013, p. 23.

7   See *sustainable* in the Indexes of *Arsy Varsy—Reclaiming The Gospel in First Corinthians, Varsy Arsy—Proclaiming The Gospel in Second Corinthians, Colossians—Christos Singularis, Rock Mountain Creed—The Sermon on the Mount, The True Mystery of the Mystical Presence, Peter's Vision of Christ's Purpose in First Peter, Peter's Vision of The End in Second Peter.*

tory sense, and is related to pheromones, a secreted chemical that triggers a sexual response in members of the same species.

SEX

And speaking of pheromones, Paul continues to address sexual issues.

> "But sexual immorality and all impurity or covetousness must not
> even be named among you, as is proper among saints" (v. 3).

Paul's concern is not sexuality per se, but identification with the sexually immoral. The Greek word (πορνεία) is more specific. The *Authorized Version* calls it *fornication*, which in Paul's day referred to illicit sexual intercourse, to include adultery, homosexuality, lesbianism, intercourse with animals, close relatives, or involving a divorced man or woman. Not only is all sexual activity outside of biblical marriage forbidden, but Paul's point was that all personal identification with such things should not occur (ὀνομάζω). Paul was not simply saying that such things should not be spoken of, but that Christians must not be identified with such immorality.

The biblical idea of naming involved a kind of character identification, such that the thing named would be accurately associated with the meaning of the name. We can think of last names, in the sense that Smiths were metal workers. Often the surname was given because of an occupation, i.e., Carpenter, Baker, etc. The name Jones and Johnson were originally a patronymic name meaning "son of John."

Paul's point was that we must not get our human identity confused with sexual immorality, such that we call ourselves homosexuals, whores, prostitutes, lesbians, etc. This error is made when people say, "I *am* a homosexual, whore, prostitute, lesbian," etc. *No,* said Paul.

> "There is neither Jew nor Greek, there is neither slave nor free,
> there is no male and female" (Galatians 3:28),

to which we can add *homosexual, whore, prostitute, lesbian*, etc. All of these are false categories of human identity. It is to obscure and occlude the image of God in which all humanity is being recreated *in Christ*.

Paul was not saying that there were no such people, but that those in Christ who used this kind of language had a false sense of

self-identity. They were still clinging to the ways of Sin, to the categories of the world that were false and Godless. Paul was not saying
that such sinful immorality was unreal or untrue, but that Christians
have no business identifying themselves as such, and much less acting
on the basis of any such identities. Rather, Christians are to crucify
the flesh.

> "But I say, walk by the Spirit, and you will not gratify the desires
> of the flesh. For the desires of the flesh are against the Spirit, and
> the desires of the Spirit are against the flesh, for these are opposed
> to each other, to keep you from doing the things you want to do.
> But if you are led by the Spirit, you are not under the law. Now
> the works of the flesh are evident: sexual immorality, impurity,
> sensuality, idolatry, sorcery, enmity, strife, jealousy, fits of anger,
> rivalries, dissensions, divisions, envy, drunkenness, orgies, and
> things like these. I warn you, as I warned you before, that those
> who do such things will not inherit the kingdom of God. … those
> who belong to Christ Jesus have crucified the flesh with its pas-
> sions and desires." (Galatians 5:16-21, 24).

IDENTITY

Paul went on to call this non-identification with false human
subgroups *proper* (πρέπω). This characteristic of common identity
was to stand out as uniquely Christian in a world filled with sin. It
was to be conspicuous and eminent, in that Christians were to identify with Christ alone, and not with any sort of group that was less
than the wholeness and holiness of humanity in Christ. This even applied to nationalities. Christians were not Gentile Christians or Jewish
Christians or Greek Christians or slave Christians or free Christians or
male Christians or female Christians or Afro-American Christians or
Irish Christians or Calvinist Christians or Roman Catholic Christians
or Baptist Christians or Charismatic Christians, etc. No subgroup was
to be named as part of our common Christian identity.

Rather, we should refer to ourselves as Christians who happen to
live in this or that nation, who have this or that heritage, who are
with or without debt, who are male or female, etc. Our sinful tenden-
cies encourage us to identify more with the adjective than with the
noun, more with the Gentile, Jewish, Greek, slave, free, male, female,
etc. than with being first and foremost *Christian*. Doing the former
undermines unity, but doing the latter encourages Christian unity by
highlighting our first, primary, and most significant identity as being

simply Christian. We see this ongoing sinful perspective today as sociologists and pollsters continue to emphasize the distinctives of various Christian subgroups in their work, and pander to them in the same way that the world does. Such sub-grouping simply must stop, especially in the church.

Paul called for an end to all such practices of subgroup identity. But we have misunderstood Paul's intent by thinking that Paul was forbidding cussing, potty talk, and slander. While it is not wrong to include these things in Paul's meaning, it is an error to think that such was Paul's central concern. These things are included in v. 5 where Paul said that it was out of place for Christians to engage in filthy talk, foolish talk, or crude joking. And the fact that they are specified in v. 5 suggests that they are not what Paul was talking about previously.

This is a very important issue that contemporary Christians have failed to understand. The more that Christians embrace church growth strategies from the world that are based on marketing segmentation programs and customized to various subgroups, the more this error wreaks its havoc in the church. The more we try to appeal to Hispanic Christians or Baptist Christians or Presbyterian Christians or nondenominational Christians or young Christians or any other subgroup of Christians, the more we undermine the unity of the church. We shouldn't even refer to born-again Christians because to be a Christian at all means to be born-again.

EUCHARIST

Rather, said Paul, "let there be thanksgiving" (v. 4). The *Authorized Version* translated εὐχαριστία as "giving of thanks." It's the same word Paul used in 2 Corinthians 4:15:

> "For it is all for your sake, so that as grace extends to more and more people it may increase *thanksgiving*, to the glory of God."

And in Colossians 2:6-7:

> "Therefore, as you received Christ Jesus the Lord, so walk in him, rooted and built up in him and established in the faith, just as you were taught, abounding in *thanksgiving*."

To Timothy Paul wrote:

> "For everything created by God is good, and nothing is to be rejected if it is received with *thanksgiving*" (1 Timothy 4:4).

Note the centrality of thanksgiving in the lives of Christians. Paul did not mean what the Roman Catholic Church thinks he meant by the word *eucharist* (εὐχαριστία). Nor did he use it the way the Roman Catholic Church uses it, by turning Holy Communion into a kind of relic, complete with magical powers (mystical properties).[8] The Roman Catholic Church (and others) have correctly understood the centrality of the Eucharist in worship, but have misunderstood what both the Eucharist and worship actually are. They have confused the reality with the symbol, the substance with the ceremony.

What did Jesus mean when He said,

"Do this in remembrance of me?" (Luke 22:19).

He meant to share bread and wine with friends regularly as a way to discuss, determine, and remember what God has done through Jesus Christ. Honestly, the Lord's Supper has become so sacrosanct in the churches, so encrusted with the traditions of men—yet accepted as divine instruction—that we have a difficult time disillusioning ourselves of our various historical assumptions about Holy Communion. If there is any tradition associated with the Lord's Supper it should be that it followed a Seder dinner because that was its original setting in the Upper Room.

In addition, the Jewish Seder was not practiced like Christians practice it, in part because it was done from memory not from a script. The children who asked the traditional Seder questions would get traditional answers, but not scripted answers. The adults would genuinely interact with the children with a give and take dynamic that would engage the attention of the children, and at the same time would quote Moses. It was fun for all involved! It would have been more like what we know as a Thanksgiving dinner with extended family and friends who were actually interested in the Thanksgiving holiday, and who discussed the details of it over wine and food. There would have been both formal and informal aspects of the celebration.

WORSHIP

Biblical worship began as simple prostration (שׁחה), which was a physical act or representation of submission to God. From this, God dictated an elaborate system of sacrificial worship that served the purpose of focusing Israel culturally on God, on serving God with honor and obedience.

---

8   See footnote 6, p. 174.

In the New Testament this prostration was expressed by the word προσκυνέω. There are other words that are translated as *worship*, and they all suggest some sort of reverence or honor. New Testament worship forms that made several changes in the light of Christ were adapted by the Apostles. Initially Christian worship took place in homes and in a few synagogues before it was banned. This means that worship would have been quite simple in comparison with the formalities of Old Testament Temple worship. When Christianity was legalized in 325 A.D., it became more formal and ornate because it was adopted by the Roman state, which had a passion for pomp and circumstance.

But regardless of the form that Christian worship takes, the biblical ideal of worship exceeds what we call *Sunday services*. There is nothing wrong with the idea of corporate worship, though some of our contemporary practices need to be reevaluated. However, corporate worship is like an iceberg, and the corporate aspect of worship is the part that is above the water line. This means that most of the worship iceberg is below the water line, unseen because it is private or personal and not part of Sunday meetings. And this element of Christian worship is nearly completely forgotten today.

People mistakenly think that personal worship means reading sappy devotionals before bed or first thing in the morning. Reading Scripture and good books is better, but there is much more to personal worship than reading. Jesus taught the disciples to pray, presumably because they didn't know how. They undoubtedly thought that prayer was done by the priests, not the people. And Paul advised praying "without ceasing" (1 Thessalonians 5:17).

> "For God is my witness, whom I serve with my spirit in the gospel of his Son, that *without ceasing* I mention you always in my prayers, asking that somehow by God's will I may now at last succeed in coming to you" (Romans 1:9-10).

> "Remembering *without ceasing* your work of faith, and labour of love, and patience of hope in our Lord Jesus Christ, in the sight of God and our Father; Knowing, brethren beloved, your election of God" (1 Thessalonians 1:3-4, *Authorized Version*).

> "And we also thank God *constantly* for this, that when you received the word of God, which you heard from us, you accepted

it not as the word of men but as what it really is, the word of God, which is at work in you believers" (1 Thessalonians 2:13).

"Through him then let us *continually* offer up a sacrifice of praise to God, that is, the fruit of lips that acknowledge his name" (Hebrews 13:15).

Worship, prayer, adoration, submission, honor, etc. are to be continuous. The idea is not to break away from ordinary life for worship, but to integrate worship into our ordinary lives in the midst of everything that we do—twenty-four-seven. This is what it means to live morally, to live a principled life, to have Christian values and to be a Christian. Worship means bringing our worth to God by imitating Christ, by receiving and practicing Christ's character qualities. The Holy Spirit is never apart from regenerate believers—never.

BE ASSURED

Because of all of this, referring back to vs. 1-4, Paul said that people who practice certain things will be excluded from having any inheritance in the future. God cannot tolerate sin. Yes, He sent Christ to forgive sin and make a way for people to repent of their sin and begin a new life in Christ. And all who are consciously and willingly in Christ will inherit the kingdom in spite of their sin.

However, it seems that a circumstance had arisen where some people claimed to be Christians, but lingered in their sin. Sure, we all linger a bit as we move from the kingdom of Sin to the kingdom of God. But persistence and the failure to make progress in overcoming sin suggests a deeper problem that Paul needed to address here. Rather than call people out by name, Paul called them out by their sin. Persisting in these sins leads to certain death.

"Sexual immorality" (πόρνος, v. 4) heads Paul's list. The *Authorized Version* calls it *whoremongering* and elsewhere *fornication*, the same root word used in v. 3. Sex is reserved for traditional, biblical marriage—end of story. Period. *Fini.* No questions are taken because none are allowed. None are needed because it is a simple idea. And yet, as simple and clear as this instruction is, this sin remains one of the most prevalent sins today, in the church and out.

The word *unclean* (ἀκάθαρτος) is usually attached to *spirit*, but not always. There is a long tradition regarding the issue of clean vs. unclean. It can be applied to food, circumstances, and people. The word *contaminated* puts it positively. The Old Testament majored on this distinction—and on fixing it ceremonially. Of course, the ceremony was not simply a talisman, but involved a procedure that would help remedy the problem functionally. For instance, unclean hands were treated ceremonially by washing them.

We often say that Jesus ended the Old Testament ceremonial laws, and He did bring them to a conclusion. But this doesn't mean that we stop washing our hands. Not at all! Rather, we are more clean today than any society in history. Our hand washing abounds! And we even do it ceremoniously, in the sense that there is a proper way to do it. Its not generally considered to be part of our worship, but it should be.

Personal cleanliness is very much a part of our Western, biblical heritage, and is a direct descendant of the ancient biblical concern about clean and unclean. My mother would instruct me to get cleaned up for church. She knew that cleanliness is next to godliness, as the old adage goes. God wants His people to be clean in every sense of the word. It's a function of health and the suppression of disease. It contributes to our healing. It actually is part of our personal worship.

And the same argument can be made for a lot of things we do. And even if you don't understand it, Paul said to pray without ceasing. So, we need to pray while we are washing. As odd as that may sound, it is simply true. To be *in Christ* is to do everything that we do in life *in Him*! Indeed, living in Christ is living in a constant state of worship. And this constant state of worship is Christian worship correctly understood. It doesn't mean that we fail to attend corporate worship at a local church. We are called to not neglect the assembly (Hebrews 10:25), but neither are we to neglect the call to a life of worship.

Gimme!

Paul also tells us that covetousness is a kind of idolatry in v. 5. The current definition of *covet* is "yearn to possess or have (something)." But the Tenth Commandment is more specific.

> "You shall not covet your neighbor's house; you shall not covet your neighbor's wife, or his male servant, or his female servant, or his ox, or his donkey, or anything that is your neighbor's" (Exodus 20:17).

The commandment does not forbid all desire. Some desires are good. Nor does it forbid wanting something similar to what your neighbor has. If he has a great marriage, it's okay to want to have a marriage like his. But it is not okay to want *his* wife. If your neighbor has a great car, its okay to want a car like his. But its not okay to want to have *his* car. Although, I suppose it would be okay to offer to buy it from him.

Christians are not called to become like Buddhists who practice the denial of all desire. But we are called to monitor our desires because human desire is like a dangerous chemical that can potentially do a lot of harm if it is not properly cared for. The commandment forbids desiring what is forbidden by God, so it encompasses the whole of the Ten Commandments. For instance, it is not a sin to desire to have sex with one's own lawful spouse. But it is a sin in all other circumstances. Similarly, it is not a sin to want to succeed, unless the means of your success are contrary to God's will.

To desire to satisfy God's will in your life is not a sinful desire, unless you slip into idolatry by failing to understand the difference between God-in-Christ and some false god. The satisfaction of the Tenth Commandment against covetousness requires having the correct understanding of exactly who God is, the God who said,

"You shall have no other gods before me" (Exodus 20:3).

To have any idea or understanding about God other than what the Bible teaches is to be guilty of idolatry.

This includes atheism because atheism is a theological belief about God. To believe that God does not exist is to be unaware of the role of God as lawgiver in the world. Law exists, including the laws of physics. God is the most fundamental source of law. And to think that God does not exist is to posit that law has no source other than man. Thus, atheists are humanists by default, in that humanity is understood to be the highest source of law for humanity.

Kingdom Inheritance

Contemporary Christians speak of being born again, of having a personal relationship with Jesus, and of *deciding* for Jesus. But seldom do they speak of *inheriting* the kingdom. First of all, inheritance is a gift not a decision made by the person inheriting. The decision about who inherits what is not made by those who receive the inheritance.

That decision is made by someone else, or by the law, which is also not dependent on one's own decision.

The idea of *inheritance* (κληρονομία) opposes the idea of making a personal decision for Christ as the determinative factor regarding salvation. Of course, there are personal decisions regarding Christian faithfulness, but not regarding the inheritance of the kingdom—other than the decision to deny or neglect the inheritance. The Greek word is composed of two words: κλῆρος, the stones or pieces of wood used to cast lots (dice), and νόμος, law. We can think of it as *the law of the lot or dice*, perhaps even *destiny*. Indeed, the inheritance of the kingdom of God is destined, even predestined. It has been previously determined. That's the good news of the gospel.

The good news is not simply that God loves you, Jesus died for you, so let Him into your heart. Rather, the good news is also that God loves humanity—the species. Jesus, who is God Himself, died for humanity and the kingdom of Christ, which is the inheritance of God's children. The good news is that ownership transfers on the death of the testator. But along with the blessings of ownership come the responsibilities of maintenance. The gift is free, but the responsibility for the maintenance comes with it. You cannot receive the one without also receiving the other.

Notice also Paul's conflation of the kingdom of God and the kingdom of Christ. The two kingdoms are one. The two kingdoms provide the model for Christian unity in that they are unified because God and Christ are unified in the Trinity. The Trinity is the model for Christian unity.

31. SAGACITY

*Let no one deceive you with empty words, for because of
these things the wrath of God comes upon the sons of disobedience. Therefore do not become partners with them; for
at one time you were darkness, but now you are light in the
Lord. Walk as children of light (for the fruit of light is found
in all that is good and right and true), and try to discern what
is pleasing to the Lord.* —Ephesians 5:6-10

Empty words bring God's wrath because they are contrary to
God's will. The Greek literally means vain (κενός) speech or
thinking that is devoid of truth (λόγος). We might call it bad
thinking, illogical reasoning, or some such thing. It is thinking, talking, or communication that is disassociated from reality, that fails to
take into account the reality of God or the wholeness of reality.
Empty words are purposeless words. Empty words neglect God, and
to neglect God is to court disaster. The easiest kind of empty words to
understand are mere abstractions. Not all abstractions are empty, not
all are unconnected from reality, but many are. We can also call such
abstractions *false*. They are simply not true. They don't mean anything because they are not viscerally connected to anything but our
imaginations.

In contrast, beneficial words conform to reality and are therefore
true. Beneficial words do not neglect God. The difference between
empty words and beneficial words is the same as the difference between true and false words or ideas. Sometimes it is not easy to tell
the difference. It takes discernment and discrimination, and these
skills have fallen on hard times in our current passion for diversity and
toleration.

In fact, the Bible does not teach diversity or toleration as they are currently understood. The Bible teaches unity and conformity to God's Word. Christians are not to be in unity with or obedient to what is evil, as defined by God in Scripture. Confusion comes when we inadvertently or unconsciously change categories of comparison. The issue is not unity vs. diversity generally, but the character of our unity and diversity. There can be much diversity with regard to unity in Christ, but we must not be so diverse as to be in unity with what is not in Christ. Similarly, we can tolerate much diversity within the bonds of unity in Christ, but we must not celebrate the diversity that falls outside of that unity. Discrimination is required to understand the difference.

Christians are never to simply be in unity with one another. Rather, Christian unity means being in unity with Christ first and foremost. Then all who are in unity with Him will also be in unity with one another. Christian unity cannot work any other way. We are to identify the character of Jesus Christ biblically, using both the New and Old Testaments, and imitate His character in our lives. We must not identify with all who call themselves Christian and then construct the character of Jesus Christ on the basis of *our* unity with one another, as is commonly done today by both the ecumenical movement and sinners who claim to be Christian, but don't repent of their sin. The Jesus of the Bible is the model, not the various churches, creeds, confessions, beliefs, denominations, or theologies.

Similarly, our creeds and confessions need to be associated with Jesus Christ, with the Bible, not simply with the various denominations or churches. When we associate our creeds and confessions with denominations and churches, we put ourselves in control of Christian unity by trying to force it into our own church and denominational standards. The result is that we create sects. Churches should not be grouped according to creeds, confessions, theologies, or beliefs. Rather, churches should be grouped geographically, according to their closest neighbors. This is how churches were originally grouped, and it allows for real unity and real diversity.

We use the word *real* to contrast that which is based on creeds, confessions, denominations, and theologies—abstract thinking—with what is viscerally real or concrete—concrete action. Those who are married understand the difference as being similar to the difference between the wedding and the marriage. The wedding is a ceremony. Of course, it is real and important. But when people live together over time, true character is revealed by the intensity and continuity of mutual exposure. The longer a couple lives together, the better they understand their differences because over time love both reveals them and smooths them out. This is the kind of unity that is more real than abstract, more life than ceremony, more love than law. At first, the unity of love and marriage is an abstract idea, but over time it grows more real because it survives more difficulties. Overcoming difficulties increases the strength of love. Thus, unity grows deeper as difficulties are weathered. Conversely, tragedy happens when the difficulties are avoided, not worked out.

PARTNERS

Paul's point in verses 5-6 is that the religious words of unbelievers are empty—vain, and that the Ephesian believers must not share in this error. The reason that Paul mentioned this was that it was happening. Many of the Ephesian believers had committed this same error. It was common among new believers. Still is.

New believers come to Christ from some other theological understanding, a false understanding that issues from sin, often from a mindset that has been saturated in sin from birth. This is true of everyone to one degree or another. And that sinful mindset originated in the Garden when the categories of the Serpent came to dominate the categories of truth. The Serpent convinced Adam and Eve in the Garden that the essential categories of reality are the moral categories of good and evil as they understood it. The Serpent said that God did not want humanity to be like Him, knowing good and evil (Genesis 3:5). But this is a lie!

God does want people to know good and evil in the same way that He knows them. God wants people to imitate Him, to imitate God-in-Christ, to become like Jesus, to incorporate Jesus' character qualities into their own lives. That is the purpose of the Bible.

The Serpent presented Adam and Eve (humanity) with a false dichotomy. That false dichotomy is false, not because of its contending positions, but because both good and evil are understood from this perspective of empty words (v. 6). Both issue from the human mind and are without God, who distinguishes between the two trees in the garden, between life and mere knowledge that results in death. Satan distinguishes only between good and evil according to his own measure, but has no concern for sustainable life. It's not that Satan's dichotomy is false because it violates logic, but because it has no visceral connection to reality. It is purely abstract.[1]

New believers invariably come to Christ from a pagan perspective that is saturated in the categories of sin, categories that are devoid of the perspective of the biblical tree of life. This is only to say that people tend to trust themselves, their own experience and understanding. New believers have very little experience with biblical categories, biblical faith, or the biblical God. There is a world of difference between knowing *that* one is a sinner, and knowing *how* one is a sinner. Our initial conversion comes from knowing *that* we are sinners.

Understanding *how* one is a sinner, understanding how the categories of sin function, and the false dichotomy presented by sin takes years of patient biblical study, prayer, and instruction. It also takes the unfolding of history and the progressive revelation of Jesus Christ through history in order for the consequences of sin to manifest, in order for us to see the true distinction between the two trees (systems) and make it increasingly plain. Truth is more than an abstract idea.

A few people are gifted with the vision to see all of this before it is completely manifest, but not many. John of Patmos was one such person, and he recorded his vision in the Book of Revelation. And although he made his vision clear, most people will not be able to see its reality until it is sufficiently manifest in history, until it affects them personally. It works in the same way that it is difficult to clearly identify growing trees until they produce fruit. John's vision is about the two trees growing in the garden to maturity, per Jesus' parable of the two crops (Matthew 13:24-29).

---

1 "Traditional systematic theology is more akin to Gnosticism than to the wholeness of thought and practice that Beecher calls for. Systematic theology has been an effort to arrange the various pieces of academic Christian theology in the abstract, to make the ideas fit into a grand scheme. In contrast, Beecher has in mind not just theological ideas, but habits of thought and behavior, the physics of nature—not just the laws of physics but the actuality of the material world, and even the reality of astronomy. When Beecher uses the word *system* he means to indicate much more than mere ideas, he means the wholeness of everything in human experience, both subjective and objective. Indeed, when God spoke to Adam about the 'tree of life' and the 'tree of the knowledge of good and evil' (Gen. 2:9) He was speaking of these trees as systems in a Beecherian sense." The trees in the Garden of Eden are systems in this Beecherian sense. Beecher, Edward. *Concord Of Ages, Or The Individual And Organic Harmony Of God And Man*, Pilgrim Platform, 2013, Phillip A. Ross, Editor, p. 3; see also "Appendix: Note On Logic," p. 514.

John also spoke of two women: the harlot and the bride of Christ. To the unregenerate and ill-informed, they look alike. These two women represent two churches, two bodies of people, two ways of life. For most of their lives they appear to be frighteningly similar, except to the groom. The difference between them is about their faithfulness to the groom and the fruit they produce. The one produces death and the other life eternal. Seeing this difference is difficult because one must him- or herself be faithful in order to know what to look for. It takes discrimination and discernment, skills that our contemporary society has branded as politically incorrect and to be avoided.

The unregenerate see these skills as evil and to be avoided because they do not result in the same evaluation and treatment of all people. The unregenerate value the principle of equality over the discernment of truth. It is more important that all people be treated equally—the same—than for truth to be known. Knowing the truth requires discernment, discrimination, and sagacity—the ability to understand and discriminate between similar things.

For example, equality demands that I treat all of my uncles the same because they are all family. But truth requires that I evaluate and treat my sexually abusive uncle differently than my biblically moral uncle. Both are uncles, so the principle of equality says that they should be treated the same. But the principle of truth says that they should not, because doing so will either punish the one without cause or will allow the other to engage in sexual abuse without consequence.[2]

Thus, Paul was complaining that new converts bring their false dichotomies with them into the church, and cautioned them against partnering with unbelievers, partnering with those who speak empty religious words by casting the logic of their thinking into various false moral dichotomies that are devoid of sustainable life. Perhaps a diagram of the two dilemmas is needed:

Satan's False Dichotomy

Good **vs.** Evil (Determined by humanity)

God's True Dichotomy

Life (Determined by God) **vs.** Good / Evil (Determined by humanity)[3]

---

2 This example is fictional and does not represent any actual family members.

3 See also Appendix: False Dichotomy, p. 415

Dark/Light—Walk

Paul then turned to an example of this same concern about true and false dichotomies to illustrate the issue in a practical way,

> "...for at one time you were darkness, but now you are light in the Lord. Walk as children of light" (v. 8).

First, Paul set out the moral dichotomy of darkness vs. light. The two things are mutually exclusive, though at dawn and dusk there are many intermingling shades. This analogy is found throughout Scripture and Paul's intention was to imply all that Scripture says about it, and to apply it to Christ. The Ephesians were in darkness before receiving the gospel of Jesus Christ. And when we apply this culturally rather than individually, we see that the darkness was far greater than what we can imagine. Our imaginations are limited because we currently live in a world that has already been greatly changed for centuries by the gospel of Jesus Christ. These Ephesians were new Christians in a sense that is difficult for us to understand, and certainly different than what new Christians bring to the church in our day.

Be that as it may, the darkness vs. light dichotomy is not new to Jesus Christ. The Old Testament is replete with it. Knowing the difference between spiritual darkness and spiritual light is the false dilemma in this case because it is patterned after Satan's ruse in the Garden. Satan's dilemma is the knowledge of good vs. evil, or in this case, the knowledge of light vs. darkness. The point is that both sides of Satan's dilemma are knowledge-based, not reality-based.

To this knowledge-based dilemma, Paul brings the reality of God-in-Christ by adding the reality factor. Having knowledge about the difference between darkness and light, or good and evil, is impotent unless it is illuminated by God-in-Christ. The real dichotomy is not between darkness and light, but between the limitations of knowledge and life. It's like the difference between ethics and morality. The ethical person *knows* the difference between right and wrong, whereas the moral person knows and *acts* upon the difference. The false dichotomy is between darkness and light. And the real dichotomy is between knowledge and behavior.

And yet there is more to this issue because there is a perspective from which Satan's moral dichotomy between good and evil is not entirely false. This dichotomy can be real. But for it to be real, it needs to escape the bonds of human opinion. It needs to be enlightened by Scripture. As long as good and evil are determined by humanity, the dichotomy is false because both positions are more imaginary than true. But when the dichotomy is framed by God, whose perspective is outside of or beyond humanity's, the dichotomy between good and evil is real because God knows the real difference.

Again, when people determine the definitions of good and evil apart from God, those definitions are always a matter of opinion and experience. But when God determines them, they are true because God's perspective is the closest to pure objectivity. For God it is pure objectivity with regard to humanity. But for us it is always filtered through our brains and is limited by our own subjectivity. Nonetheless, through regeneration, study, practice, and instruction our understanding of God's determination of good and evil can achieve an appropriate and effective level of reliable application. We cannot know God's objectivity as thoroughly as God knows it, but we can know it reliably.

This is a particularly applicable teaching about this issue because Christ, having dispensed the Holy Spirit to His people, provides the means to engage true knowledge. One of the major lessons of the Bible is that the Old Testament provided all of the knowledge needed to be the people of God. Yet, Old Testament Israel failed to share the grace of God with the whole world. So, God sent Jesus Christ, His Son, to atone for human sin and to dispatch the Holy Spirit to dwell with believers. The Holy Spirit then provides the means by which the people of God can be faithful: by the power and presence of the Holy Spirit through regeneration. Summing up the real dichotomy Paul added clarification:

> "for the fruit of light is found in all that is good and right and true" (v. 8).

Discernment is needed because Satan's false dilemma is not entirely false. Again, there is a real difference between good and evil, and between darkness and light. But as long as the difference that light brings is not based in reality—which does not deny God, the dilemma is false because it does not escape the realm of mere knowledge (human opinion).

Paul shows that light is to be associated with reality, not mere human knowledge, by speaking of the *fruit* of the light of Christ, which is in everything that is good, right, and true. The *International Standard Version* says it well:

"for the fruit that the light produces consists of every form of goodness, righteousness, and truth" (v. 9).

This is the basis for Van Til's insight:

"Only the Christian theory of knowledge, based as it is upon the absolute authority of the word of God speaking in Scripture, makes communication of any sort possible anywhere between men. Without this presupposition man would have no integrated selves and the world would be a vacuum. Without this presupposition of the Christian theory of being there would be no defensible position with respect to the relation of men and things. Neither man nor things would have discernible identity. There would be no science and no philosophy or theology, for there would be no order. History would be utterly unintelligible. Finally, without the presupposition of the Christian theory of morality there would be no intelligible view of the difference between good and evil. Why should any action be thought to be better than any other except on the supposition that it is or it is not what God approves or disapproves? Except on the Christian basis there is no intelligible distinction between good and evil."[4]

PROVING

Verse 10 brings in a translation difficulty in the *English Standard Version*, which reads,

"and try to discern what is pleasing to the Lord."

Try to discern is the translation of the word δοκιμάζω, which the *Authorized Version* translated as *proving*. The word does convey the idea of discernment, so the translation is not wrong. But it doesn't get to the point of the verse.

The previous verses have been about the discernment to correctly identify the false dichotomy in order to see the true dichotomy that is based on reality issues from regeneration. We must understand what pleases the Lord, so this discernment is necessary. But the idea of this verse is not to *try* to figure it out. The idea of verses 7 and 8 is the futility of belief apart from commensurate behavior, and this is the idea that is continued here. It's not that Christians are to *try* to discern a lot of things. Of course, they are! But here Paul said that we are to establish the *proof* of God's reality by acting on it. It's a different nuance of

---

4   Van Til, Cornelius. *The Doctrine of Scripture (In Defense of the Faith*, Volume I) den Dulk Christian Foundation, 1967, pgs. 61-62.

the meaning of *try*: to prove. We can prove what pleases the Lord by engaging with Him and then watching for confirmation of His reality in our own lives. Or we could say the same thing this way: we learn by doing.

32. This, Not That

Take no part in the unfruitful works of darkness, but instead
expose them. For it is shameful even to speak of the things
that they do in secret. But when anything is exposed by the
light, it becomes visible, for anything that becomes visible is
light. Therefore it says, "Awake, O sleeper, and arise from
the dead, and Christ will shine on you." Look carefully then
how you walk, not as unwise but as wise, making the best
use of the time, because the days are evil.

—Ephesians 5:11-16

Paul was never a popular preacher. He paid no attention to what was popular. His attention was on Christ. These verses are surely among the most unpopular words he ever penned because they are damming to the whole world of popularity, particularly in the contemporary world of computers and social media. We might be concerned that computers and social media have interconnected society in such a way that almost all computer use results in participation in "unfruitful works of darkness" (v. 11).

And while it is true that computers have given both saints and sinners the same tools, it is not true that such tools must be avoided. Computers have made it easier for sinners to pursue sin and to extend the reach of Sin's corruption. But they have also made it easier for saints to pursue Godliness and to extend the reach of evangelism. Suggesting that Christians must avoid all use of modern technology because modern technology is used by sinners is like suggesting that Christians must avoid all speaking because sinners speak.

The tools of technology are not the problem. The problem is taking part in the unfruitful works of darkness. Calvin said of this verse:

"We must beware of joining or assisting those who do wrong. In short, we must abstain from giving any consent, or advice, or approbation, or assistance; for in all these ways we have fellowship. And lest any one should imagine that he has done his duty, merely by not conniving, he adds, but rather reprove them."[1]

Matthew Henry added,

"We must therefore have no fellowship with these unfruitful works; as we must not practice them ourselves, so we must not countenance others in the practice of them. There are many ways of our being accessory to the sins of others, by commendation, counsel, consent, or concealment. And, if we share with others in their sin, we must expect to share with them in their plagues."[2]

However, the modern world has succeeded in uniting more people in various ways than ever before in history through banking, investments, and common markets. The uniting factor biologically is blood, and the uniting factor culturally is money. Both are mediums of exchange. And the result today is that even the most stringent Christians are involved in various unfruitful works of darkness through the monopoly of money. But our observation must not end here.

Rather, we need to inquire and assess whether there has been an historic increase in the depth of personal sinfulness, or whether the historic increase of sin involves a decrease of personal sinfulness, but an increase in the raw number of sinful persons.

Imagine a scenario in which the total sin of the world could be measured historically, such that a population (p) produces a measurement or volume of sin (s). The sin factor would be p times s. Putting some numbers to the calculation, let's say that sin can be measured on a ten-point scale, where 0 equals sinless and 10 equals totally sinful. At the time of Christ the population was about 300 million worldwide, and because Christianity was in its infancy with regard to saving people from sin, we might imagine an average sinfulness factor of 8. Thus, the volume of sin in the first century was about 2.4 billion (8 x 300 million). Today, there are 7 billion (or 7,000 million) people. Let's imagine that Christianity has succeeded in reducing the average sinfulness of the world by half. The sinfulness factor is now 4, which

---

1   Calvin, John. *Complete Commentary*, public domain, 1548, Ephesians 5:11.
2   Henry, Matthew. *Commentary on the Whole Bible,* public domain, 1710. Ephesians 5:11.

is a tremendous reduction of sin per individual. However, the volume of sin in the world today would be 28 billion. While the level of individual sin has decreased dramatically, the volume of total sin in the world has increased far more because of the increase in population.

The volume of sin comparison numbers are 2.4 billion in the first century to 28 billion in the twenty-first century. Thus, there has been a ten-fold increase of sin in the world, while the sinfulness of individuals has decreased by half. This fits Jesus' parable of the wheat and tares in that both wheat and tares are growing.

While this is a completely imaginary scenario with almost meaningless numbers, it demonstrates that there is a relationship between sin and population such that personal sin can be decreasing in the light of Christ worldwide, while at the same time the total level of sin in the world increases because of population increase. The lesson to be drawn from this hypothetical scenario is that greater populations require less personal sinfulness in order to be sustainable.

Applying this scenario to Paul's words we might say that the unfruitful works of darkness can increase while personal sinfulness decreases. This analysis accounts for both pessimism and optimism among people, depending on what factors are considered and how they are valued. This scenario also suggests the importance of teaching Christianity and the values of Christianity as a way to avoid future catastrophic consequences of sin, assuming that the Bible is correct in its assessment about sin and its social consequences.

EXPOSURE

Paul's solution to the sin problem is *exposure* to the light of Christ. The *Authorized Version* translated it as *reprove* (ἐλέγχω, v. 11), and elsewhere as *convict, convince,* and *rebuke.* Strong's tells us that the Greek word is generally associated with a suggestion of shame regarding the person convicted; and can mean to bring to the light, to expose; to find fault with, correct; to reprehend severely, chide, admonish, reprove; to call to account, show one his fault, demand an explanation; and to chasten or punish. Exposure is part of it, but the heart of it is to see what is exposed in the light of Christ, to see it for what it is in reality, and then to tell the world what is revealed.

Shame is involved in the exposure. Paul went on to say that it is shameful to even speak about what is done "in secret" (v. 12), apart from the light of Christ. As the light of Christ increasingly shines in this world, things are increasingly seen for what they actually are. Imagine that people have been living in a room without light for a very long time, when suddenly someone brings in a light. The first thing that the light will reveal is the dirt and filth that is not seen without the light. As people adjust to the light they will begin to clean up the squalor, and over time their living conditions will improve because of the light. The presence of light reveals the lack of perfection and the presence of sin. If the FBI were to do a thorough investigation on any of us, they would find much that would be embarrassing. And this parallels Paul's meaning here. Paul was capitalizing on Jesus' assertion,

"I am the light of the world" (John 8:12, 9:5, 12:46).

This is not an analogy, but is to be understood literally. It is in the role of the archetype of humanity that Jesus is able to be the very light of the whole world. In the same sense that the eye is the light of the soul, Jesus is the light of the world. He provides illumination to help us see reality better.

Regardless of how it was done, if we can accept the fact that God created the world, we can understand that everything in the world is in some sort of relationship with God, the ultimate Creator. To say that God created the world simply means that the world fulfills the purposes of God, the purposes for which God created it. And everything in the world is related to God's purposes. Beyond the issues of mechanics and science, the statement that God created the world simply means that the world was created to serve the purposes of God. The discussion of the mechanics and science of creation tends to obscure this fact. The opposition to the idea that God created the world is not interested in winning the argument. The opposition is interested in obscuring the truth with the argument. The argument against God is itself the mechanism of denial. And if it is not continuously engaged, the facts will simply overcome the denial. It takes a lot of effort to deny the truth.

Arguing with people who argue against God is frivolous. Such arguments simply add vain words in favor of God to vain words that oppose Him. Such arguments are locked into the categories of Satan's false dilemma, the moral argument between good and evil that issues from various positions of human opinion. Such an argument cannot be won, but neither can it be lost. And this is why it has continued unabated throughout history. In the same way that the gospel is not a matter of piety, morality is not a matter of good defeating evil. We cannot defeat evil. Our job is to live in obedience to God's will, and the reality that issues from that will defeat, or actually *dissolve*, evil.

The whole scenario of good vs. evil falls almost entirely into the categories of Satan's false dichotomy. That is to say that it does not incorporate or encompass God's dichotomy of life vs. knowledge (or various opinions regarding good and evil). The gospel is not an argument, it is a way of life (Acts 19:9, 19:23, 24:14, 24:22). People are not argued into the kingdom, they are led, drawn into it by it's truth. And this leading is not a matter of words, but of example, attitude, and behavior. To lead someone to Christ is not a matter of defeating all of their arguments against God, but of demonstrating the reality of God in one's own life. To be a leader is to manifest the character qualities of greatness, not by being popular, but by manifesting the fruit of the spirit—love, joy, peace, patience, kindness, goodness, faithfulness, gentleness, self-control (Galatians 5:22-23). Lead this life and you will be a great leader.

The Call

In verse 14 Paul calls the Ephesians to wake up, and arise from death, for the light of Christ has come. Paul insisted that preachers and missionaries go out and wake people up (Romans 10:5). But spiritual awakening is more than waking up from sleep. It is waking up from death. It is awakening from captivity by the false categories of good and evil, which keep people involved in Satan's false dichotomy, and keep people from the true dichotomy of God, which is life and death (the struggle between sustainable life in Christ and reliance on human opinion apart from God-in-Christ). There is a spiritual war that has been raging since Adam and Eve left the Garden. Humanity understands this war as being between good and evil, and have been actively fighting this war ever since. This fight is also called *history*, and human history has been dominated by this struggle.

However, this is not how God understands the spiritual war. God sees the opposing sides of the war differently. God sees them as the forces of death arrayed against the forces of life, where the forces of death generate both sides of the struggle of good against evil. The conflict between good and evil produces real warfare and causes much suffering and loss of life. This conflict is the engine of war that inflames people to take up arms against one another. And both sides, both the good and the evil, understand themselves to be on the side of good, according to their own best thinking. Both sides understand themselves to be motivated by genuine concerns of goodness and righteousness.

But each side values different aspects of the truth, and pits them against one another. Each side devalues the other side by identifying it with evil, while identifying itself with good. But God sees both sides engaging in analysis and evaluation on the basis of imaginary (or imagined) philosophical categories that are limited by their own minds. Each side trusts only its own analysis of what is true, each side only values its own sources, which keeps them from seeing truth from another perspective. By trusting themselves and their own sources, they close themselves off from the greater truth, of which their perspective comprises only a part. Again, each side of the good vs. evil struggle see themselves on the good side.

The struggle of good against evil is the cause of human war, and it actually serves the cause of death rather than life. Because God is greater than humanity, He stands apart from this struggle and is able to see it for what it actually is. God knows that the real conflict is not between what we call good and evil, but is between life and the death of war, where war is the result of the conflict between good and evil.

Thus, the call to wake up is a call to stop relying on one's own understanding as an adequate means to comprehend reality. Human beings are not designed for self-reliance or self-sustainability. We are social beings, which means that we require others to sustain human life. This is true biologically and spiritually. But neither is humanity as a species designed to be self-reliant or self-sustainable. Rather, just as males and females need one another to procreate, so humanity and God need one another in order to manifest in time.

It's not that God needs humanity in any sort of ultimate sense, but that as far as we can know, in order for God to manifest in time, as time is configured for the earth, He needs a body or vehicle that can operate in time. Thus, He sent His Son, Jesus Christ in bodily form, who then sent His Holy Spirit, who is Himself by the reality of the Trinity. God does not need humanity for His existence, but humanity needs God for its sustainable viability. Apart from God, humanity will simply engage in the war of good against evil, either keeping humanity in a state of perpetual war, poverty, and destruction that attends war, or eventually destroy itself completely.

Thus, the call is to awaken from the false dilemma of the categories of death and embrace the God-given categories of life in

Christ. And the call necessarily comes from Another, because only by hearing from Another can we awaken from the captivity of self-reliance. In addition, the hearing of the call must also be heard through Another, through the Holy Spirit in the life of the believer, through the power and presence of God-in-Christ through regeneration, wherein the Spirit actually dwells within. Anything less leaves us in self-reliance. Only thus can people arise from death in Adam to life in Christ who shines through them.

Walk wisely, admonished Paul. The *Authorized Version* translated ἀκριβῶς as *circumspectly* because the word literally means exactly, accurately, and/or diligently. To be circumspect is to be heedful of potential consequences. It is to be future oriented in the sense of considering the outcome of one's thinking and behavior.

To walk at all is to go somewhere. The purpose of walking is to get to the end of the journey. To walk without a destination is like being lost. Sometimes the destination is simply around the block, or for the exercise, or for the beauty of the trail. Of course, the journey is to be enjoyed. But contrary to the popular idea, a journey without a destination or purpose is unwise because the world is a dangerous place—particularly wildernesses and poor neighborhoods.

Paul advised not to be unwise, but to be wise (σοφός)—skilled, intelligent, cultivated, learned, smart. Wisdom is more than knowledge. Wisdom is understanding how to apply knowledge. Wisdom involves discernment, discretion, and discipline. Wisdom involves prudence, knowing how to determine the subtle differences between similar things. Wisdom knows that political correctness is foolishness. Conversely, fools think that political correctness is wisdom.

REDEMPTION

Christ redeems us (Galatians 4:5, Titus 2:14) and we are to redeem the time (v. 16, καιρός) or moment. The Greek word for *time* here is not analog clock time, but the time of special events. *Kairos* time is like the time of harvest or the moment at which dinner is ready. It is a kind of fulfillment of time, a time of expectation, or the culmination of a process. A better English translation here might be *moment.* We are to redeem the moment.

Paul has been dead for millennia. So, this verse won't have the same meaning for us that it had for Paul, but it will have a similar meaning and a similar application. But without wisdom, without discretion and discernment the application cannot be made.

To redeem a thing is to buy it back, knowing that ownership brings control. We do not have control of things we do not own. When you own a thing, you can pretty much do with it what you want, within the bounds of the law and your ability. When Christ redeemed His people, He purchased them. Or He purchased their debt. Whatever debts are owed by a company are transferred to the new owner. Christ purchased the debt that had been accrued by the sin of humanity by paying for it on the cross. He suffered the consequence of the debt—death. In a sense, Christ paid the debt holder—God. And the consequence of that debt payment is that humanity's debt for sin is now held by Christ. He is free to collect it or forgive it. And He has forgiven believers, but unbelievers are still subject to collection.

The reason that Paul gives for redeeming the time is that the days are evil (πονηρός). The Greek word is consistently translated as *evil* or *wicked*, but literally means toilsome, painful, and difficult. This evil of the world is the consequence of sin (Genesis 3:17-19). The difficulties of this world are the result of Adam's sin. And the moment that Paul had in mind is that which contributes to the momentum of Jesus Christ in history to reverse the curse of sin.

We often call this moment *receiving Christ*. While it is true that people receive Christ, it is also true that what is received is itself ancient and does not belong to those who receive it. Rather, they belong to It or Him. And while it must be received personally, the result of receiving it brings the receiver into social conformity with Christ over time. It is both personal and social (or corporate).

Thus, we see that life apart from Christ is evil in the sense of being toilsome, painful, and difficult. The cure for human toil, pain, and difficulty is the reception of Christ or conformity to Him, to His character qualities. As more and more people conform to Christ, the more they manifest the fruits of the spirit, which include integrity, honesty, industry, and consistency—to which we can also add cooperation. These things then provide the necessary foundation in human character for the development of science and technology. The proper use of science and technology, in conformity to Christ, is to alleviate toil, pain, and difficulties—or evil (πονηρός).

To redeem the moment is to make the best possible use of our lives, in cooperation with Jesus Christ by the power and presence of the Holy Spirit through regeneration toward the fulfillment of God's purpose for Jesus Christ.[3] In the natural world everything is subject to

---

3   See footnote 1, p. iii.

the Second Law of Thermodynamics, or dissipation over time—the increase of entropy, rot, and corruption. Thus, eternal life or sustainable life in the natural world is a matter of the reduction and eventual elimination of biblically defined corruption, personally and corporately. Indeed, this effort will seriously help solve most of the problems our world currently faces.

The accomplishment of God's purpose for Jesus Christ is both the means and the end of true worship. True worship is more than mere corporate liturgical celebration. It includes this, of course, but for it to be true, it must issue from the lives of individuals who are making significant progress regarding the actualization of Christ's character qualities, which are fruits of the spirit.

Those actually engaged in this enterprise compose Christ's church on earth. And such a church is not limited to any particular humanly defined corporate entity. Nor does membership in any particular humanly defined corporate entity guarantee participation in Christ's body on earth. However, saints recognize fellow saints and enjoy communion, fellowship, service, and study with other saints. To be Christian is to participate in Christ's body on earth.

33. THANKFEARFULNESS

*Therefore do not be foolish, but understand what the will of
the Lord is. And do not get drunk with wine, for that is debauchery, but be filled with the Spirit, addressing one another in psalms and hymns and spiritual songs, singing and
making melody to the Lord with your heart, giving thanks
always and for everything to God the Father in the name of
our Lord Jesus Christ, submitting to one another out of reverence for Christ.* —Ephesians 5:17-21

The usual contrast to foolishness is wisdom, but here Paul con-
trasts foolishness with knowing God's will. This contrast
then suggests that wisdom is equated with knowing God's
will. In addition, the secret of answered prayer is knowing God's will
because God will always accomplish His own will. Conforming our
lives and prayers to God's will puts people into conformity with it.
When we know God's will, we also know the future because God intends to accomplish what He wills, and He has all power to do so. We
may not know the timing (Mark 13:32), but we can know the outcome.

The art of knowing God's will is a life-long pursuit that is not
found through seeking, but through trusting. People seek what they
do not have, and once they have it they stop seeking it. Thus, we
cannot find God by a process that involves seeking Him because to
seek Him is not to have found Him. The harder one seeks, the less
one actually has. Rather, God is found and/or engaged by trusting
Him, trusting His Word to be reliable. To know God we must trust
Him, not seek Him. The simple act of seeking requires the admission
of non-possession. We seek what we do not have.

What unbelievers—and too many self-proclaimed Christians—accept as wisdom about God is mostly wrong, which means that their analysis and understanding of God is erroneous. For instance, thinking of God's Word as being *inerrant* turns it into an abstraction that can then be analyzed. In fact, an inerrant thing cannot be known to be inerrant without standing in judgment of it—and that then sets the evaluator above the evaluated, in this case, above God's Word. One must be inerrant one's self in order to to judge a thing to be inerrant. It is more productive to think of God's Word as being *reliable* than *inerrant*. This way, even what we call textual errors can provide helpful information about God's character and increase the value of trust and fidelity as tools to help us understand God.

The truth is that we have no original manuscripts of the Bible. All we have are ancient Hebrew and Greek fragments of copies of the various books of the Bible. And Christians trust these translated and assembled fragments to be the best possible expression of God's Word in all of history.

It is helpful to trust that God intends for us to have to translate His Word from ancient languages because the process of translation and text assemblage is itself part of God's will for us. The process engages people in activities and procedures that God intends for our benefit. It forces us out of our individual self-reliance because we have to rely on so many other people in the process. We must trust the integrity, competence, and fidelity of others who have worked to translate and assemble the Bible. While the truth of God's Word involves abstract reason and propositional truths, these things are secondary to our fidelity and loyalty to God-in-Christ because they determine how we value God in our thought process. If we value God highly, even poor reasoning skills will serve us well. But if we value God poorly, the best reason we can muster will lead us astray.

Buzzed

Paul set an example of true religion versus false religion in his contrast between getting drunk on wine and getting filled with the Spirit. When the Apostles were filled with the Spirit (Acts 2:13), people mistook them for being drunk with wine. The two things are both similar and different. And their similarities encourage false analysis, while their differences encourage true analysis.

Alcohol consumption reduces inhibitions, making people more aware of and sensitive to the presence of others. It also reduces stress, reducing the ability of multivariate concentration, which increases some aspects of univariate concentration. Under the influence of alcohol people pay less attention to the multiplicity of things going on around them, and more attention to fewer things closer to them. Thus, driving is impaired while interpersonal communication appears to be magnified. Social taboos are ignored while personal sexual interest is heightened. And what drives most of this is the fact that alcohol tends to numb sensitivity, which reduces discrimination and various sensations of pain, which increases the sense of euphoria.

All of this is related to being filled with the Spirit because being filled with the Spirit also releases endorphins, which increase euphoria. The gospel is about freedom (John 8:36), and the release from captivity to the consequences of the law (Romans 7:23). Drunk people tend to be easily excitable, as do those in the Spirit. What excites them is different, but the manifestation of excitement is similar.

Drunkenness is referred to as *debauchery* (ἀσωτία), or *excess* in the *Authorized Version*. The Greek is a compound word that begins with a negation (ἀ), meaning *not*. The root of the other word is usually translated as *save* and sometimes as *whole*. There is a similarity of the subjective experiences of being mildly drunk—buzzed—and being filled with the Spirit. Both increase euphoria, enthusiasm, and sociability. However, over time drunkenness leads to irresponsibility, debauchery, and laziness, whereas as being filled with the Spirit leads to greater responsibility, productivity, and discipline. Subjectively, they feel similar, but objectively, they lead to opposite results. We make the best use of being filled with the Spirit by

> "addressing one another in psalms and hymns and spiritual songs,
> singing and making melody to the Lord with your heart" (v. 19).

Paul has worship in mind, but not mere Sunday morning liturgy. Sure, this needs to be done on Sunday mornings because it is worship. But to worship *only* on Sunday mornings is to put worship into a straitjacket that Paul does not recognize.

WORSHIP

To worship (שׁחה) originally meant to prostrate or yield to the presence of a superior. And to worship faithfully was to live a life of submission to God, to God's law—the Ten Commandments. Submission or obedience was to manifest, not just at the Temple or synagogue, but always and in every circumstance. Temple and synagogue worship were simply ways to formally remember God's law and better understand it.

This sense of worship is carried into the New Testament and is translated by the Greek word προσκυνέω, which according to Strong is like a dog licking his master's hand. If this image injures your pride, you need to reconsider who you think you are.

Another Greek word that is often translated as *worship* is λατρεύω. It is more often translated as *service*, and suggests the performance of religious rites and rituals. It also means to perform service for hire or what we call *work*. Thus, work is also a form of worship wherein our worthiness is sanctified as we offer ourselves and our abilities to God.

Related to worship and sometimes translated as such is δόξα, which is more an attitude of worshipfulness. Here the root meaning suggests an opinion, judgment, view, or supposition of high favor that results in praise and honor. It is often translated as *glory*.

Elsewhere I have described this approach to Scripture and its worldview as *presuppositional trinitarianism*,[1] a fancy way of saying that I assume the reality of the biblical, Christian Trinity. It is a presupposition in the sense that it functions as an axiom, a premise or starting point of reasoning. This axiom functions as the foundation for the proof of the existence of God. But the proof is not a mental, logical, or verbal construct. Rather, the proof unfolds as my actual life. I am the proof of the existence of God, but not just me personally.

All believers provide the same proofs. I speak of myself as a participant in the body of Christ. My life proves and establishes the reality of God to me. In the same way, the life of Christ, His Church, proves and establishes God to the world. Such proofs are not merely intellectual, logical, or spiritual, but are biological, visceral, and splanchnonic,[2] as well. The proof unfolds as the character of God increasingly manifests in the world through God-in-Christ. Inasmuch as I am a new person in Christ, a different person, a renewed person, a reborn person, a regenerate person, and imitate the character of God-in-Christ as a consequence, God is real. This is what it means to be

---

1   I have been working to describe this perspective most of my life. My books on First Corinthians explicitly identified it, and those since have endeavored to clarify it.

2   The inward parts; the heart, affections, seat of the feelings. *Varsy Arsy—Proclaiming The Gospel in Second Corinthians*, Pilgrim Platform, Marietta, Ohio, 2009, Index: *splagchnon*.

filled with the Spirit, and it is encouraging, motivating, and inspirational to be personally involved in it. This is also the essence of Christian worship. Faithfulness is the art of becoming living proof for the reality of God in Christ.

Here, belief and passion are wedded in harmony as believers share themselves, their new selves, with others. Those involved in choirs, orchestras, or bands understand the centrality and satisfaction that music can play in life. At first, practice seems daunting, but as you improve, your own abilities, practice, and performance become increasingly central and satisfying. Paul quoted from hymns and psalms liberally,[3] suggesting that he demonstrated this admonition in his own life.

EUCHARIST

When Paul directed Christians to give thanks always and for everything (v. 20), he used the word *Eucharist* (εὐχαριστέω). The word is used in the New Testament thirty-nine times, and only a handful are used in reference to the Lord's Supper. It makes sense to use the word as the New Testament uses it, which usually means being demonstratively thankful. No doubt such thankfulness is an aspect of the Lord's Supper, even the central characteristic of it by believers.

History and tradition have institutionalized the Lord's Supper by insisting that the Supper be administered in particular ways, according to particular formulas. Every approach to the Lord's Supper today is formulaic. While the content of the various traditional formulas are different, they all tend to freeze the Lord's Supper into an established standard. They formalize the Supper, which is not necessarily a bad thing, but over time formalism tends to become increasingly rote and habitual—unconscious, which becomes problematic. The Lord said to Isaiah:

---

3   Hymns: Ephesians 5:14, Philippians 2:6-11, Colossians 1:15-20, 1 Timothy 3:16, 1 Timothy 6:15b-16, 2 Timothy 2:11-13, Hebrews 1:3.
    Old Testament, many were musical: Isaiah 40:13 in 1 Corinthians 2:16; Isaiah 49:8 in 2 Corinthians 6:2; Isaiah 54:1in Galatians 4:27; Isaiah 42:5 in Romans 2:24; Psalm 50:6 in Romans 3:4; Psalm 14:1-3 in Romans 3:10-18; Gen. 15:6 in Romans 4:3, 9, 22; Isaiah 1:9 in Romans 9:29; Isaiah 28:16 in Romans 10:11; Joel 3:5 in Romans 10:13; Isaiah 53:1 in Romans 10:16; Isaiah 65:2 in Romans 10:21; Psalm 68:23-24 in Romans 11:9-10; Isaiah 40:13 in Romans 11:34; Isaiah 45:23 in Romans 14:11b.

"Because this people draw near with their mouth and honor me
with their lips, while their hearts are far from me, and their fear of
me is a commandment taught by men (Isaiah 29:13).

This is the problem of having an unconscious, rote, habitual relationship with the Lord. Things that move away from intentionality,
usually move into personal unimportance. Yet, our contemporary
problem with the Eucharist, the Lord's Supper, is farther removed
than being merely unconscious. It has moved into the realm of petri-
fication. When Paul provided instructions to the Corinthians regarding the Lord's Supper, following the other Apostles, he said:

"For I received from the Lord what I also delivered to you, that
the Lord Jesus on the night when he was betrayed took bread, and
when he had given thanks, he broke it, and said, 'This is my body
which is for you. Do this in remembrance of me.' In the same way
also he took the cup, after supper, saying, 'This cup is the new
covenant in my blood. Do this, as often as you drink it, in remembrance of me'" (1 Corinthians 11:23-25).

These words are repeated in every Christian communion liturgy,
as they should be. But the celebration of the Lord's Supper on Sunday
mornings is only the tip of the Eucharistic iceberg. The Eucharist is
not the bread or the wine. The Eucharist is the thankfulness. This
means that the Eucharist is celebrated during the Lord's Supper, but is
not limited therein. *Thankfulness* is another word for love, and while
love is no stranger to formalities, rote, habitual unconsciousness stifles
it. Active love is bright-eyed, willing, eager, and determined. Active
love is awake, conscious, and attentive.

Paul said that all Christians are to give thanks always for everything (v. 20). Thus, *Eucharist* is a verb not a noun, and it is not under
ecclesiastical control or supervision. It is a way of life, an attitude, a set
of the jib, an outlook, and a worldview. *Eucharist* is a spiritual orientation and activity. The reason that the denominations cannot celebrate the Lord's Supper together is that they diminish it. They
conceive of it in unbiblical ways. They are barking up the wrong
proverbial tree. They have standardized their churches by creating legalized entities, creatures of law—and human law at that! The problem is that

"the letter kills, but the Spirit gives life" (2 Corinthians 3:6).

By *letter* (γράμμα) Paul meant legalized, standardized descriptions and procedures that constrain God. We are not to constrain God!

English dictionaries know nothing about any definition of *Eucharist* other than it being the body and blood or bread and wine of the Lord's Supper. This misunderstanding took hold very early. It appears to have originated in the *Didache*, which dates to the late first or early second century. The *Didache* was considered to be part of the New Testament until the Council of Nicea (325 A.D.) set the cannon, and excluded it. This means that while the *Didache* is very important, it is not infallible—though it has too often been treated so.

This is not a contradiction of anything that the *Didache* says. It is simply the observation that its definition of the word *Eucharist* and its description of the Lord's Supper is erroneous because the Bible never uses or defines the word that way. That error has since been compounded a thousandfold. And there is no good reason not to correct it. Nor is there any need to blame this or that denomination or group. All are guilty in one way or another, in that every historical attempt to correct it has only made it worse.

DIRECTED GRATITUDE

And yet it is not enough to simply be thankful. Generic thankfulness becomes a sin of omission because it ignores the source of the gifts that give rise to the gratitude. Thankfulness is a response to graciousness. Thanking one's lucky stars amounts to the ignorance or denial of the source of the gift, the grace. Paul was not ignorant, and always directed his gratitude toward God-in-Christ, and directed others to do the same. The object of our gratitude is always "God the Father in the name of our Lord Jesus Christ" (v. 20).

Being grateful is better than not being grateful. Yet, thanking the wrong person is worse than not thanking the right person. It's as bad as a scientist crediting the wrong cause of some outcome. It's an error. It's just wrong, and one error in a chain of causality can breed additional errors later on. The failure to credit God for His graciousness is a failure of infinite proportion because it is evidence of unbelief or false belief—wrong belief.

Thankfulness directed to God-in-Christ is the central Christian attitude, and unbelief, false belief, or wrong belief reigns where thankfulness is not demonstrably manifest. One cannot be a Christian without also being thankful. Just as the sun produces light, and water produces wetness, so Christian faith produces thankfulness to God. Of course, thankfulness can be directed to the wrong object, but that's a different issue. The result of thankfulness to God-in-Christ is

"submitting to one another out of reverence for Christ" (v. 21).

The *Authorized Version* translates it: "Submitting yourselves one to another in the fear of God." Thankfulness produces mutual submission among Christians because the Trinity is real, and the reality of the Trinity not only means that the Father, Son, and Holy Spirit are mutually intertwined in one another, but also that the Holy Spirit intertwines believers with one another. Reverence for God-in-Christ is reverence for God, for Christ, for the Holy Spirit, and for other believers in whom the Holy Spirit is manifest. The reality of the Trinity means that believers are bound to the Godhead by the Holy Spirit.

This union of believers with the Godhead through the power and presence of the Holy Spirit through regeneration *is* the church of God-in-Christ on earth. This is what it means to be *in Christ*. It's a Trinitarian thing. We might think of the Trinity as being like the three primary colors: red, yellow, and blue. Each color is uniquely individual, yet the reality of light includes them all in various strengths or degrees. And the highest degree of all three produces white, which is also uniquely individual.

Fear

The *English Standard Version* errs in the translation of v. 21b: "out of reverence for Christ." It is not that people should not have reverence for Christ—we should. But that's not what the verse says, at least not entirely. The Greek word translated *reverence* (φόβος) literally means *phobia*, as in fear, dread, and terror. This side of God (let's call it His powerful love of justice that can result in His wrath) is often ignored or denied, which is a curiosity because Scripture clearly testifies to it. Nonetheless, many people have a conception of love, particularly the purity of love that Jesus Christ represents, as being without the kind of justice that would consign anyone to eternal damnation.

The root of this problem is the misunderstanding of the character of God in its fullness. It is a misapplication of God's unconditional love for humanity (the species) as a whole or kind that is mistakenly applied to every individual. While God does love humanity unconditionally, and has promised not to destroy the species (Genesis 9:15), this love cannot be simply transferred wholesale to every individual. The fact of God's ultimate judgment of individuals at the end of history (Matthew 5:21-22, 11:22-24, etc.) testifies, not to the limits of God's atonement, but to the unrelenting corruption of unrepentant sin. Christ's atonement cannot apply to people who refuse to acknowledge it. This does not mean that Christ's atonement is insufficient, or that sinners can trump the power of God. Rather, it means that God uses repentance as the means of distributing His grace.

The idea of eternal damnation in hell is the source of the fear of God, and to deny any aspect of eternal damnation in hell is to misread the character of God, who alone provides the authority for such consignment. A healthy respect for God requires embracing the wholeness of God's character in a way that comes to terms with God's passionate love of justice. The perversion of God's justice result in a one way ticket to hell. The fear of damnation is healthy inasmuch as it keeps people from further violation of God's law.

Yes, Jesus paid the price for the sin of all humanity. And yes, the value of Jesus' sacrifice on the cross is sufficient to cover all of humanity. However, the failure to appreciate and receive God's forgiveness in Christ is the result of the stubborn willfulness of self-reliance. There are many manifestations of this willfulness, but they all track back to the Garden, to self-analysis and self-determination of good and evil, right and wrong.

Those who deny the fear of God do so on moral grounds. They refuse to believe the biblical account of the character of God, and engage their own idea of God's character—or any idea other than the fullness of the biblical account. Such people are vitally disgusted with any conception of God that does not recognize the ultimate sanctity of human individuality. Any denial or violation of the ultimate sanctity of human individuality—even by God Himself—is observed with disgust. Their freedom as individuals to stand in judgment against the Bible's portrayal of God's ultimate sovereignty to consign unrepentant sinners to eternal damnation in hell trumps the plain reading of Scripture. They are blinded by their own ideas about God's love because they fail to properly understand the Trinity and its implications.

This, however, does not mean that God is not gracious toward such people. Many such people self-identify as Christians and can be morally superior people who demonstrate an excellence of Christian character in every other way. Such people often have thought through various biblical issues in the light of Christ and can provide credible evidence for their own faithfulness. It is for people like this that God tarries (2 Peter 3:9).

God's purposes and ways cannot be perfectly clear until they are fully manifest in history to everyone extant. Only when both the wheat and the tares grow to full maturity can their true characters be clearly known to all. Only at that point will God draw the line to divide the wheat and tares and consign them to their differing destinations. At that point the tares will be glad to be grouped with other tares, and the wheat will be glad to be with other wheat. Only then will the great harvest take place. Only then will it be perfectly clear who will and who will not abide in stubborn self-reliance through the denial of the fullness of the biblical character of God's mercy *and* His judgment, God's love *and* His justice. Indeed, such characteristics can only exist in the only real and actual Triune God of biblical Christianity.

34. Bride Of The Lamb

Wives, submit to your own husbands, as to the Lord. For the husband is the head of the wife even as Christ is the head of the church, his body, and is himself its Savior. Now as the church submits to Christ, so also wives should submit in everything to their husbands. Husbands, love your wives, as Christ loved the church and gave himself up for her, that he might sanctify her, having cleansed her by the washing of water with the word, so that he might present the church to himself in splendor, without spot or wrinkle or any such thing, that she might be holy and without blemish.

—Ephesians 5:22-27

To understand why Paul launched into an analogy of marriage here we need to see the reason that he gives for it in v. 32. He is using the marriage analogy to describe the relationship between Christ and His church.

"This mystery is profound, and I am saying that it refers to Christ and the church. (v.32)"

Keep in mind that Paul was not talking about marriage per se here, but about the church, about how the church is to function like marriage and how it is to be covenantally related to Jesus Christ.

Notice also that this analogy considers the church to be a corporate whole. The whole church is in covenant with Christ like a wife is in covenant with her husband. Paul was not simply talking about the covenant between individuals and the church. He was talking about the church as a whole and also about Christ. Christ is the head of His body, the church, which means that Christ, not some aspect of the

church, is the head of individual Christians. The body or church is
not the head of itself. The body is subject to the head, as the wife is
subject to her head—her husband. The foot does not consider the
stomach to be its head.

The church is composed of members as the body is composed of
parts—arms, legs, feet, hands, etc. According to this analogy, the body
or church is subject to the head or Christ. In addition, bodily parts are
also subject to other bodily parts (v. 21), but this submission is mutual.
One part is not to "lord it over" (Matthew 20:25) another. And inasmuch as people do lord over one another, they usurp the role of
Christ in the lives of other believers. Christ's headship is both spiritual
and real.

We are to give one another spiritual counsel and hold one another accountable. But we are not to demand conformity of one another to one another because the standards of conformity never match
the principles of Scripture. The Bible calls all people to perfection in
Christ, whereas our denominational standards aim at the lowest common denominators. These two things or approaches point people in
opposite directions. The Bible insists on continuous growth and maturity in Christ, where denominational standards are satisfied with a
few commonalities. Denominational criteria lead members to be like
one another, where biblical criteria lead members to be like Christ.
The latter, not the former, is the model.

THE MODEL

Wives are to submit to their own husbands, as to the Lord.
Rather than seeing this as a command, we need to see it as an example
of how submission is supposed to work in the church. No one is to
lord it over anyone else, including husbands over their own wives. All
chauvinistic domination is a violation of mutual submission, and it always has been. All chauvinism is therefore an expression of faithlessness. Submission must issue out of the wife's willing honor of her
husband, not from the husband's demand. Husbands are to love, not
demand. We are called to conform our lives to Christ and hold one
another accountable—men, women, and children. It is never a sin to
point fellow believers to Christ when they stray from the path. In fact,
it is an obligation, but it must be done lovingly, gently.

Thus, we are to live in submission to one another, "as to the
Lord" (v. 22). We are to live in submission to the Lord—not through
blind obedience, but in conformity that issues out of willing agree-

ment with God-in-Christ. We read Scripture, but are not expected to comply with perfect obedience. Rather, we are to dialog with the text and with other believers (both living and dead—through fellowship and books) in order to understand it, knowing that our own love of God comes more from compliance than intellectual achievement. The more we endeavor to live in biblical compliance to the Lord, the fewer problems we will have with other believers.

In case we failed to grasp his meaning, Paul repeats the analogy:

> "For the husband is the head of the wife even as Christ is the head
> of the church, his body, and is himself its Savior" (v. 23).

Paul was trying to clarify through repetition. The analogy is that husbands protect their wives as Christ protects His church: he sacrifices himself for her safety and well-being. That's what husbands do and that's what Christ did. That's the model. Christ does not lord it over the church. Even when people refuse to conform, He gives

> "them up in the lusts of their hearts to impurity, to the dishonor-
> ing of their bodies among themselves" (Romans 1:24).

He lets them suffer the consequences of their sins and errors, knowing that their faithlessness will serve as a lesson about the importance of conformity to His will for humanity in the future.

Those who refuse to learn will suffer the consequences of their own behavior, not because God is not gracious and all-loving, but because that's just how the world is. This world is a habitat, which means that it is governed by laws—laws of physics, laws of nature, laws of economics, laws of biology, laws of health, laws of music, laws of electricity, etc. Reality is composed of patterns. There is an order to the world, and we human beings did not establish that order. Rather, we live in the midst of it.

And the better we understand and conform ourselves to it, the better our lives will be. Conversely, the less we understand and conform ourselves to it, the worse our lives will be. It's like rocket science —the more we know about the world, the less damage we will cause. With science and technology we can use that order to our benefit, and we can also abuse it to our detriment.

Paul was saying that Christ is the savior of the body, the body is not the savior of itself. Christ is the head of His body, the body is not the head of itself. The church violates this principle or law when it thinks that some part of the body of Christ, other than Christ Himself, is to function as the head of the church. Christians are to be in mutual submission. Christians are not to demand things from other Christians. Christ is the head of the whole body, and the head of each of its parts.

The body is subject to the head, just as wives are subject to their husbands. The duty of the church, of believers, is to submit to Christ's headship in their own lives. Thus, men should submit to Christ just as they think that their wives ought to submit to them. And when they do so submit to Christ, faithful wives will shout with joy! Men who complain about their wives not being in submission to them need to check their own submission to Christ.

While the obligation of the wife and the church is submission, the obligation of the husband is to love his wife like Christ loves the church. Again, we see the idea that husbands need to be willing to lose their own lives to protect their wives. That's what Christ did, and He's the model. However, the goal of Christ's sacrifice was not the mere preservation of His church. He has a higher goal in mind. Christ's goal is to sanctify and cleanse His church. God's purpose is to increase the maturity and purity of the church, and of individual Christians.

Here we see that God is not interested in achieving or maintaining a static-state church, nor to return to some previous historic condition. Rather, God intends for the church to grow and mature historically, over long periods of time, and for individual Christians to grow and mature over their lives. These two things are not the same, but are related.

Some people think that Paul's reference to washing (λουτρόν) suggests baptism (βαπτίζω), but they are not the same word. If there is any comparison between them, it is not that baptism is like washing, but that washing is like baptism. It's not that baptism should be thought of like washing, but that washing or the ongoing effort of cleanliness is part of baptism. While the ceremony of baptism does serve as a kind of entrance ceremony into the church, there is more to baptism than an entrance ceremony. Just as personal cleanliness is a function of diligence in washing over time, so baptism is a function of the diligence of becoming increasingly sanctified over time. Baptism is not the end, but the beginning of a Christian life of ever-increasing maturity and purity *in Christ*.

Rhema

How this washing takes place is significant. It happens

"by the washing of water with the word" (ῥῆμα, v. 26).

This phrase by itself is odd at best. Paul used the analogy of marriage to talk about the church, which is washed with water by the word. He doesn't mean that church people need to bathe together, nor read in the bathtub, nor that the Bible is the source of cleanliness. Clearly, none of this can be taken literally. The language is analogous and symbolic.

The end goal is the sanctification and purification of the church, which means the maturity and purity of individual Christians, as well as their corporate organizations. We might also call this process the growth and maintenance of the church. The allusion to baptism suggests entrance into the church, and the allusion to washing suggests ongoing maintenance. The process of this washing or cleansing is "water with the word" (v. 26). As water is the means of regular washing, the word is the means of gaining spiritual maturity. Both are important.

However, *word* (ῥῆμα) here does not refer to the Bible. It is not God's Word that is in view, but our words. We grow by talking about God-in-Christ. Some people think that ῥῆμα refers to a charismatic language. And there is a sense in which they are right, depending on what one means by *charismatic language.* However, there is no sense to be made of babbling (1 Corinthians 14:19),[1] so that is not in view here.

Rather, ῥῆμα suggests speaking about the God of the Bible meaningfully and truthfully in one's native tongue or language. The miracle of tongues begins with *hearing* the gospel in one's native language, in one's own head (Acts 2:6). It means discussing God-in-Christ with the Holy Spirit in the privacy of one's own thoughts. The miracle of tongues manifests as we discuss God-in-Christ meaningfully and truthfully with one another through the power and presence of the Holy Spirit through regeneration. The miracle of tongues is the Holy Spirit coming to the Gentiles. Nothing more, nothing less.

The goal is to make Christ's church presentable to God. Christ has already saved His people, already forgiven their sin by His propitiation on the cross. Paul was not talking about becoming saved, but

---

1 Ross, Phillip A. *Arsy Varsy—Reclaiming The Gospel in First Corinthians,* Pilgrim Platform, Marietta, Ohio, 2006, p. 234.

about being saved. He was talking about what saved people do, not about how individuals get saved. The purpose of salvation is to present the church without spot or wrinkle. The purpose of salvation is growth in sanctification and purity. The goal is for Christ's people to be holy and without blemish.

To be holy is to be complete and not broken. The two things are not the same. *Broken* implies a problem with some part, whereas *complete* implies the sum that is greater than all of the parts. Note that it is not individuals that are to be presented without spot or wrinkle. Rather, the subject is the church. Nor does Paul mean some abstract idea of Gnostic, individualistic, hyper-perfection. Rather, the perfection of the church is its wholeness, its completion in history. Perfection is not an individual expectation or accomplishment. It is the permeation of human culture by the gospel. It is the fulfillment of God's purpose for history in the lives of His people.

35. Revealed

In the same way husbands should love their wives as their own bodies. He who loves his wife loves himself. For no one ever hated his own flesh, but nourishes and cherishes it, just as Christ does the church, because we are members of his body. "Therefore a man shall leave his father and mother and hold fast to his wife, and the two shall become one flesh." This mystery is profound, and I am saying that it refers to Christ and the church. However, let each one of you love his wife as himself, and let the wife see that she respects her hus-band.   *—Ephesians 5:28-33*

Paul gave us a marriage analogy to help us understand how the church is to operate. Christ is to the church as the husband is to the wife. The wife submits to the authority and leadership of her husband because she knows that her husband loves her. She is to support and serve his authority and leadership because he has her best interest in mind, and as a model for their children to emulate.

The husband has a different role. Where the wife bears and cares for the children, the husband protects and provides for the family. The husband is to love his wife and children sacrificially. Jesus modeled this kind of love, and in this analogy He serves as the symbolic husband to the church. The symbolism of the relationship between husband and wife serves as the model relationship between believers and Jesus Christ. Incidentally, this symbolism is destroyed when women serve as church pastors because the ideal norm is not for women to serve in the role of the husband. Norms, roles, and ideals are important because they provide concrete examples for social organization, and the church is a particular kind of social organization, and its symbolism is important.

Paul was not talking about romantic love or fleshly bodies. Rather, the kind of love specified is agape (ἀγαπάω), and the kind of body (σῶμα) is corporate. Men are to love their wives with no expectation of reciprocity—that's what agape love is, because their wives constitute an extension of their bodies, in a similar way that group identity is greater than individual identity. This does not mean that wives are exempt from the responsibility to love their husbands. Rather, it suggests that love is experienced and expressed differently by men than it is by women.

Men are not to expect women to behave as men, nor are women to expect men to behave as women. Men and women have different biologies, social roles, and psychologies that require different kids of fulfillment. It's part of the social economy and efficiency of the division of labor. Or rather, it models the basis for the division of labor within the larger society. Christ's church is a model for the division of labor that is modeled on the family, the initial social unit. Paul talks about this model in terms of gifts (1 Corinthians 12-14). The church is a kind of fundamental social fractal.[1] Thus, the arrangement of roles, the order of the social unit, is fundamentally important because it is repeated throughout society. It provides social glue and cultural sustainability, and increases social familiarity with people outside of the family structure.

LOVE

Paul said that

"he who loves his wife loves himself" (v. 28)

because human identity is trinitarian, neither exclusively individual, nor merely social. The family—husband, wife and children—compose the most basic unit of humanity. Species are not composed of mere individuals, but of reproducing pairs. No individual human being is self-sustainable because individual human beings do not live eternally,

---

1   Fractal: a set or arrangement that has a fractal dimension that usually exceeds its topological dimension and may fall between numeric integers of measurement. Fractals are typically self-similar patterns, where *self-similar* means they replicate their arrangement whether viewed from near or far. Fractals may be exactly the same at every scale, or they may be nearly the same at different scales. The definition of fractal goes beyond self-similarity per se to exclude trivial self-similarity and includes the idea of a detailed pattern repeating itself.

nor do individuals reproduce. It takes two to tango. Thus, like the Godhead—Father, Son, and Holy Spirit, one unit of humanity is husband, wife, and Holy Spirit. The Holy Spirit is the bonding agent[2] for the cohesion of the unit, the marriage. Without the bonding agent functioning properly, the marriage will be weak at best, and likely to degrade the strength of the social fabric and the bonds of honesty, integrity, and industry that provide the foundation for science, technology, and commerce. The strength of the human units—unity in Christ—also provide protection against corruption and degradation.

Individuals do not hate their own flesh, but strive to feed and care for it because it is their life. People are hard wired to care for themselves. They don't always know the best ways to do so, and when they do know, they don't always act consistently on the basis of that knowledge. But the general rule stands: people care for their own bodies, their flesh. Jesus Christ does the same thing:

"just as Christ does the church" (v. 29).

The church is His body, and He

"nourishes and cherishes it" (v. 29).

This insight helps us understand the degree and passion of Christ's motivation to love and care for His people. Christ has the same kind of motivation for self-preservation as we do, but His operates at what we call the corporate or social level. This does not mean that Christ is not involved with people personally. Of course, He is! But He also has greater responsibilities. Particular individuals are expendable, humanity—the whole—is not.

We note that husbands are to have agape love for their wives, which suggests that Christ has agape love for His people. This means that Christ's love for us is not a product of our responsive love for Him. He loves us even when we don't reciprocate, and He even loves those who never reciprocate. Of course, reciprocated love is experienced differently by all parties because of the reciprocation. And reciprocated love is better—stronger, fuller, richer. This means that Christ does not love everyone the same, not in the same ways and not to the same degrees because not everyone reciprocates in the same ways or degrees.

---

2   Agent (international law): One who is employed by a prince to manage his private affairs, or, those of his subjects in his name, near a foreign government. Wolff, Inst. Nat. Sec. 1237. The Holy Spirit serves as such an agent.

The idea that He or we should love everyone the same is a figment of our fevered imaginations. To treat everyone the same actually destroys love because it ignores or denies the reality of the uniqueness of individual personality. People have different needs, desires, and ideas. To love someone means to hold them in higher regard and esteem, and to love everyone with the same regard or esteem empties love of its central meaning. Christ does not love everyone the same. He loves people uniquely for who they are, not for what they do or how they behave. He loves people even when they can't, don't, or won't love Him in return.

His agape love, which is not unconditional but is without expectation of reciprocation, then draws out our response, like sunshine that draws plants to grow toward the light. It's difficult not to smile at someone who has smiled at you, or to bark at someone who has barked at you. When Christ greets us with love without expectation of return, we are encouraged to mirror that love back to Him. That's how grace works. He does it because

> "we are members of his body" (v. 30).

Christ's relationship with His church, then, compares to marriage, when a man leaves his father and mother in order to cleave with his wife and the two become one flesh (v. 21, Genesis 2:24). The Christian covenant between Christ and His church is like the marriage covenant between husband and wife. Again, we see the emphasis on Christ's headship of His church, His people, which implies that the church is not the head of itself. Every element of the church is an element of the body because headship is reserved for Christ. The church is a self-similar pattern, a fractal, or design of Christian marriage, wherein the Holy Spirit acts as the binding agent of the family with one another, and with God. The Head alone is the head of the body.

Paul calls this a great mystery, by which he means that there are many depths that he has not plumbed regarding the analogy between marriage and Christianity. They remain mysterious—known in part but not in whole. Nonetheless, His focus here is not on marriage, it's on the church.

Church

We are so used to thinking that we already know what Paul meant when he used the word *church* (ἐκκλησία) that we don't give it a second thought. But we should, because it is unlikely that our ideas about the church and Paul's are the same. The Bible continuously warns people about replacing something real with something imaginary in their thinking. It's the issue of false gods and false belief, and it runs throughout both Testaments. We are in error when we think that human words *are* the things that they represent, that there is no difference between the sign and the thing signified. We are in error when we confuse the words with the reality. Words represent things, but the words are not the things they represent. We see this in science as scientists use computer models to forecast real events. The models are reliable to a degree, but the model is not the reality.

Paul used the word ἐκκλησία (*church*) to describe the group of Christians who gathered for worship, teaching, fellowship, and the breaking of bread. The Greek word refers to an assembly of people convened at a public place for the purpose of counsel and deliberation. As Christian persecution increased in the early church, the meetings were moved from the synagogues to homes and were kept from public view. Yet they were intended to be public meetings, meetings that dealt with issues that required public deliberation. We can think of them as political meetings that dealt with various social concerns—local concerns. We would call them town council meetings.

The word literally means *called out*, and we have come to think of the church as a group of people who are called out of the ordinary social order. And if we think of the ordinary order as the order of civil government, we can (and have) thought of the church as an alternative political order that operates differently than pagan (unbelieving) civil government. However, such a line of thinking led to the establishment of the Christian ghetto, an order where Christians mostly relate to other Christians and tend to shun those who remain captive to the ways of the world. Rather than solve problems, thinking of Christianity in ghetto categories sets up several additional and unnecessary problems, and leads to the conclusion that the Bible does not have ghetto Christianity in mind.

A better model for the church is not to understand it as people who are called *out*, but people who are called *up*, up to a higher *modus operandi*, a more refined way of life, a better covenant of improved discrimination and discernment that produces a better social order. But we must understand that Christian discrimination and discernment are not based on worldly and sinful values and modes. Unfortunately, such discrimination and discernment are open to misunderstanding because they are widely misunderstood and misrepresented by both believers and unbelievers. The central focus of such discrimination and discernment is the difference between good and evil, truth and falsehood, true religion and false religion, true belief and false belief—not based on one's opinion or the opinion of scholars, but upon the veracity of God's Word. Unbelievers fail to correctly perceive the historic, generic, Christian understanding of Scripture. What makes Christians Christian is that they read the Bible in the light of Christ, or in the love of Christ. They see the difference that Christ makes, where unbelievers do not and cannot see the difference—*because* they don't believe! Unbelievers don't trust God. It's really is that simple.

The church was never intended to be a private group or to be exclusively concerned about personal matters. Today we think of Christianity solely as a matter of personal belief or personal faith, which unbelievers interpret as *private* belief or faith. There are private matters related to Christianity, of course—and they are very important. But in general, Christianity was never intended by any regenerate Christian to be *merely* private. The historical emphasis on personal faith that came out of the Second Great Awakening was an effort to engage and motivate people who professed the faith but showed few signs of actual belief in their lives. Those who responded to the Second Great Awakening tended to demonstrate their faith publicly as a kind of compensation for the apparent lack of faith of so many church members.

The original conception of the church was that it was a governing body, but was unlike civil government in the same ways that grace is different than law. The biblical function of civil government is to keep the peace and enforce the law. However, just as police departments do not and should not establish law, neither should civil government. God is the law giver, and He has already given law that is sufficient for His purposes—the Ten Commandments in the light of Christ. And Christ has fulfilled the law, which puts God's law in a different light for those who are *in Christ*, those who share or participate in His fulfillment. The Ten Commandments remain in force for everyone, but Christians are to move beyond the mere outward fulfillment of the law and to consider and apply its more subtle nuances. For instance, the outward obedience to the Sixth Commandment against murder does not exhaust its fulfillment. As Jesus said:

> "You have heard that it was said to those of old, 'You shall not murder; and whoever murders will be liable to judgment.' But I say to you that everyone who is angry with his brother will be liable to judgment; whoever insults his brother will be liable to the council; and whoever says, 'You fool!' will be liable to the hell of fire" (Matthew 5:21-22).

Jesus raised the bar of compliance to God's law from simple outward obedience to subjective attitude and motive. Christians are not to simply obey God's law, but are to love God so much that they want to do what pleases Him, and be what He has created them to be.

The job of civil government is outward enforcement, which requires understanding and interpretation, not legislation. It's not that God forbids civil government from legislation, but that God forbids all legislation that is not a function of the clarification and understanding of Scripture in the light of Christ. This does not suggest the return to some idyllic period of history, but rather suggests the extension and application of biblical wisdom and its categories of understanding to the trials and tribulations of the progressive revelation of Christ in history. The caveat "in the light of Christ" is very important, and has barely begun to be understood—even today. There is still much work that needs to be done, and will continuously need to be done because of Christ's progressive revelation in history. The more we grow *in Christ*, the more we learn how much we still don't know.

This, however, does not mean that the contemporary world needs to revert to Old Testament law, literally or woodenly interpreted. The Ten Commandments were given for the foundation of the church, which means that progress beyond the foundation cannot proceed until the foundation is complete. Thus, the Old Testament needs to be understood and applied *in the light of Christ*, because Christ's fulfillment of the law resulted, not so much in the curtailment of the Old Testament, but in its understanding, adaptation, and conclusion. The Old Testament provided a foundation for the advent of Jesus Christ. Just as the foundation of a house is not changed by the completion of the building, the function of the house is not centered on the foundation, but in the living areas. The foundation remains as it was when it was designed and built, but the instructions for its construction are not needed for the rest of the house. Rather, once the foundation has been completed, the builders move their attention to the building plans for the living areas.[3]

---

3 Ross, Phillip A. *Rock Mountain Creed—Jesus' Sermon on the Mount*, Pilgrim Plat-

In the case of the church, the process of construction is dynamic because the church continues to exist beyond the lifespan of individual Christians. New Christians are continuously coming into the church, and need to refer to the Old Testament foundation instructions for themselves. Every aspect of the living areas are built on the foundation, and are in a fundamental relationship with the foundation. And all efforts of remodeling must conform to the foundation.

The confession (observation and adoption) of the reality of the Holy Spirit sent by Jesus Christ for regeneration signals the completion of the Old Testament foundation, and the beginning of the construction of the living areas. In other words, Christians move from concern for outward obedience to the law to the celebration and applications of grace. But this does not mean that the law is not still in effect. Rather, it means that Christian motivation no longer comes from the fear of sin's consequences, but from the desire for love's opportunities. And as Christians grow in grace, the law plays the role of the guide who knows the terrain and the discipline it takes to complete the job of building the house.

HUSBANDS & WIVES

While the purpose of this conversation about husbands and wives is to provide an analogy for the church, it will not work unless husbands and wives continue to relate to one another as the Bible teaches. If the family breaks down and fails to manifest the patterns specified in the Bible, then this analogy regarding the church will also fail. The old adage that the home is the cradle of civilization is true because the family is the first order and authority that people know. And people are genetic, meaning that people function in culture like genes function in biology—they tend to maintain the existing order. People tend to replicate the culture in which they grow up. What has worked in the past is more likely to continue working in the future— most of the time.

Obviously, there are times of change and adaptation to new circumstances. And the Advent of Christ inaugurated such a time because Jesus Christ fulfilled the mission of the Old Testament, which set the new cultural pattern or archetype for humanity. However, that new pattern did not change the traditional roles of husbands and wives. Eve was created to be a helper to Adam. That does not change, though the light of Christ illuminates the subtleties of marriage be-

form, Marietta, Ohio, 2011.

cause of the dispensation of the Holy Spirit, and the Spirit's involvement in the marriage. Christ reset that pattern to its original intent, through a better covenant in which the Holy Spirit is a full partner. This is true in both church and family, or it will fail in both church and family. And this is why it is important to understand the role of the Holy Spirit in marriage. To ignore or deny the role of the Holy Spirit in marriage sets up the ignorance and denial of the Holy Spirit in the church. And visa versa. Therefore, genuine biblical marriage relationships—not corrupted traditions, duties, and responsibilities—are to be maintained in the light of Christ.

36. Generational Transfer

Children, obey your parents in the Lord, for this is right.
"Honor your father and mother" (this is the first command-
ment with a promise), "that it may go well with you and that
you may live long in the land." Fathers, do not provoke your
children to anger, but bring them up in the discipline and
instruction of the Lord. —Ephesians 6:1-4

The relationship between children and their parents mirrors the relationship between humanity and God, and doubly so for sons and fathers. I suspect that the tension between sons and fathers has to do with the issues of authority and responsibility because these are the central elements that are to be successfully transferred from generation to generation.

Generational transfer is just another way of talking about inheritance. To inherit is to receive from a natural or legal predecessor, from someone who died before you will die, with whom you have a natural or legal relationship. Children inherit goods, traits, and habits from their parents. Parents and children share likeness (Genesis 1:26). Children are not duplicates or replicas of their parents, but they are similar in spite of a wide range of differences. The parent/child relationship provides a window into the many degrees of human identity and difference, of similarity and uniqueness.

Indeed, family introduces the idea of sets and set theory[1] as an area of theological study. Humanity, like every class of living things, involves individuals within set matrices. I mention this because it is important for a deeper understanding of the Trinitarianism of the Godhead, and provides a perspective that is rich in unmined ore. Yet,

---

1   See "Membership & Set Theory," p. 405.

neither the Godhead nor the perspective are novel. They are, in fact, as old as Scripture itself. Understanding the elements and intricacies of set theory provides an understanding of the ancient doctrine of the Trinity in ways that make sense, and may be helpful to people who too quickly dismiss some of the mysteries of Scripture (John 14-17).

Understanding how Jesus Christ is related to the Father and the Holy Spirit provides a lot of help understanding our own families, as well as the church generally because families and churches are composed of membership sets. The social dimensions of humanity are very set like. And even though set theory has limitations in its application to people, it also has a valuable range of useful analogies and applications.

To be obedient to the rules of the set is to be a member of the set. Paul expressed family membership as obedience to one's parents. But not merely to one's parents. Paul added the phrase *in the Lord*, and because the Lord he referred to is Jesus Christ we can understand the phrase to be equivalent to *in Christ*. He envisioned that the obedience of the children to the parents takes place *in Christ,* the aleph-null[2] regarding the set of church members. This analogy and the establishment of its mathematical reality may help many people reconsider the reality of God and the truth of Scripture.

RIGHT

The rationale for such obedience is its righteousness (δίκαιος), v. 1). The idea of biblical righteousness in our day and age has fallen on hard times. Most people, even most Christians, think of biblical righteousness in terms of sin and pride. Righteousness is too often understood to be a kind of overstepping of one's abilities and calling. And there is some truth to this that issues from the call for Christians to be humble rather than proud. However, humility and righteousness are not in biblical conflict, which means that they can both exist in the same person, as they did in Jesus Christ. Sure, Christians aren't going to exercise them perfectly, as He did. Nonetheless, by the power and presence of the Holy Spirit through regeneration, Christians can exercise them adequately. Indeed, to be less than righteous to our best ability in the light of Christ is to fall short of our calling to be in Christ.

The concern for righteousness is the concern for truthfulness, the fullness of truth, fully considered. To speak of the whole truth is to

---

2   See Aleph-null ($\aleph_0$), p. 407.

speak of the truth of the whole, of the wholeness and holiness of life. And such truth is greater than the wholeness of death by the measure of holiness, or the absolute uniqueness of God-in-Christ. Life is more whole than death because it includes life. Life issues from another dimension or measure than mere materiality. Life provides a measurement that is completely unknown apart from life. And philosophically, that which encourages life issues out of love and is a kind of forgiveness that is greater than that which encourages death. That which issues out of hatred is a kind of vengeance.

True righteousness is saturated in humility because the truly righteous know that they are not truly righteous. They correctly perceive an extent of true righteousness that is greater than themselves, and correctly perceive the paucity of their own development and maturity. They know that they fall short of true righteousness. Yet, they persist in their faithfulness to the biblical ideal that they cannot attain in this life, knowing that genuine progress can be made and is appreciated by God-in-Christ.

HONOR

Verse 2 switches from *obedience* to *honor* (τιμάω), which is defined as fixing the correct value to a thing. We are not used to linking morality and math, but various similarities are instructive. *Math* is defined as the science that deals with the logic of quantity, shape, and arrangement. It is a discreet science in that it distinguishes between true and false results. There are a variety of ways to solve mathematical problems, but usually only one correct or right answer, though there may be a variety of equivalent expressions.

The most common methods for solving mathematical problems are 1) correct memorization of the rules, and 2) correct discernment of the problem. Method 2 necessarily includes method 1, but method 1 does not necessarily include method 2. The two ways are almost the same, but the first can be used without real understanding. And even though these methods may produce the same answer, the second is a better solution because the process includes understanding and discernment.

Discernment is like kilning. Compare two pieces of pottery made by the same potter with the same clay, with the same tools, and in the same shop. But one is kilned and one is not. The kilned piece will be better than the unkilned piece because kilning strengthens the clay. Yet, it takes discernment to tell the two pieces apart.

Set Theory is all about the quantity, shape, and arrangement of the members of various sets. Set Theory has application to groups, which include families, churches, nations, etc. Discernment is about getting the set theory of families, churches, nations, etc., right. It is about getting their quantities (membership rules), shapes (inter-relationships), and arrangements (intra-relationships) right. It is about correctly distinguishing between good and evil, right and wrong. It's about the correct understanding and analysis, and not simply memorizing the rules of life.

Honor requires discernment. To honor both father and mother is to honor the wholeness of life. It is another acknowledgment of the wholeness and holiness of life. And in the same way that children are the product of father and mother, so the commandment to honor them comes with the promise of future life. Promises are always future oriented. The promise is not simply about the possibility of the future, but when linked with the commandment it provides an actual bridge to the future.

SUSTAINABILITY

Verse 3 is about human sustainability on earth. God's plan all along has been to nurture sustainable human development

"on earth, as it is in heaven" (Matthew 6:10).

The eternality of heaven must include human sustainability. These first few verses of chapter six are about the longevity of humanity on earth, inasmuch as the central problem of history has been the development, maintenance, and transfer (inheritance) of God's blessings. And yet, from the beginning in the Garden, both God's blessings and curses have multiplied, as in Jesus parable of the wheat and the tares (Matthew 13:25-30).

The family is at the heart of human sustainability because it is the source of population and the training camp for cultural engagement. Until recently children simply absorbed the values of their families because they were almost exclusively exposed to family life. However, in the modern age mass media broke into the family through the publication of books and the advent of public education. Then radio and movies were invented. Soon after, television intruded into family life in significant ways. And now the Internet nearly dominates, if not the time, then the attention of most children. Today mass media has replaced the family in most cases as the primary cultural agent in the lives of children.

In ages past the family provided a buffer between the culture and the children. Families protected children from the harsh realities of sin that exist in the culture. Sure, there has always been sin in families, too. But because exposure to culture was limited, the exposure of the children to sin was similarly limited. Today, children are simply exposed to more culture and therefore more sin through the advent of mass media. But it is not just children, today everyone is exposed to more culture than ever before because we can communicate with more people from all over the world.

Whether this is good or bad depends on the values that are broadcast over mass media. Humanity is an adaptive species. We are wired to adapt to our circumstances, to our environment. That's the strength of humanity, as long as the adaptations are made to our actual environment and not some pseudo-environment. When we make cultural adaptations that do not serve our actual longevity and sustainability, those very adaptations then contribute to our harm. So, whether or not mass media exposure will contribute to our sustainability or our harm is the central issue of our day.

DADS

The Bible speaks a lot about fathers and sons. The long arc of the biblical story is about the relationship between God The Father and His children. But it is also about human fathers and sons as well. Fathers—husbands—are to play the leadership role in families, and boys must learn how to play that role. And learning how to play the leadership role in a situation where you are not currently the leader but are to learn from the leader can be tricky. It can easily lead to conflict when the source of authority becomes unclear in the learning process.

Just saying that men are to play the leadership role in families sets the conflict in motion because biblical leadership is not a matter of self-assertion, but of earning trust and honor through one's own submission to the Holy Spirit, and modeling the division of authority in the Godhead. Paul has been talking about love and honor and mutual submission among believers. And the key to understanding this is Jesus' leadership model (Matthew 20:25). Jesus, who has been given *all* authority, exercises that authority through submission and service. Jesus modeled leadership as submission and service. The strength of humanity as a species is not the strength of individuals, but is the strength of cooperation. And cooperation does not mean that people are without leadership, it simply means that leadership is flexible, depending on the task at hand and who has the requisite skills for the task at hand.

Jesus Himself lives in submission to God. Yet, He both follows and sends the Holy Spirit. We say that God created the world, but the Holy Spirit actually did the heavy lifting. Understanding the interpersonal relationships of the Godhead helps us understand how authority can be shared.

Paul spoke to the two sides of this concern. Fathers should not provoke their children to wrath. The fact that this is specifically mentioned suggests that it was a problem. And the problem still exists today. It is quite easy for fathers to come on too strong to their children, or to simply insist on obedience without explanation or understanding. It is instructive to note that Paul put the blame on fathers and not on the children. Clearly, fathers are in the superior position. Both the responsibility for getting it right and the blame for getting it wrong fall to the fathers.

Thus, Paul tells them how to do it right. Train (ἐκτρέφω) them, nourish them, cherish them. Nurture (παιδεία) them, or we could translate it as *teach* them or *tutor* them. Whatever else this might mean, it means giving them individual attention—a lot of it. In addition we are to admonish (νουθεσία) them. This last term means everything that is involved in Nouthetic Counseling,[3] which uses the Bible as the primary guide for dealing with psychological issues.

Putting all of this together, fathers are to not merely teach their children, but train them, disciple them, which obviously requires loving and providing for their health, growth, and maturity. And fathers are not to merely teach them, but tutor them, where tutoring means a lot of one-on-one time. Lastly, Scripture is to provide the foundation for what is taught, the doctrine, content, or meat of the lessons.

The final phrase of v. 4 is "of the Lord," which means that the Lord is to have ownership of the process. The training is His training in biblical discipline, biblical doctrine, biblical love, biblical care, biblical responsibility, biblical maturity—all of which lead to biblical discernment. Children are to learn biblical discernment, or how the Bible defines, identifies, and distinguishes good from evil.

---

3   Institute For Nouthetic Studies, www.nouthetic.org, National Association of Nouthetic Counselors, www.nanc.org.

37. WORKING

*Bondservants, obey your earthly masters with fear and trem-
bling, with a sincere heart, as you would Christ, not by the
way of eye-service, as people-pleasers, but as bondservants of
Christ, doing the will of God from the heart, rendering service with a good will as to the Lord and not to man, knowing that whatever good anyone does, this he will receive
back from the Lord, whether he is a bondservant or is free.
Masters, do the same to them, and stop your threatening,
knowing that he who is both their Master and yours is in
heaven, and that there is no partiality with him.*
—Ephesians 6:5-9

While technically bondservants worked to pay back a bond
or debt of some kind, and didn't receive wages, they
usually received food and shelter during their service.
The central difference between bondservant and freeman was that
one was in debt and one was not. And while not all workers were
bondservants, it was a widespread practice. So, I'm taking some liberty by suggesting that what Paul said about bondservants applies to
employees and those who are in debt. And yet, not really. Today debt
is our way of life. Hardly anyone has no debt, so there is a sense in
which we are all bondservants, though wages are paid in lieu of free
food and shelter.

It sounds a bit over the top to suggest that obedience should be
done with fear and trembling, but that's what Paul said and that's
what the words mean. And that it meant then what it means now—
that our obedience should be strict. If we take what is said about
Christian service seriously, we should anticipate the needs of those we

serve and provide for them before they ask, which should be even more true regarding bondservants.

Having a sincere (ἁπλότης) heart means not being duplicitous, not pretending, not scheming, not working some angle. Again, this is not just good advice for bondservants and employees, but for all Christians. Paul was simply applying ordinary Christian morality to the work of servants and employees. It's not brain surgery or nuclear physics, but just simply Christian common sense. Well, maybe it used to be common, but not any more.

Christians are to work as if they are working for Christ, because they are. It is not that we are to simply please our boss, but that we are to please Christ with what we do at work, and how we do it. We are to please the Lord because we will do our best when we follow our gifts and calling regarding our occupation. We please the Lord by imitating Christ's righteousness to the best of our ability.

Division of labor is also at the heart of Christianity. That's what 1 Corinthians 12-14 is about. Paul was not simply talking about how to organize the church as we understand the organization of churches today. He was talking about how to organize the church as Jesus Christ understands it, as the central cultural driver of human organization. Our vision and understanding of what constitutes Christ's church today falls far short of the biblical model.

We work for Christ by fulfilling His expectations of us and anticipating His needs, and the needs of His people. The elements of such work include honesty, integrity, industry, loyalty, and honor, as previously mentioned. Paul tells us how not to do it: not with *eye-service* (ὀφθαλμοδουλεία). The Greek word is just what it is in English: *eye-service* or *eye-slavery*. It suggests that real integrity is not just for show when we are being watched, but that we should do what is right even when no one is watching, even when no one would know —because God is always watching. God always knows. We may fool others, but we cannot fool God. This is the sense in which we need to rethink what Paul calls works-righteousness. We have traditionally defined the term too narrowly, and missed the important relationship between ordinary work habits and faithfulness. We are to engage our calling, what we often think of as secular work, with righteousness— honesty, integrity, industry, loyalty, and honor. Doing so does not contribute to our salvation, but it does contribute to our faithfulness.

Nor are Christians to be *people-pleasers* (ἀνθρωπάρεσκος). Again, the Greek meaning is the same as the English. While on the one hand we are to work to please the boss, on the other hand, if the boss is not a Christian, not moral or honest, then pleasing the boss may put us in conflict with pleasing Christ. And should such a conflict ever arise, we are to remain obedient to Christ. Yet, our work and behavior must be above reproach. We are not to pride ourselves on our righteous efforts—because they will always far short of the mark. Rather, we are to provide a good example of Christian morality at all times. Our desire must be first and foremost to please Christ in all things,

> "as bondservants of Christ, doing the will of God from the heart"
> (v. 6).

To make it even more clear Paul added that we are to work as benevolent slaves of the Lord, and not as if we are slaves to some person or group. We are to serve the needs of others, but not when the perceived needs of others conflict with the revealed will of God for all people. Christians must always be free to follow the Lord, to do what He wants for His people. Christian freedom is not the freedom to do what *we* want, but is the freedom to do what Christ wants us to do. Similarly, pastors are not duty bound to do what their congregations want them to do, but are duty bound to do what Christ wants them to do, while remaining in mutual submission (Ephesians 5:21). This is widely misunderstood in our day.

We are to do God's will "from the *heart*" (v. 6, ψυχή). However, the Greek word here is not *heart*, but *psyche*. And while we usually understand the use of the word *heart* to suggest emotionality, the dictionary definition of *psyche* is "that which is responsible for one's thoughts and feelings; the seat of the faculty of reason." The dichotomy between emotion and reason is false, yet most people still tend to assume it. Emotion and logic can no more be separated than one's heart and head. One can lead and the other can follow, of course! In addition, emotions may be shallow or deep, just as logic can be coherent or incoherent. But both are always involved. Paul's point was that emotion and reason are to be in harmony in Christ.

KARMA

> "knowing that whatever good anyone does, this he will receive
> back from the Lord, whether he is a bondservant or is free" (v. 8).

Verse 8 sounds a bit like the doctrine of *karma:* if one sows good, one will reap good, if one sows evil, one will reap evil. The old adage is that you get what you give. But v. 8 does not contain the negative regarding evil. And this is a significant difference because the idea of *karma* denies God's grace. *Karma* is tit for tat, where God's grace is a free gift without precedent or expectation.

Paul's emphasis is on doing good as an expression of self-interest. Because God is both good and graceful, His emphasis is on beneficent grace. Jesus commanded people to

> "love your enemies, and do good, and lend, expecting nothing in return, and your reward will be great, and you will be sons of the Most High, for he is kind to the ungrateful and the evil" (Luke 6:35).

God's purpose in Christ is to flood the world with grace and mercy. Grace and mercy are given even to sinners! It could be no other way because "all have sinned and fall short of the glory of God" (Romans 3:23). If grace was to be given at all, it must be given to sinners. Indeed, this is the foundation for evangelism. God provides and models grace and kindness.

But we have confused this in our day by thinking that God's grace and mercy make no difference, that they do not change people. We continue to offer grace and mercy to sinners when they do not renounce their sin, thinking that this is what grace and mercy require. But this denies the reality of regeneration by denying that Christians are changed people. Because God is gracious to both the faithful and the faithless, we think that God treats everyone the same.

But this is a serious error. God is merciful to the faithless as a way to allow them to grow in faithfulness without the fear of ultimate damnation. But as people do not grow and mature in faithfulness they

> "are storing up wrath for yourself on the day of wrath when God's righteous judgment will be revealed" (Romans 2:5).

God's grace functions to defer judgment, not to eliminate it. Those who respond to God's grace will find that the ultimate consequence of God's judgment—damnation—is removed. But those who do not respond, will find that it is not removed—not because God does not want it removed, but because the sinner does not want to renounce sin. God initially treats everyone the same by extending grace and mercy, but ultimately God's intention is to separate the sheep and the goats (Matthew 25:31-46).

SUPERVISION

Christian masters, slave owners—those who I'm calling the bosses or supervisors—are to behave the same. The advice that Paul just gave to slaves also applies to masters. Today, this kind of advice is about as exciting as watching paint dry. But in Paul's day it was revolutionary, and it confirmed Paul's injunction that

> "there is neither Jew nor Greek, there is neither slave nor free,
> there is no male and female, for you are all one in Christ Jesus"
> (Galatians 3:23).

Threats are poor motivators, they tend to undermine trust. Masters who threatened their slaves were doing themselves a disservice. Love and encouragement are much better motivators. Even masters who were not Christians could reap the advantages of this. Christian masters were morally obligated to follow Paul here. Rather than threaten their slaves, it would behoove them to remember that Christ is master of both them and their slaves. What unites masters and slaves is their common master, Jesus Christ. This should help create a productive relationship between masters and slaves, employers and employees.

The final argument in this section was

> "that there is no partiality with him" (v. 9),

with God-in-Christ. God doesn't play favorites, which means that He doesn't prefer one over the other, but treats human beings as a whole —categorically. The only people who will be saved are those who are in unity with God-in-Christ. All others are not whole because they deny the dimension in which whole-iness exists.

It means that God does not evaluate people on the basis of wealth, position, status, possessions, skin color, or sins committed. In contrast, the things that keep people out of heaven are

> "sexual immorality, impurity, sensuality, idolatry, sorcery, enmity,
> strife, jealousy, fits of anger, rivalries, dissensions, divisions, envy,
> drunkenness, orgies, and things like these. I warn you, as I warned
> you before, that those who do such things will not inherit the
> kingdom of God" (Galatians 5:19-21).

God's concern is compliance standards, not who is complying or not complying. God's long term goal is universal compliance, but He is not so dumb as to think that it will come any time soon. Compliance involves a process. It takes time to disengage from our errors and false beliefs. So, God is patient, but not indefinitely so.

The idea of God's non-partiality jars contemporary people because we are so invested in individualism. We read that God numbers the hairs on our heads and that we are more valuable than sparrows (Matthew 10:30-31), and we convert this into the idea that human individuality trumps everything. Of course, God does love Christians for their individual uniqueness. He created them! But we get into trouble when we try to universalize this idea. God does not love all human uniqueness. Rather, He discriminates between good and evil, the saved and the lost, between covenant keepers and covenant breakers.

This should not be surprising, we do the same thing with our laws, in that we value and treat law abiders differently that we treat law breakers. The one is encouraged and the other is discouraged. One is left alone and the other is punished. However, we confuse ourselves when we think that we are free to legislate whatever laws we want, whatever laws we can get passed. This makes us think that we are able to adjust the difference between law abiders and law breakers with our laws and politics. But all such efforts fail to sway God or convince Him to change His laws and judgments. We just end up legislating immorality and outlawing morality, because we cannot do it without legislating some reversal of the biblical categories of good and evil (Isaiah 5:20).

38. Contra Mundo

Finally, be strong in the Lord and in the strength of his might. Put on the whole armor of God, that you may be able to stand against the schemes of the devil. For we do not wrestle against flesh and blood, but against the rulers, against the authorities, against the cosmic powers over this present darkness, against the spiritual forces of evil in the heavenly places. —*Ephesians 6:10-12*

The purpose of all that Paul has written is found in v. 10. The idea is that the church or community of Christ is stronger *in Christ* than anyone or any group can be apart from Christ. This is partly a kind of strength in numbers approach that takes advantage of the fact of social cooperation. Human cooperation is the engine of civilization. The idea that there is strength in numbers is the origin or seed of civilization. The idea that larger groups could dominate smaller groups blossomed before the Tower of Babel was built and it flowered in the Tower. This idea in our day fuels what I call *the urge to merge* that we see in the corporate world as bigger and bigger businesses increasingly dominate the world.

This idea of corporate dominance has been the driving force of the world system from the very beginning. However, corporate power in and of itself is neither good nor bad. It depends on the purpose and practice of the corporate principles, those ideas and commitments that bind the members of the corporation into coordinated action. Corporate power tends toward monopolization through control of religion (monotheism) and trade (money). Both issue from the same philosophical root—unity or oneness (*mono*). This strength has always dominated in the world.

But with the rise of Christianity we find that this urge to merge acquired a refinement that caused corporate dominance to grow beyond the wildest expectations of anyone previously alive. The Bible predicted it, but couched it in religious terms, which has caused the bulk of humanity to misidentify it, even today. The development of social cooperation led to governmental control through the development of science, technology, and capitalism, which funded its growth.

SPIRITUAL

What has been missed is the actual reality of the supernatural. Just saying the word congers up visions of ecstatic revelations of the miraculous, defined by eons of church history. My intention is not to deny miracles or the supernatural, but to see them from a different perspective. And in order to do that we must suspend or set aside our usual presuppositions about the supernatural and the spiritual. Our assumptions shape our vision, so we tend to see what we expect to see. But I want to help us see what we do not expect because our expectations too often blind us to the reality in which we actually live and move and have our being (Acts 17:28).

I've been trying to get at this throughout this book—and others. I've been trying to describe a dimension, like height, width, depth, density, and time. Dimensions are measurable. We can call this dimension *wholeness* or *holiness*, and it is a dimension because it is measurable. Its standard of its measurement is righteousness and it is more real[1] than houses, cars, roads, airplanes, computers, etc. Our access to this dimension comes through thought and imagination, which causes us to think that it is purely abstract. But nuclear physicists know better. They might understand it as being similar to an *atomic* or *quantum* dimension. This dimension is not open to direct, unaided individual experience, and has historically been the domain of religious mysticism, and now of science. With the help of science and technology we have build instruments with which to probe what can only be described as additional dimensions, and to demonstrate their reality.

But for the most part, we have yet to make the connection between such dimensions and the supernatural realm described in the Bible. Actually, it may not be proper to speak of the supernatural as a

---

1   *Real* is defined here as sustainable. Things that are sustainable over time are more real, more substantial than those that are not.

single dimension, because in reality the very large (outer space) and very small (nano space) appear to have many similarities, which raise thoughts about some sort of unified realm that is both beyond and beneath what we call reality. In addition, both the very small and the very large appear to extend infinitely.[2] There has been no end to date to the exploration of the very small or the very large. The only limits appear to be our tools and abilities to conceive of and comprehend such things.

There are untapped resources in these dimensions that scientists are only beginning to imagine, which the Bible has long both celebrated and warned against. However, the only safe access to these dimensions and their resources requires what the Bible calls *righteousness* (צדקה, δικαιοσύνη). Righteousness involves a concern for and conformity to ultimate truth, and truth requires honesty, integrity, industry, loyalty, and honor from all who pursue her (σοφία). We may also call it *biblical fidelity*.

The greatest truth that is knowable must necessarily be communicated by a Person. In traditional Christian theology, God is a Person, Jesus Christ is a Person, and the Holy Spirit is a Person. At the end of the day, ultimate reality is best understood by human beings as a unified story. That's how we understand dynamic things in the ebb and flow of the forces in which we live. It's the best we can do. And at the center of every story is a person.

NOWHERE / NOW HERE

This dimension of wholeness or holiness is not located in some other place, but is very much involved in the reality in which we presently live. It is in our midst, and we are also in the midst of it. In fact, it provides the shape and character of the reality we perceive. We might conceive of it as existing the "cracks" between the extant things we perceive, like space exists between individual atoms. Look around your present environment. You see various things. Yet, when those things are analyzed at an atomic or quantum level, they appear to be nothing like what we perceive. Yet, we perceive them as real because they share our scale of reality—we can experience them.

The very small and the very large are beyond the range of our ordinary senses, and are foreign realms to direct, immediate human experience. We cannot relate to what we do not perceive. We only relate to the very small and the very large through the tools of science

---

2   See: Appendix, p. 416.

and technology. We enjoy some of that fruit, but some of it is poisonous—just as in the "natural" world. So, we have to be careful. We
discover poisons when they make us sick. And our society is sick
right now because it is imbibing various spiritual poisons. Discovering which fruit is poisonous is dangerous. The poisoned person usually has to have help to find a cure because it's hard to think straight
when you have been poisoned.

And this is the central concern of the Bible. God knows the cure,
and He knows what has poisoned His people. Thus, we need to do
two things: receive the cure, and quit imbibing the poison. The cure
is Christ and the poison is sin. Many people are worried about the environment and over population. But the problem is not that there are
too many people on earth, but that there is too much sin.

Paul calls us to "be strong in the Lord" (v. 10). The Lord is the
master and king of the entire spectrum of all realms that human beings can ever encounter. Being strong in Him is a function of being
in Christ, of manifesting Christ's character qualities through our personal imitation. That character imitation is the central fractal of human society at every scale of which we can have experience, whether
"natural" or aided by the tools of science and technology.

Armor

Paul's second phrase, "and in the strength of his might" (v. 10) has
to do with God's ability (ἰσχύς) to strengthen us supernaturally,
through prayer, worship, service, and study (Bible, science, and technology). Traditionally, Christian scientists have understood God to
have provided two books: the Bible and nature. The study and development of nature using God's biblical principles protects us from the
many poisons that can kill us—not just individually, but as a species.
We as a world are currently very near that precipice where care must
be taken lest we destroy ourselves by abuse and faulty dependence
upon the science and technologies that issue from sin. To protect
ourselves, Paul counsels us to

"put on the whole armor of God" (v. 11).

Armor protects soldiers, and we need it because we are at war.
But we are not at war with other people. Rather, we are at war with
Satan, who is an alternative archetype, competing against the
archetype of Christ. Any archetype other than God-in-Christ is a false

archetype, and the most prevalent one is Adam. The war is a battle of archetypes, different models of competing ways to be human.

Just as in regular warfare, the real battle is not between the soldiers fighting in the trenches, but is between the rulers and authorities who control the soldiers and the societies from which the soldiers are drawn.

> "For we do not wrestle against flesh and blood, but against the rulers, against the authorities, against the cosmic powers over this present darkness, against the spiritual forces of evil in the heavenly places" (v. 12).

Following the ancient biblical patterns we can call this a conflict between Israel and the Gentiles (not-Israel), or between believers and unbelievers, or covenant-keepers and covenant-breakers, or between the church and the not-church. However, this last comparison is not simply about the social organizations that we call *churches* today. Of course it includes them, but it is not defined by them. In an ideal world all believers would be members of churches, and churches would be composed of believers only. But this is not the reality in which we live.

Churches are mixed bags, like every other extant social organization. Ideally, all social organizations would be churches of one kind or another, by which is meant that all humanity would be faithfully *in Christ*. But what we find in the world today is a jumble of social organizations that are pulling in every imaginable direction. And what we need are organizations that are pulling together *in Christ*, whether we officially call them *churches* or not.

Paul said that the war is against rulers, authorities, and cosmic powers. The battles are fought between soldiers, but the war is waged and will be won among rulers, authorities, and cosmic powers.

THE WAR ROOM

We are tempted to think that by *rulers* Paul meant the various leaders of nations, states, and cities—kings and politicians. But he did not. The Greek word translated *rulers* (κοσμοκράτωρ) might better be translated as *worldviews*, except that Paul did not simply mean philosophies. He meant enfleshed philosophies or the personification of worldviews such that they might better be called world powers. Strong's defines the word as "lord of the world, prince of this age and the devil and his demons." Upon hearing such a definition our minds immediately fly into various realms of fantasy and imagination. It is very difficult for us to understand the reality of Satan's worldview.

We can get a glimpse of it when we understand that ideas have consequences, that causes are related to effects in actual ways. This is better seen with what the *Authorized Version* calls *principalities* (ἀρχή). The Greek word means *beginning* or *origin*. It refers to the first person or thing in a series, like an archetype. In fact, this is exactly what it refers to—a way of or model for being human, a human fractal, the source of a recursive process of imitation. Paul was talking about Adam, the Old Testament archetype, who should also be known as Satan because Adam followed Satan's model in the garden and became the leading historical proponent of Satanism, of Satan's methodology.

He and Eve abandoned God's model for humanity and imitated the pattern of the Serpent, and passed that pattern, that fractal of human behavior, down the ages through their children. It must also be noted that the model of the Serpent is individualistic, following Satan, rather than the Trinitarian God in Christ, following the Godhead, God's original manifestation (Genesis 1:26). God created man in community, but Satan alone confronted Eve as an individual. The importance of this cannot be underestimated. The issue that captured Adam and Eve was not so much between men and women as it is between individuality and corporality (the power of cooperation).

WILES

The purpose of wearing the armor of God is to

"stand against the schemes of the devil" (v. 11).

Schemes (μεθοδεία) is translated *wiles* in the *Authorized Version*. It is a compound word that literally means *method* or *meta-journey*. The meta-journey of an individual is quite different than the meta-journey of a community (a Trinity). The individual is not ultimately focused on relationship, as are communities. The value of Trinitarianism is found in its inherent relational character, where ultimate identity is both individual and corporate, and not merely monotheistic or pantheistic, religiously speaking. The schemes and ideas of the devil are atomistic and individualistic, whereas the plans of God are Trinitarian or communalistic.

However, this does not mean that the values of the community trump the values of the individual. God's ideal is not communistic.

Rather, God's ideal is Trinitarian and relational, where authority and responsibility are shared—divided, as they are in the Godhead. Such sharing does not violate the ultimacy of the individual, nor of the corporate group. Rather, it harmonizes them such that appropriate authority and responsibility are dispatched as needed by the circumstances requiring them. The group does not simply trump the individual, nor does the individual trump the group. Authority and responsibility are shared, distributed.

Thus, authority and responsibility cannot simply be replaced by an algorithm, rule, or principle. Rather, the call for authority and responsibility must always be personal—living, whether individual or corporate. This means that ultimate authority and responsibility are both unique and are shared by all parties of the corporate body, dynamically and in differing degrees. For the Godhead it means that Father, Son, and Holy Spirit are each and all ultimately unique Persons who have a shared essence, to describe it in traditional terms. And for human beings who are created in God's Trinitarian image, ultimate authority and responsibility are shared in union with Christ—not perfectly nor completely, but adequately for the circumstantial need.

Standing against the devil (διάβολος) means standing against slander and accusation. Those who stand with the God of love and goodness are subject to slander and accusation because the enemies of God do not perceive or understand Him correctly, as He actually is. They misunderstand and misrepresent Him to be something that He is not, but which they mistakenly believe He is. God's purpose is to eradicate evil from the world, and that is a *good* thing. However, the definition and character of evil is the object of dispute by unbelievers. The two sides do not agree about what is evil and what it is not. To disagree with God about this is to side with Satan, who reverses the definitions of good and evil. So, unbelievers call God what God calls *evil*, and tend to perceive themselves to be under the threat of ultimate eradication by God.

Thus, those who fear that God intends to eradicate *them*, and who will not agree with God, hurl accusations at Him and His people out of fear, thinking that God intends to destroy *them*, their personhood. But this is an error because God is no respecter of persons (Deuteronomy 16:19; Ephesians 6:9; Colossians 3:25; James 2:9). This means that God is not after them as persons, but is after their false belief, their false thinking, their false ideas—their misunderstanding of Him. He is not after them individually, but is after their false worldview, their false belief. God's desire for the eradication of evil does not mean that God is out to eliminate certain people. Not at all! God does not want people to die. He wants them to stop believing in evil things because it causes them to act in evil ways.

Unfortunately, too many sinners identify with their sin. They think that they *are* their sin, that their sin is an essential part of them, an essential part of who they are as individuals. They tenaciously cling to their sin, rather than change their minds and agree with God. This tendency is especially strong among unrepentant homosexuals, but is not limited to them. All who are sufficiently habituated to their sin tend to commit this error.

WICKEDNESS

Christians are also called to stand against what the *Authorized Version* calls *spiritual wickedness* (πονηρία), and the *English Standard Version* calls *spiritual forces of evil*. Again, note that we are not called to oppose people, flesh and blood, but wrong thinking, wrong believing, false religion, and false gods—ideas.

And we run into the same difficulty here, inasmuch as unbelievers are unwilling to separate their person from their thinking and behavior. It is curious, because personal growth and maturity require that we outgrow and discard old modes of thinking and behavior. People tend to think that they are quite mature because they have outgrown their old ideas of Christianity, which were acquired in their youth, and were simply wrong to begin with. Christianity itself continues to grow and unfold over time. But rather than taking their faith with them into maturity, people too often find it easier to abandon it for the platitudes of godless science that have been drilled into them through public and higher education. And this has been going on in education over the past hundred or so years as educators have endeavored to keep on the cutting edge of popular science.

Again, we see the age-old conflict between God and Satan, or good and evil that was inaugurated in the Garden. I have said much about this issue, and all that has previously been said applies here as well. Remember that we are to stand against false belief, false religion, and false ideas, but not against the people who hold them. This is the heart of Paul's concern here.

HIGH PLACES

Christians are not to fight "against flesh and blood" (v. 12). People are not the enemy. And even if they are so perceived, Jesus insists that we love our enemies (Matthew 5:44). Even when people define themselves as enemies against God or against us, we are not to buy into their delusion by thinking of them as our enemies. Of course, the more tenacious people hold to their delusions, the more difficult—and important!—it is to maintain this position. Nonetheless, we are to follow Jesus' lead here and

> "forgive them, for they know not what they do" (Luke 23:34).

Jesus did this as an act of evangelism, and so must we.

Such forgiveness is evangelistic because it provides an excellent model of what it means to love. Jesus established the model, and as we follow it we demonstrate our commitment to Jesus and His Way as the only means of human sustainability. The more it costs us, the more effective it will be down the line. It may not immediately effect the person you have forgiven, and maybe it never will. That's God's call, not ours. Our call is to be faithful to the model. And as the story of our faithfulness gets out, the Lord will make evangelistic use of it. The religion of forgiveness must displace the religion of vengeance. Indeed such displacement is equivalent to heaven conquering hell (Matthew 16:18).

People are so used to acting out of the religion of vengeance that all opposition to them is understood personally. People habitually deal with opposition by revenge, lashing out at others. That is the human default mode. So, we need to *not* trigger it whenever possible. And the way to not trigger it is to not paint others as enemies. We must not oppose other people. Rather, our opposition is to be directed at false ideas and beliefs, not at people.

Many Bible translators have difficulty with this when they translate Paul as saying that we wrestle "against the authorities" (v. 12). But the Greek is quite different. Strong's defines ἐξουσία (*power, authority*) as the "power of choice, liberty of doing as one pleases." We wrestle against *doing as we please*. We wrestle *against authority*. Sure, there is a dimension of this that pertains to civil law. We are to obey the law, and the authorities of the law. But to think that Paul was simply talking about opposing other people is a serious mistake. The central concern of this opposition is *doing as you yourself please*, apart from God-in-Christ.

The *English Standard Version* translates ἐξουσία as *the cosmic powers*, where the *Authorized Version* translates it as *powers*. *Cosmic* must be thought to be implied by the idea that the power comes from *high places* (*Authorized Version*) or *heavenly places* (*English Standard Version*). But even the word *places* is implied, because it is not in the Greek. Again, Strong's defines (ἐπουράνιος) as the "power of choice, liberty of doing as one pleases." My experience has been that most Christians get glassy-eyed when they refer to this verse, meaning that it becomes mystical for them, an abstraction that is without any practical application.

Heavenly powers is likely to be an allusion to the common belief in astrology that was popular Paul's day in. The common understanding was that the stars or heavenly realm somehow ruled life on earth through various gods. Like it or not that was the common view of the first century. In addition, these gods were involved in the governments and kingdoms of nations. So, there was a link between heaven and national or earthly government. Heaven was thought to dictate to kings and emperors. Or perhaps we can turn it around and say that kings and emperors consulted with heaven. Either way, the point remains that Paul's allusion to *high powers* was aimed at both heavenly powers and the highest earthly powers—government. And we would do well to remember this and not get all glassy-eyed at the mention of *heaven*.

Unfortunately, there have always been many people involved in government who do just as they please. In fact, politics is too often understood as the art of doing as you please to get what you want, usually money and power. We call it *lobbying* today, but God has always called it *sin*. I'm not saying that all lobbying itself is a sin, but that lobbying our own desires is our sin. The problem is not the lobbying, but the serving of our own desires. Governmental people and lobbyists are often found together in high places, living the high life and enjoying the high times. Christians do find themselves in opposition to such people. But again, our opposition is not to be directed at them as individuals, but at their false ideas, false beliefs, false gods, etc., because these false things create hardships for other people.

This is actually pretty hard to do in practice, not because Christians cannot discern the difference between the person and his or her worldview, but because non-Christians can't or won't or would rather not. The old adage for Christians is to "love the sinner, hate the sin." But unbelievers too often identify themselves with their sin.

They identify their behavior with their person, so when Christians criticize the behavior, it is received as a personal criticism, a personal attack. Unbelievers correctly understand that they would not be who they think they are if their behaviors changed. They cling to sinful behaviors as if they are qualities of character. And there is a sense in which they are! Again, Paul said that

> "we do not wrestle against flesh and blood, but against the rulers, against the authorities, against the cosmic powers over this present darkness, against the spiritual forces of evil in the heavenly places" (v. 12).

We might be tempted to read this in terms of law and grace, thinking that the rulers, authorities, and powers refer to what we call *civil law* today. And this is true, to a degree. But because we know that there is no real conflict between God's law and God's grace we must adapt our understanding. The conflict, for there clearly is a real conflict, is not between law and grace, but between God's law and bad law, between good and evil written into law. The conflict is not between some abstract, Gnostic notion of eternal, Platonic sense of good and evil, but is between the good laws that are an extension of God's discernment and bad laws that contradict God's discernment. The conflict is exacerbated when governmental officials are sworn to uphold laws that contradict God's discernment, made by rulers with authority and power, that go against what God recommends.

CULTURE WARS

Indeed, this was the immediate context of Paul's letter. Christ's church has always been hounded by both establishment traditionalists and civil authorities. And while the American experiment was able to put this issue on the back burner for most of its existence, that pot has continued to simmer. And of late it appears to be coming to a boil. While it was on the back burner, the American experiment was able to take advantage of much Christian fruit (science, technology, etc.) with minor engagement of the conflict. However, unbelievers have been able to chip away at the traditional Christian worldview until, beginning in the 1960s, the paucity of that accepted worldview became increasingly obvious.

For a century, science and technology have been portrayed as leading the attack against Christianity, and Christians bought the bait because unbelievers controlled the debate by setting the terms. We

see this kind of thing more generally when unbelievers insist that believers prove the existence of God from the presuppositions of unbelief. Unbelievers believe themselves to be objective in their unbelief,
that unbelief is itself an objective position. But it is not!

Rather, the issue between believers and unbelievers is as much
about the definition of *objectivity* as it is about belief in God. Thus,
unbelievers set the conflict as being between Christianity and science
(reason, objectivity, or intelligence), ignoring the reality of God's
grace, which provides the foundation of science—honesty, integrity,
and industry, which were widely embraced in young America.

During this time Christians could not counter the newly developing scientific ideas that the future would prove the unbelievers to
be correct. Christians were unable to argue against the logic of the
newly developing sciences and concluded (falsely) that science undermines Scripture. So, they began to look backward, hoping to return
to a time when the conflict was not so intense. Knowing that Scripture testifies to God's call to return to the right paths (Jeremiah 6:16)
and the old ways, they sought to return to the nineteenth century, or
the seventeenth, or the sixteenth. Some even thought that the answer
was to return to the church of the fourth century, or even the first.
But history does not run backwards!

Only when Christians understand that Christianity is the source
and foundation for science and technology can they harness them to
properly serve the progressive revelation of Jesus Christ. Future generations will prove and establish that the progressive revelation of Jesus Christ is a worthy journey without end, that Jesus Christ is
actually sufficient for all time.

39. WHOLLY TAKEN

Therefore take up the whole armor of God, that you may be able to withstand in the evil day, and having done all, to stand firm. Stand therefore, having fastened on the belt of truth, and having put on the breastplate of righteousness, and, as shoes for your feet, having put on the readiness given by the gospel of peace. In all circumstances take up the shield of faith, with which you can extinguish all the flaming darts of the evil one; and take the helmet of salvation, and the sword of the Spirit, which is the word of God, praying at all times in the Spirit, with all prayer and supplication. To that end keep alert with all perseverance, making supplication for all the saints, and also for me, that words may be given to me in opening my mouth boldly to proclaim the mystery of the gospel, for which I am an ambassador in chains, that I may declare it boldly, as I ought to speak. —Ephesians 6:13-20

Before we talk about the various parts of armor, we are instructed to take it *all* up wholly, totally, completely. It's okay to call it armor, but the Greek word is richer. Παόνοπλία is composed of two words: παν, which means ·*all* and οπλία, which Strong's defines as "any tool or implement for preparing a thing." It includes all of the various accouterments of armor, but can be many other things as well. Paul was alluding to Jesus' comment in Luke 11:21-22:

> "When a strong man, fully armed, guards his own palace, his goods are safe; but when one stronger than he attacks him and overcomes him, he takes away his armor in which he trusted and divides his spoil."

The strong man Jesus referred to was Satan, who had been the strongest man or archetype on earth. The stronger man was Himself, who had come to overcome Satan and divide his possessions, the wealth of the earth, among His people. Christ came to take from Satan what Satan had taken from God, possession of the earth, and to divide it among His people. It is important that Christ is not simply giving what Satan had, but *dividing* it up. It is an allusion to the distribution of power and authority that has been the hallmark of Protestantism until recently. Protestants have always been interested in the division of power and authority because power and authority tend to corrupt sinners. The damage can be controlled by keeping power and authority distributed among many people. Whenever power and authority amass, abuse is sure to follow—even by the best intentioned. There are always unforeseen consequences, even when no malice is intended.

Whole Armor

And of course, the armor is not actual armor, but is an allusion to the parts of the armor—truth, righteousness, peace, faith, salvation, and the Word of God. When we put all of these things together we have holiness or wholeness in Christ. The allusion is to wholeness, as has been discussed previously. That wholeness is the object of salvation, faith, peace, righteousness, and truth, and is the central topic of Scripture.

Unfortunately, the allusion to armor has tended to obscure Paul's point. This idea might be translated as: *Therefore take up the wholeness of God that is accessed with the various tools or implements provided (truth, righteousness, peace, faith, salvation and the Word of God).* That wholeness or holiness provides protection against the wiles of Satan. Satan wants to destroy that wholeness, and he does it by getting us focused on the various parts rather than the whole. Our focus on the whole is the very thing that destroys Satan's effectiveness. He cannot destroy the wholeness while we are giving our attention to it. In fact, he cannot destroy it at all. All he can do is get us to ignore it by paying attention to the parts rather than the whole.

This is easier to describe than to accomplish. We have been trained from birth to pay attention to the parts, to narrow our focal-length rather than widen it. Notice that our eyes cannot focus on everything all at once. When they focus on something near, the distance blurs, and vice versa. Our attention is similar. We easily pay attention to this or that particular thing. But it takes practice and commitment to pay attention to context and history. The key to wholeness is seeing the long arc of God's plan and history in the world. What is God's long term objective? How does He plan to achieve it? Where is the world in that story or plan right now? What is God doing right now to move His plan forward? And what can we do to be of help?

The evil day (v. 13) is a particular day of great difficulty for many people. It is a day of cataclysm and calamity. That's what makes it evil —horrible. And yet it is part of God's plan—not that He wants it or intends it. But it cannot be avoided—not because of who God is, but because of who we are. God is certainly powerful enough to avoid such difficulty. But in order for us to become who God wants us to be, in order for sinners to become perfect (τέλειος, lacking nothing necessary for completeness), whole, and holy, we must confront and triumph over every difficulty. If the difficulties are avoided, the end purpose cannot be accomplished because it uses them as a fulcrum.

Consequently, suffering and pain cannot be avoided. They are part of this world. Satan balks at this idea, and slanders God for creating such a horrible world. Satan cannot see beyond the suffering, and is captivated by the pain—as are his followers. Satan actually tries to avoid the suffering and pain, and by doing so short-circuits God's blessings. People then follow suit, which locks them into patterns, beliefs, and behaviors that receive God's curses.

God uses pain and suffering as a platform for spiritual maturity (Genesis 50:20). God uses these things as building blocks for discipline and training in the logic and ways of this world. Pain and suffering are pedagogical in God's hands. They teach lessons that cannot be learned any other way. However, the point is not the pain and suffering, nor even the discipline and training. Rather, the point is the lessons learned, lessons in patience, commitment, love, passion, sacrifice, worship, and duty. These are the things that instill Christ's character in us. Following Christ into pain and suffering establishes Christian character or God-likeness in both the personal and the social genome.

STAND

We find a similar problem with Paul's phrase, "having done all" (v. 13). It's not wrong, but there is much more to it than is suggested. The idea of *having done* (κατεργάζομαι) might be better expressed as *having been fitted into*. In addition, *all* (ἄπας) here is not the usual word for *all*. This word suggests wholeness and unity rather than a mere aggregation. Thus, the phrase conveys the idea of *having been fitted into a unified whole*. Wholeness and/or holiness is the idea, not the mere expenditure of labor.

The final command of the verse is to *stand firm* (ἵστημι). Again, *stand* is not wrong, but there's more to it than standing in a line. It means *stand the ground*, or *maintain your position*, or *be established in your position*. It's not a command to fight, but to *be*. It is not a call to action, but a call to identity. Being in unity is not an activity to be undertaken or a goal to be accomplished. It is more of a character to inhabit, or a way of being in the world. It's a state of mind, not a mass movement. It doesn't require anyone to *do* anything. Christ has already done all that is necessary. It's not a call to revival in the way that we think of revivals of the past. It's not a call for reformation as we think of the Protestant Reformation. It's not a position taken by the church, it is the reality of the *church*, the people of God. It's not something to do, it's someone to be. It's not a change to make, but is the culmination of changes that have been made by Christ. It is a matter of *being* not of *doing*.

We are to stand in truth and righteousness (v. 14) at all times, as if they were garments to be worn for protection against the elements. We are to practice them. It's easy to get caught up in the analogies of belt and breastplate, but the analogies pale in comparison to the importance of truth and righteousness. Perhaps we overlook the analogy because people no longer wear or value armor. We understand it, but have no real appreciation of it. It's old school, a thing of the distant past with which we cannot relate.

PEACE

We are to walk in peace (v. 15), to practice peace, to live in peace, to be a peaceful and peace loving people. This means that we do not threaten or attack other people. It means that we always lead with forgiveness, grace, and mercy, that we model these things in our own lives, and teach them to our children. Peace is not simply a condition of the absence of war, it is a lifestyle that is both self-sufficient and productive. We are to contribute locally to the social and economic fabric of society in positive, loving, supportive ways that encourage others to do the same.

To be at peace is not to be enslaved to debt. It means that we personally produce more than we use, that the world is better for our being in it. This is what science and technology can do for us. Science and technology help us to harness and multiply our effectiveness in the marketplace, such that we produce a positive net gain or surplus of goods and/or social good in our local communities.

To be at peace means that we don't hoard resources for ourselves, but rather we teach and train others to do for themselves what they are able, by the grace of God, to do for themselves. To be at peace means that we are generous to a fault in this regard, not rewarding sloth but encouraging self-reliance. To be at peace means devaluing Godlessness, crime, lying, and cheating, making them socially unacceptable and unappreciated as story lines for media exploitation.

And yet, Paul's call for peace does not require the full-fledged accomplishment of it, but the *readiness* (ἑτοιμασία) for it. "having put on the readiness" (v. 15). The *Authorized Version* calls it *preparation*. We are to be prepared for an outbreak of peace. The fact that most of the history of Western civilization is the history of war likely means the vast majority of people have no idea of what biblical peace really is, or how to live in its midst.

This is particularly true since the advent of World War I. Human society prior to WWI and after WWII—and especially now in the twenty-first century—are literally worlds apart. And most of the cultural developments since WWI are related to offshoots of war preparation that have issued out of science and technology.

We can only speculate about what all of this means regarding an impending outbreak of real, biblical peace. And anyone who says that they understand biblical peace for sure is mistaken. Biblical peace or *shalom* (שלום) is defined as completeness, soundness, and welfare, which are very much like wholeness and holiness. We must take care here not to imbue *welfare* with our modern ideas associated with it. We tend to think of it as governmental assistance, whereas the biblical idea is more inclusive in the sense that it is having the tools and resources to take care of ourselves (self-dependence), but also the ability, desire, resources, and compassion to help others during times of need. Of course, such need might include governmental assistance, as in the times of Joseph and the famine in Egypt, but would also include much more than mere governmental assistance.

FAITH

The most important element of Paul's advice here is to have faith (πίστις), to use it as a shield (θυρεός). According to Strong's, the root word of θυρεός (shield) is θύρα (door), probably because the shield was shaped like a door, and provided door-like protection when a door is shut. Fiery arrows are stopped by the closed door.

In very olden times serfs, who labored for the castle owner, would seek shelter in the castle when bad guys came to rob or destroy them. And once in the castle, the door or drawbridge would be closed for protection. That is likely the analogy intended by Paul here, which means that an individualistic understanding of the shield would not have been in view. The protection afforded by the shield was not like that of a warier who used the shield in battle, but was more like the serfs who sought the protection of the castle by getting in and closing the door to shield them from danger.

Here the *shield-as-door* functions first as a door into the castle, where the door itself is faith, by analogy. Thus, faith is more a matter of getting people into the safety of the castle and of being *in Christ*, than that of defending them in battle, though the defense analogy is not wrong. The great defenders of the faith can use faith as a shield. But most people will need to use it to get into the castle for protection.

Note also that the shield of faith not only stops the fiery darts of Satan, but extinguishes (σβέννυμι) or suppresses them. It keeps them from occurring. By keeping our minds occupied with the things of faith, Satan's fiery challenges are simply not launched in our minds. Thus, faithfulness is the best protection against Satan's evils. And it is here that the importance of the role of the community comes to the fore. The web of faithfulness that is created by an entire community of faith is much, much stronger than the faithfulness of a few individuals in the community—and far stronger than the faith of a single individual. Faith itself is every bit as much a corporate affair as a personal affair. However, true faith is never one or the other (individualistic or communal), but is always both.

MORE GEAR

Salvation is paired with a helmet, which protects the head—but only if your head is in it. The idea of salvation, of being saved is a head thing. It's an idea or a rationale. Salvation provides the justification for the believer, which also means that being saved is not something that one does to or for him- or herself. Salvation comes from without, from God-in-Christ, from His work on the cross, not from our work in the fields. He provides, and we receive it. We must remember that in days of old, knights could not get suited up by themselves. They needed help. And so do we.

The sword (μάχαιρα), which is the Word of God, is wielded by the Spirit, or perhaps *in* the Spirit. The sword is the only offensive weapon mentioned, which also means that the Word of God is offensive by nature. It offends the flesh, as Paul mentioned many times in many places, which is why it needs to be wielded by the Spirit. When the flesh tries to wield the Word, it proves to be completely inadequate at it. Wielding the Word of God without or apart from the Spirit, which is entirely possible and actually happens far too much, results in a worldly faith that depends on one's own personal efforts, and sidesteps or bypasses the necessary reliance upon the Holy Spirit.

We are to pray

"at all times in the Spirit, with all prayer and supplication" (v. 18).

We are to pray *in the Spirit,* which is not simply a matter of extemporaneous prayer. The Spirit is certainly capable of working in advance through liturgy and planning. Neither formal liturgy nor planning ahead for prayer are impediments to the Spirit. In fact, because God loves order and planning, He often prefers to work in the midst of liturgy and advanced planning.

The idea of

"praying at all times ... with all prayer" (v. 18)

is complex. The phrase *at all times* comes from three Greek words: διά (*through*) πᾶς (*all,* which can mean each of every instance, or the collective totality) and καιρός (*kairos, time,* which is not clock or calendar time, but is more like the time of fulfillment or completion of something). The *American Standard Version* does a good job of translation:

"with all prayer and supplication praying at all seasons in the Spirit, and watching thereunto in all perseverance and supplication for all the saints."

As does the *International Standard Version*:

"Pray in the Spirit at all times with every kind of prayer and request. Likewise, be alert with your most diligent efforts and pray
for all the saints."

ALERT

The final instruction Paul gives is to

"keep alert with all perseverance" (v. 18).

Alertness is not simply a matter of staying awake, though sleep is the
antithesis of alertness. Rather, it is a matter of circumspection, of being aware of how things play out and what consequences they bring.
Circumspection is really a matter of being able to follow logic and
understand cause and effect relationships in the world.

The Greek word (ἀγρυπνέω) literally means not being asleep.
But there is more to not being asleep than avoiding literal slumber.
When one is asleep one is not aware of this world. Analogously, it
means that we are not to be unconscious, and that we are to be conscious. We are not to be shallow thinkers, but deep thinkers. We are
to teach and encourage deep thinking, analysis, and comprehensions
of deep things.

"Making supplication for all the saints" (v. 18)

can also be understood as making supplication for the sanctification of
all. This might even be preferred because ἅγιος (*saints*) functions as
an adjective not a noun. God's ultimate desire and plan is to sanctify
the human race, which of course means the sanctification of specific
individuals because there is no such thing as the human race apart
from specific individuals—and that's the point, the goal! Yet, the purpose of the goal is not for any specific individual or group of individuals to achieve it, but for all to strive for it. To believe that the goal
has been accomplished at any point, is to stop striving for it, which
will result in its failure. As long as new human beings are being born,
the goal has not been achieved. Every human birth requires a new
birth in Christ.

Such rebirth does not have to be loud and flashy. We don't need
to know the day and the hour, anymore than we can remember the
day and hour of our natural birth. Yet, we celebrate our natural birth.
So, we should also celebrate our spiritual rebirth. There will come a
time in life when we can freely admit that we have been reborn, that
we recognize that our rebirth is different than our ordinary birth, that

at some point something changed in us. Paul said that we are to sup-
plicate—to beg—for this awareness to come to all people.

AND FOR ME

> "...and also for me, that words may be given to me in opening
> my mouth boldly to proclaim the mystery of the gospel, for which
> I am an ambassador in chains, that I may declare it boldly, as I
> ought to speak (Ephesians 6:19-20).

Paul wanted to boldly and correctly proclaim the mystery of the
gospel. However, this does not mean that Paul intended for the gospel
to continue being a mystery. For him to proclaim the mystery means
that he would explain it correctly, to clear it up so that it would be a
mystery no longer. Paul's intent was to clarify the mystery of the
gospel in order to free it from its occlusion, to set it clearly before the
world so that the whole world would know that the mystery of the
gospel ends and concludes in Jesus Christ. Paul did not intend to per-
petuate the mystery, but to clear it up—not completely, of course, but
adequately.

Have you ever prayed that God would use you to accomplish His
purposes? If not, please do so now. I've been praying that very thing
for you, that those who read this book will "get it." So, if you get it,
please also pray for me, and for God's mission through this book.
Share it with a friend. Get together and discuss it. If it has stirred you,
it will stir your friends.

SENIOR MEMBER

Paul described himself as a πρεσβεύω (*presbyter, v. 20*). We
think of it as a noun, but the Greek word functions as a verb. It describes, not what Paul was or what he thought himself to be, but what
he was doing. He was representing Christ, and he could do that because he was older in the faith than most of his readers were. The
word means an older member of the council, which for Christians at
the time would have meant the highest level of local government.
Christians separated church and state because they separated Roman
government from church government. Paul was a senior member of
the high council of Jerusalem. He was a representative, an ambassador
who served as a communication channel between the high council
and the local churches.

But he was also an ambassador in captivity, a prisoner of Rome—
but a willing prisoner (Acts 23-24). He refused to be set free because

he appealed his case to Felix, the Roman governor, in order to bring the gospel of Jesus Christ to the highest levels of Roman government he could reach. Marcus Antonius Felix was the Roman procurator of Iudaea Province from A.D. 52–58. Paul talked to Felix

"about righteousness and self-control and the coming judgment" (Acts 24:25).

Felix responded

"Go away for the present. When I get an opportunity I will summon you" (Acts 24:25),

but he never did. After

"two years had elapsed, Felix was succeeded by Porcius Festus" (Acts 24:27).

The Bible leaves Paul in Rome as a prisoner following that conversation with Felix.

40. Love Incorruptible

So that you also may know how I am and what I am doing,
Tychicus the beloved brother and faithful minister in the
Lord will tell you everything. I have sent him to you for this
very purpose, that you may know how we are, and that he
may encourage your hearts. Peace be to the brothers, and
love with faith, from God the Father and the Lord Jesus
Christ. Grace be with all who love our Lord Jesus Christ
with love incorruptible.   —Ephesians 6:21-24

Paul made an effort to keep personal stuff out of his letters to the churches. He didn't always succeed. Nonetheless, that is why they continue to resonate with Christians of every stripe. His concern was always to proclaim Christ and the gospel for the benefit of humanity. Sure, he was concerned about the church. But as we have seen in this study, Paul's idea of the church and ours barely overlap. The church is never limited to any particular group of believers, and yet is always manifest as some particular group of believers.

His understanding of Christianity was neither individualistic nor communalistic. The ideal is neither individual dominance, nor collective dominance, but trinitarian distribution because God owns "the cattle on a thousand hills" (Psalm 50:10). And because God owns everything, His ownership is distributed through the Godhead. And Christ's church should be a reflection of God, with authority distributed throughout the church. With authority comes control, and because the fundamental structure of the church is local, church authority and control should be local. Christians are stewards of God's treasure, which is to be shared.

The separation of church and state can only be accomplished biblically because the Bible is all about the distribution of power and authority. People, on the other hand, are all about the concentration of power in order to get things done. However, Christianity is not about getting things done. It's about the works of God that culminate in the rest (sabbath) of God.[1]

PRACTICE

Tychicus was from Asia and traveled with Paul. He was there when Eutychus fell from a third story window during one of Paul's late night sermons (Acts 20:9-10). Tychicus was there when Paul revived the boy who was thought to be dead. Tychicus would tell people how Paul was because Paul did not want to waste time and effort writing about himself.

Tychicus' job was not to just tell about *what* Paul was doing, but *how* Paul was doing it. Verse 21 might be translated as *that you may see how I practice (the faith)*. Paul taught imitation. He imitated Christ so that other Christians could imitate him. And Tychicus would demonstrate how he imitated Paul. Thus, the faith was handed down through imitation (1 Corinthians 4:16, 11:1; Ephesians 5:1; Philippians 3:17; 1 Thessalonians 1:6, 2:14; 2 Thessalonians 3:7, 3:9; Hebrews 6:12, 13:7). It's not simply that Tychicus would *tell* (γνωρίζω) people about Paul so that they could imitate him. Rather, Tychicus would *make it known*. Telling people is one thing, making something known to people is another. The telling ends with the speaking, but the making known is not over until there is evidence of the success of the communication in the lives of the recipients.

Tychicus' job was to *encourage* (παρακαλέω) their hearts. We have the image of back-slapping, tear-hugging embraces, of bolstering their self-esteem, and making them feel good about being Christians. But that's not really what the word means. Literally, it means *call near*, and is alternately translated as *beseech, comfort, entreat, desire,* and *exhort*. It is more a pleading and begging that borders on demanding that their hearts be open to Christ and to Paul and to Tychicus and to one another. Tychicus

"shall make known to you all things" (v. 21, *Authorized Version*).

---

1   Ross, Phillip A. *Rock Mountain Creed—Jesus' Sermon on the Mount*, Pilgrim Platform, Marietta, Ohio, 2011, *Introduction*.

Tychicus would not rest until they knew what they needed to know about Paul's practice of the faith. His job was edification.

You'd think that peace and love would be the natural condition of people whose hearts have been encouraged. But Paul specified again that they were to be in peace and love (*agape*) with one another, probably because he knew the difficulties involved in being a believer and maintaining peace and love in the church. From Paul's repetition of the command, we can surmise that peace and love were not the natural or usual responses, but needed to be specified—again! I'd change the punctuation of the verse to read:

> "Peace be to the brothers, and love, with faith from God the Father and the Lord Jesus Christ" (v. 21).

Peace is the fruit of agape love, so peace and love go together. And *the faith* belongs to Jesus Christ. He can give it because it's His.

He then dispatched the Holy Spirit to bring us a measure of *that* faith, of *His* faith. If the faith is ours, then it is limited by our ability to work it up. But if it belongs to Christ, then it depends on Him. I'm glad that the faith I have doesn't depend upon me. I'd screw it up! But because it depends on Christ and not on me, it is safe with me. I can trust it, even when I can't trust myself—and that's truly good news!

Paul's final sentence to the Ephesians was that grace unites all who love Christ sincerely. Therefore, the unity of the church issues from loving Christ sincerely. Where the one thing is lacking, so will be the other. But where the one thing abides, so will unity abide. Thus, the unity of the church is not a matter of councils or synods or making decisions or church revivals or denominational reformations or doctrinal statements or legal agreements, etc. Rather, the unity of the church is a matter of loving Christ sincerely.

No one can do that for anyone else, but we all can demonstrate love to everyone else. This is the number one job of every Christian, and given the state of disunity in the churches, it appears that this job has gone long neglected. Perhaps its time for a change. Perhaps one person *can* make all the difference in the world. Well, at least I can make a difference in *my* world. You?

Appendix

Whole & Holy

The etymology and origin of the word *holy* confirms that *holy* implies *wholeness*. *Holistic* and *wholistic* are one and the same, and are etymologically traceable to 1 Thessalonians 5:23:

> "And the very God of peace sanctify you *wholly* (ὁλοτελής); and I pray God your *whole* (ὁλόκληρος) spirit and soul and body be preserved blameless unto the coming of our Lord Jesus Christ."

The Greek words are from the root ὅλος, which is a primary word meaning whole or all that is complete (in extent, amount, time, or degree) especially (neuter) as a noun or adverb: *all, altogether, every whit,* and *throughout whole.*

Of course, the Bible uses other Greek words that are translated as holy. But that does not negate this understanding of holy.

Membership & Set Theory

Understanding the relationship between membership and mathematical set theory is critical for a realistic understanding of membership in the body of Christ, which is the new creation established by the regeneration of humanity (both individuals and society or culture) in Christ. The math involved in set theory can help provide analogous information about the spirituality of Christianity. Not only are science and Christianity not incompatible or contradictory, but they are actually in a harmonious and helpful relationship. This appendix addresses the issue of parts and wholeness in order to explore the idea that the whole is larger than the sum of the parts as a spiritual analogy regarding church membership and participation in Christ.

405

Cardinal Numbers

Set theory as conceived by Georg Cantor assumes the existence of infinite sets. The argument is that the body of Christ is an infinite set because of Christ's divinity. As this assumption cannot be proven from first principles it has been introduced as an axiom of set theory by the axiom of infinity, which asserts the infinite existence of the set N of natural numbers. Every infinite set which can be enumerated by natural numbers is the same size (cardinality) as N, and is understood to be countable. Examples of countably infinite sets are the *natural numbers*, the *even numbers*, the *prime numbers*, and also all the *rational numbers*, i.e., fractions. Thus, the body of Christ is countable, and exists as a specific number at any specific time. These sets have in common the cardinal number $|N| = \aleph_0$ (aleph-null), a number greater than every natural number. The divinity of Christ is the spiritual axiom that grants Him infinitude and an analogous cardinality regarding the set defined by participation in Christ.

Cardinal numbers can be defined as follows. Define two sets to have the same size by: *there exists a bijection (a one-to-one correspondence between the elements of the sets) between the two sets.* Then a cardinal number is, by definition, a class consisting of all sets of the same size. To have the same size is an equivalence relation, and the cardinal numbers are the equivalence classes.

Ordinal Numbers

Besides the cardinality, which describes the size of a set, ordered sets also form a subject of set theory. The axiom of choice guarantees that every set can be well-ordered, which means that a total order can be imposed on its elements such that every nonempty subset has a first element with respect to that order. The order of a well-ordered set is described by an ordinal number. For instance, 3 is the ordinal number of the set $\{0, 1, 2\}$ with the usual order $0 < 1 < 2$; and ω is the ordinal number of the set of all natural numbers ordered the usual way. Neglecting the order, we are left with the cardinal number $|N| = |\omega| = \aleph_0$.

Ordinal numbers can be defined with the same method used for cardinal numbers. Define two well-ordered sets to have the same order type by: *there exists a bijection between the two sets respecting the order: smaller elements are mapped to smaller elements.* Then an ordinal number is, by definition, a class consisting of all well-ordered sets of the same order type. To have the same order type is an equivalence relation on the class of well-ordered sets, and the ordinal numbers are the equivalence classes.

Two sets of the same order type have the same cardinality. The converse is not true in general for infinite sets: it is possible to impose different well-orderings on the set of natural numbers that give rise to different ordinal numbers.

There is a natural ordering on the ordinals, which is itself a well-ordering. Given any ordinal α, one can consider the set of all ordinals less than α. This set turns out to have ordinal number α. This observation is used for a different way of introducing the ordinals, in which an ordinal is equated with the set of all smaller ordinals. This form of ordinal number is therefore a canonical representative of the earlier form of equivalence class.

Power Sets

By forming all subsets of a set S (all possible choices of its elements), we obtain the power set P(S). Georg Cantor proved that the power set is always larger than the set, i.e., $|P(S)| > |S|$. A special case of Cantor's theorem proves that the set of all real numbers R cannot be enumerated by natural numbers. R is uncountable: $|R| > |N|$.

For more on the various paradoxes related to set theory see: http://en.wikipedia.org/wiki/Paradoxes_of_set_theory.

This brief discussion provides the math involved in the maxim: the whole is greater than the sum of the parts. It actually is!

To see the application of all of this to spirituality consider the function of $\aleph_0$ (aleph-null).

Aleph-null ($\aleph_0$)

The set theory symbol $\aleph_0$ refers to a set having the same cardinal number as the smallest infinite set of integers. The algebraic numbers also have cardinality $\aleph_0$. Some rather surprising properties satisfied by $\aleph_0$ include:

1. $\aleph_0^r = \aleph_0$ for $r > 0$
2. $r\aleph_0 = \aleph_0$ for $r \neq 0$
3. $\aleph_0 + f = \aleph_0$, where f is any finite set. However, $2^{\aleph_0} = \aleph_0^{\aleph_0} = c$, where c is a continuum.

Notice that no operations on $\aleph_0$ have any observable effect on it. Why not? Because $\aleph_0$ represents a whole, which exists in a different dimension (basis of measurement) than the sum of the parts. The whole requires a different kind of measure than the parts, and that's what is meant by a different dimension.

Renteln and Dundes (2005)[1] provided the following humorous mathematical analog of the "99 bottles of beer on the wall" drinking song, which refers to its property that $\aleph_0 - 1 = \aleph_0$: "$\aleph_0$ bottles of beer on the wall, $\aleph_0$ bottles of beer, Take one down, and pass it around, $\aleph_0$ bottles of beer on the wall" (repeat).[2] This illustrates the economy of infinite sets.

The smallest set of integers is 3, which is found in the set {0, 1, 2}. Spiritually, this corresponds to the Father, Son, and Holy Spirit, or the Trinity of God. Deciding which number corresponds to which Person in the Trinity is moot because the Persons of the Trinity are identical though distinguishable, and unique but in unity. This corresponds to Christ's dual nature—human and divine. This is used here as an analogy, not a mathematical description.

Each and all of the equations regarding $\aleph_0$ above testifies to the same thing: that in the realm of the infinite ($\aleph_0$) ordinary functions, calculations or measurements operate differently. The presence of the realm of $\aleph_0$ is not observable in the natural order, though it is very real. The economy of $\aleph_0$ is not a zero-sum, but is open or infinite.

BAPTISMAL PARALLELS

INFANT BAPTISM	**BELIEVER'S BAPTISM**
Symbolizes God's initiating action in salvation.	Symbolizes believer's response to God's salvation.
1. **Infant baptism ceremony** (a symbol of God's grace)	1. **Infant dedication ceremony** (a symbol of God's grace)
• To be baptized as a symbol of God's Covenant is to be brought under God's eternal covenant with all its attendant promises and threatenings (Deuteronomy 28, 2 Samuel 7, Jeremiah 31:31-40, Matthew 26:26-30, Acts 3:12-26) by the	• To be dedicated as a symbol of God's Covenant is to be brought under God's eternal covenant with all its attendant promises and threatenings (Deuteronomy 28, 2 Samuel 7, Jeremiah 31:31-40, Matthew 26:26-30, Acts 3:12-26) by the

1   Renteln, P. and Dundes, A. *Foolproof: A Sampling of Mathematical Folk Humor.* Notices Amer. Math. Soc. 52, 24-34, 2005.

2   Weisstein, Eric W. "Aleph-0." From *MathWorld*—A Wolfram Web Resource. http://mathworld.wolfram.com/Aleph-0.html

blood of Christ and the power of the Holy Spirit in the hope of salvation, symbolized by the washing of water by sprinkling or pouring, and the parents' commitment to God's covenant.

2. Profession or Confirmation of Faith

(a symbol of personal response to Spirit's work)

- Public confession of faith in Christ as personal Lord and Savior, and a period or process of instruction or testing.

3. Dedication ceremony (taking the vows of faithfulness).

- Confirmation or dedication is a symbol of personal regeneration that involves the laying on of hands as an outward sign of an inward and spiritual receiving or the acceptance and forgiveness of Jesus Christ as personal Lord and Savior (Acts 9:17).

4. Church Membership

- Requires baptism and profession.
- Public assent to God's personal calling to unity in the Body of Christ through the common commitment of believers in a local church.
- Requires public assent to the local church constitution, by-laws, and Statement of Faith.

blood of Christ and the power of the Holy Spirit in the hope of salvation, symbolized by the laying on of hands upon the infant and the parents' commitment to God's covenant.

2. Profession or Confirmation of Faith

(a symbol of personal response to Spirit's word)

- Public confession of faith in Christ as personal Lord and Savior, and a period or process of instruction or testing.

3. Baptism ceremony (taking the vows of faithfulness).

- To be baptized as a symbol of personal regeneration involves sprinkling, pouring or immersion with water of an individual as an outward sign of an inward spiritual grace, or the acceptance and forgiveness of Jesus Christ as personal Lord and Savior (Romans 6).

4. Church Membership

- Requires profession and baptism.
- Public assent to God's personal calling to unity in the Body of Christ through the common commitment of believers in a local church.
- Requires public assent to the local church constitution, by-laws, and Statement of Faith.

THE AMERICAN DREAM

Martin Luther King, Jr. (1929-1968) was an American clergy-
man, activist, and leader in the African-American Civil Rights Movement. He is best known for his role in the advancement of civil rights
using nonviolent civil disobedience, and has become a national icon
in the history of American Progressivism. From his most famous
speech:

> "I say to you today, my friends, so even though we face the
> difficulties of today and tomorrow, I still have a dream. It is a
> dream deeply rooted in the American dream.
>
> I have a dream that one day this nation will rise up and live
> out the true meaning of its creed: 'We hold these truths to be
> self-evident: that all men are created equal.'
>
> I have a dream that one day on the red hills of Georgia the
> sons of former slaves and the sons of former slave owners will
> be able to sit down together at the table of brotherhood.
>
> I have a dream that one day even the state of Mississippi, a
> state sweltering with the heat of injustice, sweltering with the
> heat of oppression, will be transformed into an oasis of
> freedom and justice.
>
> I have a dream that my four little children will one day live
> in a nation where they will not be judged by the color of their
> skin but by the content of their character.
>
> I have a dream today.
>
> I have a dream that one day, down in Alabama, with its
> vicious racists, with its governor having his lips dripping with
> the words of interposition and nullification; one day right
> there in Alabama, little black boys and black girls will be able
> to join hands with little white boys and white girls as sisters
> and brothers.
>
> I have a dream today."

(King, Martin Luther; King, Coretta Scott. *The Words of Martin
Luther King*, Jr.: Second Edition. Newmarket Press, 2008, p. 95.)

Jefferson's constitutional phrase, "We hold these truths to be self-
evident: that all men are created equal," has become a popular perversion of the biblical doctrine of the universal application of God's law.
It is a popular perversion because it is often used to *replace* the biblical
doctrine of the universal application of God's law. (Of course, as soon
as such a thing is uttered aloud, offense is taken, which impedes the
further efforts of communication and clarification. And all forthcom-

ing answers are immediately met by the passion of umbrageous indignity.)

Nonetheless, King, an ordained Christian minister, laid the burden of his concern for justice on the traditions of men—on history and civil law, rather than on the kingdom of God. King's intent was to change American civil law, which had perverted justice by not treating all people equally. Equal treatment before the law is an Old Testament mandate (Exodus 12:49). King's concern and work was noble, but misdirected. He made a name for himself by engaging in politics and protest in order to bring attention to the problem of disparity in the South. The problem was and is real. And King's success exceeded his expectations.

King built upon Jefferson's error—Jefferson's disdain for the fullness and comprehensibility of God's law. The U. S. Constitution itself is a compromise document. And understanding the two sides of the compromise is the key to understanding and revealing much unknown American history. It is not unknown because it is unavailable, it is unknown because it is ignored and/or rejected.

If the U.S. Constitution was a compromise document, who were the parties of the compromise? As the American Founding Fathers worked to develop a constitution for the fledgling nation, they worked against the backdrop of the history of Europe, which was awash in similar sentiments. The European constitutional model since Constantine involved invoking the name and incorporating the spirit of Jesus Christ in some way into national constitutions. Prior to 1776 every European constitution did so. Similarly, treaties between Christian nations conventionally began with an invocation of God up until the late nineteenth century.[3]

France, whose revolution completely repudiated Christianity by establishing a secular state, was an effort by France to establish the state's religious neutrality. While there are many differences between the American Revolution and the French Revolution, the religious issue was perhaps the most important. France had been predominately Roman Catholic and had just emerged from the Seven Years War, which nearly devastated the French monarchy. And Europe had been subject to various ferocious and long-standing religious wars and conflicts since the Reformation.

---

3   Lesaffer, Randall. *Peace treaties and international law in European history: from the late Middle Ages to World War One.* Cambridge University Press, 2004, p. 79.

In contrast, America had been populated early on with disenfranchised European Calvinists, who sought to escape from religious persecution and sought the right to worship freely. These were the people who dominated the early American public offices. In addition, it included those fleeing the European wars in exasperation, and who also sought freedom of worship. But in their case they wanted the freedom *not* to worship. These were the two parties of the American Constitutional compromise: Protestant Christians on one side, and those who remembered Europe's fractured Christian history and opposed the Protestant Christians on the other. One group emphasized the Bible, the other emphasized the Enlightenment. Obviously, this is an over-generalization, but it shows the two dominant perspectives that were woven into the Constitution, and later in to the American political parties.

The Christians wanted to name Jesus Christ in the American Constitution and worked to do so. But the others, following the French idea of secular government that was in discussion at the time among the Founders, did not. Jefferson was in agreement with the French idea of a secular government, and made various general allusions to God, but kept the name of Jesus Christ out of the Constitution. Thus, the American Constitution broke with the historic tradition since Constantine of invoking Jesus Christ by name, to the disappointment of many.

The parties of the American compromise have continued to struggle against one another ever since. Both have their own versions of the self-evident doctrines regarding the equality of all people, and they have gravitated to different political parties. Christian equality is centered in Christ, where secular equality is centered in man. Thus, the two sides can also be broadly described as Evangelical Christian versus secular humanism. And the two sides have coalesced into what we know today as conservatives and liberals or progressives, broadly speaking.

Today, conservatives generally understand the doctrine of human equality as being treated equally before the law, and the liberals understand it as equal opportunity for self-expression, which increasingly challenges and reverses historic American law. Clearly, the reality is far more complex than this simple model, but the model communicates the essential issue in a general way.

And at the same time, it relies on a false dichotomy—the idea that truth is either conservative or liberal. Actually, it is both, and neither.

Jesus was conservative about some things and liberal about other things. There is a real division between believers and unbelievers. The two groups hold different assumptions and presuppositions about reality, which cause them to speak past one another. They don't define things in the same ways, though they use common words.

Familiarity with the Bible actually bridges this gap because the Bible recognizes an element of truth in both liberal and conservative ideas. It teaches people to discern subtle differences that help each group understand the other. And with the decline of biblical literacy and familiarity, the two groups experience increasing difficulties of communication with one another. Unfortunately, biblical illiteracy is growing among both unbelievers and believers. Nonetheless. the burden of proof falls to believers because they are charged with greater biblical familiarity.

Under God

The story of how that phrase was added to the Pledge of Allegiance takes us back to examine a previous era that was more Christian. Louis A. Bowman, an attorney from Illinois, initiated the addition of "under God" to the Pledge. The National Society of the Daughters of the American Revolution gave him an Award of Merit for the idea. Bowman lived in Chicago and was Chaplain of the Illinois Society of the Sons of the American Revolution. At a meeting on February 12, 1948, Lincoln's Birthday, he led the Society in swearing the Pledge with two words added. He said that the words came from Lincoln's Gettysburg Address.

In 1951, the Knights of Columbus, the world's largest Catholic fraternal service organization, also began including the words "under God" in the Pledge of Allegiance. On August 21, 1952, the Supreme Council of the Knights of Columbus adopted a resolution urging that the change be made and copies of this resolution were sent to the President, the Vice President and the Speaker of the House of Representatives. The National Fraternal Congress meeting in Boston on September 24, 1952, adopted a similar resolution upon the recommendation of its president. Several State Fraternal Congresses followed suit.

In 1952, Susan Anald wrote a letter to President Truman suggesting the inclusion of "under God" in the Pledge of Allegiance. Representative Louis C. Rabaut of Michigan sponsored a resolution to add the words "under God" to the Pledge in 1953, but it failed to pass.

Some American presidents honored Lincoln's birthday by attending services at the church Lincoln attended, New York Avenue Presbyterian Church, by sitting in Lincoln's pew on the Sunday nearest February 12. On February 7, 1954, with President Eisenhower. The church's pastor, George MacPherson Docherty, delivered a sermon based on the Gettysburg Address titled "A New Birth of Freedom." He argued that the nation's might lay not in arms but its spirit and higher purpose. He noted that the Pledge's sentiments could be those of any nation, that "there was something missing in the pledge, and that which was missing was the characteristic and definitive factor in the American way of life." He cited Lincoln's words "under God" as defining words that set the United States apart from other nations.

President Eisenhower, who was baptized in the Presbyterian church the same year that he was elected President (1953), responded enthusiastically to Rev. Docherty in a conversation following the service. Eisenhower acted on Docherty's suggestion the next day, and on February 8, 1954, Rep. Charles Oakman introduced a bill to that effect. Congress passed the necessary legislation and Eisenhower signed the bill into law on Flag Day, June 14, 1954.

That was not very long ago, yet long enough for many Christian values, assumptions, and practices to have been since removed from society. Most people think that the dechristianization of America began in earnest with the two landmark decisions of the U.S. Supreme Court, Engel v. Vitale (1962) and Abington School District v. Schempp (1963), which established what is now the current prohibition against public prayer in public schools. But reaction against prayer in public schools actually began in the 1800s, and gained traction when the Roman Catholic church became officially opposed to such prayer because the character of the prayer was consistently Protestant, when there was still strong anti-Catholic sentiment throughout the nation.

The point of this departure is to demonstrate that those who claim that America has always been a secular nation have had to overcome an awful lot of Christian values, arguments, and practices along the way. And their success has been amazingly consistent, accumulative, and effective. My speculation is that this anti-Christian sentiment infected the highest echelons of the Federal government as the American Experiment began to be exported all over the world as a movement for *democracy*, a term rejected by the Founders. They undoubtedly believed that it would be easier to export democracy than Christianity, and rightly so because Christianity cannot be imposed upon people. But democracy, which is in effect just another name for socialism, can be.

False Dichotomy

In the Garden of Eden God set before Adam and Eve the dichotomy of life versus death as the central concern of humanity. This dichotomy was presented as two trees: the tree of life and the tree of the knowledge of good and evil (Genesis 2:9). The central challenge was to understand the difference between them and live in obedience to God's proscription against their own determinations of good and evil, which opposed life. Thus, God said that the central concern of discernment was *life versus death*, but Satan said that the central concern of discernment was *good versus evil*.

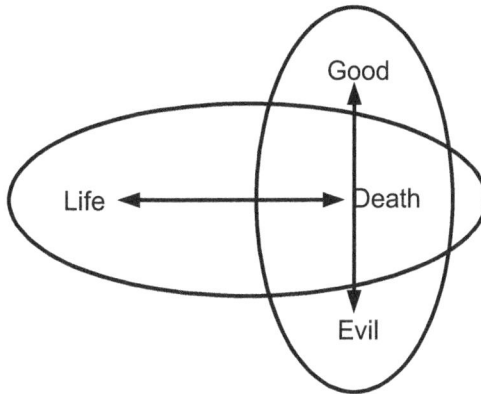

MEASUREMENT SCALE OF THE VERY LARGE AND THE VERY SMALL

				Metric prefixes		
Prefix	Symbol	1000^m	10^n	Decimal	English word[n 1]	Since[n 2]
yotta	Y	1000^8	10^{24}	1 000 000 000 000 000 000 000 000	septillion	1991
zetta	Z	1000^7	10^{21}	1 000 000 000 000 000 000 000	sextillion	1991
exa	E	1000^6	10^{18}	1 000 000 000 000 000 000	quintillion	1975
peta	P	1000^5	10^{15}	1 000 000 000 000 000	quadrillion	1975
tera	T	1000^4	10^{12}	1 000 000 000 000	trillion	1960
giga	G	1000^3	10^9	1 000 000 000	billion	1960
mega	M	1000^2	10^6	1 000 000	million	1960
kilo	k	1000^1	10^3	1 000	thousand	1795
hecto	h	$1000^{2/3}$	10^2	100	hundred	1795
deca	da	$1000^{1/3}$	10^1	10	ten	1795
		1000^0	10^0	1	one	–
deci	d	$1000^{-1/3}$	10^{-1}	0.1	tenth	1795
centi	c	$1000^{-2/3}$	10^{-2}	0.01	hundredth	1795
milli	m	1000^{-1}	10^{-3}	0.001	thousandth	1795
micro	µ	1000^{-2}	10^{-6}	0.000 001	millionth	1960
nano	n	1000^{-3}	10^{-9}	0.000 000 001	billionth	1960
pico	p	1000^{-4}	10^{-12}	0.000 000 000 001	trillionth	1960
femto	f	1000^{-5}	10^{-15}	0.000 000 000 000 001	quadrillionth	1964
atto	a	1000^{-6}	10^{-18}	0.000 000 000 000 000 001	quintillionth	1964
zepto	z	1000^{-7}	10^{-21}	0.000 000 000 000 000 000 001	sextillionth	1991
yocto	y	1000^{-8}	10^{-24}	0.000 000 000 000 000 000 000 001	septillionth	1991

1. ^ This table uses the short scale.
2. ^ The metric system was introduced in 1795 with six prefixes. The other dates relate to recognition by a resolution of the CGPM.

Source: http://en.wikipedia.org/wiki/Nano-

This is the sense in which the earth is the center of the universe, and suggests that other dimensions may exist in both directions.

Alphabetical Index

SCRIPTURE INDEX

www.ingramcontent.com/pod-product-compliance
Lightning Source LLC
Chambersburg PA
CBHW060037100426

42742CB00014B/2619